CIVILIZED AMERICA

SERIES IN AMERICAN STUDIES

Editor-in-Chief: Joseph J. Kwiat

PROGRAM IN AMERICAN STUDIES
UNIVERSITY OF MINNESOTA

CIVILIZED AMERICA

By THOMAS COLLEY GRATTAN

Volume 1

With a New Introduction by
MARVIN FISHER
PROFESSOR OF ENGLISH
ARIZONA STATE UNIVERSITY

JOHNSON REPRINT CORPORATION
New York and London
1969

The edition reproduced here was originally published in 1859.

Library of Congress Catalog Card Number: 70-79657

Printed in the U. S. A.

INTRODUCTION

I suspect that very few present-day readers, whether British or American, could read Grattan's *Civilized America* and keep their composure. Even the most insular Englishman would shudder while asking himself "Were we really that snobbish and complacent"? But those were still the great days of Empire; and while perceptive Englishmen saw significant change within England itself as well as in international relations, Grattan did not. His tone was imperial in its broadest implications, imperious in most personal respects. The United States seemed to him the land of constant change, of grandiose aspiration but decidedly mediocre achievement. When he came to write his account of experiences and impressions as British consul to Massachusetts from 1839 to 1846, he did not try to conceal how his sensibilities suffered during his cultural exile and how he longed to return to the stability of a securely structured society with its aristocratic privileges and its comfortable literary coteries.

Grattan made some shrewd observations concerning American character, attitudes, and values, but his perspective has a kind of built-in obtuseness that blurs his best points and baits every American reader, no matter how objective or self-critical he may be. In abstract formulation many of Grattan's judgments resemble Tocqueville's estimate of America (with which Grattan was very familiar) but where Tocqueville's reasoned presentation gained increasing currency because of the way it balanced criticism and admiration within a framework of liberal and humane sympathies, Grattan arouses the chauvinistic defenses in even the most cosmopolitan American readers. The coarseness, vulgarity, and crassly commercial character of American life spurred writers like Charles Dickens and James Fenimore Cooper into long essays in social criticism and sharply pointed critiques in fiction, and they too roused the anger of American reviewers. The difference with Grattan is that he often vitiated his criticism through his gratuitous self-esteem and managed to sound like a caricature of an English aristocrat. I wonder whether any but the most stereotyped character in the tritest of comedy situations could get away with the following lines:

> To meet anything quite coming up to English notions of a finished gentlemen is scarcely to be expected [in America]. . . . Everyone knows that it takes three generations to make a gentleman. And as that implies three generations of liberal education and all of the appliances of gentility, ergo, it is very rare, if to be found at all among Americans. (I, 189)

In Grattan's time these sentiments might make a man seem pretty stuffy; in our time they might be appreciated as one species of "camp."

The excessive gentility of Grattan's sentiments is reflected also in his stilted and unrealistic approach to the spoken language in America. He objected, for example, to the disagreeable sound of American abbreviations of English terms – *hack* for hackney-coach, *cab* for cabriolet, *bus* for omnibus. He was critical of Americans for using an expression like "I don't care a *copper* for him," instead *of farthing* for the same idea; of American women for *fixing* their hair, instead of *dressing* it. These barbarisms, as he viewed them, linked the way Americans spoke and the way they ate and drank. Only a people of debased tastes could esteem a New England fish chowder, concoct such items as "slap-jack, flap-jack, rye-cake, ris-cake, Johnny-cake, and dough-nuts," and imbibe mint-juleps, sherry-cobblers, and gin-slings. Grattan admitted sampling a mint-julep and it stimulated his wit, if not his palate: "The first I *did* try, and found it guilty; I thought it detestable; bad as a cordial, and worse as a physic."

On another occasion Grattan's manner provoked a kind of humorous retort in the style of "The Arkansas Traveler" dialogue, but he did not seem aware that he was being put down. The incident occurred while he was on a journey that required a transfer from train to steamboat. As he stepped off the railroad coach, he learned that the locomotive had struck a carriage with two women in it some distance back but had failed to stop. "Good God!" said Grattan, "Can't you send back to know what state they're in?" The conductor, apparently realizing the sort of person he was dealing with, answered, "Well, mister, I reckon they're in the State of Delaware; but you'd better jump into the steamer there, or you're like to lose your passage."

This was no proper way to speak to Her Majesty's representative to Massachusetts, a diplomat who had already distinguished himself as author of histories of Switzerland and of the Netherlands, of multivolumed historical romances and plays for the London stage. He translated French poetry and contributed to the *Westminster* and *Edinburgh Reviews*. He was a man who mattered and too many Americans lacked the social instincts to recognize this.

Civilized America is to some extent Grattan's revenge. The title not only limits his coverage of the New World, it also has distinctly sarcastic overtones. His overall view is that anyone who has "the means of enjoying even the moderate refinements of Europe" would be wise to stay away from life in the United States. In his own case he felt moderately fortunate to have his consular office in Boston, which was not only more English in flavor but possessed "a superiority over the other cities of the Union [in regard] to the refinements of his society and the literary taste of its inhabitants." It was a minor oasis in a cultural desert:

> Altogether I looked on Boston as the greenest spot in the comparative waste, to explore which my fate had sent me; and as a residence in the New World must at best be felt by the man of European tastes and habits as a banishment, I over and over congratulated myself on the good fortune which made me for a while a part and parcel, as it were, of the most desirable portion of its vast extent. (I, 29)

He does not pretend to any real knowledge of that vast extent and obviously did not feel that his official position obliged him to stray much beyond Boston, New York, Philadelphia, and Washington. Richmond was far enough south to permit viewing a slave auction, and as for the rest of the country,

> There are many portions . . . which I have not seen, and much which I had little wish to see. The parts with which I was familiar are the most settled, containing the circles of greatest

> refinement. The days are passed when I would have more enjoyed the adventures of the prairie, the forest, or the mountain range, the rude eccentricities of half-cultivated men, and the wild romance of nature. (I, xii)

Instead he focuses on the very limited northeastern and Atlantic coastal area that he considered "the better part of the American people – an established community, who being heirs of an earlier wisdom than it falls to the general lot of nations to inherit, form the materials of a grand experiment in civilization, for others to follow or to shun."

In defense of his generalizing from such limited experience, Grattan minimized geographical or sectional differences. Regardless of variations in religion or politics, whether slaveholder or abolitionist, every American seemed to Grattan "essentially the same with his fellows." This sounds a little like what Tocqueville observed or what Whitman celebrated, but Grattan did not mean quite the same egalitarian characteristics. What he meant was that a rather unflattering "Yankeeism is the general character of the Union." Because New England was the source of this widespread influence, he felt that whatever he found true of New England would "apply to all portions of the nation at large" as the "civilization" of the Eastern seaboard pushes westward.

Probably because he saw the culture of the South as simply the geographical dispersion of "Yankee" civilization, Grattan even as late as 1859, saw little likelihood of sectional conflict. He did not minimize the evil of slavery, and he chided the business interests, North and South, that supported it overtly or covertly. He recognized that slavery was admitted by Americans to be the issue "most likely to endanger the continuance of the federal pact." In his own voice he termed it "the touchstone that will try the strength of confederation." But despite these rather obvious presentiments, he confidently asserted that "the time for trial is, in my opinion, yet far off, unless the policy of England may produce an interference that would hurry on a crisis. I see no chance of a speedy collision between the north and the south on the mere merits of the question." (II, 288.)

Since Grattan had left the United States in 1846, he could not be as familiar with subsequent developments as he would have been had he remained on the scene. But he was succeeded in his diplomatic post by his eldest son who should have been able to counter his father's confidence as 1860 approached. To Grattan's mind, I fear, there was no difference in signification between a Yankee, a Damyankee, and a Secessionist.

The Yankee clearly does not come off well in this account. Late in the second volume Grattan tells of having lost from forty to seventy percent of his investment in a number of enterprises and suggests that some form of corruption or chicanery was involved in each instance. Yankees are clearly not to be trusted in such financial matters. Yankee shopkeepers, on the other hand, seemed scrupulously honest in adding up their bills. Generalizations regarding other ethnic groups seem less relevant and perhaps illustrate one mode of Grattan's thinking. We are informed that modern Greeks are men of "faithless levity," that Dutchmen are characterized by selfishness, and that Scotchmen and Jews have cupidity in common with Yankees. Though opposed to slavery, he clearly considers Negroes an inferior race. Toward Indians, who also seem to him basically inferior, he mercifully extends his hope for a relatively painless extinction. Surprisingly, the Irish, in the Old World and in the New, are treated far more charitably than these others – surprising, that is, until one discovers to what land Grattan traces his ancestry.

All this, however, slights the significant social and political comment in Grattan's volumes, and this constitutes their primary substantive value. The main lines of Grattan's response to American social and political life resemble Tocqueville's earlier analysis, but as I have suggested, lack some of the Frenchman's profundity and humanity. What Grattan offers that Tocqueville could not match is a kind of behind-the-scenes glimpse of the far from smooth workings of diplomacy – particularly the boundary disputes from Maine to Mexico to Oregon – and some detailed and vivid descriptions of major figures in local and national politics. Grattan's position brought him into frequent contact with men like Edward Everett, who was Governor of Massachusetts when Grattan took up his consular duties, Martin Van Buren, John C. Calhoun, Daniel Webster, and Henry Clay. Grattan's particular perspective – as a consciously genteel, anti-slavery outsider – is quite apparent in these analyses of power and personality in America, but they are quite balanced in tone and frequently, as in the case of Calhoun, very incisive (or, in the case of Webster, most unflattering).

In his overall view of the American republic, Grattan found citizens at every level of society justifiably proud of its political principles, which they were ever ready to explain to foreigners. But these same individuals were in many instances "ashamed of the narrowness of their social system . . . [and] would hide its workings, not only from the world, but from each other." (I, viii-ix.) Sounding far more contemporary than in most of his pronouncements, Grattan concluded, "There is much of what is political to praise, and so much that is social to condemn."

He was criticizing not simply the gross paradox of slavery in the land of the free, but the tyranny of the mass in many social circumstances and the constant pressures toward conformity. According to his account, he recognized this frightening uniformity on his initial trip from New York to Boston:

> The varieties of human nature all round or below me were not so marked. Character seemed moulded, for the time, into one regular standard, as though the weight and measure of each separate mind had a national stamp affixed to them, to give them a common value. There was difference of countenance, but sameness of expression. So it was as to cloth, in distinction from costume. The features of many faces were finer or coarser, as the fabrics of the garments worn by their possessors. But one unvarying cut and pattern was seen throughout. . . . The tone of the men and women was common-place; the fashion of their dress the same. Equality was more evident than liberty, in as far as the latter implies the power of gratifying individual whim or fancy. The movements of all were as nearly as possible alike. There was nothing curved or angular in any of their actions. They walked in straight lines, sat erect on the stools or benches, smoked their cigars and spat on the upper, and chewed their

> quids and spat on the lower deck, or read their newspapers and spat in the cabin, and had their 'drinks' and spat at 'the bar,' with a marvellous regularity. It was, take it all in all, a most curious specimen of living mechanism, completed and brought into action by the irresistible force of public opinion and general habit. (I, 26-27.)

The underlying metaphor in these observations is that of a factorylike society and a mass-produced population. "God's destiny" for the United States, according to Grattan, assures "the greatest well-being of the greatest number; but that well-being is to be found in a simple, economic existence, which makes the country a paradise of mediocrity, but of nothing more." (I, 222.) His analysis implies that no significant civilization, in the fullest sense of lasting cultural accomplishment, can develop in the New World. In life as in art, he believed, democracy limited achievement: "I have endeavoured to show that the true philosophy of the democratic principle consists in the great truth, that a medium civilization is alone feasible for those who are opposed to social inequalities. If mountains were levelled, and the chasms between them filled up, the plain could have no pretensions to the romantic or picturesque." (II, 471.)

It should come as no surprise, then, that Grattan found the state of literature and the arts quite sad at mid-century and the future dim and hopeless. In this area his myopia becomes monumental. The period of his consulship was a time of great ferment in American literature, but one finds no hint of that possibility in Grattan's discussion of the literary situation, the bulk of which is devoted to ridiculing an Arkansan's defense of tobacco chewing. By the time Grattan published *Civilized America,* Emerson had become a respectable sage and such works as *The Scarlet Letter, Moby Dick, Walden,* and *Leaves of Grass* had appeared, unnoticed of course by Grattan, whose chapter on "Speculative Philosophy" urged more serious attention to phrenology, graphology, mesmerism, and spirit rappings. In short, he found no American writer, apart perhaps from Washington Irving, worthy of recognition; and in the case of the several painters and sculptors whose names and works had become known, Grattan's awesome pronouncement restates his metaphor of the enduring infertility of the New World's cultural wasteland:

> The artist of America is but a weed or a wild flower in his natural state. To give him grace or delicacy he must be removed to the hot-bed of Europe; and if many specimens fade in the transplanting, they almost all pine and wither when sent back to their original soil. (II, 110–111.)

We have in these volumes an extended exercise in arrogance and condescension. Grattan's friend Sydney Smith had asked, in a question that has accorded him an unenviable immortality, "Who reads an American book"? Grattan, who seems in the end to have been more influenced by Mrs. Trollope than by Tocqueville, has earned that same sort of immortality.

Marvin Fisher

SELECTED BIBLIOGRAPHY

Published Works of Thomas Colley Grattan

Agnes de Mansfeldt, an Historical Tale. London, 1836. 3 vols.

Beaten Paths and those who trod them. London, 1862. 2 vols.

Ben Nazir, the Saracen, A Tragedy. London, 1827.

The Boundary Question raised and Dr. Franklin's Red Line shown to be the right one, by a British subject. London, 1843.

The Cagot's Hut and the Conscript's Bride. London, 1852.

Chance Medley of Light Matter. London, 1845.

Civilized America. London, 1859. 2 vols.

Curse of the Black Lady and other Tales. London, 1857.

England and the Disrupted State of America. London, 1861.

The Forfeit Hand and other Tales. London, 1857.

The Heiress of Bruges, a Tale of the Year Sixteen Hundred. London, 1831.

Highways and Byways, or Tales of the Roadside picked up in the French Provinces by a Walking Gentleman. London, 1823, 2 vols. Second Series, 1825, 3 vols. Third Series, 1827, 3 vols.

The History of Switzerland. London, 1825.

The History of the Netherlands to the Belgium Revolution in 1830. London, 1830.

Jacqueline of Holland, an Historical Tale. London, 1831. 3 vols.

Legends of the Rhine and of the Low Countries. London, 1832. 3 vols.

The Master Passion and other Tales. London, 1845. 3 vols.

Philibert, a Poetical Romance. Bordeaux, 1819.

Traits of Travel, or Tales of Men and Cities. London, 1829. 3 vols.

Secondary Sources

Allibone, S. Austin. *A Critical Dictionary of English Literature.* Philadelphia, 1898. I, 722.

Dictionary of National Biography. London, 1921–2. VIII, 425–426.

CIVILIZED AMERICA.

BY

THOMAS COLLEY GRATTAN,

LATE HER BRITANNIC MAJESTY'S CONSUL FOR THE STATE OF MASSACHUSETTS;

HONORARY MEMBER OF THE AMERICAN INSTITUTE ; THE NEW YORK AND BOSTON HISTORICAL SOCIETIES, ETC., ETC.

AUTHOR OF "A HISTORY OF THE NETHERLANDS;"
"HIGHWAYS AND BYWAYS,"
ETC.

IN TWO VOLUMES.

VOL I.

LONDON:
BRADBURY AND EVANS, 11, BOUVERIE STREET,
1859.

ADVERTISEMENT.

Proving a title, whether in Law or Literature, is sometimes a difficult process. I feel that the name I have given to this book may be considered rather ambiguous, according to the rules of logical evidence; and it requires a few words of explanation.

The Work relates exclusively to but a portion of those vast countries comprised in the general appellation of America. Yet the dominant influence of the United States justifies me in conceding to them the designation recognized by most European nations; and in spite of any demur on the part of Spain, or until Columbia, Alleghania, or some other of the proposed alterations, is adopted, the great federal Union must retain the name originally, though perhaps unadvisedly, given to the whole continent.

It is next necessary to explain what portion of the Union I consider entitled to be called Civilized, and in what degree that term may be applied to its various parts.

Of all the definitions attached to the word Civilization, the idea of progress in civil life, and the development of Society in the different relations of men among themselves, seem best to comprise the essential attributes of the term. To trace the gradations of this development in the United States would be extremely difficult. But by reference to the accompanying map, the Author's attempt to illustrate the subject may be perceived, and the attention of the reader be more directly drawn to it.

INTRODUCTION.

THE following work is intended as a practical essay on a great nation. It is a record of events, a gallery of portraits, and a miscellany of opinions. It is the result of several years' acquaintanceship with the people of whom it treats; a people easy of access, but difficult to understand; offering to the observer a mass of incongruities, and swayed by agitations which defy a steady description. With this qualification, the work must be taken for what it seems worth to each individual reader. The author is conscious that he must not put any higher estimate on it. No one who writes about the United States of America should be considered an oracle.

Among the most embarrassing problems of philosophy are the relative effects produced on mankind by climate and by institutions. A brief or rapid conclusion on so important a question would be unbecoming in any one who has consulted the works of those who have profoundly treated it. Montesquieu, Hume, Charles Comte, and Guizot, are among those eminent men. Mr. Buckle, in his recent most erudite work, "The History of Civilization in England," has gone deep into the subject. But, though I hesitate to enter on its subtle intricacies, with the chance of being lost in the labyrinth, I am nevertheless satisfied that writers who ascribe to climate and topographical formation such great influence, have assumed an exaggerated value for their reasonings, an error common to philosophers from Bacon back to Plato. And I believe that those reasonings, however applicable to remote times, have little comparative weight applied to a period in which civilization has modified the primitive rules of society.

That the Athenians were lively from the effect of the vivifying air they breathed—that the Hollander of old acquired his habit of dogged industry from the monotonous war he waged against the ocean, we may admit: *Bœotûm in crasso jurares aëre natum.* But we cannot so account for the faithless levity of the modern Greek, or the selfishness of the Dutchman of to-day. The "skiey influences" are at present confined more to imaginative than to real results. Bentley was right when, in one of his sermons, alluding to a people overcome with vice, he scouted the idea that difference of climate inclines one nation to sensuality and another to blood-thirstiness. Manners, and the more evanescent feelings dependent on them, are no doubt affected, to a certain degree, by climate; but I cannot understand how great moral principles could become subservient to its control. It is for casuists to argue, and, if they can, elucidate, this question. They may find it comparatively easy while they confine themselves to the distinctively defined communities of Europe; but when they come to the consideration of the North American continent and the varied characteristics of its people, the profoundest theorists are at fault. The early effects of climate on the accumulation of wealth are not applicable to the existing national character of the United States, where the acquisition and distribution of wealth are points settled beyond theoretic inquiry; while the action of natural phenomena on the human mind must be discarded in all speculations on the present state of American civilization. That civilization was brought from Europe and naturalized in America. Whatever might have been the influence of climate on the imagination or the intellect of the aboriginal inhabitants, it has little or no connection with the social state of their conquerors and destroyers. It is with these I have to deal; and among these, with climate of all varieties, and institutions widely different, we find general results of entire similarity. There is more homogeneity in some localities than in others. Peculiarities of race form strong contrasts, in a geographical extent of several thousand miles. National traits are flagrant in settlers and their immediate descendants from various European stocks. But still the distinguishing attributes of the whole people are alike, and not to be mistaken.

Meet an American where you will, let his pursuits in life or his every-day language be what they may, be he slaveholder or abolitionist, of whatever religious sect or political party, he is essentially the same with his fellows. And although the genuine Yankee is only he who belongs to the part of the country called New England, the term "Yankee," as the cognomen of the entire national family, is now as appropriate to the natives of the Union at large as are the distinctive national appellations given to the people of other countries.

Yankeeism is the general character of the Union. Yankee manners and feelings are as migratory as Yankee men. The latter are found everywhere, and the former prevail wherever the latter are found. Yankee connections and interests are spread throughout the land, and are gradually neutralizing all opposing influences. The

Yankee mind, in short, is stronger than that ot the other races, and is subduing them all. It is consequently important, towards the knowledge of American character, to study that of the section which gives the prevailing tone to the rest. New England is therefore of surpassing interest. It is right and fair that she should enjoy her moral pre-eminence. Liberty was cradled, and Independence founded on her soil ; and a frame of government exists there now, a practical scheme of polity, unsurpassed in any country of the earth. But the observations in this book are not confined to New England alone. They are meant to apply to all those portions of the nation at large which are fairly entitled to be called Civilized America.

The States of which that vast union is composed present themselves, more particularly than any other country existing, in two distinct aspects, the political and the social. But the institutions that act on these conditions are infinitely less blended than those of the European communities, which have been commingled for centuries, like the various races composing the population.

No people offer greater facilities than the Americans to him who would politically examine them. There is so much publicity in the proceedings of their government, so little reserve in its treatment of all questions; personal character and private objects have such obvious influence on matters of state, that by studying the movements and motives of leading politicians, one may soon acquire a knowledge of party measures. But the extreme caution which prevails on the subject of social economy, repels the hasty inquirer, and puzzles even the resident foreigner. Proud of the breadth of their political scheme, the Americans willingly lay it bare to inspection. Ashamed of the narrowness of their social system, they would hide its workings, not only from the world, but from each other.

Nowhere else is the individual at once of so much and of so little importance as in the United States. He directly affects every question by his voice or his vote. But he is insignificant as one of the mass, a majority of which carries everything before its aggregate will. We should well understand the American man before we pass judgment on the institutions which he creates and which control him.

Many clever attempts have been made to give to the people of Europe a clear idea of the politics and character of America. But I cannot help thinking that some of the works which embrace the first of those branches are too theoretical; those which depict the latter, too practical. The essays on government have not sufficiently shown its effect on the popular mind; while the strictures on manners fail to trace their connection with the laws from which they spring, but which are nevertheless subservient to them—as parents who become dependent on their children. Much has been written on this extraordinary country. Very much more may be written usefully and agreeably. It is a theme of unbounded variety. No research can be too deep, no sketch too light. It is equally difficult to fathom and to span; at least within the reasonable limits of one work.

I consider it next to impossible to produce a book on the United States that would be extensively circulated and generally approved of among the inhabitants. If all is painted *couleur de rose*—and such has been done by English writers—the flatterer finds but few readers; because the Americans know their own defects, however they may deny them; and they have no faith in their over-ardent eulogists. If a bold hand and independent mind point out errors and keenly satirize, the book is devoured, but the author detested. No European who writes honestly on America should look for general popularity on either side of the ocean. There is so much of what is political to praise, and so much that is social to condemn, that one is sure to shock home prejudices while wounding foreign pride ; and the double offence brings a double punishment. Whether you approve or blame you are doomed to suffer. By professional critics you are, in either case, identified with the object you pourtray ; and the public will not always take the trouble of separating an author from what he would depict. But the prospect of this fate should not deter him who has no personal purpose to subserve, and who can see both sides of the question. Nor should he be checked by the reproach of apparent contradictions in his views. The anomalies he has to deal with often baffle every effort at analysis. In short, his task is one of extreme difficulty, and his execution of it should meet with great indulgence. With a full understanding of the difficulty, and taking chance for the indulgence, I began this work. But to lessen the first, and to give me a better claim to the latter, I resolved not to write until I had duly reflected on what I was about to say. I was aware that men who hastily commit themselves to an opinion, may deceive themselves as to its value, and persist in what they should abandon ; for the pride of consistency is often stronger than the love of truth. I have not, therefore, forced the utterance of crude notions, which that false pride might have induced me to stick to, right or wrong. If I have erred in my opinions it has not been from haste.

The English public will, I am sure, take this book as it

is meant, because they will understand the author's feelings even if they dissent from them. I am not so confident as regards America. But it is only my imagination, not my conscience, that takes the alarm. I can safely say that the work is faithful and sincere.

Yet I cannot expect that my disclaimer of all unfair bias will protect me from the fate of those who have already offended against the notions entertained by the Americans as to whatever concerns themselves. Aware of what I risk on this score, I protest by anticipation against the looked-for censure. Admitting their right to vaunt the value of everything American, I denounce the inconsistency with which all parties in the State contradict themselves by turns. What they gild with praise to-day they dash with blame to-morrow. What they glorify by wholesale they vilify in detail. Smarting under evils inseparable from all forms of Government, and of abuses to which their own is peculiarly liable, they, nearly in the same breath, cry it up as perfect and run it down as corrupt; exercising a kind of political ventriloquism, which belies in individual undertones the loud-speaking voice of the masses. Yet if foreigners are deceived by, or blame the inconsistency, they are abused as dupes or slanderers.

This proneness to vituperation is, by the Americans, miscalled sensitiveness. For, sensitiveness is a nervous consciousness of one's own defects, or an over-sensibility to injustice, making us shrink from collision with the object which assails or slights us. But the coarseness of American retort proceeds from an obstinate conceit far removed from modesty or diffidence. So long as that serious blemish is paramount in the national character, improvement, even of palpable defects, cannot be hoped for; nor can an impartial observer of the country meet with toleration. Had I suffered personal feelings to influence me they would have given a far different colouring to the following pages. But he who paints a whole people from his attachment to a few individuals does great injustice to those for whom he writes. It is better far to leave such individuals to their sense of conscious merit. Were I about to make a record of personal enjoyment or private excellence, I should only treat of pleasant visits in town and country, and of those who made them so pleasant. But this book has a broader view ; and I must avoid partiality while I steel myself against reproof.

My volumes do not pretend to embrace all the topics of importance connected with the United States. There are many portions of the country which I have not seen, and much which I had little wish to see. The parts with which I was familiar are the most settled, containing the circles of greatest refinement. The days are passed when I would have more enjoyed the adventures of the prairie, the forest, or the mountain range, the rude eccentricities of half-cultivated men, and the wild romance of nature. The reader has, therefore, to expect in these pages observations on the better part of the American people—an established community, who, being heirs of an earlier wisdom than it falls to the general lot of nations to inherit, form the materials of a grand experiment in civilization, for others to follow or to shun.

Justice has been done, as far as I was capable, to the peculiar traits of the living picture I studied so closely. My purpose was not to present only shallow reflections of humanity—mere sketches to be filled up by fancy or caprice. I have no pride in leaving matters doubtful from a show of impartiality ; nor do I presume to decide boldly for a display of vigour. But, having made up my mind,

I speak it freely. I think that every book should have an object and a moral. The object of this one is to tell the truth respecting the New World in a way to be understood by the Old. The moral it would inculcate is this :—

The United States, with their Federal Constitution fairly carried out, and wisely modified according to the spirit of successive ages, are better adapted than any country on earth for securing the greatest amount of good to the greatest number of mankind; but the beings so blessed must be satisfied with a far more restricted happiness than is aimed at by the ambitious malcontents among them. The democratic forms of America are widely inconsistent with the instincts, traditions, and capabilities of the European nations. To force those forms upon the people of the Old World would be almost impossible; and could be effected only at the cost of a struggle more terrible than the object is worth. The political events which agitated Europe in 1848 and 1849, and their miserable result, may justify this opinion.

The author would add, for his own sake and for that of all who have the means of enjoying even the moderate refinements of Europe, that he should be sorry to exist for ever under such a system as that of which he has here related his experience. As a sequence to this avowal, he would disclaim any desire to treat his subject flippantly, or to speak with asperity of a people with whom he lived so long on friendly and familiar terms. He has followed the bent of his natural style of writing, taking his topics as they occurred, treating them without constraint, and striving to blend the light and the serious in fair proportions.

With the exception of the first two or three chapters,

none of the book was written till after the author had been some years in the United States. After that time, and since his return to Europe, he has performed his task by snatches, and in a very desultory way. But his judgment being decidedly formed, on whatever subject he undertook to discuss, he has found no reason to recall any of the opinions thus put on record.

CONTENTS.

CHAPTER I.

THE VOYAGE.

CHAPTER II.

FIRST IMPRESSIONS.

CHAPTER III.

BOSTON.—NAHANT.

CHAPTER IV.

NAHANT.

CHAPTER V.

NATIONAL CHARACTERISTICS.

CHAPTER VI.

NATIONAL CHARACTERISTICS—(*Continued*).

CHAPTER VII.

THE SOCIAL SYSTEM IN NEW ENGLAND.

CHAPTER VIII.

EDWARD EVERETT.

CHAPTER IX.

MY FIRST VISIT TO WASHINGTON.

CHAPTER X.

WASHINGTON.

CHAPTER XI.

CHAPTER XII.

AMERICAN ARISTOCRACY.

CHAPTER XIII.

POLITICAL ULTRAS.

CHAPTER XIV.

DANIEL WEBSTER.

CHAPTER XV.

SERVANTS.

CHAPTER XX.

INAUGURATION OF PRESIDENT HARRISON.

CHAPTER XXI.

THE NORTH-EASTERN BOUNDARY QUESTION.

CHAPTER XXII.

THE NORTH-EASTERN BOUNDARY QUESTION—(*Continued*).

CHAPTER XXIII.

THE NORTH-EASTERN BOUNDARY QUESTION—(*Continued*).

CONTENTS

CHAPTER [illegible]

[illegible]

CHAPTER [illegible]

[illegible]

CHAPTER [illegible]

[illegible] (Continued)

CHAPTER [illegible]

[illegible] (Continued)

CIVILIZED AMERICA.

CHAPTER I.

THE VOYAGE.

Departure from London—The "British Queen" Steam Ship—Passengers—Incidents of the Voyage—First Gale—"Ship on Fire" Alarms—The Flying Dutchman—Deserted Ship—Banks of Newfoundland—New York Harbour—Arrival.

MY voyage across the Atlantic has been so rapid that my mind cannot entertain those ideas of expanse, distance and separation, with which our friends in Europe are at this moment filled. I can trace in every league of ocean a link in the chain of time and space, while they are sensible of only the extreme points at which we severally stand. For them there is but a wide blank, across which they throw their fears, hopes, and wonderings—all things of the imagination; but without one matter of fact on which to rest. The various events of the voyage are to me so many punctuations, breaking the monotonous lapse into fragments of thought.

And can it really be that I have traversed 3,230 miles—for so say the charts and the captain's log—in fifteen days? That I have so easily performed the once formidable feat of crossing the Atlantic? That I am treading the soil of the New World? What a double action there is in my mind this moment! How I am excited by the scene of novelty before me; yet how depressed by recollections of the distant and the past!

Slight as is the effort which leads us to the change, the change itself is great between the Old World and the New. Less in the external appearance of things—for nature, human and inanimate, wears nearly the same dress—than in the whirlwind of associations, in reference to bygone days, and of fancies as to the future. Columbus and his fellow-adventurers, he had no peers—Raleigh, the red men, the pilgrim fathers, the wilderness, the frail barks traversing the waste of waters, chivalry, adventure, witchcraft, as the mind looks back—civilization, corruption and decay as it rushes on. We are lost in bewilderment. The present is forgotten or despised. We feel that we were born too late or too soon. The dissatisfied heart tortures itself with self-born regrets, like some unquiet reptile writhing from its own sting.

The first stage on this great journey is the voyage. Of this let me say briefly—I was disappointed. I had been often at sea before; had more than once crossed the Bay of Biscay; been for several weeks at a time cooped up in transport ships; and on two occasions made European passages in small merchant vessels, of a fortnight's duration each, and innumerable short trips between England and the continent. But a real, downright, Atlantic *voyage* had excited extraordinary expectations of the wonderful and sublime. I pictured to myself the mountain billows, the monsters of the deep, the splendour of the skies, all on a scale that defied every common measurement. But the reality fell far short of all this.

The narrow horizon, not more than what I had so often observed when out of sight of land between England and Holland, France or Spain ; the quiet sea, in comparison with the storms I had encountered—the scanty glimpses of grampuses or porpoises now and then—the every-day appearance of sky and ocean—was all very common-place. I was just sick enough at times to make the ship uncomfortable to me, and the monotony of idleness was overpowering. Reading was not "made easy" in any sense. I never attempted to write. Thought seemed stagnant. But there was a good deal of desultory conversation among the 150 passengers in the "British Queen."

This crowd of strangers from so many different countries formed a very incongruous assemblage ; and they were forced to mix together in spite of all discrepancies. The saloons and the deck were eminently inviting and capacious, while the sleeping dens were (with a few exceptions called "state rooms") inconvenient in the highest, or rather let me say, the *lowest* degree. None of the passengers stayed in their berths a moment longer than they were forced to do by tired nature, for which however those said berths were by no means *sweet* restorers. By some awful mismanagement, a prodigious quantity of tarred coal bags were stowed away in the close neighbourhood of the cabins, and a diabolical odour of creosote, enough to cure the tooth-ache in an ocean of sharks, pervaded all the best parts of the ship. Five-sixths of my sickness during the voyage arose from this cause ; and, to escape from it, I, as well as scores of others, resorted at all possible times to the upper air.

The majority of the passengers were British subjects. Next came a great many Americans from all parts of the Union ; then French and Germans, a few Spaniards,

Swedes, Italians, and one Russian. I need not say our ship was a floating Babel—the image will at once rise up to all imaginative minds. But with all this confusion of tongues there was really no discord, except indeed when the boisterous after-dinner choruses flayed the ears (as the French say) of the musically organised. And was there not singing and speechifying enough, ye Tritons! Voices that never before attempted music, and that never should have been tempted to attempt it, seemed to burst into song, from some unharmonious instinct. And others little attuned to eloquence, daily bellowed forth toasts and sentiments. A few of the passengers, however, both sang and spoke well; and there was some very rational conviviality.

We sailed from London on the 10th of July, 1839; reached Portsmouth on the 12th; quitted the shores of England the same day; and made the land near New York on the 27th. Several members of the company which owned the steamer that carried us and our fortunes, accompanied us to Portsmouth. It was the first voyage of the splendid vessel, the largest that had been launched in modern days, and much interest and excitement prevailed as to the issue of her voyage across the Atlantic. I had all along been anxious to make one of those who joined in it, and had considerably delayed my departure for the purpose, in defiance of the dissuasions of many friends, and the public forebodings which promised failure and foundering, a "broken back," and sundry other calamities to the floating palace, for such her costly decorations entitled her to be called.

The commander, Captain Roberts, was a frank and energetic Irishman. His first officer, Franklin, an Englishman, and also a Lieutenant in the Royal Navy, was more polished but more reserved. The second officer, Stewart, an obliging, courteous Scotchman; and the third and youngest, Watson, as active and handsome a fellow as ever left old Ireland for a seafaring life. Among the passengers were the Commissioners sent by the English Government to make a survey of the topographical peculiarities of "the (then) disputed territory;" a radical member of Parliament; numerous mercantile men of many countries; the Consul General for Sicily to the United States; a General from Georgia; a Judge from Montreal; and other specimens of our species, from Prince Edward's Island all the way to New Orleans.

To detail the various objects of this crowd of passengers would be amusing enough, if I were merely writing a sketch-book of amusement. But I am anxious to get through this preliminary trifling, in the hope of recording observations less worthless. Still I cannot help mentioning one or two striking illustrations of this wonderful application of steam power for the shortening of the distance—for that is now measured by time, not space—between Europe and America. The worthy member of Parliament just mentioned, was taking a two months' run, voyages both ways included, to the United States and back to England, meaning to visit half-a-dozen of the chief cities, in a length of a thousand miles from the New Brunswick frontier, to some southern parts of the Union. Another passenger, a sporting captain in the Prussian Royal Guard, had obtained six weeks' leave of absence, and crossed the Atlantic solely for the purpose of shooting a wild Buffalo, and then returning to Europe, within the prescribed period. But an old English colonel, who had visited the ship the day before we sailed from Blackwall, was induced by Captain Roberts to make the voyage totally unprepared, merely to look at America, intending to return with him to London (which he actually did) after the three days' stay at New York, to which Captain Roberts was, from peculiar circumstances, limited.

From London to Portsmouth the weather was superb; and as we sailed down channel many pleasure-boats put out from the various ports on the English coast, filled with gazers at the great steam-ship. I could not pass those shores, nor look towards the heights on the French line of coast unmoved by recollections of other days. But these were private. I strove to draw a veil across the time that was. I turned my glance on the external world. My views were all bent forward. And when the vessel plunged into the expanse of ocean, I felt as though I had shaken off the bonds which had so long bound me to the past.

What may be emphatically called the incidents of the voyage were few, though not far between. Two or three stiff gales relieved the monotony of the summer season, by rattling the furniture, smashing some of the crockery, and shaking the nerves of the ladies. But a couple of still more serious alarms occurred.

On the fifth night of our voyage from Portsmouth, at a thousand miles distant from land, I was lying in my berth, sick—if not at heart, very near to it—when a rather unusual bustle attracted my notice; and I quitted my cabin or crib, while all the passengers in the corridors at either side were apparently asleep. I made my way towards the engine-room, and soon met one of the officers who told me the cause of the disturbance. It was nothing less than that the whole mass of coal stowed away around the furnace, from which it was separated by an iron screen, had been gradually heating for five days and nights, until it at length burst out into flames, which were providentially discovered by one of the passengers before any of the wood-work had taken fire. Captain Roberts was immediately summoned, and he at once set every individual of the crew and the stokers to work to remove the burning and smoking material, which was accomplished very fortunately ; but not in less than six hours of incessant labour, and with infinite difficulty. There were not four persons in the ship, besides the officers and men, who knew anything of the affair until the next day, when all danger from that cause was over. But on that next day it blew harder than it had yet done ; and as night came on, some of the more nervous among the passengers, to whom the past danger from one element was more forcibly brought to mind by the increasing violence of others, were ready to magnify any real alarms and to imagine the existence of more. As the gale increased the huge vessel rolled awfully, and a terrible commotion took place among the splendid furniture of the main saloon. Knowing that I should be inevitably pitched out of my berth had I gone below, I stretched myself on a sofa, and looked on with I confess a sort of malicious enjoyment, as the concussion of seat against seat and table against table, knocked off one by one the corners, knobs, and other fantastic protuberances with which the bad taste of the proprietors had *adorned* the various *meubles,* to the infinite annoyance of the passengers during some previous rough weather, from a series of assault and battery against limbs and carcases, by those prominent imitations of the gothic. I was calculating the great comfort that was in store for us when all these gimcracks would be rounded off and smoothed away from the chairs, tables and settees, when a loud alarum on deck, and a sudden illumination of the saloon, from a light streaming through the hatchway-window, caused me and a dozen more to spring to our feet.

"The ship's on fire!" was the exclamation of half the party, staggering and rolling across the room.

"I knew it would come to this, by G——!" cried the long-visaged and cadaverous-looking general from Georgia.

"You don't say so!" uttered one.

"You don't really think she's on fire!" bawled another.

"I do, by the Etarnal!" coolly answered the general. drawing on his pantaloons, "and we'll be all driving to everlasting smash in no time."

Hastening on deck, and fairly in the open air, I soon ascertained that the light which had caused so much apprehension, proceeded from two or three large lanterns hoisted up to the mast head, the concentrated rays of which had found a focus in the glass of the hatchway skylight, sufficient to cause the fierce glare below. But although relieved from all dread on the score of fire, I found that a danger even more appalling, from being less easily remedied, was close upon us. It appeared in the shape of a large square-rigged vessel in full sail, which was bearing down upon us on the starboard quarter, running before the wind, without any lights visible in any part, and as it would seem, totally indifferent to those we had hung out. She was close beside us, as I leaned over the gangway with several of the crew and passengers, every instant expecting her bows to come plump against our paddle-box or hull; while the officer of the watch and others who rushed on deck, were stimulating the efforts of the men at the wheel to luff and avoid the impending crash. Loud shouts were sent out from all of us, as warnings to the stranger ; but those on board of her seemed to be all below or all asleep ; and as somebody beside me cried out in a jocular tone, "perhaps it's the Flying Dutchman," a shudder ran through many of the group, and every voice was instantly hushed. It was a moment of mysterious and irresistible misgiving, even to those who laughed to scorn all commonplace superstition, on commonplace occasions,

"D—n her, she'll not answer the helm!" vociferated our boatswain.

"Put the helm hard up!" cried the officer of the watch.

"Aye, aye, Sir," answered the rough old steersman, on the starboard side of the wheel.

"Luff it is, Sir," echoed the other to larboard.

"All's right! all's right!" shouted the boatswain.

"Away she goes—Hurra!" exclaimed young Watson, springing forward.

The bowsprit was in an instant down in the surge ; the Queen's effigy, forming the figure head, dashed deep into the waves ; a cloud of spray covered the prow, and was blown up upon us, the gazers. We cleared the intruder by several points, and as she swept fiercely past our stern, plunging into the foam, her bellying sails seemed almost to touch our mizen yards, and in a minute or two she was quite lost in the darkness.

Who, or what was she? Whence coming? where going? These questions were asked in rapid succession, but no seaman answered. The *passengers* made random conjectures, guessed, calculated, and asserted. But neither at that stirring crisis of great risk, nor ever afterwards, during the voyage, did officer or sailor utter a word on the subject ; nor could the chatter of the curious landsmen on board elicit from them even a shrug or glance, in token of either assent or denial to the various theories put forth by the babblers, in reference to the strange occurrence.

In three days more we had made 1600 miles, and were thus literally half seas-over. Just at noon, on a glorious day, the sea calm, the sky clear, the passengers almost all on deck, a sail ahead was announced by some one on the look out: and we soon steamed up, with all our canvass spread, towards a vessel, apparently lying-to, with her sails furled. This appeared strange during such fine weather; but as we got closer, it was evident that all the sails and running rigging were stripped away, and that she was under bare poles. No one appeared on board. Captain Roberts ordered two signal guns to be fired. The echoes rolled across the deep, but nothing gave evidence on board the strange craft of their being heard. Speculation then began its work among us. One calculated that the crew were all down, or perhaps dead, with some malignant disease. Another guessed the ship was abandoned. Another that she had been rifled, and all her people murdered. While the Sicilian Consul-General exclaimed, as a hundred of us stood on the forecastle gazing at the object of our inquiry, "*C'est un pirate, je n'en doute pas, qui va nous jouer un mauvais tour.*"

This last opinion seemed to catch the general taste of those who understood it, or heard it translated into English. Some treacherous shot from the mysterious vessel was looked for by the nervous; advice to the Captain to run from her close neighbourhood was given by the timid; while the adventurous urged him to lower a boat, and send a party to board her, several volunteers offering their services. Roberts took the latter counsel, and had the engines stopped; and while we lay like a duck on the water, Lieutenants Franklin and Hall (the latter a volunteer on this voyage), with six or eight men, stepped into the gig, and soon rowed alongside. We, at a couple of hundred of yards distance, saw them climb up unobstructed and spring on the deck. In half-an-hour they returned, reporting the vessel to be in capital order, quite new, laden with iron rails, evidently meant for some transatlantic road, scarcely any water in the hold; but every portable object of the least utility carried clear off, no boat being left on board, nor any relic of furniture or provisions. An old torn bible, and the broken arm of a female effigy, part of the vessel's figure-head, were the only trophies of their exploit which the exploring party could lay hold of. These they brought on board; and then a short counsel was held as to what was to be done. The vessel and cargo was estimated by the officers to be worth from 3000*l.* to 4000*l.*, if she could be taken safely to a British port. Lieutenant Hall volunteered to navigate her to England, if the Captain would give him half-a-dozen of the crew. These could have been easily spared; but to have put on board sails, rigging, and provisions for the voyage home, would have required six or seven hours delay, in addition to the two already lost. Considering, therefore, the importance of time to the proprietors of the "British Queen" on this her first voyage, Captain Roberts did not hesitate in preferring the interests of his employers to his own, for he, as commanding officer, would have been entitled to a large portion of the prize. So, putting on all steam and hoisting all sail, he turned his course once more towards New York; and it was not without regret that we left the doomed vessel to her fate, met thus by chance in the liquid wilderness, and possessing for all an interest almost equal to that excited by "a thing of life" suddenly discovered and forcedly abandoned in the populous ways of the world. We lost sight of her, little by little; and as she finally disappeared on the horizon's verge, we seemed as though deprived of a speck of companionship that had awhile relieved the monotony of sea and sky.

Three or four days more brought us into and through the thick fogs of the great bank of Newfoundland. Our only hope in that misty region was to fall in with some fishing boat, from which we might procure a few fresh cod. Our only fear was the chance of running down in the night some of the small craft which pursue that perilous trade. Neither hope nor fear was realized. We saw and spoke a few boats, but got no fish; nor did any accidental collision take place. For the rest of our voyage we had continual fine weather. We saw several vessels traversing the ocean in different directions. We watched the grampuses and sharks at their gambols, and the tiny nautilus as it floated past on the smooth surface. The rising and setting sun, a brilliant moonlight, and the increasing brightness of the stars occupied us in ardent idleness. But no voyagers across "the broad Atlantic" had ever a less favourable chance for enjoying the sublimity of ocean life. The grander scenes of nature to be felt worthily should be viewed in solitude. Companionship, unless on the narrowest scale and strictly confined to those we love, deadens if it does not entirely destroy the charm. Our populous ship, like some huge hotel launched on the waves, and mechanically urged across them, had no sympathy with outward creation. So we turned our thoughts inwards, and did the best to improve the occasion from which there was no escape. We had almost all the luxuries of the land; and as we neared the

New World the general vivacity increased, bets were made as to the day and hour of arrival, lotteries and raffles set on foot; a piece of plate subscribed for, as a present to our captain, and song and speech were the eternal order of the day and night. Everything in short wore the joyous aspect common to the occasion; and finally, the cry of "Land!" from the masthead capped the climax of our expectations.

For some hours we pushed rapidly forward towards the welcome shore. Land soon became visible to all eyes, the highlands of "Neversink" being the objects first in sight. As night closed in the lights of Sandy Hook were our beacon guides; and no pilot boat appearing as we had hoped, though we fired gun after gun and threw up several rockets to announce our want of one, the engine was at length stopped, and we lay quietly to till dawn.

By sun-rise the next morning, Sunday, July 28th, a pilot having previously come on board, we were bearing up directly for New York. But not being anxious to arrive until the morning was somewhat advanced, so as that a fair proportion of the city population might at once greet us and gratify themselves, we went quietly onwards till we made the quarantine station, three miles from the city.

As we sailed up into the harbour, our sensations—I think I may speak for almost all on board—were highly excited; and rich associations of enjoyment were lavishly combined for us. The beauty of the scenery at either side, the brilliancy of the day, the many brightly-painted and fanciful steamboats and pleasure barges floating about; several ships of war at anchor (bands of music in some, joyous cheers from all of them); repeated discharges of artillery from the battery as we approached the shore, answered by our own guns in quick succession, and the shouts from thousands of people lining the quays, formed a union of all that external circumstances could contribute to such a scene. The great variety of feeling among our motley party it would be impossible to describe. For our own parts, that is mine and my family's, we were exhilarated, and I might say, delighted. It was a stirring preparation for our landing on the long-wished-for shore ; and when at last I put my foot, for the first time on the soil of the New World, I thought I could comprehend the emotions of the early adventurers, who sought their checquered fortunes in this land of promise.

NOTE.—Readers who have seen the "Great Britain," the "Persia," the "Adriatic," or later still the "Leviathan," or "Great Eastern," may smile at the importance given in this chapter to the size of the "British Queen," a vessel of only 2000 tons. But it is not amiss, perhaps, to mark the progress of Atlantic steam navigation and ship building, from its earliest days down to the present time, a period of twenty years.

And here, I may add, that I have let the names of the officers of the ship remain on record, chiefly as a small tribute to the memory of poor Roberts and Watson, his third mate, who were both lost some years later, in the unfortunate "President," with Power the comedian and several others.

CHAPTER II.

FIRST IMPRESSIONS.

New York—Hackney Coachmen—Astor House—American Thunder—Sea and Land Journey to Boston—Steamer on the Sound—Railroad Cars—Travelling Companions—Arrival at Boston.

The record of first impressions is often looked upon as the most valuable, sometimes the only valuable, portion of a traveller's observations. If those which I mean to make during my residence in America are ever destined to meet the public eye, they must rest their claim to notice on quite another score; for my object is to give the fruits of experience and reflection, rather than the hasty remarks of impulse—frequently so deceitful. But I must, nevertheless, not pass by the first of those first impressions, which I, in common with other strangers, received in the earliest portion of my intercourse with the American people. The small matter which in my case caused this action of the intellect, was the necessity of procuring a coach to take myself and my family from the ship to the hotel we had fixed on. No sooner was the "British Queen" fast moored to the wharf, at the other side of which lay the "Great Western," looking very small indeed in comparison with the huge bulk of our vessel, than a considerable rush was attempted from the crowd on shore. The police, however, exercised a wholesome restraint on the impetuous many; and only certain well-dressed and well-behaved individuals were admitted, whom I took to be the "Commissionaires" of the various hotels, at the same time remarking how favourably their demeanour contrasted with that I had been accustomed to on the continent of Europe, or in our own seaport towns. One of these persons approached me as I stood on the deck, and with great civility inquired "if I wanted a *hack?*" Attaching the usual English meaning to the word, I answered that I was rather inclined for a drive than a ride just then, and that I should be glad to have a carriage to take me to the Astor House.

"Well, Sir, there's my hack standing ready to take you right away," replied he, pointing to a clean and comfortable looking calêche at the head of the wharf.

I of course instantly understood that the term hack was the American abbreviation for hackney-coach, and that the gentle citizen who addressed me was the driver for the particular one in question. Travellers often feign more surprise than they feel at slight differences of phraseology, I have long since become accustomed to peculiarities even more startling than the inelegant short cuts taken by the Americans to express an idea in English. Nevertheless I am quite alive to them. I shall have occasion to notice a few of them as I go on ; but shall just say in passing, that none of the abounding slang of the New World struck me as more disagreeable than the first sounds of the word cab, instead of *cabriolet,* and 'bus for *omnibus,* on the occasion of my arrival in London after an absence on the continent, during which the vehicles in question were first introduced to our streets.

The manners of these hackmen, and of the Custom House officers, obliging, but not obsequious, quiet and businesslike, impressed me very favourably indeed. And while I was making arrangements about my large quantity of baggage, settling what was to go ashore, and what to remain on board, I was accosted by a gentleman, of a burly, but cordial appearance, and apparently about sixty years of age, who announced himself as my brother-consul, being in fact Mr. Buchanan, my worthy colleague for the State of New York.

Under his auspices we soon reached the Astor House; my first impression of the city, as we drove through some minor streets and a portion of Broadway, being that it looked half Dutch, half French, something between Paris and Rotterdam. Small details of resemblance I leave to more acute observers. Great was our enjoyment on finding ourselves fairly ensconced in our several apartments in the Astor House, a really magnificent hotel, as to the extent of the building and its spacious accommodations. And we were at once struck with the unusual air of discipline in the little army of attendants who thronged the rooms and passages. The waiters seemed to be all Irish. They were dressed in a uniform of white cotton jackets and trowsers, but no aprons *à la Française;* and the ready civility of their air, and extreme neatness of apparel, gave me an instant notion of independence, in mind as well as circumstances. I was pleased to observe such an evident contrast between the condition of this class of men in America and that of their fellow-countrymen at home. And thus my very first thoughts in regard to the inhabitants of this new country, whether native or naturalised, were highly satisfactory.

What can be a greater luxury than a warm bath after a sea voyage, and after that a plunge into a comfortable bed with cool sheets; the thermometer in the shade being at 90° or more! Infinitely did I enjoy the first hour after my arrival, thus passed; and while my brain gradually recovered from the pitching and reeling sensation which seemed still to agitate it, I was roused from my resting-place, by what I thought the most extraordinary clap of thunder I had ever heard. There was a harsh, metallic rattle in it, of that peculiar tone which immediately follows the lightning's flash, and tells you that the electric fluid has been close by you. But in this case there was no lightning, and the peal was much longer in duration than any of those sudden bursts of sound which I had several times heard in the south of Europe, when a tree or a steeple had been struck very near to me. I sprang out of bed, and looked from my window upon a church built of a dull red stone, which fronted it, standing in relief against a brilliantly blue and cloudless sky, the sun brightly shining all around. "Well," thought I, "I have often heard that American thunder was very peculiar, and this is so, indeed." The rumbling crash was dying away, when my wife, who was dressing in the next room, opened the door, and asked me, if it was not very strange to have a thunder-storm in such fine weather? I replied that it *was* very strange, but not so strange as the thunder itself; and before we could pursue our observations, another clap, fiercer, and apparently closer than the first, rattled along the corridors and staircases, and seemed to vibrate from the bottom to the top of the house. I again thrust my head out of the window: saw to my amazement the same deep blue, and the glorious sunshine, and the spire at the other side of the street untottering; and again remarked to my equally astonished helpmate, that it was certainly the oddest kind of thunder, and the oddest kind of weather *for* thunder, imaginable. Hearing a footstep outside, I opened my door on the corridor, and asked a waiter who was quickly passing along—

"Pray, *was* that thunder ?"

"Was *what* tundther, sir ?" replied he.

"Why, that extraordinary noise just now."

"Is it the gong you mane, sir ?" asked my countryman, in his turn.

"The gong !" exclaimed I, "was that the sound of a gong ?"

"To be sure it was, sir, did you never hear it before !"

"Never, and hope I never shall again."

"By my sowl then, sir," said he with a smile, indescribably national, "you'll hear it often enough if you stop in this counthry, for that's the way they always ring the bell for breakfast, dinner, and supper."

It required no witchcraft to comprehend from this, that this infernal instrument was adopted by the American inn-keepers, to call their lodgers to the *table d'hôte.* I felt at the instant that this was a positive relapse towards barbarism, and that such a direful knell would be a fit summons, not to heaven, but to "the other place." I suffered a momentary shock as I bethought me of poor Lord Napier, who had been put to death by the clashing of this hideous discord under the windows of his ship's cabin near Canton ; and I felt that the war then threatened by England against the Chinese, however indefensible on moral grounds, was in some measure retributive, on behalf of outraged civilisation, against the people who had invented such a weapon of offence. But if the savage inventors merited punishment, what is due to the nation who imports in cold blood, this ear-splitting, nerve-shattering monstrosity, not for purposes of warlike assault, but as a substitute for the cheerful tingling of the dinner-bell, to drive people half deaf and three quarters crazy before they sit down to table! Old Dennis himself would have disclaimed such thunder as that. And Saint Denis, as he walked with his head under his arm, might esteem himself lucky, if his organs of hearing were consequently sufficiently impaired to make him insensible to such a sound.*

Dinner being prepared for us in a parlour below stairs, we descended about an hour after this adventure of the gong; and as we passed on along the lower corridor, conducted by the waiter, we observed on the open door of a large and handsomely furnished room, "Ladies Drawing Room," painted in large letters. I thought that was rather exclusive, and impelled by such curiosity as would urge one to peep into a seraglio, I looked into the apartment (my wife leaning on my arm), and we both involuntarily stopped and stood still, gazing at the object which attracted our attention. This was a very handsome and abundantly dressed woman, sitting in a velvet-covered armed chair, with a high back and of singular construction, for two curved shafts, of about two feet long, projected from it both in front and rear; and the lady, with arms crossed and a most vacant expression of countenance, rocked herself forwards and backwards—not sideways as in a cradle—her legs swinging, and her feet just touching the carpet. We both thought that she was some unfortunate person of feeble intellect, thus harmlessly amusing herself; and upon looking further into the chamber, we were still more surprised at observing another female

* Recounting this anecdote of my first impressions two or three years later, in one of the hospitable villas on the banks of the Hudson, an accomplished British peer, before and since then a cabinet minister, who was of the party, seemed surprised at my not having heard the gong before, assuring me that it was adopted in several English country houses, in place of the dinner bell; an instance of how ignorant my long residence on the continent had kept me of some of the *improvements* in English domestic life.

form, situated precisely as the first ; and they persevered in the motion, without seeming at all disturbed by being caught in such an absurd occupation, looking most ludicrously grave, and nodding like the figures of two mandarins in a tea warehouse. We felt for them more than they appeared to feel for themselves ; and we retreated, repressing the curiosity that would have made us stare longer, to see the result of the *tête à tête*, at which we should have laughed but from compassion to the poor creatures, whom we really and truly believed to be bordering on, if they had not passed, the limits of idiocy.

I need scarcely record, "by way of explanation," that what so much moved our pity and our wonder was nothing more than a couple of rocking chairs, those fine tributes to indolence, invented in Boston, and long since common to all America, and now not unknown in Europe. These are trivial details of "first impressions." But they are genuine ones, and I record them merely as a proof of the small matters which strike ignorant foreigners with wonderment in every new country. But for the future I shall avoid, as much as possible, indulging in anecdotes of the gong and rocking-chair genus.

The recollection of my first dinner at the Astor House lingers even now pleasantly on my palate—the place where *such* memories hold their seat. The good cooking and the good appetite, the large well-ventilated room, the pine apples, and the lumps of crystal ice in each glass of wine and water, making champagne taste as never it tasted before : these are delicious items in the account of the repast, which I covet to tot up again, even after a long lapse of time. But New York, on the whole, fell far short of my expectations. Broadway was too narrow to square with my preconceived notions, and its enormous length reminded me of a wounded snake. It is a perfect Alexandrine in street-making. The Battery, however, is really a beautiful promenade. Washington Square presents two sides of imposing appearance. Hudson Square, with its centre place of massive branching trees, is very handsome ; and there are several points of view worthy of a city of 500,000 souls. But its position between two rivers is too cramped to give sufficient verge on either side for the improvements which are called for by its increasing population and wealth. The public buildings are not remarkable, with the exception of the Exchange and the Custom House (both in course of erection when I first arrived), and they are absolutely lost in the confined space of one rather indifferent street, although they are edifices that should stand respectively in extensive areas, and to be rightly seen, should have been placed on some elevated spot, neither obstructed by crowds, nor hidden by intrusive houses.

My hurried observations during a two days' visit are scarcely fit to be set down, they were so very superficial. The extreme heat prevented our seeing much, and it probably indisposed us for the enjoyment of what we did see ; but there were many things of novelty to attract our attention, particularly the large mixture of coloured men and women flashily dressed. Any minute examination of the public institutions was of course out of the question ; and I may here take occasion to avow that I was not sorry at having a good excuse for declining every proposal to visit jails, hospitals, and penitentiaries.

The sight of suffering is to me at all times intensely painful. I pretend to no overactive sympathies with my kind, nor am I conscious of any morbid sensibility ; but I never voluntarily seek out sights of sorrow or disease from mere statistical curiosity. I like to take for granted the official reports of those matters, and to leave to overseers and guardians to ratify or correct them. Happily the world abounds with men whose taste lies that way, and whose sense of duty leads them to expose the abuses of authority. I have occasionally seen such sights at both sides of the Atlantic, to which I have been invited, but which I never courted. But I really think I never found any benefit from them. To watch the victims of disease, to mark the fitful wanderings of the insane, or to catechise the imprisoned criminal, have a harrowing effect upon me. I do not attempt to analyse it. But it invariably superinduces contempt for human nature, as well as compassion for its ills. Mankind, in its most favoured aspects, and in the intercourse of every-day life, is sufficiently capable of producing this result, without searching for it in the legalised cells of guilt or woe. I can gaze on a wild beast in its cage, but I turn from the grating which confines a maniac or a murderer.

On Monday Evening, July 29th, we embarked on board the "Massachusetts" steamer for Stonington, on our route to Boston. The arrangements on board this vessel were admirable. There were upwards of three hundred passengers, and nothing could exceed the order and regularity with which their accommodation was provided for. The discipline to which all submitted was worthy of a man of war. The evening meal, of tea, coffee, fish, flesh, and fowl, in all their varieties, was served with neatness and abundance. The cookery was certainly but mediocre, and the company was mixed. A perfectly democratic indifference to gradations of rank prevailed. Respect was paid only to the female portion of the crowd. They were first placed at table and in the best places. After them every one took his station on the cane-seated benches, ranged at each side down the double line of tables for the whole length of the immense saloon ; but there was none of the pushing and squeezing so common to a promiscuous mass of travellers in Europe. A spirit of forbearance seemed to pervade the whole. Every one decorously and silently sought his berth. And when we arrived at Stonington at three o'clock in the morning (having made the passage in ten hours, at the rate of fourteen miles an hour) they all quietly defiled from the deck to the quay, and walked to the train of carriages on the railroad close by, with the steadiness of a regiment on parade. The sailors and attendants on board, the latter being all coloured people, performed their duties without noise or bustle. Every body in fact seemed perfectly drilled. There were no materials for an awkward squad ; and what was most extraordinary, was the total absence of any appearance of control. The weather being extremely warm I found it impossible to sleep, even in the state room provided for me on deck ; so I passed almost the whole night in promenading above, and I never heard the voice of captain, pilot, or boatswain. The monotonous rise and fall of the piston, and the regular heaving of the engine gave the only notion of command. Men and machinery seemed to keep time together without any evident signal. I never before, except in military evolutions, saw anything to compare with the good management on board this fine steam-boat ; and, from ample subsequent experience, I can vouch for its being nothing extraordinary in the United States.

The early part of the passage, as long as daylight lasted, was very agreeable : the East River, as the sea route for an extent of thirty or forty miles between New York harbour and the Sound is called, presents a succession of pleasing views, though none of extraordinary beauty. The shore on either hand, Long Island to the right, and the main land to the left, is diversified with hill and dale, neat villages and country seats; while a couple of prisons, of fanciful architecture, are prominent features in the scene, and may be considered ornaments by those who see them with only an artist's eye, which does not penetrate their donjon towers. Hellgate, or Hurlgate, for it is called by both names, was to me an interesting point of observation, and my mind was carried back to "the money diggers" and the days of Captain Kidd. The tide was just at the proper height to let this celebrated pass be seen to advantage. The rocks, more than half hidden, were lashed by the angry whirlpool, our paddles increasing the commotion of the waves; and a little schooner lying wrecked on one of the rough ledges, proving the danger of the place to such small craft in foul winds. A glorious setting sun, succeeded by the brilliant moonshine, lighted us onwards; and for hours, as I paced the hurricane deck, I amused myself watching the contrasts produced by these and the stream of fiery sparks from the chimney, with the phosphoric brightness of the sea through which we cut our rapid track.

The varieties of human nature all round or below me were not so marked. Character seemed moulded, for the time, into one regular standard, as though the weight and measure of each separate mind had a national stamp affixed to them, to give them a common value. There was difference of countenance, but sameness of expression. So it was as to cloth, in distinction from costume. The features of the many faces were finer or coarser, as the fabrics of the garments worn by their possessors. But one unvarying cut and pattern was seen throughout ; and it was, both as to mere humanity and its covering, of a very ordinary kind. The tone of the men and women was common-place ; the fashion of their dress the same. Equality was more evident than liberty, in as far as the latter implies the power of gratifying individual whim or fancy. The movements of all were as nearly as possible alike. There was nothing curved or angular in any of their actions. They walked in straight lines, sat erect on the stools or benches, smoked their cigars and spat on the upper, and chewed their quids and spat on the lower deck, or read their newspapers and spat in the cabin, and had their "drinks" and spat at "the bar," with a marvellous regularity. It was, take it all in all, a most curious specimen of living mechanism, completed and brought into action by the irresistible force of public opinion and general habit. But the first aspect of this monotony was imposing, and it created a certain feeling of respect, which being partaken by each individual in regard of his fellows, was sure to be returned to him by the mass. The total absence of everything discourteous, of quarrelling, disputation, and cursing, of vehement language or violent gesticulation, gave to every group of talkers the air of a knot of business men transacting their affairs ; and the journey, by water or land, seemed merely a link in the various mercantile transactions which took them from or brought them back to home. No man in the steamboat or the railroad cars (as the carriages are everywhere called) had the slightest appearance of a traveller for pleasure's sake. Some of our fellow passengers in the "British Queen" accompanied us to Boston, and relieved the dulness which might otherwise have become oppressive.

The tract of country through which the railroad lies, in Connecticut, Rhode Island, and Massachusetts, is rather barren and unpicturesque, We passed by Providence some distance to the left. A few scattered villages, one or two of them of a straggling extent, sufficient to make them be called towns, seemed built entirely of wood, and each house being painted white, the whole had an air of glaring and naked neatness that did not look comfortable even when shone on by the rising sun. Bleak, arid, and stony, with masses of stunted trees, and pools or ponds intermixed, the ideas of forest and flood, that in spite of one is associated with every bit of American landscape, was checked on the eighty miles of railroad route. No cattle were to be seen in the fields ; and the population might be looked for in vain. We were therefore glad as we approached Boston to find the face of the country improve, while the gradual increase of farmhouses and cottages, well-peopled hamlets to the right and left, and, as we got nearer, several villas, announced the neighbourhood of a large and wealthy city. We were now soon summoned to gaze from the windows on the left at the State House of Boston, standing high in the midst of a mass of red brick buildings, and after passing by the neat villages of Roxbury and Brookline, with several others in sight on the rising grounds, and traversing a swamp of two miles extent, flanked on either side by lake-like branches of the sea, we finally reached the railroad station (invariably named in America the *dépôt,* and sometimes pronounced the *depott*) at the outskirts of the town. Good carriages were provided to convey the passengers to their various destinations ; and we were soon safely set down at Tremont House, the principal hotel.

CHAPTER III.

BOSTON.—NAHANT.

Feelings on arrival—General appearance of Boston—Road to Nahant—Description of the Place—Historical Memoranda—The Hotel—Atmospheric Phenomena—Society—Sky Scenery—Its Delusive Effects on the Imagination—Moral Analogy.

My sensations on entering the city of Boston were, in a certain degree, such as one feels on coming home after a long absence. Viewing this place as the probable scene of a residence of years, I had reckoned on my arrival there as the completion of one important stage on life's journey. And considering it in the more endearing aspect of a safe harbour, gained after hard buffeting in a stormy world, I had been for months looking forward to it with feelings of sincere and cordial good will. I had been constantly during that time talking and reading about it, endeavouring to make myself familiar with all its bearings, historical and local. Many of its leading inhabitants having been the subject of numerous conversations in Europe and on the voyage, I could not look upon myself as quite a stranger among them, and I was disposed to meet every advance from those individuals, or indeed from the citizens generally, fully halfway on the path of intimacy and friendship.

Independent of these claims to my personal regard, Boston possessed many attractive peculiarities; it is not only famous from its association with the early struggles of the American Revolution, but a superiority over the other cities of the Union seems to be generally conceded to the refinement of its society and the literary taste of its inhabitants. It is known as the birth-place of Franklin, and, in modern days, as the head quarters of the North American Review, the only transatlantic periodical which is at all recognised, or I might say at all known, in England. It was besides, when I arrived, the residence of Dr. Channing, Edward Everett, the historians Bancroft and Prescott, Mr. Goodrich, better known as Peter Parley; and a numerous body of small literati, the authors of the "Book of Boston," which musters, if I rightly remember, full fifty contributors.

Then it is the very focus of the anti-slavery party in the United States; that generous body of enthusiasts who have stamped it with celebrity in the abolition cause, obtaining for the great majority of its population a fame that is justly the property of a very few.

Altogether I looked on Boston as the greenest spot in the comparative waste, to explore which my fate had sent me; and as a residence in the New World must at best be felt by the man of European tastes and habits as a banishment, I over and over congratulated myself on the good fortune which made me for a while a part and parcel as it were, of the most desirable portion of its vast extent. And so feeling, it may be well believed that I considered the various groups in the streets, as we drove along, as my neighbours ready made, and that I entered into the system of hand-shaking, which commenced on the very steps of the hotel, with a heartiness and warmth such as sanguine-minded men give to whatever is to them a reality.

The first appearance of Boston is calculated to make a

most favourable impression. It is well-built, clean, and bearing evidence of increasing embellishment in every quarter. It is far more English-looking than New York. It has no long avenue, like Broadway, planted with trees and shaded with awnings, to remind you of the Paris Boulevards; nor are there rows of painted houses by a river side, to bring up the recollection of some Dutch scene. The plan of Boston is very irregular, like the formation of the ground it is built on. There are bits of great beauty to be selected in various of the street views; and I think the "Common," the homely appellation of a handsomely planted park of sixty acres extent, with the streets which look upon it at three sides, and the view of the sea and distant hilly country covered with villages, is altogether one of the finest things of its kind which I had ever seen.

At the other extremity of the town is a series of wharves and quays, of most solid and imposing construction. The warehouses (here called stores), mainly built of granite, with their large windows, thanks to the absence of any tax on the light of heaven, look like long lines of splendid dwellings, and only require porticos and colonnades to have the air of so many palaces. A quantity of shipping mix their tall masts with these handsome erections. The public buildings scattered through the town are not remarkable, except in general for the economical tone of their structure, and in some instances for the extreme bad taste of their style. The new Custom-house, just begun at the time of my arrival, and the Exchange, long afterwards commenced and quickly finished, are exceptions. The former, in spite of some architectural defects, is a handsome ornament to the city; the latter is a plain, but striking feature in State Street, the main place of business, of which its *façade*, with six fine granite pilasters, is the chief object of observation.

But it is not from any point within the city that it appears really what it is—the flourishing capital of a populous extent of country. To see it aright you must ascend the neighbouring heights of Roxbury, Dorchester, or Bunker's Hill; whence its dimensions, with those of the suburb villages in its immediate vicinity, seem joined in one immense mass of habitations, intermixed with spires and domes, stretching far into the land, and lining the sea-shore for several miles.

But the advantage of seeing Boston in these various favourable aspects was not to be indulged in immediately on my arrival. The foregoing sketch is from after-examination. My most lively wish in the earliest hours of my arrival, was to escape, as soon as possible, from the overpowering heat to the remotest point of rock or sand-bank visible in the harbour. We accordingly made our arrangements for removing to Nahant the following day, having been preceded to this fashionable bathing-place by a family who had been our companions from London to Boston, and who promised to make every effort to procure us accommodation in the crowded hotel.

Having duly taken possession of my office, into which I was inducted by the deputy of my predecessor, he being absent in Canada; and having left for distribution some of the many letters of introduction given to me by friends in Europe, we escaped from the fiery furnace—for so Boston really seemed to me, and proceeded on Wednesday, July 31st, by railroad to Lynn, a distance of nine miles; and thence by a stage coach to the Nahant Hotel, situated on the extreme South Eastern point of that exquisitely refreshing and picturesque peninsula.

This place is so curious, and indeed so unique, and is associated with so many interesting recollections, as being our first resting-place in America, that I must pause and dwell on it for the extent of a few pages, an hour or two, perhaps, of *writing*, not of reading, mind you, gentle individual, whoever you be, that may be startled at the promised episode, in manuscript or print.

The usual way of beginning to describe a place with an unexplainable name, is to give a variety of definitions and derivations, one more incomprehensible than the other. The only pleasing point which I can discover among the conjectures of this nature, as to the origin of the word Nahant, is that a certain wife of a somewhat uncertain chief, called Montowampate, Sachem of the Saugus Indians, bore the euphonious name of Nahanta. Now whether she was called after the peninsula, or the peninsula after her,* I do not pretend to determine, but it is pleasant to be able to associate the question with the memory of one of the fair sex, and there I leave it. Montowampate was succeeded in his sovereignty by his brother Winnepurkitt. This chieftain, the last of the Sagamores, had three daughters, viz., Petagunsk, Wuttaquattinusk, and Petagoonaquah. He died, and with him expired his illustrious dynasty. Whether or not Masconomond, the Sagamore of Agawam, was of the same family, is to this day a disputed point. So is the connection between that branch and Poquannun, or Dark-skin, and his daughter Ahawayetsquaine, and her brother Queakussen, familiarly and somewhat irreverently called by the first English settlers, "Captain Tom."

* "Pray, Mr. Murphy, were the potatoes called after you, or you after the potatoes?" was a question once put by an English gentleman to a very loquacious countryman of mine, and with a most silencing effect.

But I must resist the temptation of culling any further flowers of genealogy in this fertile field, and pass rapidly on to the celebrated individual who first disposed of his territorial rights in Nahant to the British. This was the Sachem of Swampscot, whose double *sobriquet*, handed down in history, was Duke William, or Black Will. This chieftain seems to have been rather loose in his construction of the principles of bargain and sale, having bartered his sovereignty several times to different individuals: to one of whom, Farmer Dexter, of Saugus river, he disposed of it for the sole consideration of a suit of clothes, while another claimant, one Witter, insisted that he bought it from "the Duke" for the valuable consideration of "two pestle stones."

These transactions led to a lawsuit between Dexter and the town of Lynn, the inhabitants of which occupied a portion of the peninsula, in part as a sheep pasture, and also as a convenient place for turning their swine into the woods, "that they might fatten themselves on nuts and acorns;" a fence of rails having been previously made across "the beach" to keep out the wolves, as it is notorious that these animals do not climb. Nahant was for many years the subject of litigation, but the inhabitants of Lynn finally succeeded in holding it against all claimants, and they possess jurisdiction and ownership over it to this day.

The moral to be drawn from this historical sketch is, that those Puritan sons of "the Pilgrim Fathers," the fantastic nickname given by their descendants to the early settlers—soon commenced their system of trickery on the poor aborigines; who were thus in the second generation rifled, according to law, of the remnants of the property wrenched from the first, by force of arms.

With respect to Nahant itself, the most curious feature of these records, carefully collected by Mr. Alonzo Lewis, in his "History of Lynn," is the fact of its having been a couple of centuries ago completely covered with forest trees. This seems almost incredible—at any rate apocryphal—to any one who sees it now, and who learns on all sides that it is almost impossible to persuade a clump of willows or poplars into growth. But a strong confirmation of the statement is to be found in a curious old work called "New England's Prospect," written in 1633 by William Wood, and which was undertaken, as the author assures us, "because there hath been many scandalous and false reports past upon the countrie, even from the sulphurous breath of every base ballad-monger."

The portion of this "Apologie for New England," which relates to the place I am now treating of is as follows:

"The next plantation is Saugus (as Lynn was then called), six miles North-east from Winnesimet. This towne is pleasant for situation, seated at the bottom of a bay, which is made on the one side with the surrounding shore, and on the other side with a long sandy beach. This sandy beach is two miles long, at the end whereof is a necke of land called Nahant. It is nine miles in circumference, well wooded with oakes, pines, and cedars. It is beside well watered, having, beside the fresh springs, a great pond in the middle, before which is a spacious marsh. In this necke is a store of good ground fit for the plow; but for the present it is only used for to put young cattel in, and weather goates and swine, to secure them from the woolves; a few posts and rayles, from the low water-markes to the shore, keepes out the woolves and keepes in the cattel. One Black William, an Indian

Duke, out of his generosity, gave this place in generall to this plantation of Saugus, so that no other can appropriate it to himselfe."

I will not transcribe the rest of the long description, which would have small interest for any but those who are attached by recollections (as I myself am) to Nahant. Its many visitors will perhaps smile, in the conscious pride of improvement, at these records of wild beasts and forests, in a place which has now neither wolves nor woods; and instead of an Indian Duke giving away his territory "*out of generosity*"—poor Black Will!—can show only a few Yankee Republicans, who know very little indeed of that gift-impelling quality.

The most striking feature of Nahant at the present day, as well as of the numerous islands of the great bay into which it advances, is its barrenness of aspect. Utterly denuded of those "oakes, pines, and cedars," mentioned by the old chronicler, a mass of naked surface and rocky projections form the natural appearance of the place; while art, in its least tasteful mood, has studded it with cottages, neat, but with two or three exceptions, quite unornamental.* There is now scarcely a stump to be discovered of the wolf-infested forest of which we have read so much. Nahant and the islands of the bay owe their present nakedness to having been early robbed of their trees for firewood, and to the absence of all taste for ornamental improvement, unconnected with profit, in

* The chief among those few exceptions is the residence of Mr. Tudor, a gentleman who has liberally striven for the improvement of Nahant; and whose cottage, gardens, and young plantations, are models of good taste and enterprise. His example has not as yet been followed by any of the other wealthy proprietors. Indeed, they look upon Mr. Tudor's innovations as rather objectionable—"workings against nature," as a learned neighbour of his once called them, in reply to my expression of approbation.

the rich people of Boston; or indeed for any kind of outlay that does not promise a large and quick return.

On the 13th of June, 1668, Robert Page, of Boston, was "presented," as is shown by the town records of Lynn, "for setinge saile from Nahant in his boate, being loaden with woode, thereby profaning the Lord's daye." The offence in this case did not consist however in stealing the wood, but in carrying it away on Sunday. In fact the town of Lynn, had in the year 1656, made an order for clearing the land, inflicting a penalty of fifty shillings on those who neglected to clear their lots within six years from the date of their grants; but the order of the town meeting concludes with a strict prohibitory clause, in the following words:—

"And it is to be remembered that no person is to raise any kind of building at all."

How long this bar against settlement remained in force does not appear. But the usual gradations of civilisation may be regularly traced; the savage Indians having driven out the wild beasts, and being in their turn expelled by the pious Puritans, by force or fraud. In the hands of these conscientious proprietors, the place became first a pasture for "cattel and swine;" next a station for the catching and curing of fish; afterwards a depôt for fuel for the neighbouring towns; then as a cleared and cultivated tract; and finally, about the beginning of the present century, a resort for pleasure parties from Boston, and so on by regular improvement until it became the most fashionable watering-place in New England.*

* On reading the above sentence, three or four years after it was written, I find another of the many instances of rapid change which take place in the United States. Newport, in Rhode Island, which was, until very lately, one of the most secluded summer haunts for a few Southern families, its yearly visitors, has now become a crowded, bustling, and rather boisterous resort of company of

Cottage-villas rose up rapidly; and in a few seasons there appeared a church, a school-house, a large hotel, and a couple of small ones. Stages were established, to cross the beach to Lynn several times each day during the season; a steamboat was regularly employed to carry passengers to and from Boston, a distance of twelve miles; and the opening of a railroad between that city and Lynn —but reaching much farther to the eastward—completed the facilities for communicating with the Peninsula, which indeed was all that was hitherto wanting to make it the crowded resort of company during the summer months.

Nothing can look more barren and uninviting than this place, seen on the right of the railroad leading from Boston to Lynn. The country to the left presents a succession of wooded elevations, forming what is commonly, and I need not say absurdly, called an *undulating* landscape; for except in cases of earthquake that epithet is without meaning, applied to the solid hills and vales of *terra firma*. Stretching at the foot of these elevations and widely scattered in the meadow-land, is a long succession of white wooden houses, with their little gardens and enclosures, composing the town of Lynn. This place extends for a length of two or three miles, and contains a population of about 10,000, nine-tenths of which are shoemakers, whose labour supplies the South with some hundreds of thousands of pairs per annum; but the trade of this locality in this article being rigidly wholesale, I have been repeatedly assured, by persons

all possible kinds. Hotels of enormous size have sprung up; villas have been profusely built; old boarding houses enlarged and new ones erected; and by these results of fashionable caprice, Nahant has sunk into comparative obscurity.

who made the vain attempt, that it is impossible to purchase a single pair of shoes in the town, and that nothing short of a case containing some dozens can be had for love or money.

Between this far-stretching settlement and the sea is a marsh, over which the railroad has been constructed, and at three or four miles distance from the shore on the right hand Nahant is seen rising above the water, and joined to the main land by a curved beach of nearly two miles in length. The latter is the first portion met with after crossing the great beach; it is at high water almost an island, containing about fifty acres, and being joined by a second beach, about a quarter the extent of the former one, to the much larger division of territory, which consists of 600 acres, of irregular formation, and gives its name to the whole. On Little Nahant there are as yet no habitations; but a great part of it is under cultivation, containing, like the principal portion (to use the description of old Wood) "store of good ground fit for the plow." There are several other shorter beaches around the two Nahants; but excepting these sandy curvatures at intervals, the shore is entirely rock-bound, "the very aspect of the place" (I quote again from the same authority) "being fortification enough to keepe off an unknowne enemie."

To this general description I must add a few historical and characteristic memoranda, which bear upon some of the individuals already mentioned, or the other productions indigenous to the district.

In 1663, Thomas Dexter, the purchaser of Nahant (I call him so by courtesy), was ordered to be "set in the bilbowes, disfranchised, and fined x£; for speakinge reproachful and seditious wordes against the government here established." And in August, 1646, the same worthy was presented at the quarterly session, as a "common sleeper in meetings for public worship," and heavily fined.

But previously to this last offence (it was in the year 1633), an event took place which might have caused him some unquiet dreams. The poor Indian, Duke William, or Black Will, who had been choused out of his patrimonial rights by this same "Farmer Dexter," in the way already mentioned, was hanged, "in revenge," says the record, "for the murder of one Walter Bagnall, who was killed by the Indians on the 3rd of October, 1631." It does not, however, appear that the poor "Duke" had any hand in the murder, so as to justify this most unchristian act of vengeance on the part of the pious sons of the Pilgrim Fathers; but, even if he had, Governor Winthrop bore testimony that "Bagnall was a wicked fellow, and had much wronged the Indians."

In 1634, on "training day," Captain Turner went from Boston with his company to Nahant, to hunt the wolves by which it was infested.

On the 6th March, 1704, the town of Lynn took measures, but too late, to check the spoliation of the natural treasures of Nahant, which had been so strictly enjoined half a century before. Being informed that several persons had cut down several trees or bushes in Nahant, "whereby there is likely to be no shade left for *the creatures*" (the sheep), it was voted that no person thereafter should cut any tree or bush there under penalty of ten shillings.

In the great snow storm of 1717, a great number of deer came from the woods for food, and some fled to Nahant, and being chased by the *wolves*, leaped into the sea and were drowned.

In 1749, the summer was extremely dry and hot. Immense multitudes of grasshoppers appeared. They were so numerous at Nahant, that the inhabitants walked together, with bushes in their hands, and drove them by thousands into the sea.

But I must not indulge in those old extracts, which, *in*-elegant as I admit them to be both in subject and in style, have nevertheless more interest for me, for reasons before mentioned, than many a modern matter on which I shall have to dilate as I proceed. And having thus given a general notion of Nahant as it was, I must leave much of its actual aspect to the imagination of my readers.

Nahant is really so unlike any other "watering-place," so little is done for it by its owners or inhabitants, and so much of its attractions depend on association, that it might be hard to account for the great charm it contains, for most of those who frequent it. Seen only on a wet, or foggy, or stormy day, by the "transient visitor," to use a funny phrase common all through America, he must have a poor idea of the place, and of those who love and praise it. But to him who has lounged in the cool piazzas of the hotel or his cottage residence, when the thermometer a few miles off ranges between 90° and 100°; or walked the smooth sward, or mused among the jutting crags, or sat in some granite niche, and let his mind keep time to the murmur of the surge in the caverns around; or dreamily watched the ripple on the sandy coves; or gazed at such gorgeous sunsets as Italy cannot rival, or at moon and starlight of such intense brilliancy as no one sees in Europe; to such a one, the impression made by this delicious place, is such as words can feebly tell.

But there are frequent atmospheric phenomena almost peculiar to this spot, which give it still better claims to notice. I speak not of the glorious thunder storms, when piles of thick clouds come rolling from the westward, and lightning flashes seem to pierce down through the foaming waves,—nor of the mists which rush in suddenly from the sea, veiling for awhile the whole peninsula in vapour, then breaking off as quickly, while the dazzling sunbeams bring out every rock and shrub, as it were, into a new creation of light. Nor of visitations of aurora borealis, more expansive and vivid than I had ever seen before. I mean more particularly than all these the magical *mirages*, which in the heats of summer rise all round the bay, giving to the islands which stud it, to the wood-covered and town-sprinkled shores of the main land, and to the shipping which is scattered on the waters, appearances so fantastic, as to realise our imaginings of fairyland, and endow "airy nothings" with the tone and colouring of fact.

Ah! if this wild spot on such occasions, when it seems as if heaven has come down to earth, or earth been raised up towards heaven, were bereft of those human realities which too plainly recall us to truth,—if, in place of the vain and vulgar, no forms but the shadowless beings of fancy were near—if, instead of those twanging voices which syllable men's names, no sounds reached us but the hum of insects or the murmur of the waves, how elevated might the mind become, how softened the passions, how improved the heart! But the utmost stretching of imagination cannot convert the beautiful into the perfect. The alloy of humanity is everywhere mixed with nature's purest creations. And we catch these glimpses of paradise, only to feel the more keenly that it is desecrated by man.

I am disposed to dwell somewhat longer on my

description of Nahant and its associations than the place may seem worth, because it affords a fair specimen of the summer life of American gentility, and from my residence there having allowed me admirable opportunities for observation on national character and the workings of institutions.

On our first arrival, the large and uncomfortable hotel was so crowded that we were compelled to be content with very scanty accommodation. But at best it could afford but little besides pure air and pleasant company. Constructed for the purpose of stowing away as many lodgers as possible, it was nothing better than a huge pigeon-house, with a number of sleeping cribs wretchedly furnished, a couple of drawing-rooms (for the common service), as many parlours to receive parties of "transients," and a dining-hall capable of accommodating about two hundred persons. But it was surrounded by two piazzas, on the ground-floor and the first story, of sufficient width to make most agreeable promenades, either in warm or wet weather. On the upper of these the ladies congregated in groups for walking, or in gossiping parties on the settees; while the lower one was destined to the exclusive use of the gentlemen to smoke, chew, and drink drams, from early morning until late at night. Sometimes a few stragglers came up and joined the parties above, particularly in the evenings when the most natural hour for flirtation arrives. But, in fact, it is only then that much intercourse between the sexes can be expected; for nine out of ten of the male visitors to Nahant are obliged to go off at a very early hour to Boston, by stage or steamboat, to attend their daily drudgery. When they return in the evening they are tired, and not much inclined for anything but indulgence in the delights of the bar-room or the lower balcony. The great majority of men in America having small taste for female society, the lighter duties connected with it consequently devolve upon a few.

The genius of republican institutions and of the Nahant Hotel being opposed to the comforts of privacy, and irregular hours for eating, there are no private sitting-rooms tolerated there, and no family ventures on the luxury of dining alone. The infernal gong summons you to table at fixed and unvarying periods; and the unrefined habits of the people carry early hours to a ridiculous excess. The first meal begins at seven, the second is served at two, and the third at six in the evening. Some latitude is allowed for late risers in the morning, that is to say those who cannot get up at sunrise, or late comers in the afternoon. But one of the things which first struck me as most singular is the pride which almost everyone seemed to take in being strictly punctual at meals, and the extreme rapidity with which they were despatched. I had, of course, read and heard enough of these American peculiarities before I left Europe; but I did not expect to find them carried into the customs of a fashionable watering-place, where everybody might be supposed to be devoted to comfort, not to say idleness; and where the greatest difficulty is to kill time by the easiest possible death. But I soon found it was considered as a serious reproach to be a quarter of an hour late to breakfast or tea, and not much less so to linger that much after the many had bolted their dinner. This meal does not, in fact, form in America an epoch for social enjoyment. It, like all others, is transacted purely as a matter of business. The pleasures of the table, as combining indulgence of appetite and taste with intellectual intercourse between the sexes, are wholly unappreciated by the persons assembled in this hotel. The tone for such pleasures must be given by men ; and the male portion of this company are quite incapable of giving it. Either absorbed in business, or addicted to a mean order of amusements, they want altogether the required taste. I was soon convinced that the women possessed all the conversational talent, and the love for literature and the fine arts. But even in them this is but a theoretic love, and there are no opportunities for its becoming practical. A mere abstract taste for the arts will make scarcely one woman or man in a thousand a good musician, painter, or poet. The harmonies of colour, sound, or thought may be in their souls ; but the fostering sympathy of beholders, listeners, or readers is essential to their full development. Taste for the arts is not a solitary passion. It was meant by Providence for the advantage of mankind, not for isolated individual indulgence. That mutual dependence on each other which forms the great link of connection in our social system throws us of necessity on the encouragement of our kind. A visionary abstractionist may now and then perform a miracle of composition in utter seclusion. But these rare exceptions only prove the general rule, that the arts can only flourish in the atmosphere of social sympathy. And this rule establishes the truth, that a passion for art in the abstract is not only inferior but subservient to the kindly associations of nature.

Deprived, then, of the chief essential to improvement, the Boston ladies, of whom Nahant in the summer season furnishes a fair specimen, are but indifferent instrumental performers, have the rudest notions of singing, and can at best but execute a feeble pencil sketch. A few good voices may be heard; but the unfortunate nasal pronunciation of New England is a positive, and the want of scientific instruction a negative, drawback on the advantage. About half-a-dozen young persons, in what is considered the fashionable circle of Boston, have the hardihood to attempt Italian music in a small way. But the great majority of those addicted to "the harmony of sweet sounds" confine themselves to the plainest English songs; and the piazzas of the hotel, or the rocks of Nahant, echo nothing more *récherché* than a duet from the "National Melodies," or "Auld lang syne," in a somewhat discordant chorus.*

The attractions of female society here are therefore owing in but a small degree to acquired accomplishments. They are nevertheless considerable. They consist in pretty faces, gay, unaffected manners, and a prevalent command of temper which is indeed quite a national characteristic. Light literature has numerous votaries among these fair ones. Reviews and magazines are discussed with avidity; and any English author of novels at all popular is sure to have been generally read and highly esteemed. These ladies are quick in conversation and fond of good small talk. Judging from the goings on in this hotel (and after-experience confirmed the impression), I should say that no proportionate given part of the Old World, can furnish anything approaching to the quantity of flirtation which is consumed in this section of the New. I find myself so much infected with the spirit of the place, as to rank almost everything as a commodity of barter and sale. The article just specified is of such very flimsy texture that it costs nothing and is worth nothing. This

* It must in justice be mentioned that, of late years, very considerable improvement in the practice and encouragement of music has taken place in American society.

accounts for its being so freely thrown away. But these are only passing observations. I shall be sure to devote a chapter elsewhere to the women of America and their peculiar pursuits, in which some better digested remarks will find a place.

We found so general a disposition to receive us well and to make the place agreeable to us, that we soon formed several pleasant acquaintanceships with various families belonging to Boston and the neighbouring towns. Nothing could be more easy and familiar than our intercourse with them ; and we considered ourselves fortunate in thus gaining in a few weeks a footing with many of those in whose society we were destined to live, and which a year of formal visiting and occasional parties would have failed to ensure us. On first taking possession of our little, cabin-like bed-rooms,* and walking the piazzas as we so recently walked the deck, or attending the long table at meal times, it was difficult to divest ourselves of the notion that we had only moved from one ship to another, and that we were still at sea. Look which way we would, the ocean seemed to surround us ; vessels of various sizes were constantly passing. The bracing air blew freshly upon us. And it was only when we descended to the rocks which lie at foot of the hotel, that we could quite realise the notion of a land life. Within the house there was a constant bustle. Walking, talking, eating, singing (such as it was), piano dances, reading parties, whist parties, and the everlasting noise of children, formed the staple productions of the day and night. There were also riding and driving parties, boating parties, billiards, nine pins

* The old hotel above described has been pulled down, and replaced by one of much larger dimensions and far superior accommodation.

(a favourite game with both sexes), sentimental musings on the crags, and, most interesting of all, occupation for hours of delight, in the sunsets, and the frequent occurrence of those *mirages*, which I have before mentioned, and on which I could dilate for page after page if there was no risk of tiring any one but myself. It really often happened to me to gaze on the mockeries so vividly pictured on the false horizon, until I believed for a moment that the forests, the ruins, the splendid edifices were all real, and that I was transported back to the scenery of Europe, in some of its most picturesque and brilliant sites. But when the cheatery passed away, and left behind mere shrubs and rocks and wooden houses, which had been so falsely magnified and beautified by the vapoury medium they were seen through, the re-action was proportionably painful, and the truth appeared even less attractive than it really was.

And analogous to this feeling is the moral re-action which oppresses almost all Europeans, who remain in this country for more than a short period. At first they see everything in bright and flattering hues. Vivacity of manners, professions of regard, dinner parties, and balls, look like sincerity, friendship, and hospitality. But the erroneous impression is soon dissipated. The astonished stranger, who has believed himself revelling in the cordial enjoyments of the old world, is quickly satisfied of his mistake. He is painfully taught that he felt through a false medium. That the charms which had bewitched him lay only on the surface of society. That the roses which gave their hue to everything had no root in the soil. That the affections in America are without any solid basis. That men are too much absorbed in self to enter on the cultivation of the nobler feelings. And that even women are so driven by the force of things from the impulses of their nature, as to have little more than the semblance of those generous qualities which elevate them, in other parts of the world, to the very height of human excellence.

But I am widely anticipating. The experience on which these conclusions are founded came by slow degrees ; and the opinion so advisedly recorded, in winding up my sketch of our earliest notions at Nahant was not permanently formed until after several seasons passed there, with ample opportunity for remark and reflection in the intervals, in various portions of the country.

CHAPTER IV.

NAHANT.

Indians—Sea Serpent—Church Service—Religious Feeling—Cookery—Drinks—National Slang—Passionate love of Pork—A Tirade against Tobacco: Smoking, Chewing—American Gentlemen.

My summer's residence gave me many glimpses of insight into the national character, and it must be observed that I made, like the rest of the male visitors, almost a daily trip to Boston, by which means, and the constant reading of newspapers, I soon acquired a general knowledge of public events. But as I knew well the immense mistakes which are constantly made by hasty travellers, who feel bound to form fixed opinions on the most imperfect premises, I took care not to pronounce a decisive judgment on any matter of importance relative to the people or the institutions of America, without ample time for reflection. Some light symptoms of character, lying loose, were too easily picked up; for even these, as indications of more solid matter beneath, were liable to be mistaken for other than they really were. Of these I might specify many instances. It may be enough just to mention "love-making" (so to call it) as an evidence of passion; hand-shaking, of cordiality; hob-nobbing, of good fellowship; smiles, of warm-heartedness. I admit myself to have made a few such mistakes as these at starting. But in the process of undeceiving myself, I acquired an increase of caution to save me from more serious errors.

We had not been a week at Nahant when our attention was called one evening to a little squadron of bark canoes making for the land, and we then saw, for the first time, a group of Indians, who, throwing aside their paddles, dragged their fragile vessels high on the strand of one of the coves, not far from the hotel. In a very short time men, women, and children had disembarked the scanty baggage and cooking utensils; and as soon as some curious observers, of whom I was one, could reach the landing place, preparations for the rude encampment were completed. Three or four stakes stuck upright into the earth, close to the sheltering rocks, with a couple of old sails hung above and at the side, from which the wind blew, and some skins spread on the ground, formed the "parental roof," or "domestic hearth," or both, under and around which groups of dark-skinned, long-haired, little Indian boys and girls quickly began to disport, some amusing themselves with bows and arrows, while the women and elder children, wrapped in loose cotton gowns, incontinently squatted down before the tents and began with a mechanical air, and in melancholy or moo ly silence, to make wicker baskets from materials ready at hand. The men, who were dressed in the ordinary ga ·b of fishermen, were busy in preparing their cargoes for the market, or in spreading out their nets to dry. The scene altogether, first observed in the glowing sunset and subsequently by the glare of the watch-fires, was most picturesque. It was also particularly appropriate to the place, for it formed a fine medium through which to direct the mind back to the days when the Sachems of Swampscot, or the Sagamores of Agawam, pitched their tents in the forest of Nahant, happy and powerful at the head of the tribes of whom the poor creatures now before me were the degenerate descendants. These belonged to the remnant of the Six Nations, generally known as the Penobscot Indians, whose chief settlement is at some distance from Bangor, in the State of Maine. They are little other in character and habits than the gipsies of Europe, but without their vagabond vivacity. These Indians, with their dark brown skins and lounging and listless air, are far different in appearance from the people among whom they exist on precarious sufferance ; and it requires no stretch of fancy to see in them a tone of hereditary regret for the soil which was theirs by natural right.

No one could look with an eye of indifference or of calculation on this fragment of a ruined people, except the accustomed Yankees, the descendants of the spoilers, who speculate on turning the labours of the semi-savage wanderers to account. I am not, however, going to insert a sentimental palinode in this place on the political crimes of former days or the heartless system of the present time. I mention this small incident of scenery, for it pretends to be nothing more, only as one of those casual accessories which were mixed with my earliest experience of the New World.

Another visit to the shores of Nahant during my first stay there, of which I had good evidence, must find a record here. I allude to no less a circumstance than the advent of the celebrated sea serpent, the existence or non-existence of which had formed for several years a topic of animated discussion, and furnished matter for many a fable, many a sarcasm, and innumerable squibs, good, bad, and indifferent. On our first arrival we soon heard a great deal, half in jest, half in earnest, about the monster which, fabulous or real, had given so much notoriety to the shores of Massachusetts bay. It was in the year 1817 that the sea serpent was first said to have been seen at Gloucester, near Cape Anne. Between that period and the 5th August, 1820, many doubtful reports of its appearance, with contradictory assertions, were promulgated; but on that day it made its first absolutely evident visit to the Bay of Nahant, and it was distinctly observed during calm and warm weather within a quarter of a mile of Phillips's beach on the western side of the bay. Three inhabitants of the place, men of veracity, went out in a boat on a voyage of discovery, and got within 30 yards of the illustrious stranger before he sank beneath the waves. They observed him minutely at that short distance, and their accounts were positive and unhesitating as to his appearance. He was seen again the next day farther out from shore, and for twenty successive years numbers of persons of respectability and good sense, credible witnesses as to any fact, made various depositions as to the time, place, and circumstance of their seeing the occasional visitations of this monster of the deep, with a coincidence as to general characteristics, and occasional variations as to certain details, in the highest degree confirmatory of the common assertion, that an animal known by the appellation of the sea serpent was frequently seen in the waters of the neighbourhood.

My own notions on the subject had not acquired any particular consistency. When I thought on the matter at all it was in the same spirit that actuates me in respect to any well-authenticated statement of extraordinary events. Without actually believing what I do not myself see, I never feel justified in altogether doubting what is pronounced on respectable testimony to have taken place. I have really seen so many things beyond the pale of usual occurrence, that I have great toleration for reports which many persons deem extravagant ; and I was in fact quite prepared to see and believe in the sea serpent, whenever it might chance to appear. An opportunity was very soon afforded to me.

On a Sunday afternoon in the middle of August, above a hundred persons, at that time in and about the hotel, were called on to observe an extraordinary appearance in the sea, at no great distance from the shore. Large shoals of small fish were rushing landwards in great commotion, leaping from the water, crowding on each other, and showing all the common symptoms of flight from the pursuit of some wicked enemy. I had already more than once remarked this appearance from the rocks, but in a minor degree, and on these occasions I could always distinguish the shark, whose ravages among the "manhaidens" was the cause of such alarm. But the particular case in question was far different from those. The pursuer of the fugitive shoals soon became visible ; and that it was a huge marine monster, stretching to a length quite beyond the dimensions of an ordinary fish, was evident to all the observers. No one, in short, had any doubt as to its being the sea serpent, or one of the species, to which the animal or animals so frequently before seen belonged. The distance at which this one was for ten minutes or a quarter of an hour, visible, made it impossible to give a description of its apparent dimensions so accurate as to carry conviction to the sceptical. For us who witnessed it, it was enough to be convinced that the thing was a reality. But one of the spectators, Dr. Amos Binney,* a gentleman

* This most worthy and respectable gentleman has since died in Italy ; a real loss to Boston.

of scientific attainments, drew up a minute account of it, which is deposited in the archives of one of the Philosophical Societies of Boston. I was and am quite satisfied that on this occasion I had a partial and indistinct but positive view of this celebrated nondescript. But had the least doubt rested on my mind, it would have been entirely removed by the event of the day following the one just recorded. On that day, a little before noon, my wife was sitting, as was her wont, reading on the upper piazza of the hotel. She was alone. The gentlemen, including myself and my son, were as usual absent at Boston, and the ladies were scattered about in various directions. She was startled by a cry from the house of "the sea serpent! the sea serpent!" But this had been so frequent, by way of joke, since the event of the preceding day, and was so like "the wolf, the wolf!" of the fable, that it did not attract her particular attention for a moment or two, until she observed two women belonging to the family of the hotel keeper running along the Piazza towards the corner nearest the sea, with wonder in their eyes, and the cry of "the serpent, the serpent! He is turning, he is turning!" spontaneously bursting from their lips. Then my wife did indeed fix her looks in the direction in which they ran; and sure enough she saw, apparently quite close beyond the line formed by the rising ground above the rocks, a huge serpent, gliding gracefully through the waves, having evidently performed the action of turning round. In an instant it was in a straight line, moving rapidly on; and after coasting for a couple of minutes the north-west front of the hotel, and (as accurately as the astonished observer could calculate) looking as it stretched at full length in the water about the length of the piazza, that is to say about ninety feet, it sank quietly beneath the surface, and was seen no more.

The person who was thus so lucky as to get this unobstructed view, is one so little liable to be led astray by any imaginative impulse, that I reckon on her statement with entirely as much confidence as if my own eyes had demonstrated its truth. And so I give up this topic to other inquirers, unless some future circumstance calls for a recurrence to it, before the word *finis* is put to the concluding page of my work.

In selecting from the occurrences of the earliest period of my residence in America, when materials for remark crowded on me, in the "admired disorder" usual to new comers in a strange country, I reject many subjects which were endowed by novelty with an undue importance, and the mistaken impressions of which were soon effaced or modified. There is one, however, of such paramount interest, that I must record it as it appeared to my first experience, so that any later observations in relation to it, may have the benefit of the inductions that decided my permanent opinion. I am now about to speak of Religion as it first presented itself to me in practical operation in America. And of all the many instances, in which "first impressions" have been in my case erroneous, this is, I think, the most striking.

I need hardly say that I expected to find New England the very hot-bed of fanaticism. The history of the early settlers was fresh in my mind, as well as recent accounts of Yankee violence in matters of sectarian belief. The persecutions of the Quakers of the past century were mixed up with the Revivals and the Camp Meetings of the present; and I came prepared to find on every hand either the bigotry of puritanical zeal or the harshness of its pretence. It was therefore with some misgivings that we accepted the invitation of some fellow lodgers, to accompany them to church-service on the Sunday following our arrival at Nahant, in a modest-looking, Grecian temple-like wooden building within sight of the hotel. Unwilling to risk any discussion on the delicate matter of sectarian differences, we made no inquiry as to the particular doctrines of the clergyman who was to officiate, nor of the congregation. It struck us as remarkable that literally every lodger in the hotel who was not incapacitated by indisposition, made ready on the ringing of the church bell; and supposing of course that they were going respectively to their various places of worship, we set out with our own group. On reaching the little church, we were somewhat surprised to see all the hotel lodgers, with many persons from the neighbouring cottages, making their way together—so many votaries coming to lay their offerings at the same shrine. The plainness of the little chapel, and its utter want of distinctive marks, evidently told that it was not sacred to any particular sect; and the simple service which followed—a prayer, a chapter from the New Testament, a hymn, a sermon, and the parting benediction—were in all points so free from any allusion to doctrinal differences, so imbued with the essence of true morality, so catholic in sentiment, that I felt as though transported back to the primitive ages of Christianity, when the priest was personified piety, and religious worship the type of practical virtue. Happy to let my mind rest on such a fancied analogy between the past and the present, I would not allow it to pursue the theme, even for the sake of contrast, into epochs of bigot zeal and brutal persecution. I felt really better for this attendance on worship which *had* something divine in it.

And I looked round, with feelings of respect I can scarcely describe, at the congregation, which joined so decorously in a service that combined all that seemed required by religion and philosophy. As soon as it was concluded, my first inquiry was as to the name of the pastor, who so becomingly performed his duties, whose excellent discourse, amiable demeanour, and simple eloquence, were made more remarkable by a tinge of foreign accent which told me he was a German. I learnt that he was Dr. Follen, a professor of Harvard University, and that he was considered a man of superior endowments, but had not that reputation for eminence which had been ascribed to him by Miss Martineau in her work on America. I may here say, in passing, that I felt great regret in having had no opportunity in cultivating the acquaintance of this excellent man, whose melancholy fate is recorded in the account of the burning of the steamboat "Lexington," in which he perished, one of nearly 150 victims to a combination of circumstances, which gave to that fearful catastrophe the air of an inevitable doom.

Great as was my admiration, in the first instance, for all those who formed the congregation of this exemplary person, it was increased tenfold on my being informed that they individually belonged to almost every variety of sect into which Christianity is split, with the exception of Roman Catholicism; and that they gathered together for the performance of their duty in the little church of Nahant (there being only one in the place), by an understanding that no doctrinal points should be touched on in the service; so that during the eight or ten weeks which constitute "the season" at this neutral ground, as many clergymen of different pursuasions—the Calvinist (which is called the orthodox church in the United States), the

Unitarian, the Baptist, the Episcopalian, and several et ceteras—came down on the successive Sundays from Boston, free from all the bitterness of theological dissension, and one vyeing with the other in offering up prayers and preaching sermons, to which all denominations of believers might conscientiously listen, without having their scruples or their prejudices shocked in the slightest degree. The effect produced on me by this information may be easily imagined. It was in an inverse ratio with all my preconceived notions on the state of religious feeling in America. I was now satisfied, and I thought on just grounds, that the new people among whom I had arrived, were the most truly tolerant, and the least divided in essential opinions on the most sacred subjects, that anywhere existed. I had known instances, in Germany and elsewhere, of different sects performing their religious services in the same place of worship, one succeeding to another at hours of mutual convenience. But this mingling together in the same form of devotion, with a common pastor addressing a flock composed of all the heterogeneous specimens of dissent, seemed to me not only surpassingly christian-like, but incompatible with the possibility of a violent or acrimonious aggregate opposition.

But in forming this conclusion, jumped to, I confess, and too hastily, I was woefully at fault. I very soon found out that this sabbath assembling at Nahant was a mere meeting of convenience for decency's sake, a matter of form, to chime in with the general feeling that a Sunday ought not to be passed without going to church, a mere salve on the consciences of those who, in escaping from the heat and the week's labours of the city, could not be content with a cool day of rest and with the informality of mental devotion, in a place where nature itself appealed to every religious sentiment. I too soon discovered that in the touching observances of that day, and the others which followed it in like simplicity, not one out of a hundred of the listeners of Dr. Follen and his fellows sympathised with what they heard. No one entered thoroughly into the spirit of these admirable moral discourses, or quite approved of them. For some they were too tame, for others too lax. One hearer wished they were more orthodox, another that they were more episcopalian. Nobody, in fact, acknowledged them as particularly speaking their own sentiments, though all might have been proud to claim a participation in them. In one word, this sabbath service at Nahant is but a mockery. It is not inspired by morality or holiness. It has neither the odour of sanctity, nor the flavour of philosophy. And I greatly fear that most of the ministers who come to do the duty, at so many dollars a-head, do it rather like students reciting a theme as part of their task-work, than as gospel teachers, offering a banquet of wholesome food for the minds and not for the passions of men.

The discrepancy of this whole arrangement with the sectarian animosities which I subsequently found to be so prevalent in the population, may be briefly explained by the fact, that the Yankees can, on all and every occasion of necessity, make their strongest prejudices bend to the general convenience. A deep discussion on their religious tenets and practice would be out of place here. For the present, it may be enough to state my conviction that the true spirit of piety is not in the wealthier and more educated classes of society ; but that they hold to *forms*, with a tenacity equal to that of the vulgar. Hereditary pride in those grotesque old characters of history nicknamed "the Pilgrim Fathers," is wide-spread throughout

New England. They are held in an abstract veneration which has all the force of a religious belief. Not one man in a thousand attempts to analyse their actions; or examine into their motives, to separate the good from the bad. Every one reads the records of their deeds. All admire their intrepidity in quitting the Old World and seeking liberty of conscience in the American wilderness. But no one reflects that it was for themselves alone they sought and found it, and that what they obtained for themselves they fiercely denied to others. The descendants of these stern adventurers, anxious to do homage to their merits, uphold the forms they established, forgetting that it was alone the spirit which created those forms that made them fitting to the days of yore; and that the spirit being now extinct, the forms are but so many mummies—curious relics of the time that was, but now valueless, because out of keeping with the present. A vain emulation of England and all that is English is one of the leading features of the Yankee mind. To have had an ancestry is the prevailing point of pride. To go back between two and three centuries—as far as they can go—and to take what they find there as superexcellent in all things, are the obvious consequences of this most natural sentiment. Chivalry they cannot claim for their recusant forefathers, and therefore they set up Puritanism in its stead. One of the living writers of America goes so far in his indulgence of this vanity as to have inserted a piece of wordy sophistry in his works, to prove the superiority of the latter over the former.* But to whatever pitch of faith they have raised their reverence for the "fathers" of *their* church, it is certain that the modern New Englanders have no sentiment in common with them,

* History of America, by George Bancroft.

any more than a British peer may possess for the barbarous Paladins from whom he traces his descent. Therefore, their feelings are at constant variance with the principles they boast of; while the forms in which those principles are supposed to be embodied are piously preserved. Men who are incapable of burning a witch from superstition, or hanging a Quaker from bigotry, nevertheless maintain a deep respect for the memory of their ancestors, who acted such atrocities. They worship their wisdom, they vaunt their virtue. While shrinking from their example in acts, they stick to it in ceremonies. Yet as this is the general rule, it has like others its exceptions; and an exception is always justifiable to a Yankee conscience, when it can tend to the common good. I hope that I have thus clearly, though perhaps hastily, explained why the various denominations of Yankees who reciprocally hate and despise each other's religious opinions, can meet for convenience sake, on a common ground of pretended piety; and, while casting aside for a moment the mantle of intolerance, be still far from walking in the naked truth of Christianity.

My family and myself having been accustomed to live in foreign countries, we found little difficulty in conforming ourselves to the general ways of the people among whom we might happen to be resident. Yet I confess there were some things in America which were more repugnant to our tastes and feelings than many which embarrassed us when travelling in Europe. But it would be ungracious to stop at such trifles as tripped us up on the threshold, particularly as I shall have to mention more important obstructions, over which we stumbled when we got fairly within the house. Among the minor matters with which I strove to become familiar were sundry condiments and combinations of cookery, new to me even by name, and which varied the scanty and ill-dressed supplies of fish, flesh, and fowl, in their European aspect. I started from the very first day with a plate of *chowder*, a thick mess, made of haddock, onions, butter, biscuit, and fat pork; an odious compound, held in infinite esteem in these parts.* I afterwards ate of hominy, tautaug, squash, and mush. I tried slap-jack, flap-jack, rye-cake, *ris*†-cake, cup-cake, Johnny-cake, and dough-nuts. It was even a matter of conscience with me to taste, for once at least, some of the beverages technically called "drinks," such as mint-julep, sherry-cobbler, gin-sling, gin-cocktail. These two latter delicacies I never tried. The first I *did* try, and found it guilty; I thought it detestable; bad as a cordial, and worse as physic. The second being simply a glass of sherry, with sugar, lemon, and ice, is delicious. Snakeroot bitters, timber doodle, egg-nog, and some others I have only heard of, but have never been tempted with.

The bad taste, in giving vulgar names to their articles of food or refreshment, is an obvious defect in American manners, and is certainly unpleasing to a foreign ear. But it should be known that this people are very ambitious of establishing a sort of quaint and coarse phraseology, as the distinctive national humour; and, moreover, that their standard notions of politeness in language are very far indeed below European refinement. Expressions that are usual with only the lowest orders in England are very

* This mixture afforded me one out of numberless examples of the anxiety of the Americans to give a foreign origin to their indigenous slang. A gentleman of Boston strove to prove to me that *chowder* was a French dish, and the name a corruption of *échaudé*. A cabinet minister of Washington once assured me that the phrase "going the whole hog" was *a splendid orientalism*.

† *Ris*, the participle of the verb active "to rise."

common from the mouth of American gentility. "I don't care a *copper* for him," or such a one "is not worth a *copper*," is an every day phrase, instead of our home word *farthing* to express the same idea. In this it will be perceived that an American only generalises, while a *Britisher* specifies ; and there is no really better reason for our rejecting the word "copper" than there was for the celebrated antipathy of the epigram writer to Dr. Fell. The under part of the sirloin of beef is called by some of the best people in America "the tender line," an intense vulgarism according to English notions. When a lady talks of "fixing" her hair, meaning to talk of dressing it, we are, in spite of us, struck with the inelegance of the word. These few out of dozens of instances may serve to point out certain peculiarities of speech usual among the most refined. There are a hundred downright vulgarisms that they shrink from as much as the most fastidious member of the best London society. But I confess myself very tolerant on mere conventional points, either in language or manners. Words are of no value but as being the types of thought. The arbitrary adoption or rejection of certain phrases is a mere question of taste ; which is in itself, according to the dramatist, a very questionable concern, "much talked of, not to be defined."

Many quaint proverbial expressions of doubtful gentility are admitted into polite discourse in England ; and America has quite as good a right as we have to establish a standard, or to pass above or below it at pleasure. If the gentry of America would in all things show as much independence as in this one of mere words, I should find no fault with then on the score of good or bad taste, or *sense* either. And I am infinitely more annoyed by instances of their affected fine speaking, to which I shall advert in another place, than to the frequent homeliness of which I have given two or three examples.

But there are two things, and matters of *taste* too, in its sensual meaning, which I cannot pardon in Americans or any other people—a passionate fondness for "pigs' meat," and an immoderate use of tobacco. Nothing can persuade me that there is not much grossness in the cookery that puts lumps of fat pork into fish soup, or layers of it on fish fried, or that invariably serves a piece of it on the same dish with a boiled chicken. But what language can express our decent abhorrence at seeing it served up as an accompaniment to a leg of mutton! All these and many more methods of using this beloved nourishment might be adduced. Probably the most fearful is when it is eaten with treacle, by way of sauce, and then playfully called pork and 'lasses (molasses). But, notwithstanding these enormities, it is strange to say that the most favourite accessory to a leg of pork with certain English people, to wit, pease pudding, is not known in the United States. And for the sake of civilisation it may be hoped that no new writer on domestic cookery will ever send out a receipt for its concoction.*

* I am happy to append, by way of note, the following paragraph from a newspaper (February, 1845) which gives some hope of an abatement in the national appetite for pig's meat. The amount in figures of the "falling-off" is most appalling, from the evidence it gives of the prodigious quantity still consumed:—

"The Pork Market of the West.—In addition to what we gave a day or two since, in relation to the falling-off in the slaughter of hogs this year in the great West, we gain the following statement from the Alton (Ill.) Telegraph, which says that from intelligence carefully collected from all quarters, the indication is that the decrease 'will fall far, far below that of the previous season. The deficit in Illinois is estimated at 85,800 head. It is thought by those best acquainted with the business, that the falling-off in Cincinnati will amount to about 90,000; and the Chillicothe Advertiser, on the authority of a competent judge, calculates the decrease in the Scioto Valley, at not less than 73,450. Supposing these various estimates to be correct, the deficiency at the points above-mentioned

As to writing a tirade against tobacco, it would be as hopeless as blowing a penny trumpet against a hurricane. The love of this pestiferous weed must be a natural failing of humanity, like original sin or total depravity. Since the day when King James puffed his "counterblast," volumes (not of mere smoke) have been ineffectually directed against this habit. Good sense, good feeling, good taste, have been appealed to in vain. The custom gains ground among men.* The most refined take the intoxication in one shape, while the most inelegant take it in another. The difference between smoking and chewing is, no doubt, immeasurable; and to those gentlemen who attend to cleanliness and cold water after the occasional use of a cigar, some allowance may be made for a propensity that is nearly universal. I know from the experience of my early life, that a Turkish pipe, or if it can be come at, a hookah, with good canaster, is a seduction hard to resist, and it may be yielded to in the open air, after dinner, as

—without including Indiana, Kentucky, and the other western states, where the falling-off is also believed to be considerable—will not be far from 250,000 hogs; which, computing them to average 200 pounds each, will give a gross amount of 50,000,000 pounds—or, according to the usual calculations, 100,000 barrels of pork; 15,000,000 pounds of bacon; and 5,000,000 pounds of lard—a quantity sufficiently large to affect the market throughout the Union. In fact, this is already apparent; a gradual rise in the price of hogs having taken place from the commencement of the season to the present time; and no less than 16,000 barrels of pork have recently changed hands in a single day in the city of New York.'"

* Official accounts, furnished in compliance with a call of Congress, 1842, established the astounding facts that the annual consumption of tobacco in the United States amounts to 100,000,000 pounds weight—giving seven pounds for each man, woman, and child of the population; and that the sum annually paid by the consumers of this quantity, in its manufactured state, has been computed at 20,000,000 of dollars, between four and five millions sterling! I do not know what has been the gradual yearly increase. The quantity, manufactured and unmanufactured, entered in the United Kingdom for home consumption in the year 1848, amounted to 27,305,134 pounds, including 206,581¾ pounds of manufactured tobacco and cigars, and 238¼ pounds of snuff. Gross total amount of revenue received on this tobacco and snuff, 1848, £4,365,223.

a gentleman may yield to it, when it is followed by the copious use of Eau de Cologne and some odorous dentifrice. Nor can one help regarding as admissible the delicate little *cigarito,* formed of the purest possible preparations of "the weed," rolled neatly in fine *Papel de Hilo,* such as I have seen used by luscious-lipped women beyond the Bidassoa, and, indeed, more lately on the banks of the Seine and the Thames. Even the twisted leaf of Havannah, manufactured in short, stumpy rolls, held daintily betwixt finger and thumb, and not suffered to get quite between the teeth, the vapour gently puffed forth immediately after being partially inhaled—even this may find excuse, particularly if the before-mentioned antiseptic appliances form the afterpiece of the performance. But he who smokes cigars from morning to night, who thrusts the bitter firebrand for a couple of inches into his mouth, who mumbles one half while he burns out the other, swallows a large portion of the smoke, and lets it accumulate in his throat, like soot in the flue of a steam-engine, he is—I say it with all possible respect—a nuisance. The approach of such a person towards a being of even ordinary purity in a drawing-room, or his close neighbourhood at a dinner-table, is among the pestilent anomalies of refined society. Such abominations are at times met in the best houses in England, under an excess of courtesy towards foreigners. I need not say that they abound in the United States.

The habitual chewer of tobacco is an animal I do not wish to describe. Nor is it necessary to waste words in depicting his nastiness. Every one knows what he is, and every one is aware that he is as commonly met with in American "parlours," as are alligators in the swamps, skunks in the woods, or other nauseous things in their chosen localities. That a sailor on deck, or a soldier in the trenches, hungry, tempest-tossed, and storm-pelted, should have recourse to stimulants even as gross as this may be conceived. But how well-fed, warm-lodged, educated men, in the gluttony of a depraved taste, can adopt a habit so abhorrent to common decency baffles imagination. No one can chew tobacco in ignorance of the disgust he creates in those who do not chew it. He must be aware of the noxious effluvia he emits with every breath, of the filthy appearance of his mouth, of the offensive spittle which he voids around him. He cannot, with the best intentions, escape from this last-mentioned necessity. He must expectorate when it is impossible to swallow. And, Spirit of Elegance! contemplate the only resource which a gentleman can fly to in partial concealment of his dirt—the spitting-box! I protest that I see scarcely a difference in point of indelicacy between this revolting instrument, as I have often and often seen it, introduced into the "parlours" of American refinement, and the sentry-box conveniences, not uncommon in Dutch sitting rooms, of middle-class occupancy.

I have no measure in my loathing for this vile habit—no terms in which to express it. How civilised men can practise it, or how lady-like women can countenance it, moves my especial wonder. When my fancy sometimes flew with unclipped wings, farther, perhaps, than it had a right to do, and I imagined the lips of delicate-looking wives pressed by the kisses of a tobacco chewer, I have many a time turned in irresistible antipathy from some thing of beauty, who legally lent herself to its desecration.

But I stop my pen. The case is hopeless. I have no notion that as many pages as I have written lines on the subject, would produce any effect on the practitioners of this vice. Legislation cannot touch it, religion is above the subject, and fashion below it.* Yet if this manuscript should ever be transferred to print, and if it might be the means of inducing one female to spurn some tobacco-tainted suitor, or of making one youth to pause before he was tempted by the nauseating quid, in the belief that it is manly to do what is usually done by men, that one ought to go with the crowd, or follow the stream, or from any such common excuse for low pursuits, I shall be quite satisfied, and shall think my philippic not altogether thrown away.

It will be seen that sundry impediments towards perfect enjoyment in the society of America awaited our very introduction into it. Yet, taken altogether, it was in the first instance very pleasant. But that was chiefly from the agreeable manners of the Boston ladies, visitors at Nahant, and the constant round of unformal intercourse, which promised us so cheerful and hospitable a circle for our winter acquaintanceships in town. From what I have already said, it may be inferred that the other sex did not bear their share in producing this impression. They were almost all dry and cold in manner, *bornés* in general information, mere business men, or lawyers of narrow practice and no great breadth

* Among the celebrated blue-laws of Connecticut, nearly two centuries back, there was one which goes far to redeem the absurd intolerance of some of the others. No person under twenty years of age was allowed to use tobacco without a physician's certificate that his health required it. *All* were prohibited from using it in company, whether at their labours or in travelling, and in any case permitted to take it not more than once a day upon a penalty of sixpence fine for each offence. This was a virtuous attempt of the pious Puritans. It was a pity they did not alter a little and transpose one of those sumptuary laws, namely, "that no woman shall kiss her child on the Sabbath-day" into the following enactment —"No woman shall kiss her husband on tobacco-day." I know a few ladies who would joyfully hail the passage of such a law in America now: but I fear that the mass of women are too much vitiated by custom to care about it.

of mind. A few exceptions existed among them; and as we value things in proportion to their rarity, I put a higher estimate on the persons in question than was warranted by their intrinsic merit, viewed in comparison with the associates of other days and other lands. But I was soon confirmed by experience in what I always instinctively felt, that it is unfair and absurd to measure the gentlemen of America by a European standard. They have no resemblance but to Englishmen, and their inferiority to those is undoubted. It strikes me at every turn, and on every possible occasion—in society, in business, in literature, science, art. They can bear no comparison with the stock from which they sprang. They are of the same blood, but of a different breed. The Anglo-Saxon race deteriorates with transplantation. It requires the associations of Home to preserve its lofty attributes; and under Republican forms, it must be content to exhibit a mediocrity, conducive to the general weal, but fatal to individual distinction.

CHAPTER V.

NATIONAL CHARACTERISTICS.

National Good Temper—Yankee Honesty—Speculators—Bankrupts—Curiosity about Strangers—Neglect of Native Talent—Public Dinner in Boston—Harvard University Commencement—Phi Beta Kappa Society—Corporations—New England Character—The Masses—Want of Individual Independence—Public Enterprise—Failures—The Refuge of the Destitute.

It must here again be borne in mind that I am in these remarks recording the results of some years' experience, and at the same time giving their full value to all the peculiarities of character which attracted my early admiration. Among those I must specify the general good temper and civility evident in all the people; the accommodating air of the shop keepers, hotel keepers, masters of steamboats, managers of railroad cars, &c. And, for the justification of Yankee reputation, I must state that I never knew in any country more correctness in shop accounts. Indeed I can recollect very few instances of charges a second time made after payment, in our dealings with the tradesmen of Boston or elsewhere. The only attempts at actual dishonesty worth mentioning were confined to a printer and publisher (a low fellow), and a lawyer, a person of good connections, and who is considered a "smart" practitioner. I must admit that a total want of conscience in laying on high prices, extreme sharpness, and illiberality in matters of business, are the common characteristics of the New Englanders towards each other. But in all the smaller transactions, such as totting up accounts, I believe a cautious probity to be the rule, and cheating the exception.

Of the many mercantile failures, and ruinous speculations in lands, stocks, and other gambling concerns, I cannot speak with certainty. Having had no intimate acquaintanceship with such matters, and associating but little with the persons interested in them, I had neither opportunity nor inclination to know much about them. The keen practices of trade tend in all countries to make men selfish and tricky; and the gradations are rapid towards deceit and roguery. Instances have been frequently pointed out to me of fraudulent bankrupts, among the twenty-four hundred who, in Massachusetts alone, availed themselves of the Act of 1841, and of wealthy insolvents. But I am not prone to believe reports to the disadvantage of persons in embarrassed circumstances. They have a *primâ facie* claim on compassion and forbearance. A man with the most upright intentions may become liable to the suspicion of unfairness; a misplaced confidence in others, a liberal taste for expense, a sanguine reliance on chances, expose such a one to failure; and failure superinduces the necessity of shifts and expedients, and is followed by slander and persecution. The man in embarrassed circumstances is always under a cloud. He walks in a false light, and his best qualities are seen in shade. The sunshine of prosperity is wanting to show them in relief. Till that bursts forth again let no man pass judgment on him.

Within a fortnight after our arrival at Nahant, I had formed many pleasant acquaintanceships, independent of the hotel company and the residents of the cottages around. A number of Boston gentlemen came out to visit me and do honour to the introductions I brought with me. Many called on me out of respect to my office. And it may be added that my connection with literature was a passport to consideration, and above all things an incitement to curiosity. Any one at all known in the world of letters is sure of being lionised more or less in America. The public mind has a feverish thirst after knowledge in all shapes; and is intensely inquisitive as to the personal appearance and habits of foreign authors. The crowds by which they are assailed, the invitations they receive, the entreaties to sit gratuitously for pictures and busts, the request for their autographs, and all the other acts of homage paid to notoriety, are by no means so complimentary as they seem to be. All this is very much more for the gratification of personal or local motives than out of regard to the individual. Each city in the Union has a pride in vyeing with the others in a reputation for hospitality to strangers, and in apparent admiration for talent. That these are but spurious pretences is proved by the general neglect of their native writers and scientific men. Dr. Channing, a prophet in our country, was but a pamphleteer in his own. Beyond a very small circle he was neither read nor talked of in Boston. Bancroft, the historian, is, on account of his political tendencies, even more than his shifting and frivolous character, shunned as a black sheep, against whom the white sheep of the opposite party are afraid to rub. Prescott, a writer far beyond the common run of his compatriots, an amiable man, and half blind, receives no popular marks of consideration. I might swell out the list of estimable and talented individuals, male and female, whose productions are constantly before the public, who are lauded in the newspapers and reviews far beyond their merits, but who are kept in a social position far below them ; who are never asked to dinner, or soirée or ball ; who are in fact utterly unknown, in the very places of which their names form the chief ornaments.

Owing, however, to what were considered my claims to notice, I and my son had soon many invitations, and among them was one to a public dinner, to be given at Boston early in August, on occasion of the annual examinations at the public schools. I was not sorry of an opportunity of seeing *en masse* some hundreds of the individuals who had not singly any strong attraction for me. We accordingly, after first attending some of the examinations in the school rooms, repaired to Faneuil Hall, a building set apart for political celebrations, and endeared to the people of Boston, under the appellation of "the Cradle of Liberty," as the spot in which the principles of national independence were first publicly proclaimed, in the early periods of the revolutionary struggle, to a generation now fast disappearing from the earth.

This dinner, like all others of the kind, had been preceded by a procession through the streets formed of the principal·*convives*, with a band of music and banners, the usual "pomp and circumstance" of such occasions in the United States. When we reached the celebrated place of rendezvous, the company was assembled ; and after a formal reception by the mayor of the city, who was to preside at the feast, and by the governor and other state dignitaries, we proceeded towards the dining hall, to enter on the great business of the day.

I must here admit, strange as it may appear, that I had never been present at more than two public dinners in England, and these had an interval of a dozen years between them. One was on the nomination of sheriffs for the City of London. The other was on an anniversary of the Literary Fund Society. I had also *assisted* at a farewell dinner given to Tom Moore in Paris, and at one on St. Patrick's Day in Brussels; and once was chosen to preside at a complimentary repast in honour of a worthy individual at Ostend. These three last-mentioned were scarcely to be called public dinners, for the party on neither of the occasions numbered more than sixty, and almost all the individuals were more or less acquainted with each other. When, therefore, I entered the great room of Faneuil Hall, and saw tables laid for nearly a thousand persons, with a taste and elegance in the decorations of which I had no previous notion, the crowd of coloured waiters, in their white jackets, circulating (as the French say) between a profusion of the gaudiest flowers, a band of music sending down streams of harmony through flags and banners, shining in the sun and floating in the breeze from the open windows, and the immense company, well dressed and decorously arranged; the effect was at once startling and delightful. I felt a thrill of pleasure, not alone from abstract enjoyment in the scene, but from the consciousness that the sense of another new excitement existed within me.

I occupied a seat on the left hand of the chairman. Governor Everett, with whom I had previously become acquainted, was on his right. Several of the foreign Consuls, my colleagues, with sundry state functionaries, civil and military, and some English officers who were passing through Boston, occupied the principal table, elevated on a platform at the upper end of the room, arm-chairs being placed only at one side of it, so that nothing intercepted the view of the animating scene below, and no one sat with his back to the rest of the company. Long tables stretched down to the other extremity of the hall, and several were placed under and in the side galleries, the band occupying the one fronting the main table at the other end. No ladies were present; and this absence of bright faces and brilliant dresses was the only drawback to the picturesqueness of the spectacle.

Whether it was that the admirable arrangements for the feast greatly facilitated its dispatch, or that the company got through the eating with the wonted national vivacity, or that I was myself so exhilarated as to make no count of time, I cannot exactly say. Perhaps it was a combination of these causes which made me almost start with astonishment when the chairman rose to announce the first toast, proclaiming very plainly that the feast of *sense* was at an end, and that of *reason* about to begin. Mr. Eliot, the mayor, performed his duties right well. He introduced the "regular sentiments," prepared by a committee, with fluent and apt remarks; and opened out a view of the public exertions for the great object of general education that gave me ample food for reflection and inquiry, some of the results of which I may take an opportunity of developing.

A toast complimentary to the Governor brought Edward Everett on his legs, and he responded in what was indeed a beautiful speech, occasionally playful, highly finished, full of good sense, and gracefully delivered, in spite of the drawling and quivering tone that savoured somewhat too strongly of the conventicle. Three or four of the speakers, Mr. Quincy, the President of Harvard University, among the rest, acquitted themselves extremely well. All seemed prepared and no one at fault. But I was utterly taken by surprise when the chairman, turning to me, said,

"I am now going to give a toast which will bring you out," and in an instant he proposed a most flattering sentiment, in honour of "the mother country." To hear old England thus spoken of in a large assembly of American Republicans and in the "Cradle of Liberty," to listen to the thunders of applause and to the band pealing forth "God save the Queen," while a thousand pairs of eyes were fixed on me, as the unworthy representative of all that was implied in the sentiment and its accompaniments, would probably have overpowered me had I made any preparation for the occasion. But as it was I felt nothing but a desire to acquit myself creditably in the entirely new task which I saw I *must* perform. I therefore "spoke to the toast," as the phrase goes, to the best of my ability. And I had every reason to be pleased with the courteous indulgence with which my extempore effusion was received by the company.

This first public display which I had witnessed in America impressed me with a conviction, which day by day grew stronger, that it is in masses that the people of this country are to be seen to the greatest advantage. Their tact in the management of all matters in which they act in bodies is scarcely to be believed compatible with the mean and timid tone of individuals. The enthusiasm exhibited at their meetings is inexplicable to him who has observed them in cold and cautious singleness. There is no greater moral phenomenon than this mighty difference between the man and the multitude. It is as if a given number of ice-blocks fermented, exploded and rushed abroad in streams of lava. This school dinner forms an epoch in my New World experience. It gave me a clew to the secret of popular power. I left the hall, with the Governor and others, during the height of the evening's enjoyment. But although Champagne and other wines had been freely partaken of, I ascertained that no one showed an appearance of excess, and that the large party broke up at a reasonable hour, and dispersed as though they had been dining quietly in their respective homes. I have thought it right to mention this here, not as a singularity, but as a peculiarity in this country. The rule is so general that the only exception I have met with was on one occasion of an Irish St. Patrick's Day dinner at New York; and even that had no riotous result—only a little extra noise in honour of "the old country."

Another opportunity was soon afforded me of seeing an assembly of Yankees of another description. Invitations were sent to us to take part in the proceedings on "Commencement day" at Harvard University, including the usual exhibitions, recitations, and dinner. And for the day following we were asked to dine with the *Phi Beta Kappa* Society (a college club formed of men who had been the first of their respective classes), by the official politeness of its president, Judge Story of the United States' Supreme Court, who had paid me a visit at Nahant, and whose ardent loquacity and amiable egotism made him a companion highly agreeable to meet with occasionally.

The orations, poems, and other exercises on Commencement day were dull enough, except for the parents and relatives of those who had an opportunity of distinguishing themselves. The venerable associations clinging round our colleges, and hallowing even their intolerance and pedantry, were all wanting to throw a charm of antiquity over these ceremonies. Nor had they any of that dignity which covers a multitude of bigotries in our divines—of that lofty tone which marks the royal and noble patrons of each particular *alma mater*—of the bold frank bearing of the students—of the *ensemble*, in a word, of European talent, taste, and fashion. The dinner was every way mean and meagre. And I was altogether a good deal disappointed by what I had looked forward to as a series of superior exhibitions.

But though disappointed on the first day, I was amply repaid by the agreeable surprise which awaited me on the next. I confess that I started from Nahant on the following morning, on my fifteen miles journey to Cambridge, in a hot sun and with rather a heavy heart—under that most oppressive of sensations, the reluctant performance of a disagreeable duty. Knowing that I had a great deal to observe in the United States, and uncertain as to the length of my residence, I had resolved from the first to lose no opportunity that was offered to me of seeing what was to be seen, so for some months I refused no invitation, public or private, that circumstances allowed me to accept. This University club-dinner would have held out great attraction to me, had it not been for the intense stupidity of the previous day; and when I sat down in the same hall, at the same table, and to a repast no better served, I was only anxious for the hour of separation, that I might escape from the dust and dulness of Cambridge, to the coolness of the Nahant hotel. I must also premise that I had been warned, on leaving England, by a friend well versed in the observation of American character, against any indulgence of pleasantry in conversation, and most particularly against my natural inclination for a joke, and occasionally the perpetration of an intended *bon mot*. This adviser assured me that the grave and matter-of-fact Yankees would not relish, or indeed comprehend, those sharp trivialities—those *pun*gent spices which season social converse in Europe. And I had consequently hitherto abstained from any attempt of the kind; except, now and then, a sly innuendo or insinuated pleasantry, when talking nonsense to the ladies, on the piazza or the rocks. I had not yet observed in the general conversation of the men anything to belie the accuracy of my friend's judgment. No gleam of wit (not even at the school-dinner) had broken forth from those I associated with. Great, then, was my surprise when, quick following the grace after meat, seriously pronounced by one of the clergymen, the worthy president rose up, and began the real enjoyment of the day, by a speech, half Latin, half English, rambling, jocose, and admirably delivered, prefacing the usual toast in honour of the Society.

This was the signal for a series of the most rapid and animated succession of jokes, epigrams, puns, quotations and off-hand speeches, that I had ever heard in any part of the world. There was no formality or restraint. From the one elevated table at which the president and invited guests were seated, and the two long ones, running down the room, containing altogether above two hundred members of the University, a continued fire of sharp-shooting was kept up, the whole connected together by the tact of the chairman into a regular *feu de joie.*

He must have been a dogged fellow who would not have entered into the spirit of the hour, and freely given his mite to the general contribution. I paid my tax like another—to the best of my ability. But there was no assessment—no forced loan—nothing "on compulsion." Nobody was mulcted. But every one threw in his voluntary offering, so many weapons of fun and frolic for the killing of old Time; just as the Roman ladies used to fling their ornaments into a common heap, to raise a fund for the destruction of the common enemy.

I should have been greatly inclined to attempt a more particular record of the sayings and doings of this day, had not a gallant officer, Colonel Maxwell, of the 36th Foot, in his "Rush through the United States" (or his *Run*, I do not exactly recollect the title) given a sketch of what occurred at the anniversary meeting the following year, which in general resemblance was very nearly the same thing. But it was not, after all, the same. For me, the freshness, the surprise, and consequently much of the charm, was past. But still quite enough of the spirit of the scene was there to make me now enjoy its recollection, as another of the pleasantest public days I have spent in America.

And this first dinner with the *Phi Beta Kappa* Society forms another of the epochs of my awakening to the anomalies of the American mind. This concentration of humour, in a people so generally unfacetious, is only one among many instances of the national instinct for classification, supplying the place of the distinction of ranks which prevails in other countries. As there are no social grades, with artificial limits positively marked, they have substituted certain other methods of separation between man and man. Not satisfied with the boundaries supplied by age—and nowhere else are the youthful, the middle aged, and the old, so sundered in the social relations of life—they do not allow learning or literature to mingle, in a general way, with commercial, manufacturing, or legal knowledge. Were all their materials for enjoyment well mixed through society, instead of being thus confined to so many particular sections, it would present a far different aspect from that which makes it now so unattractive.

Almost immediately after the feast of fun just described, I met several of the most agreeable members of the Club, at private dinners in Boston, and found them there as reserved and unanimated as the particular merchant or manufacturer who then entertained me in one sense, as they had previously done in another. This change of manner, even in social intercourse, resolves itself into the category of national traits before noticed, which makes *association* an essential requisite to success. No man ventures anything single-hand, not even a joke. Even humour cannot be attempted without a corporation being formed for its fabrication. And here, forestalling the results of my long experience, I must introduce a few remarks, which may be not quite inopportune, but which, had I been writing a journal of consecutive events, would be somewhat out of time and place.

In observing the great mass of good, and its natural result of general well-being among the people at large, throughout the United States, I must admit that it is produced by a sacrifice of individual eminence, and consequently of personal enjoyment. Each man at all elevated in the social scale seems to pay a certain *per centum* of his better qualities—a sort of intellectual property-tax—into the public treasury of morals. But he is thus left comparatively poor. And in proportion as the greatest good of the greatest number is secured by this aggregate contribution, each person singly is reduced to a still lower standard; and this, with other conspiring causes, leaves very few indeed able to stand alone in manly independence.

No other country, perhaps, shows so great a proportionate deficiency in that noble characteristic. Few Americans, in the settled and civilized portions of the country, are of any note or worth in their separate existence. Instances of isolated superiority are rare indeed. There is no self-confidence—no consciousness of power—no defiance of the world. They must congregate and combine, for the smallest as well as the most important objects. To carry out every commercial enterprise there must be a partnership. All manufacturing undertakings, or works of public improvement, or banking establishments, are in the hands of joint-stock companies; all such being technically designated "corporations," and considered, by the democratic majority of the people, as equivalent to a band of designing capitalists, leagued together for their own aggrandisement and the ruin of the public liberty.

Now, although it is notorious that the members of those corporate bodies are almost entirely of the Whig or "aristocratic" party in politics, I believe that another cause operates powerfully in making them thus unite. I attribute their doing so mainly to that deficiency of self-reliance before alluded to; and I think that much of the evil-doings of such institutions as the late United States Bank and others, in various parts of the Union, has arisen from that spirit of association which gives men the courage to become rogues in a company, who might have remained honest from fear had they carried on business alone.

An individual Yankee is not a very elevated specimen of human nature. Cold, timid, cunning; watchful for opportunities to overreach, fearful of being outwitted, he is always like a man on his defence, looking for something to lean his back against, and apprehensive that every one wants to take the wall of him. He creeps cautiously on, when he ventures to move at all. He has little cordiality of manner—is never at ease himself—and has not the knack of putting other people at theirs. He cuts his way through the world as he cuts his path through the woods, every step on calculation. He shrinks from acknowledging a favour, and is insensible to the delight of having received an obligation. To give nothing for nothing is notoriously a Yankee motto. To take nothing for nothing is equally a principle with him. If you make him a present, he will give you another in return. He is always ready with his *quid pro quo.* He has it (may I be pardoned the pun ?) ever ready in his waistcoat pocket. It has more than once happened to me to be offered a piece of tobacco or a cigar in payment for some small civility, or a cent or two (sure to be neither more nor less than its value) for the newspaper I had been reading on board a steamboat, and had lent to some knowledge-seeking neighbour.

Such being the outline of the Yankee character in individuals, and it being admitted that the Yankee type is effacing all others in the national mind, the chance of anything bold or vigorous would be small for the country at large, did its greatness and prosperity depend on individuals alone. Happily, however, the necessity of seeking support gives them a tendency to coalesce, and they find in numbers an element of courage which makes them appear collectively of a totally different race. The single brick, offered as a specimen of the Grecian house, was not more unfitting than any one given Yankee would be as a sample of the people he is a part of.

Let the Yankees congregate for any specific purpose—and no people on earth are so prone to assemble in large bodies—and they become the most excitable and enterprising people in the world. Their pent up feelings all then find vent. The caution which held them back singly degenerates into fear of now being behind-hand. Each man is anxious to take the lead. At their public dinners, suppers, caucuses, stump meetings, camp meetings, conventions, in Congress, in the State Legislature—wherever, in short, they come together in masses, they show surprising ardour. Individuals who in private society are prolix and prosy, become on these occasions brisk and fluent. The timid shake off their caution ; the taciturn are all at once talkative ; the men of doubts and apprehensions, fearless and often desperate. There can be no better audience for a public speaker to address. A spurious but fierce enthusiasm arises on the slightest stimulus. While it lasts, it carries all before it. Resolutions or subscriptions, as the case may be, are passed or filled up with reckless rapidity. Each man is emulous to out-talk or outbid his neighbour. Thus it is that doctrines of the most ultra nature in politics, morals, and religion are put forth, and the most extravagant projects entered into by acclamation. The wildest speculations are decided on in this way, and a union of over-cautious individuals forms an aggregate of over-adventurous people.

But fearful consequences ensue as soon as difficulties arise. Individuals have then no confidence in others any more than in themselves. As soon as differences of opinion spring up—as they must always do in large undertakings—the principle of general distrust begins its work ; and every man doubts, fears, and thwarts his fellow. Great undertakings are thus followed by total failure ; and men of wealth become penniless, from having given way to the force of example. The masses can resist no temptation, and they often become themselves irresistible. Hurried away without control, they sweep all obstacles from their path ; and it is only when their object is attained that they find it leads to loss, and too often to ruin. Enormous plans for money-making, either in local or distant adventures, turn out to be feasible as to execution, but fallacious as to profit. And it is quite marvellous to see persons who singly rail at speculation and set their faces against enterprise, fall resistless victims to the epidemic, as soon as they mix with the infected crowd.

But these splendid failures are of immense value to the nation. The railroads, canals, vast clearances of the wilderness, and the many other public enterprises known under the general name of "internal improvements," have all had their origin in the spirit I describe. The large sums embarked by capitalists in the Atlantic cities are spread over a wide tract of country, and thousands are enriched, at the cost of some scores who become beggars *pro bono publico*.

The fluctuation of fortunes caused in this way, forms one of the peculiar national features. To be rich to-day and poor to-morrow is so common a case that every man holds himself prepared for a reverse, and when it comes he is not overwhelmed by it. I have known many instances of bankruptcy tripping up the heels of apparent prosperity. But elasticity of character seems the ordinary habit of the people, and no one lies down to brood under the load of his mishaps. I am moreover afraid, as I before mentioned, that fraudulent failures are not uncommon. It has been frequently remarked to me that such a one, in becoming bankrupt, had made the best hit since he began business. Be that as it may, the nominally unfortunate assuredly bear their reverses with wonderful fortitude, and they recover from them with great celerity.*

* An American merchant once remarked to me, that "honesty was the best policy." "Why, every one knows that," said I. "No, Sir," he replied, "Every one says it—but all don't know it. I do, for I have tried *both*." There was no answering this naïve commentary on the proverb.

The extreme improvidence in regard to their families calls, at any rate, for deep and just reproach. Abounding instances occur of complete destitution to wife and children, on the death of men who to the last keep up the appearance of wealth. And I was well acquainted with some who lived in handsome houses, and maintained an ostentatious air of expense, who if suddenly cut off would leave nothing for those who follow them but struggling and poverty. This proceeds from the double vice of an extreme selfishness which makes men think only of their own indulgence, and of a pride which cannot resist the temptation of enjoying the homage paid to apparent wealth, in a country where few other distinctions are common, and none other considered of much value.

Even the comparatively easy provisions of Life Insurance during the time of my residence in America, was scarcely or never made by men of good incomes arising from yearly profits, but without any secured property. They were unwilling to curtail their expenditure to the amount of the necessary annual premium. There was but one Life Insurance Company in the city of Boston, and scarcely anything was done in that branch of its business; and there were but very few in the other parts of the country.* People have been greatly astonished at my informing them that many a man in England of merely a life income, has his life insured for more or less.

It must be admitted that the accident of a family of former wealth being left suddenly in reduced circumstances, does not carry with it the painful and mortifying conse-

* Within two years after this passage was written, a perfect rage for Life Insurance had overrun the country. Boston, and the towns of New England possessed several companies with their branches, besides a number of foreign agencies for London societies. In all probability this *furore* will subside altogether or be considerably moderated in a very short time.

quences it entails in Europe, and especially in England. In the United States, loss of "caste" does not follow loss of fortune. The widow and daughters who give up the handsome mansion in which they had spent their previous life, sink into the obscurity of the boarding house, to which they are doomed on the death of the husband and father, without disgrace. They no longer meet with consideration from their rich friends, but they are not actually shunned by them. They had often before lived in this public way at watering places or in travelling. The lady who keeps the establishment is very probably their relative, or may have been one of their previous associates. Their fellow lodgers have possibly mixed in the same circle with them. In short, though they are forced to endure comparative privations, they lose nothing in social position. They enjoy new facilities for gossip, flirtation, and publicity; and although they cannot dress as finely as before, they go into company as often as the expense permits them, with just as much claim to equality as when they gave balls and *soirées* themselves.

The Boarding House is thus the common "refuge of the destitute" in America. Reduced ladies, poor widows, or fortuneless spinsters, are sure to have recourse to it, either to keep and manage for a livelihood, or as a retreat in which they can subsist on cheaper terms than in "housekeeping." And the domestic habits of American ladies, in their better days and brighter fortunes, admirably fit them for this occupation. They have been always accustomed to household employments; to mix much with their servants from the nursery to the kitchen; to know the prices of provisions; to superintend cookery and other menial work. More than half the keepers of boarding houses in America are women who have seen better days;

and there is scarcely a family, however wealthy, which has not some near connection in this line of business.* Thus the merchant, or lawyer, or any man, in short, who is quitting the world, has not his last hours embittered by any very poignant regret, even if he leave his widow and children but a pittance, compared with the expensive disbursements of which they shared the enjoyment with him. And if he only loses his fortune instead of his life, gives up his establishment and contracts his outlay, he drops quite naturally into the public retirement of the boarding house, where he can thoroughly enjoy himself in economy, without being forced to add the suffering of privacy to his other misfortunes.

In this single point of view the boarding house system is very desirable in such a country. Its defects and disadvantages I shall speak of by and by.

* Two late occupants of the Presidential Chair at Washington, have sisters or cousins who keep boarding houses in that city.

CHAPTER VI.

NATIONAL CHARACTERISTICS (*continued*).

Breaking up of the Season at a Watering Place—An Easterly Storm—Profitable Investments—Final remarks on Nahant and its Visitors—Boston—General Resemblance to England—Points of Dissimilitude—Characteristics of American Cities—Style of Living—Cookery—Hotels—The "Boarding" System—Its Evil Effects on Manners and Character—American Gentlemen.

THE breaking up of our first season at Nahant was very curious and characteristic. We had looked forward to the month of September, the commencement of "the fall," as Autumn is rather poetically called in America, as likely to afford us great enjoyment, for that time of the year is proverbially delightful in New England, and particularly so on the sea-coast. The weather up to the last week of August, had been very fine. Warm days, cool nights, sunshine, moonlight, gentle winds, mist, mirage, and aurora borealis, just chequered by a couple of thunder-storms; when on the 29th of the month the weathercocks pointed to the north-east, and the sky showed symptoms of approaching rain.

I had gone, as usual, to Boston, with my son that morning; and we were forced to take the railroad and stage on our return, instead of the steamboat, which a heavy fog prevented from running. On crossing the beach between Lynn and Nahant, we met an unusual number of carriages of various descriptions; and before we reached the hotel, it seemed as if every species of available vehicle had been put in requisition, laden with human beings of all ages, besides trunks, portmanteaus, bandboxes, cradles, rocking-chairs, and other light articles of furniture, which had been previously brought from Boston by the sojourners, to eke out the scanty accommodations. It was, in fact, evident that there was a thorough breaking up of the whole Nahant system; or rather a systematical disruption of the Nahant season. For subsequent experience taught me that every year it explodes, so to call it, after this fashion.

"And what can have caused this abrupt and total desertion?" asked I, as I found the hotel quite desolate, with the exception of its keeper, his family and servants, who were sorrowfully helping to despatch the last lingering lodgers on their departure.

"What has happened? Has part of the house fallen in? Is the foundation giving way? Has the cholera broken out? What the devil *is* the matter?" exclaimed I at length, nobody being disposed to answer my first question.

"The storm! the storm! the Easterly storm!" hurriedly replied some one, sweeping past me towards the door. When, making my way to our apartments, I found my wife and daughter in a little nook which we had converted into the parody of a sitting room, with a couple of ladies who had heroically resolved to brave the perils which had literally scattered 200 of their fellow citizens before the wind.

There never was anything more ludicrous than this dispersion. It arose from no reason whatever but the intense popular dread of an easterly breeze, which meets one so laughably in a thousand instances all along "the sea-board." This fearful bugbear is generally accompanied with rain, and the most trivial fall of rain is always called "a storm." A little wind without rain is named a dry storm. So that when heavy rain and high wind come together, there is no distinct word in use to describe the conjunction accurately; for being something more than a mere gale without being a downright tempest, the word storm is precisely applicable to it. Now the wet weather which has led me to all this description, was not certainly what we should call in Europe a storm. It was not agreeable, and it lasted for full forty-eight hours. But by lighting a fire on the two damp evenings, and keeping within doors during the day, the time passed over without harm; and it was followed by weather so delightful, as to realise perfectly our most sanguine anticipations. But alas! we had not the power of enjoying it at Nahant. Our host was reluctantly obliged to discharge his servants and close his house, for want of company; and we, to our infinite regret, were driven out on September the 1st, to seek a hot and unwholesome lodging in one of the city hotels, until the time arrived, a month later, for which we had engaged a private house.

My conversation with the keeper of the Nahant Hotel, on my remonstrating against his shutting his doors, while we were so willing to remain, and with so fair a chance of fresh visitors with the return of fine weather, afforded a proof of Yankee versatility in the ways of money-making, which struck me as new and amusing.

"I should like very well to keep the house open a month longer," said he, "but the Colonel and the Doctor positively say it must close."

"Who are they? What have they to do with it?" asked I.

"Why, Sir, don't you know that Dr. R—— and Colonel P—— own the hotel, and that I only work it under their directions?"

And a little further explanation satisfied me, that the worthy Doctor, who also managed a woollen factory, and the gallant Colonel, who speculated in land in Michigan, and opium in China, and in many other undertakings besides hotel-keeping at Nahant, actually interfered so far in the latter concern as to fix a tariff for the prices of the most minute articles furnished at the public table, and reduced every purchase to so mean a minimum, as to afford a perfect excuse to their *locum tenens* for the bad living to which he proverbially confined his guests.

This instance of a rage for "profitable investments," no matter where they are to be sought for, is one out of many which came to my knowledge, of persons putting forth the loftiest pretensions to "aristocracy," yet descending to very low methods of money-making. But numerous failures are the consequence. This very speculation of the Nahant Hotel was one of them. The partners who had thus undertaken it, having no taste for the liberal management of a place which, if made attractive, might have been valuable, carried it on on the narrowest possible scale of expense. It, consequently, instead of being frequented for months as a place of elegant enjoyment, was resorted to merely as a refuge from the scorching heat of the dog days, and abandoned at the very first symptoms of a change. For three successive summers I and my family spent a portion of the season in this house; and, being always sure to meet some agreeable people among the promiscuous crowd, it was with reluctance we at last gave it up, though for sufficient reasons, and tried a cottage in the village.

And I cannot take leave of this place, to which I have so far extended my remarks, without the utterance of a final lamentation on the fate that dooms it to linger on from year to year in unimproved capability of all that might make a watering-place perfect. Even at this epoch there is not a single bathing-machine established here, though the beaches are numerous and most convenient ; a few huts, erected by private families, besides those belonging to the hotel, being the only accommodations for ladies: the rougher sex taking to nooks among the rocks. There is no possibility of a family obtaining apartments in a cottage, with the privilege of having their own cook and living in their own way. The only resources are the badly kept hotel, or the few village lodging-houses, in which one may obtain scanty and ill-furnished quarters at high prices, and accompanied by the penalty of being supplied with eatables by the owners, of as poor a description and with as primitive a *cuisine* as can be well imagined.

I see small prospect of a change for the better. A new wooden cottage is here and there springing up ; but only one with the least appearance of good taste was built within my memory. Mr. Tudor continues his improvements on his restricted locality. With that exception, not a hundred trees or shrubs were planted ; and gentlemen of wealth are one by one selling their cottages to others as tasteless, tired after a few years' possession, or wanting to place the few hundred pounds they receive for them in some new investment. The most niggardly spirit pervades the place ; not the least advance being made towards sociability among the visitors. To enjoy cool weather at the smallest possible expense, saving every dollar they can, is their utmost ambition. To spend one in entertaining their neighbours is out of the question, unless as a *very* rare exception on some unavoidable exigency. An ostentatious dinner now and then at their town houses as a positive act of duty, or for the display of their fine things, is the extent of their summer entertainments. And I must in verity add, that although the flower of hospitality may blossom a little oftener in winter, it is not a bit more fragrant from this frequency. Those who display it when they have a purpose to serve, shut it carefully up whenever they can. Having no spring of sociability in their hearts, they are glad of any excuse for living on a mean and thrifty scale. And it is only when they meet in large hotels, eating in common and forced to mix with each other, that they enjoy any relaxation from the routine of their homely occupations.*

Boston has the reputation—and its inhabitants are not a little proud thereat—of being the most "English-like" city in the Union. Such is the prevalent idea, and in certain respects it is correct. The people are of nearly unmixed British descent. The early settlers of New England generally, and of this their capital in particular, were exclusively so. And so they remained until within the last thirty or forty years, during which a considerable accession of Irish has taken from the population its entirely Anglo-Saxon character; and, in the opinion of the majority, its purity has consequently much deteriorated. That point I will not stop to discuss; but I will merely remark

* A step towards improvement has been made with respect to the Nahant Hotel. Its "aristocratic" owners sold it, on easy terms, to a man, who, from the humble situation of porter at the Tremont House, in Boston, thus became the proprietor of a house of his own. And, with an active, intelligent, and withal a handsome helpmate, he is doing much on the scanty profits of his short seasons to give comfort and satisfaction to his customers. I trust he may thrive; and that before this work sees the light, he may be, like his wealthier, but less liberal predecessor, every inch a colonel.

that the cross between the Hibernian and the Yankee produces a breed intelligent and active, with a dash of frankness that the purely national race has no pretensions to.

With the exception just stated, there are, almost literally, no foreigners resident in Boston.* I know but one English merchant, not a naturalised citizen, who frequented "Change;" but two Frenchmen, two or three Germans, a couple of Greeks, one Sicilian, a Russian, and a Swede, who were the vice-consuls of their respective countries. There may be half-a-dozen German and Italian music and dancing masters. Among the artisans and shopkeepers are a few Europeans. The mass of Irish labourers completes the list; but as the latter form the lowest order of the community, and are totally confined to their own haunts, I may safely say, that there are no foreign settlers in Boston at all known in the more elevated circles of society. It is a common saying, that a Scotchman cannot thrive in New England, the Yankees being "too cannie for him." There are, nevertheless, several highly respectable Scotch tradesmen among the citizens of Massachusetts. Even a Jew, it is remarked, with more apparent truth, would have no chance there. Boston does not, I believe, contain one individual Israelite. But the many resemblances in character and habits between the Hebrew and the Yankee are very remarkable, and very soon become obvious. The latter shows many tendencies towards a relapse into Judaism, and a return to the Mosaic law. The Old Testament is more congenial than the New to *his* Christianity. Its maxims and

* Of late years this state of things has much changed; and seeing the advantage of an increase of Europeans to the native American stock, I must say greatly improved.

doctrines are constantly appealed to. The exclusive characteristics of the Jews are very common, and the great prevalence of Hebrew in comparison with Christian names is one of the most striking peculiarities of a people eminently pharisaical.

In an evening paper called "The Boston Evening Gazette," I find some remarks on the trial of a young man named Mercer, who murdered the seducer of his sister at Philadelphia. The editor says, among other things, "We hope young Mercer will be acquitted, but not on the ground of insanity (which was pleaded by his counsel). We consider the *removal* of such a wretch as the seducer in this case, a just sacrifice to outraged virtue. The sons of Jacob, for a similar provocation, slew the better part of a whole tribe, and the plea of insanity was the last they would have resorted to."

This is a chance specimen of many similar indications of the tendency I have pointed out.

But on the foundation of English origin is established a character in which many of the distinctive traits of the parent stock are preserved. Everything tends to foster it; the proud recollection of British descent, associations with British literature, a trade very much confined to England, her American and West India colonies, or her Eastern possessions. All the social sympathies of the people are English—but they are *old* English — exclusive, narrow, selfish. The wide-spread intercourse with other nations, which has opened the heart of Great Britain to the generous influences of philanthropy, poured into it the genial streams of taste, and elevated the national mind far above the cramped standard of former days, has had no influence in New England. So that, with a general resemblance, which strikes strangers on their first arrival, and which in individuals is of the nature of that borne by living men to the portraits of some far-back ancestors, there is really a wide difference between the two countries. This soon becomes observable in many ways. In costume, for instance, young men of any pretension are much more like ill-dressed French or German "exquisites" than like English gentlemen of the present day. They affect mustachios, tufts on the chin, long greasy-looking hair (called in their own expressive slang "soap-locks"). They remind one of the Parisian "*Calicots*" of some years back; and we are surprised to hear them talk English so passably.

The few private equipages are anything but English. They are greatly deficient in comfort or elegance, according to our notions. They are little better than ill-painted tubs on wheels with a coat of arms (picked up "à discrétion" in some book of heraldry) daubed on the panels, and hung on enormously high springs, with a narrow rickety flight of stairs, to let down or put up whenever one wants to descend or mount. The houses, though mostly built of brick, and many of them having fronts of granite, have rarely the look of London or Liverpool dwellings. The shops are generally small, with narrow-paned windows, and more like those of Paris or Brussels in the days of Louis XVIII. There is an over-abundance of glaring sign-boards, gilding, and green paint. But it is, perhaps, more in the absence of many things that constitute the general appearance of an English city of our time, than in the difference between the relative objects which are visible, that we perceive the contrast when walking the streets of Boston, New York, Philadelphia, or Baltimore. In the first mentioned a livery servant is never seen; in the others, some gaudy, ill-assorted variety of colours occasionally distinguishes the dress of domestics, particularly of black men. The absence of soldiery, or a uniformly dressed police, is very striking. No one, in fact, in uniform appears, unless on periodical occasions of muster for the militia companies. A military garrison is unknown in the United States, except in the far distant forts and frontier towns. The few thousand men composing the regular army are so widely scattered and in such small parties, particularly since the termination of the Florida and Mexican campaigns, and consequent increases of territory, that they have no where an opportunity of showing themselves in any force.

Although there are constables in all the cities, they are not to be distinguished from the inhabitants at large *; but it must appear to all new comers that no class of persons exists requiring the interference of a permanent police. Open beggary is altogether unknown. The general air of the population proclaims it to be above want, and out of the temptation of the petty crimes and disturbances of European communities. Employment is the most effectual peace-preserver; and where every man feels himself to form a portion of the Law, or at any rate of the Executive, hired guardians are little required for its enforcement. To see anything like indigence or idleness we must penetrate into the purlieus in the seaport towns, occupied by the Irish labouring population. And there even, though they be in comparative wealth to what they were in their state of native wretchedness, their home habits are too evidently traced in the filth of the dwellings, the raggedness of the bare-footed children, and the slatternly air of the women. The haunts of this portion of the inhabitants and of

* Of late years, a badge on the coat, or a blue band bearing the word "Police," has been introduced.

the coloured people form a painful contrast to the general air of cleanliness and comfort.

The season of the year at which a stranger arrives in an American city makes a greater difference in his first impressions than it would do in any other country. In summer, the foliage of the many trees planted along the streets and in the public places gives great brilliancy and softness to the scene. But in winter, particularly if it is a severe one, the scandalous way in which the ice and snow are allowed to accumulate—the day-thaw from the heat of the sun, and the night-frosts partially retarding its action—causes a mass of mud and a state of slipperiness that is dirty and dangerous in the highest degree. The middle of the streets is filled with snow several feet high, the channels overflowing, and the flag-ways, or "side-walks," covered with ice in patches, which neither respect for the corporation ordinances nor benevolence towards their species can induce the householders to clear away or cover with ashes. Dr. Franklin remarked long ago, that the test of a citizen's goodness of heart, or the want of it, was his strewing ashes before the shop door, or the neglect of it, in frosty weather. If this be a fair rule to judge by, the milk of human nature is fearfully curdled, in the cities of Boston and New York more particularly; for the neglect in question is not so severly felt in the more southern cities. But in those where the winter lasts for several months, and the snow and ice lie in the streets for many weeks, the consequences are direful. Horses plunging in a chaos of obstructions, carriages and sleighs upset, and foot-passengers continually falling, meet the eye at every turn. While to the unfortunate persons forced by business to be constantly out of doors and to wade through the *slush*, the ill effects are boundless, in colds, sore throats, rheumatism, and many other ills, of their inheritance to which the people seem proud. For it would be very easy indeed to remedy these abuses, if the magistrates had the courage to enforce the fines, or the corporation the liberality to pay for labourers to clear the streets, or individuals any pride in the decent appearance of their front premises. Partial attempts are, no doubt, made, here and there. Men and carts are employed at long intervals to break up and remove the frozen snow heaps from the vicinity of some public building. A shopkeeper is seen, now and then, sweeping his flagway; but the general rule is a shameful neglect, and frequent-recurring accidents are the consequence.

Within a short period, perhaps a couple of weeks, during one winter I knew of my own knowledge the following accidents from falls on the ice, on the "side-walks" in Boston:—

Mr. Pratt, a wealthy merchant, was killed, by fracturing his skull, close to his own door.

Mr. Inglis, a Scotch gentleman, dislocated his shoulder.

Mrs. May, a lady of great respectability, broke her leg.

Another elderly lady broke both legs.

Major Grafton, surveyor of the port, cut his knee, and was disabled for some weeks.

Mr. Richard Derby violently hurt his arm and narrowly escaped contusion of the brain; saved by the thickness of his wig, or some craniological conformation.

Several more ladies and gentlemen of my acquaintance, among them Col. Perkins, Commodore Nicholson, and Mr. Abbott Lawrence, were more or less bruised, or cut, or strained, in body and limbs.

The venerable Bishop Griswold was killed on the spot;

and the following paragraphs, the first announcing the fatal accident, the second published in the same newspaper the day after, are not bad illustrations of the levity with which such things are viewed in this civilized community :—

"We were *somewhat startled* last evening by a report of the death of Bishop Griswold ; and on inquiry, we learned that the report was too true. Bishop Griswold was about paying a visit to his colleague, Bishop Eastburn, in Pemberton Square ; he had nearly reached the front door when he slipped on the ice, fell, and struck his head very heavily upon the side-walk. Bishop Eastburn saw him fall, rushed to his assistance, carried him into the house, but he expired in a few minutes."

"☞ The unkindest cut of all was one administered yesterday, by the iron railing round the common, to a gentleman who slipped on the ice and fell against it."

But not one in a hundred of these accidents is mentioned in the papers. An occasional squib, or a sharp reproach, in the shape of a letter to the editor from some sufferer, gets into "poets' corner," or the column devoted to minor correspondence, and is either unread or unheeded.

At all seasons of the year there is an absence of much that gives a sort of speaking life to an English town. There are no morning or evening "cries ;" no bells jingling, except the church bells, for service in the day-time or a fire at night, or the bells attached to horses' necks at sleighing time, to warn foot passengers of what is coming along the snow. There is no street music, vocal or instrumental* (perhaps a satisfactory exemption) ; no dancing

* An occasional Italian organ-grinder is an importation recently admitted.

dogs, no puppet-shows, and, saddest of all privations, no PUNCH! I am not speaking in anti-temperance lamentation; but I seriously mourn the want of *Polichinel,* his mellifluous squeak, the well-wielded club with which he draws sweet melody from his wooden-headed wife and his other victims, and all those quirks, and quiddities, and personal jokes with which he makes the streets of the Old World joyous. I really wish some adventurous showman would cross the Atlantic with a well-appointed "Punch," and I think he would get as good a reception as his literary namesake, who is now so generally read, though at times so nervously winced under.

The streets of the "Atlantic cities," as the seaport towns are called, are altogether deficient in the air of lounging and lazy life, which well-dressed men of leisure and the many varieties of *vagabondage* give to the towns of the Continent, and, in a minor degree, to those of the British Isles. But there is much bustle and business-like vivacity. The thoroughfares are full of well-clad, plain-looking, serious-visaged men, and women in all the gaudiness of over-dressed pretension. The flaunting air of these ladies, their streaming feathers and flowers, silks and satins of all colours, and a rapid, dashing step as they walk along, singly or in couples, give foreigners a widely mistaken notion of them. They look, in fact, like so many nymphs of the *pavé;* for no other class of females in Europe are at all like them; and many awkward mistakes take place in consequence. But in proportion as the American ladies lose much of the retiring modesty so becoming in their sex, by this habit of independent promenading, the streets gain largely, in the glare and glitter of the fair *piétons.*

A very curious feature in the movements of Boston

is the extraordinary degree of training exhibited by the horses which draw the numerous trucks (*Anglicè* drays) through the narrow and sometimes densely crowded streets. These trucks, formed of two long shafts with transverse planks, are a most unwieldy and unmanageable kind of carriage; and, laden with barrels of flour, or other heavy articles, they require two, three, four, and sometimes five horses to drag them. The animals so employed are of a good breed, and many of them are handsome. But the matter most worthy of remark is, that none of the team, except the shaft-horse, has any sort of reins; and they being all harnessed singly to the traces in a line one after the other, they obey with amazing sagacity the word of command of the driver, who stands on the plank or bar close behind the shaft horse, with the bridle in one hand, and a short whip in the other.

I have often gazed with wonder at a vehicle of this kind coming along at a smart trot, the wholly uncontrolled leader, and the two or three equally reinless steeds which follow, winding, turning, stopping short, resuming their pace; and all the while avoiding the least contact with any object that might obstruct the path. These horses really seem possessed of reason; and the driver of them is surely something more than an ordinary charioteer. And I must here remark with sincere praise, not only the general skill of American drivers—maugre their loose, awkward, and unartist-like way of holding "the ribbons," —but the extreme civility and command of temper manifested by the whole tribe of stage, hack, cab, or truck drivers, not only to their "fare," but to each other. In the crowded streets and broken roads they often find themselves in a bad *fix*. I have frequently seen half-a-dozen or more carriages of different kinds—omnibuses, gigs, waggons, and trucks—all entangled together at a corner or a railway station in America. But I never, except occasionally at New York where Irish hackmen abound, heard oaths, imprecations, or abuse applied to as the means for unravelling the knot. On these occasions the men engaged rarely exchange word or look. They commune with their horses; and when necessary, every one puts his shoulder to his respective wheel, and thus the close-locked mass is quickly set free, without time or temper lost, and generally without damage done.

Such are some of the peculiarities of the American cities, contrasted with those of Europe. Within the houses they are still more striking. Unpapered walls, uncurtained windows and beds, the absence of what American delicacy calls "modern improvements," and the tenacity with which American indelicacy adheres to ancient nuisances, all give to the generality of houses in the United States a half-finished and half-furnished appearance. There is also a cut-and-dried look about everything. Scarcely any object seems meant for use, all are so prim and formal, in pattern and position; while the sameness which pervades the whole, makes it look as if it was done by a common measurement. Some mansions are, no doubt, more expensively fitted up than others; but they are nearly all built on the same plan, and furnished in the same style of ungraceful utility. In some, the walls are covered with tolerable engravings; in many, they are spotted with wretched pictures; but in very few, indeed, does good taste preside over the decorations, or confine them to what is chaste in art, and rare in America. A passable copy of some old European master, or a *médiocre* specimen by some living American painter, is overlaid by a number of daubs; or a small group of well-copied foreign statuary is smothered in a crowd of big busts of the native "great men." *

The method of heating many of the best houses is a terrible grievance to persons not accustomed to it, and a fatal misfortune to those who are. Casual visitors are nearly suffocated, and constant occupiers killed. An enormous furnace in the cellar sends up, day and night, streams of hot air, through apertures and pipes, to every room in the house. No spot is free from it, from the dining-parlour to the dressing-closet. It meets you the moment the street-door is opened to let you in, and it rushes after you when you emerge again, half-stewed and parboiled, into the wholesome air. The self-victimized citizens, who have a preposterous affection for this atmosphere, undoubtedly shorten their lives by it. Several elderly gentlemen of my acquaintance, suddenly cut off, would assuredly have had a verdict of "died of a furnace" pronounced on their cases, had a coroner been called, and had a jury decided on fair evidence. But no citizen is inclined to condemn the instrument which every one in "high life" patronizes, and which is congenial to the frigid temperament of all classes. Half the sickness in the Atlantic cities, north of Washington, is to be attributed to the extreme heat of the houses, without which the cold external air would do good instead of harm. Large fires of Anthracite coal and close stoves are common, in houses of moderate pretensions, where the cruel luxury of a furnace is not found. And independent of the mischief done to the health of both sexes and all ages, there is something inexpressibly cheerless, whether

* But I must in justice remark, that in the general arrangements of lately built houses, considerable improvement has taken place, both in hotels and private dwellings.

it be in Germany, Holland, or the United States, in the look of a house heated by a furnace, particularly if the rooms have grates unfilled and useless.

One extremely gratifying circumstance of domestic economy in the United States, arises from the cheapness of lamp oil. Tallow candles (the curse of middle life and moderate incomes in Europe) are never seen. Astral, solar, moderator, or other fanciful kinds of lamps, lustres lighted with gas, and wax or spermaceti lights, are to be found everywhere. English and Nova Scotia coal is much used, particularly on the sea-coast. But wood is also a favourite fuel, though becoming dear, from the constantly increasing havoc among the forest trees, in proportion to the rapid clearing of the country in all directions. A very strange and disagreeable-looking lamp, made of glass, in the shape of an urn, is common in the best houses. The wick is seen inside coiled up in oil, and having exactly the appearance of a large worm preserved in spirits. This is passed upwards through a small tin tube, and it burns openly, without covering of any kind. These lamps are the common bedroom lights; and one or more, very large and lofty, stands in every drawing-room.

The style of every-day living among even the wealthiest people, is very simple and unexpensive. But little wine is drunk in the more domestic circle; and plain English cookery is alone usual. Eating and drinking, *en famille*, is a mere operation of appetite, without any social feeling connected with it; and the more quickly and least expensively it can be performed the better. But the overloaded table, and the interminable varieties of wine, at a regular dinner given to company, form a striking contrast to the family meal. At these dinners all the good things of the place abound; and they are well served, for the best cook in the town is sure to be hired for the occasion. Poultry and wild fowl largely preponderate among the more solid portions of the repast; sometimes, indeed, to the entire exclusion of butcher's meat. A high-flavoured, but half-starved, fatless kind of venison is considered a dainty. It is always served disgustingly underdone—almost raw sometimes—on pewter or tin plates, standing over burners with spirits of wine, to enable each person to cook it in a thick gravy according to his fancy. This is a very disagreeable process to witness. I never was tempted to undertake it.

Excellent beef, mutton, veal, and lamb are to be had in all the large cities of the United States. But the national taste certainly runs on pork, salt-fish, tough poultry, and little birds of all descriptions. Two favourite condiments are cranberry jelly and tomato sauce. They form a part of every dinner. Oysters are eaten in all ways, and in great quantities. Of vegetable substances, and certain fancy dishes with uncouth names, I have spoken elsewhere.

Without wishing to enlarge on this topic of gastronomical taste, I cannot omit noticing more particularly the passion for salted provisions, which prevails so generally. Even butter is rarely to be met with, except at Philadelphia, that is not impregnated with salt to an almost incredible excess. What we understand by fresh butter in Europe is, with the above exception, in the summer season, almost unknown. Many Americans, male and female, have assured me that they could not eat the butter served to them in England and France, from its want of salt. I believe I should, in justice, attribute much of the apparent deficiency in flavour, both to myself and others, of fish, flesh, and fowl in the United States, to the excoriation of our tongues and palates from the inevitable use of the fiercely salted butter.

One word as to cookery in general throughout the country. At hotels, with a few exceptions in the large cities, it is detestable ; in private houses, very indifferent. The great evils are the odious attempts at *la cuisine française,* and the bad butter used in the sauces. You hear of French cooks very often, but you see little of French cookery. Every broken-down barber, or disappointed dancing-master, French, German or Italian, sets up as cook, with about as much knowledge of cookery as a cow has of *cow*cumbers.* In a word, the science of the table is in the earliest stage of infancy in the United States. In all the doubts and fears expressed as to their future fate, nothing sounds so terribly ominous as that aphorism in the "Physiologie du Goût," which solemnly says, "*La destinée des Nations dépend de la manière dont elles se nourissent.*"

As to the behaviour, while at meals, of the people in general, nothing very refined or graceful ought to be expected. Of the conventional proprieties of European life there is a great deficiency. Those who form their estimate of foreign manners (as I do not) on the presence or absence of certain observances amongst good society in England, must be prepared to meet grievous anomalies in transatlantic circles. Eating with the knife, loading the plate with numerous incongruous kinds of food, abruptness of demeanour, are the common habits of the *table d'hôte.* Private parties are not exempt from the first two of those offences against taste. But, in my opinion, a natural instinct of good breeding may exist in indi-

* An *Irish* illustration of ignorance, as the pronunciation of the word cucumbers specifies.

viduals sufficient to counterbalance habits like those. The stiffness and overdone efforts at propriety, of people who wish to behave remarkably well, are more offensive to me than the rough and rapid method with which others dispose of their dinner. I consider a man who picks his teeth with his fork (and I am sorry to say I have frequently sat at table in America with such a one) as a less unpleasant object than he who ostentatiously holds his napkin before his face while he performs with a gold instrument, taken out of an ivory case, the simple operation that can be so unobservedly effected by the point of a quill slipped quietly between the lips. Then the splashing, rinsing, and wiping, when the finger-glasses come into play, is far worse than having none at all. But these are small items of remark ; and at best but paltry tests of good or bad manners, and none at all of character.

When we penetrate a little deeper into the domestic arrangements of the natives, we find that the most prominent feature of their private lives is its publicity. The vast majority of the town inhabitants of the United States live in boarding-houses or hotels ; and it would be difficult indeed to calculate the small proportion of those who live alone. In the style of their country-houses the same wish to be stared at and to stare prevails. A snug cottage embowered in shrubbery, or a handsome villa shaded with plantations, is a very rare object in the landscape. Almost all is open and exposed. The *improvements* of a country place in England, mean the copses or clumps of young trees, put into the earth and fostered in their growth to rural embellishment. In America the same word means the clearance of old timber, with half-burned and unseemly stumps defacing the sward, or the huge and tasteless wooden barns and other offices of the farm. To see and to be seen constitute the staple of enjoyment in town or country. But there is none of the *nonchalance* of French, Italian, or German out-of-door life, or the easy intercourse of its *table d'hôte* existence. No graceful display —no cordial association. This mixture of cold self-exposure and prying curiosity arises from the absence of domestic resources, and from sheer niggardliness. The comparative cheapness of occupying merely bedrooms, frequenting the common sitting parlour, called the Ladies' Drawing-room, and eating all meals at the ordinary, is irresistible to the natives, when added to the luxury of seeing what other people wear, listening to what they say, and watching how they "feed." Very few, therefore, occupy private apartments in the hotels; and the accommodation for those who do is most imperfect. Every discouragement is, in fact, given to such a taste, and those who venture to act on it are considered very exclusive and "aristocratical." Few persons will risk the unpopularity attendant on such a reputation.

There is but one hotel in Boston confined to the entertainment of families on the European plan, where no *table d'hôte* exists, and where people may live alone, and have their meals at their own hours. But even in this house there is that fearful nuisance a "bar," where any one who has three pence to spend in dram-drinking, or a penny to pay for a cigar, may freely enter, to sit down or lounge about. The lodgers, however, are not exposed to much annoyance, unless they have the ill-luck to occupy the best rooms in the house, those on the first floor to which the noise and the smoke freely penetrate. And this house such as it is, ill-furnished, dirty, and dear, is the only refuge for persons who have not one of their own, who could not endure the annoyances of a "boarding house," and who object to the better-kept hotels on account of their enormous population. The Tremont House, the Revere House, and the Winthrop House, excellent of their kind, and the United States Hotel, well kept but less *recherché* in its style, constantly contain several hundred persons, the last-mentioned between four and five hundred. A residence in such a garrison, with the constant change of visitors, and the everlasting recurrence of births, deaths, and marriages, is not particularly inviting to Europeans accustomed to the comforts of private life.

The first of the troubles which beset a strange family in Boston, is the extreme difficulty of obtaining a house in a good situation. The very desirable streets are few, and much sought for; and every probable vacancy is known long in advance, by the relatives or acquaintances of the several occupants. Besides this the rents are exorbitantly high. From two to three hundred pounds a-year is the least for which a house, sufficiently spacious and comfortable for a moderate-sized family to receive company in, can be had. A ready-furnished house is almost impossible to be obtained on any terms. The only chance of that kind is in the case of some family going to Europe for a year or more, and a score of persons among their relations and friends are always on the look-out for such a contingency.

A suite of furnished apartments, or even a single room for a solitary man, with a kitchen and accommodation for one's own servants, is as unknown at Boston as at Nahant. The only alternatives are the hotels, or the houses where you are furnished with board and lodging; a combination of terms which, by the way, does not exist in the American language. "Going a-boarding" expresses the whole thing. "Where do you board?" is the only way of asking a person where he lives, if he has not a house of his own. Lodgers are invariably called "boarders." And these several expressions are foremost amongst those which give to English persons a notion of the general vulgarity. For, without meaning the slightest disparagement to the individuals who, from temporary causes, avail themselves of the boarding-house system in England, its permanent adoption for respectable families is I may say almost unknown. Its prevalence in America is certainly the most disagreeable feature in the social habits of the country. It is productive at once of the most narrow scheme of existence—inhospitable, ungenial, selfish—and of the most inquisitive and gossiping pursuits. All the delicate privacies of life are blighted. Children brought up in this way can know nothing of gentleness or reserve. The open exposure of domestic circumstances and feelings is inevitable, between women who pass their whole days in doing little or nothing, having no household occupations of their own. Family secrets become public talk; individual peculiarities, common property. Every one knows everything about everybody. The extent of Mr. Smith's business, the amount of his property, his liabilities and engagements, are as well known to his fellow-boarder Mr. Jones, through the medium of his own remarks and his wife's revelations, as are Mrs. Jones's wardrobe, purchases, and connubial grievances to Mrs. Smith, by a mutual scheme of intercourse.

Abundant disputes, quarrels, and estrangements are inevitable. And the overcharged bosoms of the belligerents find ready recipients for their outpourings in the separate circles of family connections, from whom the tittle-tattle is widely spread, until the whole city is cognizant of the most minute affairs of its obscurest inhabitants;

for, be it remarked, there is no class in the United States out of the pale of the boarding-house system.

This is in itself a great evil; but it generates a still greater. The general acquaintanceship with every man's affairs, arising from a mean spirit of inquiry, creates a still meaner one of distrust, and that again superinduces an increased caution, on the part of those "observed of all observers," which degenerates into cunning, deception, and falsehood. These painful errors of human nature are altogether national in America. Every one is tainted with them more or less. They form a general epidemic from which no one is safe. I believe that every family throughout the United States is at times, and frequently, accustomed to "go a-boarding." If they stir from home for a day, week, or month, they must submit to it, even if they do not like it; and they must all, in a greater or a less degree, be liable to its influence. It enters into their habits of thought. They cannot, if they would, shake it off. But no one would if he could. It is not felt to be an evil, nor considered at all discreditable. The most distinguished people in the country are so accustomed to promiscuous living while they are from home, that they consider it as a portion of their national nature. Governors of states, senators, judges, generals, with their wives and daughters, go to boarding-houses and "messes,"* without hesitation or repugnance. And men of all ages "double up," or "room together," as the phrase goes, as a matter of course. And they are as insensible to the mischief it does them, in blunting their perception of the delicacies of life, as are the narrow-chested, round-shouldered beings who walk the streets unconscious of their

* A technical term, confined, I believe, to the city of Washington, for families boarding together.

deformity, arising from the want of manly exercise and wholesome sports. As the latter portions of the community are cripples without knowing it, so are the people in general ignorant of their deficiency in mental straightforwardness.

The absence of an acute sense of delicate feeling is very remarkable. I had well known the stigma to that effect commonly fixed upon Americans by Europeans. But I had always attributed much of this to prejudice; and when instances of it were forced upon my observation, soon after I arrived in the country, I was anxious to believe them merely individual cases — the exceptions rather than the rule. By degrees, however, I became satisfied, by my own experience and that of others, that a want of the keen perception of right and wrong which prevails in Europe—and is too often violated there—is common to the American mind. The moral, like the political constitution of the United States is not identical with ours. The fine shades of sentiment which pervade society in the Old World are less known in the New. The intense pursuit of gain, the little cultivation of the higher order of intellect, the shifting way of life, the fluctuations of fortune, all tend to reduce the standard. "The chivalry of the South," "nature's noblemen," "the dignity of man," "a free, enlightened, and high-minded people," are the bywords of American phraseology, as applied to the Americans; and a meaning is attached to such expressions, bearing a certain degree of resemblance to that which an Englishman gives to them. But the resemblance, if put to a practical test, will be found rather fanciful than real. These grandiloquent phrases are like the "*magnifique*" and "*superbe*" of a Frenchman applied to the most ordinary objects.

I do not, however, intend to convey the opinion that American gentlemen mean to act in violation of what they believe to be implied in that character. I mean only to say that their notion of it is somewhat different from ours; but that, as far as they comprehend it, many of them very conscientiously observe it. And when a European is put on his guard, by long, and it may be costly, experience, when he expects no more than he can find, the gentlemen of America may with satisfaction be associated with. Many of them, are most agreeable and trustworthy companions; but few can rise entirely superior to the cramping influence of the home atmosphere in which they dwindle; and great allowance should be made for them, not only at home but abroad.

Nor must this general deficiency in a high order of sentiment or information, or the inability to appreciate fully these qualities in English gentlemen, be made a reproach to the class of men in question. It should be remembered that they are for the most part drawn from pursuits of an inferior order, to fill a station for which they have received small culture, and that in a generation or two the most leading families very generally sink back to their original lowness. It is quite painful to observe at present the striking change for the worse in most of the sons of the men from sixty to eighty years of age who are now fast dropping off from the scene. But painful as this degeneracy is, in an individual point of view, it would be far better for the country at large were these weak scions of good old stems aware of their inferiority, and content to become merged in the general mediocrity (I am forced to reiterate the word) to which everything in the United States is tending.

CHAPTER VII.

THE SOCIAL SYSTEM IN NEW ENGLAND.

Restricted State of Social Liberty—Fashionable Society—Men of Fashion—Exclusiveness—American "Almack's"—"Our First Men"—Extracts—General Contentment—Yankee Characteristics—Caution—Want of Originality—Public Opinion—Its effects on Social Intercourse—Dinners, Clubs, Parties—Superficial Feelings.

In proportion to the great extension of political freedom in New England, social liberty is unquestionably very much restrained. The great blessings of life depend, perhaps, more on the latter than the former ; yet, from the most impartial observation, I am satisfied that the social system at present established in the commonwealth of Massachusetts is, after all that has yet come under my experience, that which is best adapted to secure the well-being of the community. It falls very short of perfection ; but that is a mark beyond my expectation in regard to any human institution. It may be improved, and with such elements as are already in action there is a fair chance that it will be. But my notions of what constitutes improvement in this case are, I believe, very different from those which many people in England, or a certain class of society in Massachusetts entertain.

The great object among the democracy of America is to guard against a too rapid progress in the advance towards civilisation. But of this there seems to be little danger in any portion of the country, and less perhaps in New England than anywhere else. In the first place, the leading characteristic of the Yankee people is caution. Everything is weighed and measured, and by a common standard—that of utility. Next, there is a wide-spread, but still far from complete, system of education throughout the New England States, at the public expense. A prudent and enlightened people are therefore unlikely to be led astray by false and flimsy projects, or to abate that watchfulness and jealousy of overgrown wealth which have hitherto checked the advance of luxurious and demoralising habits. Refinement has, to a certain extent, worked itself into the social system. But there exists only the raw material of elegance—handsome houses, fine furniture, expensive dress—money, in short, in its various modes of disbursement. The skill for working this up into a fabric of social happiness is wanting. The longing after refinement does not make a man refined, unless a certain degree of talent, and a large portion of taste point out to the individual where fit models are to be found, and how they are to be adapted to his particular position.

There can be nothing more absurd than to hear the wealthy classes in the North American cities boast of their "fashionable society," and their "aristocracy," and make announcements of events in "high life." It would be invidious to analyse the pretensions or the practices of those who assume these distinctions. It may suffice to say that, with very few exceptions, the persons who occupy the best residences in the best parts of the towns were originally of low pursuits, not having the advantages of early education, or of subsequent leisure to cultivate polite literature or well-bred society. A few families are of respectable descent, and may have claims to gentle blood. But the host of the leaders of *ton* are all, in the still-existing generation, persons raised by their own industry and good luck from most inferior situations. Many of them have been poor country boys, who came into the cities as sweepers of counting-houses, pedlars, or incumbents of the lowest places among a large population. From these small beginnings they became clerks, grocers, linendrapers, "dry goods men," commercial travellers, supercargoes, or masters of vessels, stockbrokers, merchants, manufacturers, and—men of fashion!

From such persons and their wives, chosen in the same circle that they themselves belong to, little is to be expected but the most absurd attempts at what is in England called "exclusiveness." Often have I been amused at the airs assumed by these leaders towards their quite as respectable and frequently more agreeable neighbours. I will not launch forth into common-place praise of honest industry, working its way through life and obtaining its high honours. But I cannot help branding with a note of disparagement those who, having won this glorious victory, degenerate into self-dubbed "aristocrats," and set their faces against the progress of others who now run the very career they themselves have so successfully completed; and indulge in the cant against radicals, the rabble, and so forth, which being natural to the almost over-civilised ranks of the English nobility is not, when assumed by them, actually repugnant to reason. We can even tolerate and pity it in the gentry of England, where, rank and station being the fountains of distinction, people are driven, as it were, to slake their thirst at them or pine in arid respectability. But the independence of republican life in America should show no such weakness. Attempts at exclusiveness there are ludicrous. There being no marked lines, no titles beyond the everlasting "honourable" awarded to senators, members of Congress, governors of states, and others; and the naval and military distinctions, which latter degenerate into mere burlesque, it is hard to know whom to keep out, whom to admit, or to decide who is or who is not a member of "fashionable society." The position is one of mere assumption. Yet it is understood and to a great degree admitted by those who are not quite within the pale. Exclusion is, for the reason just mentioned, the most arbitrary in its action of anything that can be imagined. Why, Mr. A., the oil merchant; or Mr. B., the clothier; or Mr. C., the shipping agent; should not be one in the same circle with Mr. D., the ci-devant linendraper; or Mr. E., the grocer of some years ago; or Mr. F., who made his money by opium smuggling in China; or Mr. H., who is minus a finger, which was chopped off when he was a cabin boy; or Mr. G., who still bears the scar of the reaping-hook on his hand—or so on to the end of the alphabet—it would be very hard to tell. One set lives in as good houses as the other. They are all shareholders in railroads, banks, and manufactories. They dress as well, are as well informed and well mannered, one as the other. Why some should have the power to pronounce the ban, or why others should be put under it or submit to it, I have never been able to find out. We made sundry fearful mistakes, arising from this ignorance, on our early settlement in Boston. The elect and the rejected appeared to us as like each other as possible. Some of "the best set" were certainly not the least deficient. It was only on the establishment of certain assemblies for dancing which took place in the winter after our arrival, that we really found out who were, or were not, "fashionable society." About a hundred and twenty subscribers, heads of families, having the right to bring ladies, formed, as I soon discovered, the self-elected fashionables. Almost every one not on their list was to be looked on as the vulgar. These assemblies were extremely well conducted, and as pleasant as anything of the kind could be in Boston. But by far the funniest thing connected with them was that the place where they were given (the rooms of an Italian dancing master) was called "Almack's."

A curious and amusing pamphlet published in Boston in 1846, is so strikingly illustrative of this subject, and of the slashing, slangish, style of writing prevalent in the United States, that I will give a few random extracts from it in this place. It is entitled—

"Our First Men: A Calendar of Wealth, Fashion, and Gentility."

It opens as follows:—

"A great deal is said, first and last, about the 'Boston aristocracy,' sometimes more familiarly designated as 'our first men.' We hear this phrase constantly repeated in newspapers and political speeches, as well as in conversation. Yet how many of those who repeat it, have anything but the most vague and incoherent ideas about that aristocracy of which they talk!

"The present is the first attempt ever made to produce this much-talked of aristocracy,—the 'solid men of Boston'—*our first men*—visibly and palpably,—by name and enumeration,—rank and file,—head and tail,—in their own proper persons, before the eyes of the people; and so to give this hitherto invisible power and presence—

"'A local habitation and a name.'

"So far from any apology being needed for this work, there are abundance of reasons why it ought to be published, and should have been long ago; some few of which we shall mention.

"In the first place, the gratification of the curiosity of vast numbers; not a mere idle curiosity, by any means; but a liberal and reasonable curiosity. We are told and taught that all men are *born* equal; yet they do not long stay so. When we look around us, we see a very great inequality existing: this man in a hovel—that man in a palace; this man surrounded with every luxury that wealth can afford—that man subjected to all the sufferings and mortifications of poverty. Whence this difference? Who are these rich men, in whose hands such a large proportion of the wealth of the community is concentrated? and how did it get there? Are they gods,—favorites of Heaven? or are they mere puppets of fortune; mortal men and women, like the rest of us?

"It will also be an excellent thing for our rich men themselves to be put in mind of some points of their history, which they are very apt to forget. It will be well to remind them, that they were once poor themselves, or their fathers were; and that this money which so puffs them up, and makes them feel so big, came to them through toil and labor, and close shaving, and tight economy; and now and then, perhaps, a little cheating; sometimes by business not very creditable; and that, in the same way, it may come, and is every day coming to others, who are willing to use similar means to obtain it.

"But there will also be advantages in this book for those who, while they can hardly pretend to be rich, are yet very unwilling to confess themselves poor.

"Next to being rich themselves, it is for such persons a very delightful thing to have the reputation of being a friend and associate, or at least an acquaintance of those who are rich. How mortifying to a multitude of young Bostonians in the country, or in distant places, to be inquired of about this or that rich man of Boston, and to be obliged to confess that they know nothing about them! Whereas, by the diligent study and judicious use of this little book, they may appear very knowing, and may even be able to pass themselves off as a part of the aristocracy!

"It is no derogation, then, to the Boston aristocracy, that it rests upon money. Money is something substantial. Everybody knows that and feels it. Birth is a mere idea, which grows every day more and more intangible.

"It should be understood, however, that in Boston, as elsewhere, this moneyed aristocracy is divided into two sections, the old and the new, or with more precision, and in country terms, the two-year-old, and the yearling aristocracy.

"The two-year-old aristocracy is composed of those who either inherited money, or, if they have made it themselves, had the benefit of a certain standing in society to start with; or who, gifted by nature with a certain refinement, tact, and sense of propriety, have no difficulty in acting the part of gentlemen, though they were not born to it. It is of such that the best society of Boston is composed. There are admitted into this circle of society, many families, who in point of wealth do not come up to the limit which is the stopping-place in this calendar; and on the other hand, no small number of those mentioned in it, notwithstanding large sums set against their names, are still excluded from the best society, and are wriggling, working, and tormenting themselves to death, or are tormented by their wives and daughters, at an exclusion, which, now that they are rich, distresses them quite as much as they were once distressed at the idea of being poor.

"To those within this charmed circle it appears for the most part very delightful; and it no doubt contains many well informed, well bred, agreeable people. But to those without it looks forbidding, arrogant, cold, comfortless. It must be confessed that Boston manners are exceedingly wanting in cordiality. Beyond mere family circles, there is very little of social heartiness.

"As to the yearling aristocracy, that branch includes a number of individuals who have neither manners nor character to boast of; nothing, in fact, but their money. Vulgar, violent, robust, and hard-hearted. Many of these persons, notwithstanding the worship paid to the great god Mammon, and the glory reflected upon all those who seem to be his favorite, have yet so begrimed themselves in their struggle after wealth, and are naturally so unamiable, and their manners so gross, that though each one has his circle, larger or smaller, of dependants and 'toadies,' they find no admission for themselves into the two-year-old circle above alluded to. There are others, lucky fellows, and honest enough, as the world goes, but too rough and rude for fashionable drawing-rooms; and others yet, persevering old fellows, who have grown rich by long assiduous industry, who retain all the simple and economical habits of their childhood, snap their fingers at show and display, and who look upon fashion and its attendant extravagance with indifference, disgust, or contempt. But the children of all these, if they have any wish for it, as with few exceptions they do, if they are not engulfed in the whirlpools of dissipation, pass as a matter of course into the two-year-old aristocracy, which indeed is principally maintained by such accessions. For, as a general rule, though some few instances to the contrary may be found in this list, wealth does not long remain in the same families, but frequently in the second, very frequently in the third, and almost always by the fourth generation, vanishes and disappears—a process which the equal distribution of the property among all the children greatly facilitates."

An alphabetical enumeration of the "First Men," with a statement of their supposed fortunes, are then given. This public interference with purely private affairs is not only inquisitorial, but impertinent, and is highly characteristic of the country where every man freely meddles with his neighbours' secrets, and assumes a control over them. The biographic sketches are historically and socially instructive, and bear with great force on the subject to which this chapter is devoted; but being rather too personal I shall abstain from introducing any of them here.

Yet these somewhat coarse, but graphic sketches might explain in some measure the difficulty of classification for those who would establish an exclusive set. In fact, the real "upper class," which should form what is called in America the Aristocracy (an absurd misnomer, as I shall show elsewhere), is that which contains the successful members of the learned professions, with literary men of eminence. These alone are entitled in this republic to the distinction of forming the first order. Individual merchants, manufacturers, and men of leisure, of educated and refined habits, should be admitted into this circle by a general understanding. But, as the matter is now established, it is woeful to behold specimens of sordid vulgarity in the high social position accorded to them by virtue of their money, and that alone; while individuals, in every rational advantage their superiors, are excluded from that magic circle, or only called into it now and then on sufferance, as the attendant sprites at the bidding of a wizard.

This creates, of course, great jealousy and much heart-burning. But, all things considered, I am still disposed to believe that there is a much greater amount of general contentment here than I have ever seen elsewhere. There is also an absence of all great causes of suffering. All the elements for social good in a reasonable degree abound. There is less servility, more self-respect, and a juster appreciation of the relative value of men and things.

These are wholesale qualities. But, when we come to details, there is much that is defective. The elements are not yet formed into those delightful combinations which make society more of a pleasure than a business. Large fortunes are gained; but men unaccustomed to a liberal use of wealth, are afraid of spending the income they have earned. They are ignorant of the fact that money has no intrinsic worth, and is valuable only in proportion to the amount of enjoyment it can buy. They gaze on the fruits of their industry, but dare not pluck them; and they leave to their successors to squander what they have toiled to produce.

There is very little originality in the American mind; and not much variety in the national manners, except in some occasional specimens of a keen "down-easter"—the Sam Slick genus—or a rough "far-wester"—of the Colonel Crocket school. The sameness among people in the Atlantic cities is perfectly tiresome. On all great questions of morals or conduct, every one *seems* to feel alike. An inordinate timidity pervades the whole surface of active life. We talk of moral courage in Europe. Moral fear is painfully prevalent in America, and in men and women alike. There is no lack of kind manners. On the contrary, there are, a good deal of general civility, an almost universal good temper, or command of temper, which comes to the same thing, and an abundance of superficial attentions. Indeed, small instances of kindliness are more numerous than in those countries where powerful impulses absorb the mind, and leave it no leisure for the *petits soins* of life.

There is, in America, very little indeed of what *we* call heart. People are afraid to go any great length on the road of the affections. There is small chance of their tumbling into the pitfalls which passion digs by the way-side. No one ever died for love in New England, except an unfortunate Italian music-master who shot himself one morning, much to the surprise of his cold-blooded pupil, who quietly married immediately afterwards.

To these defects I am obliged to add a great deficiency of benevolence in a general and extended sense. The happy absence of wretchedness and destitution among the working-class may account for, and in some degree excuse this. The Yankee is civil and courteous, but neither cordial nor candid. The want of benevolence and the excess of caution are satisfactory phrenological causes for these peculiarities.*

The development of caution is certainly immense in the

* There are numerous charitable "institutions" throughout the country, supported by city taxes as well as by voluntary contributions, the result of a judicious system of government, rather than of a spontaneous philanthropy.

Yankee mind. Prudence is its use, cunning its abuse; and mankind is more prone to abuse than rightly use its faculties. Therefore, I do not see in America that noble species of prudence which, mingling sense with sentiment, can go great lengths out of the common track, convinced that happiness is wisdom, and that to make others happy is virtue. As rashness is seldom exhibited in individuals, generosity is rarely seen. I have known people varying from the straight line for their own indulgence, but never an inch for that of others. The deeper passions are unknown to the Yankee, in the European sense. He (or she) cannot comprehend the intensity which makes one hold everything light in comparison with the object to be attained. Their blood simmers up at times, but never boils. To take a thing to heart is a phrase they do not understand. Self-interest and appearance-sake are the ruling motives. No one would be believed who might profess a disregard for the first, or esteemed who is indifferent to the latter, in the most trifling as well as the most serious cases. This may appear contradictory to what I have said as to the general absence of servility. But one thing is easily reconciled to the other. Servility is the meanness of veneration; subserviency to general opinion is the baseness of caution. It is not from respect to the public, but from fear of it, that people submit to its sway. The effect is cruel, as it acts on the private relations between individuals, checking confidence, and cramping affection, but salutary in a general application, by keeping ostentation within bounds, and holding luxury and its attendant corruptions at arm's length.

This dread of public opinion prevents many a man from driving four horses, going on the turf, or flaunting his wealth in the face of the world. But it need not restrain works of charity, or interfere with the purchase of books, pictures, or statues, with the patronage of talent, or the exercise of hospitality. But the great majority of the rich men are glad to make it an excuse for the absence of all this ; so that there is small encouragement for the arts, literature, or science ; and very little social enjoyment in its more liberal sense. Entertainments are given often enough, but not freely enough, Stiff dinner-parties are common, of from twelve to twenty men, all of them with gray hair or *none*—and the one unhappy lady of the house, without a single female friend to share her suffering. *Soirées* are abundant, with dancing and supper and refreshments of all kinds. Musical parties are rare. There are very few tolerable *amateur* performers ; but a great fancy for music itself, good, bad, or indifferent, and not much taste to discriminate between them.

The classification of society according to age is a fearful defect. Girls of fifteen and sixteen give parties to each other and to their *beaux*—that hateful vulgarism. Old and elderly people herd together to the exclusion of the young ; men dine together, as I have before mentioned, or meet in *coteries* (called clubs) on stated evenings at private houses, to discuss a hot meat supper and its accessories. But I have, in several years, been at only about as many dinners, where both sexes and all ages were mixed in anything like sociability. It is rare, indeed, to be asked to a family dinner, or to spend an evening off-hand, unless one happens to be a client or a customer.

Notwithstanding all this, society is tolerably good in its way. If there is not much cordiality, there is not much visible conceit. Nothing delights, but nothing offends. Good temper stands instead of high breediug. An intercourse with these people is altogether pleasant enough to strangers, for a passing visit or a short sojourn. But for any European who has not business to occupy, or a family to sympathise with him, it offers but few permanent advantages; and the instances are indeed rare of those who have thoroughly taken root in the country.

The want of originality in the American people—or rather of individual originals, for as a nation they are original enough—resolves itself entirely into the dread of public opinion, which they carry in some points, and pretend to carry on others, to the greatest excess. I say *pretend;* for the fact is that this bugbear of public opinion is a most convenient excuse for many things that individuals do not wish to do, and yet would be ashamed not to do, if they had no better apology than their own disinclination. This applies to a thousand things difficult to enumerate in the arrangements of social life, some of which I have before touched on. The whole of their way of visiting and entertaining company is a continuous illustration of it.

Taking Boston, for instance, I will give a sketch of the manner in which social intercourse is carried on.

The visiting circle of what is considered in that city "fashionable society," embraces, I should say, at a rough guess, from two hundred to three hundred families; though the *élite*, the *créme*, as I have already intimated is confined to a much smaller number. In this large body, reinforced by numerous stragglers from the country round, by the young men students at Harvard University, officers in the army and navy, and travelling strangers, native and foreign, it may well be supposed that almost all the elements for a good social circle are to be found. And so it is, in fact. Everything essential to the most agreeable society exists among them, with one exception—

and that one is the spirit of sociability. It is actually unknown. Entertainments in abundance are given, in every form of dinners, suppers, balls, *soirées*. The whole outward appearance of hospitality is there, but the soul is wanting. There is a strong mixture of ostentation and bad taste in the way they manage those things. The weight of the dinners—the sixteen or twenty elderly men, and the one solitary lady, forming a heavier portion than even the aliments that load the table—is oppressive beyond description. The quantity of wine that is drunk is very great, chiefly, almost entirely indeed, Madeira, but of such exquisite quality that it carries in some degree its excuse with it. A great variety is produced; and I observed that this favourite wine is generally distinguished by the name of some individual or some event, which has made each particular sort remarkable. These great dinners, with a very few exceptions, were disappointing to me during my earlier sojourn in Boston. Taking but little wine, unable to enter entirely into the spirit of the conversation, disliking mere eating and drinking parties, where there was no mixture of female animation or of youthful vivacity, it required an effort to preserve an appearance of satisfaction at these repasts. There were certainly exceptions. I have dined occasionally—but the occasions were *very* few and far between—with mixed parties of ladies and gentlemen in Boston, which made a delightful contrast to the general rule of entertainment.

There are several friendly associations among the gentlemen, such as "The Agricultural Society," "The Humane Society," which entail on each member the necessity of giving a dinner in his turn to the others, and to which a few strangers are invited. Besides these, there are those minor and more restricted associations before mentioned, called clubs, such as the Wednesday and Friday clubs, being merely meetings of a certain number of acquaintances at each other's houses, on those evenings, to chat, eat supper, and smoke cigars. These latter reunions I could not stand at all. The heavy meal at nine o'clock, the quantity of Madeira, the nuisance of the tobacco smoke, and the accompaniment of spitting on mats laid down for the occasion, were too much for me. I very soon renounced them on one excuse or another; and I sincerely regretted that those favourite forms of social intercourse in Boston were such as I could not become naturalised with, for I found it impossible to improve the several pleasant acquaintanceships I formed at first without falling into the habits of my neighbours. It was in vain to attempt to lead them into mine. The light evening parties of from a dozen to twenty, a little music, a carpet dance, slight refreshments, and absence of *gêne*—which for twenty years of a continental residence had been to us one of the charms of social life—were quite exotic in New England; and though some persons came to us in that kind of way, almost as often as we asked them, and were evidently pleased, and lamented that such was not the style of society in Boston, still they never, with one or two exceptions, followed our example or entertained us in the same manner. Often have I remonstrated with several of them who had been in Europe, and had seen the way things are done there, and several of them have quite agreed with me; but the excuse for not doing as we did was invariably the impossibility of getting others to join them. "Public opinion" did not sympathise with those lighter ways of enjoyment, and it would be in vain to oppose it. No three families ventured to make an original move and commence a reform; and one lady who did so, and fixed a regular evening in each week for receiving her friends in the French fashion, was wondered at by many of them as a person of great *moral courage!* * As to the seniors of the respective families, they either would not come to us in this way at all, or if they did so now and then, it was clearly from a forced effort to meet our good intentions. Altogether, we soon gave up our friendly war against the inveterate habits of our neighbours; and when we saw them at home it was to entertain them as they did us, by regular invitations to meet in rather large parties, eat, drink champagne, and then—the business of the evening being done—retire.

I grieve to record it, but it is very true that the great object of these social meetings is the eating and drinking. At such dinners as I have described, it is a matter of course; but at the evening parties, the musical *soirées* (for such things were at long intervals attempted), and the regular balls, the preponderance of animal appetite over intellectual feasting was flagrant. The time for assembling is generally understood to be nine o'clock; but few, except some old relatives of the family, appear till half-an-hour later, and the greater number of the guests do not come till ten. At that hour, or perhaps somewhat earlier, the music is going merrily. The house is generally beautifully prepared and decorated with a profusion of flowers and lights; the dresses are expensive; the women pretty; and everything seems combined to provoke and keep up excitement. At half-past ten the host leads a lady to the supper-room; the hostess follows, under charge

* I am glad to hear that, after many years, and even while these pages are going through the press, those cheerful "Thursday Evening" parties are continued, so greatly enjoyed, but so little, if at all, imitated.

of her cavalier; the married ladies, duly escorted, go off in files; and as soon as the movement becomes general, the dancing rooms are deserted, the young couples take the same path, and the supper room presents what is technically called in America a "reg'lar jam."

This is pretty much the course of things in all the countries of the world, I believe; but here the similitude ceases. For, while in England and on the continent of Europe, the effect of all this music, dancing, flirting, and champagne, is to exhilarate, animate, and in a certain degree to turn the heads of both young and old; *here*, each of these incitements seems a sedative, and the tremendous execution done at the supper-table is followed by decided evidences of *ennui*. Dulness is the order of the hour that remains. A few return to the ball-room, and the waltz or cotillion (as the quadrille is always called in America) is resumed for a short time. But with the demolition of the supper the delights, or, as I have before said, the business of "the meeting" is over. At eleven or half-past, hooded women and cloaked men emerge from the muffling room and disappear; the carriages rattle away; and at twelve o'clock not one of the party remains. The coldness with which people take leave of the host and hostess is chilling to the last degree. No one seems to have had any enjoyment, or to regret this early breaking up. They all have had their appetite satisfied. To the last moment pyramids of ice, dishes of stewed oysters, and chicken or lobster salad, are brought in in fast-succeeding relays by the black servants hired for the occasion. Wine is given without stint—and when all have had enough, each makes his or her stiff bow or curtsey and escapes.*

* This description is much less applicable to New York, or the more southern cities, than to Boston.

Often and often have I wondered at this uniform breaking-up of those promising parties, at the very time when "pleasure, like the midnight flower," really does begin to bloom, surprised that there should never be one exception; that no group of young men, under the joint effect of wine and beauty, ever showed any exuberance of joy—ever turned the usual current of the time into tricks or jollity, or strove to prolong even the regulated course of amusement. And it has then amazed me, when looking at the rooms left empty in all their brilliancy, and taking more particular note of the arrangements, and thinking of the great trouble and expense that was lavished on them, that any family could have done all this, with the certainty that it was but for two hours' enjoyment. Surely it is not worth while to meet at all in this costly way, for so very poor a result. Many persons in Boston agree with me in this opinion. But they admit that there is no use in striving to stem the current of custom. A contemptible imitation of English manners is adopted in one point, namely, in coming to these parties at a late hour; for ten o'clock is comparatively very late for people who dine at two; and public opinion condemns sitting up after midnight, for seven o'clock in the morning is the general breakfast hour, at which every Yankee merchant or lawyer expects (and I am sorry to say too often insists) on his wife and daughters meeting him, to make his tea, or cut his bread and butter. Such hours as those which prevail for the daily meals may be very convenient and very wholesome; but for people who adopt them to attempt anything like the style of European society can only result in a vulgar parody. Those who rise at six are perfectly right in going to bed at ten or eleven, the usual hours; and the man who dines at two is naturally hungry by nine at night. The only thing objectionable in these domestic arrangements is their inevitable clashing with social enjoyments. The indulgence in such primitive and business-like habits utterly incapacitates people from the delicious, but perhaps deleterious, elegances of refined life. And if they would escape from the ridicule that attaches to them now, they really must learn to meet at seven, or at latest at eight o'clock, or give up ball-going altogether. And, if they cannot contrive to dine later, they should eat their evening meal at home, so as to remove the necessity of the "feeding" which is so very unpleasant to the lookers-on.

But these defects, and others of a similar kind, in the social system of America, have an origin so wide-spread and obstinate, as to defy any very speedy remedy. They arise from the extremely superficial nature of all the moral qualities among the people. No one feels very deeply on any subject. Nothing profound can be cited as characteristic of the United States. The word passion in its best and most solemn sense, has no application here. And even its commonest meaning is rarely exemplified. Intense emotion does not exist, and a fiery temper is seldom, if ever, met with. Violent things are frequently done in the South and West, and now and then elsewhere, but they are rarely done in sudden outbursts of violence. Desperate encounters with bowie-knives, rifles, and revolvers take place; murders are committed; crime abounds. But while nature and civilisation are shocked by such events, the extenuating plea of a fierce temper, so often dangerously allied to a generous heart, cannot be urged. The assassin almost always lies in wait for his victim, or seduces him to some sequestered spot, where the implements of murder are arranged for use. The duellists go to the ground by preconcerted agreement, armed to the teeth, and ready for their savage work. In both cases it is the spirit of calculation and design that directs the actors. They are ever "of *malice prepense.*" Even in the ruffian conflicts that take place in the streets and bar-rooms, and at times in the senate chambers, the parties all have provided their weapons beforehand, and come to the place prepared for butchery; and they stab, shoot, or cut each other to pieces with a coolness as proverbial as their courage. Public opinion, in fact, sanctions such scenes; advocates excuse them, newspapers palliate them, juries refuse to punish them; and they are more the result of admitted custom, than of any impulse, right or wrong. The northern and eastern sections of the country are very rarely disgraced by these events; but the Yankee dandy in a ball-room shows a want of passionate feeling, quite analogous to the character of the cold-blooded bravo of the South. Neither the one nor the other is hurried away beyond his purpose. They are not either of them, perhaps, quite dead to occasional starts of feeling; but in ninety-nine cases out of a hundred they do their several doings quite according to rule, and not once in a thousand times do they exceed them from any irresistible emotion. All the affections, so to call the sentiments of this people, are the result of habit or of a sense of duty. Not having their roots in the heart, they are plucked up as easily, and thrown aside as carelessly, as garden flowers, whenever they show the least failure in fragrance or bloom. The capricious indifference towards close acquaintances, friends, or lovers (save the mark!) shown by the people of New England is without parallel. Nobody seems to care about the persons met with the oftenest and known the best. Of a room filled with agreeable people on the most familiar terms with each other, scarcely any two—certainly no six—are on a footing of real friendship. They meet at *soirées* or balls at long intervals, but know nothing more of each other, except when they are occasionally thrown together for a week or two at a watering-place. There is no easy intercourse between neighbours; no real sociability; though they sometimes ask each other "socially," as they call it; but that merely means that a meeting of a dozen or more are not to eat as heavy a supper as if they were asked to "a general party." Anything of close intimacy is almost entirely confined to the circles of relationship. There is a dull decorum of intercourse between all others that is chilling and hopeless of reform. Morning visiting is entirely confined to the ladies, who leave cards for themselves and their husbands. But not once in twenty attempts is one admitted on these occasions. Men very rarely call each other by their sirnames familiarly. Mister is, I may say, always prefixed. Old schoolfellows, college chums meeting in after-life, counting-house companions, partners in business, and even brothers sometimes address each other as a general rule, "Dear Sir," and end their letters with the word "respectfully," the prefix "yours" never being considered necessary. Anything more familiar is disapproved of by public opinion. What possible chance, then, of social enjoyment, or free companionship, as we understand it, can there be for such a people?

CHAPTER VIII.

EDWARD EVERETT.

Visit to Governor Everett—His appearance and Public character—His Qualifications as Preacher, Professor, Editor, Politician—Episode of the Montgomery Guards—Mr. Everett's inconsistency on the Question of Slavery—Appointed Minister to the Court of London—President of Harvard University—Secretary of State.

THE first man of any particular note with whom I became acquainted in America was Edward Everett, then Governor of the State of Massachusetts. I had several letters of introduction to him, all of which I forwarded to the State House (the official place of business, not the residence of the state officers) as soon as I arrived in Boston. Mr. Everett was at that time in the country, at Watertown, about six miles from the city, one of those straggling villages which lie scattered over New England, giving no idea of a village in "the old country," but rather presenting the notion of an irregular settlement by some recently-arrived inhabitants, where every man pitched his tent (in the shape of a wooden cottage, painted white, with green window shutters) as best suited his whim, and as far as he could conveniently pitch it from his next neighbour.

Mr. Everett called on me a couple of days afterwards at the Tremont Hotel, where, I being absent at Nahant, he was received by my son, to whom he said many polite and obliging things. Two days afterwards I drove out, accompanied by a gentleman of his acquaintance, to return the Governor's visit. We passed through Cambridge, the seat of Harvard University, where my companion pointed out all that was of external interest in his Alma Mater—the old brick buildings of the college, the new library and dining-hall, built in very good (Gothic) taste ; besides Washington's tree, a venerable elm, where the hero halted on the first day of his taking command of the revolutionary army ; and other points of local interest. Three miles more brought us to the door of Governor Everett's neat residence, close by the roadside, with its pretty shrubbery and grass-plat ; and which, being of course built of wood, realised completely the title of "box," which is applied in England to every specimen of red brick vulgarity that defaces the environs of our towns.

A rough-clad stable-boy took charge of our gig and horse, a woman servant ushering us into a little drawing-room (or parlour, as such apartments are invariably called in America) and going smilingly off to inform the Governor of our visit. Announcing us by name was out of the question ; for one of the most annoying customs of the country is the omission of that branch of etiquette, by which strangers either paying or receiving visits are constantly exposed to much embarrassment.

It is certainly unworthy of the philosophy of travel to be disappointed at any man's appearance or address. As to forming previous conjectures of what an individual is probably like in mien and manners, I have long given it up. I had therefore no preconceived idea of Mr. Everett's outward man. I was warned that he was cold and formal, but I had irresistibly associated with him expectations of dignity and classical polish. He did not come up to that mark, as he walked into the room—it was just after his dinner—in his black coat and trousers and green slippers. He struck me as a plain man in every sense; but a pleasing one notwithstanding. He was not exactly cold, but very formal, without any ease, or tone of society. Yet his voice was agreeable, though his utterance was rather monotonous; his conversation possessed a measured fluency that smacked of the professional lecturer; and there was a strain of kindliness and good sense that left an impression of respect for the individual, but a conviction that his proper sphere was the Presidency of the neighbouring college, rather than the "Gubernatorial chair" (as the phrase goes) or a seat in Congress.

No man, as far as I may presume to judge, was ever less fitted than Edward Everett for the work of public life. He is a scholar, a student, and somewhat of a pedant; and was for several years a preacher, and editor of a Review. I have repeatedly heard his post-prandial orations—after-dinner *speeches* is not the name for them. I have listened to him as a public lecturer; I have met him frequently in society; I have had several *tête-à-tête* talks with him on general affairs. I can therefore pretty safely venture to say that although he has gracefully filled several situations, though he was a respectable member of the national legislature, a decorous Governor of his native state, and a conciliatory minister to the Court of St. James's, he can never be a distinguished politician in his own country until the world of politics is reformed, "its rough places made smooth, and its crooked ways made straight."

I could scarcely pay Mr. Everett a higher compliment than this. While I knew him, he was uniformly kind, attentive, and considerate to me and my family. Whenever a public meeting or lecture of any interest was to take place, and in which he, as Governor or private individual, bore a part, he never forgot me ; and I particularly recollect the occasion of the Establishment of the Lowell lectures at Boston, the opening one of which was given by Mr. Everett. For this he received a handsome remuneration from Mr. John A. Lowell, the sole trustee and manager of the fund left by his cousin, and which amounted to about 200,000 dollars, 40,000*l.* This munificent legacy to the public might certainly have been turned to better purposes than the payment for lectures, however important the scientific subjects discussed. They produce but a temporary and superficial effect on the indiscriminate crowd of listeners, and leave no lasting benefits proportioned to the amount of money expended.

Mr. Everett's writings and speeches—the latter being all prepared compositions—are finished specimens of artificial eloquence. They are before the world, and it is not my intention to review them in these desultory notes. I have seen some of his letters written during his travels in Europe. I remember one of them, from Florence, a mere common-place description of churches and monuments, larded with Latin quotations, and altogether in the most guide-book style. Everett has yet touched no subject of a powerful nature with a master-hand. He wants boldness. He is not a man to originate a great conception, or even to execute a daring design. On the only occasion on which his nerve was really tried, as far as I have learned, he signally failed. I allude to the affair of the "Montgomery Guards," a matter worthy of being recorded.

The volunteer company which bore that title was composed of Irishmen, or the sons of Irishmen, and was, I understand, one of the most effective of these trained-band bodies, of which there are several in Boston. The Irish have always been very unpopular in this city. In the year 1834 a grievous outrage was perpetrated by the mob, in the pillage and destruction by fire of the Ursuline Convent, established at Charlestown, one of the suburbs. This wanton attack on a family of inoffensive and unprotected females is a foul stain on Massachusetts. At the time it occurred, the resentment of the Irish Roman Catholics must have been highly excited, and reproaches were no doubt freely uttered by them, adding to the dislike which previously existed against them by the citizens at large. Some honourable exceptions were however to be found, foremost among them was Mr. Austin, the Attorney-General, who used great exertions to bring the offenders to justice. But every attempt to procure a conviction was ineffectual. Jury after jury acquitted them. In the midst of the excited state of feeling arising from this event, the "Montgomery Guards," together with several other of the military companies, held a parade on some day of public duty, and they marched in their turn to the "Common," the general muster ground where the review was to take place. No sooner did the Irish corps appear on the ground, than five out of eight of the other companies, who were already assembled, deliberately shouldered their arms and marched away into the city, with such plainly spoken avowals of their hostility to the Irish, as prepared the mob to follow up the insulting movement.

The effect produced by this mutinous conduct may be imagined. The superior officers were astonished and confounded. The whole "order of the procession" was broken up. Company after company disappeared. And as the Montgomery Guards retired in order through the streets, they were assailed with yells from the mob, and assaulted with stones and other missiles. They kept their ranks like soldiers, and their tempers as citizens. But how, as Irishmen, they could do either one or the other under such gross provocation is to me a marvel. They did not retaliate by a blow. On the score of discipline their conduct was perfect. No possible cause of complaint existed against them. Yet within a few days, instead of receiving thanks or some badge of distinction from the commander-in-chief—for the governor of the commonwealth bears that title also—the Montgomery Guards were abruptly disbanded, in common with the five offending companies whose misconduct was the cause of their ill-treatment. But in a very short time afterwards those same five companies, disgraced as they were, were all re-organised and restored by the governor, while their victims, the Montgomery Guards, have never since been able to recover their charter, filched from them so shamefully.

This transaction was by far the most important in the administration of Edward Everett. It was a test of his capacity for public affairs, and of his moral courage. Its consequences were fatal to his political career. They not only deprived him of the attachment of the Irish inhabitants throughout the State, but must have lost him the confidence of even the native citizens, who saw that he possessed, if not the fury of a partisan, at least the weakness of a participator. He was to all intents and purposes an accessory after the fact. And although he was not to be reached by remonstrances, hedged round as he was by the clamorous support of the prejudiced masses, still the injured parties had their sure redress in the ballot-box, the best and often the only security for public justice.

An organised system of opposition was carried on

against Mr. Everett, by the naturalised Irish. It took some sime to bring it to a head: but at the contested election for governor in the autumn of 1839, the votes of the Irish were, with very few exceptions, cast for Marcus Morton, Everett's chief opponent; and the majority for the former, which was about 400 over all the combined votes for Everett and others, was formed of the Irish in the city of Boston.

I remember having talked with the defeated candidate on this result, which I, on personal grounds, regretted, for a bad exchange was certainly made in a social and intellectual point of view. I had long previously preached to my Whig acquaintances, and particularly to Governor Everett, the policy of conciliating the Irish generally, but especially the naturalised portion of them, having the privilege of the franchise. I had laboured hard to induce him to attend the St. Patrick's day dinner that year (1840); to which, as a matter of courtesy, he received an invitation, though I admit it was without cordiality. Had he done so, accompanied by 50 or 100 of the better class of merchants and lawyers of the place, I am sure that the feelings of the Irish might have been turned to such account as to have secured the approaching election of Everett; for Morton's majority over him was but one solitary vote. Had there been a tie between them, they being the only real candidates (the "scattering" votes amounting, out of 90,000, to but a few hundreds) the choice of governor would have depended on the legislature of the state, the greater part of which being Whigs, Everett would surely have been chosen.

When I talked all this over with him, the day after the official announcement of his defeat, he admitted the conclusion I drew from the premises, but he confessed that he could not venture to confront the ill-used Irish even as their guest, and under the sure protection of their hospitality; while he took much pains to convince me that in the disbanding of the Montgomery Guards he acted from the best motives towards them, and by the wish of some of the Irish inhabitants of Boston.

This transaction was strikingly illustrative of Everett's character. He was a fine preacher, a graceful lecturer, a seductive orator on occasions where his audience felt with him. He was well adapted for floating on the tide of public sympathy and going with the stream. But to breast a torrent, to frown at a storm, to check a mutiny, or by calm audacity to neutralise a foe, were acts beyond his conception and his power. He was consequently a man unfitted for a lead in public life, particularly in America; and had there been any chance of eminence for a mere scholar following the pursuit of letters, I am satisfied that Everett's ambition would never have led him into politics. But he is only another instance of that subserviency to party which is the general disgrace of American statesmen; scarcely one of whom takes up for conscience' sake a position opposed to the faction to which he has pledged himself, and to the absence of this courage in individuals is owing many of the evils that are charged upon the people, or the system that regulates their conduct. The American people are in my opinion pre-eminently alive to the influence of energy and daring in their public men. If those men had a corresponding confidence in themselves, or a true devotion to the cause of liberal principles, they would not hesitate to tell the people their faults, and put them in the way of right. But the fact is, that the men who seek public distinction, do so more from the love of place than the love of truth. Their ambition is for gain rather than for glory. Scarcely an individual of independent fortune enters the political ranks. Almost all public men are adventurers in America. Politics are with them a speculation, not a sentiment. They consequently bend to the prevailing opinion of the party they espouse, and they espouse that party from interest, not principle. Faction has absorbed the public morals of the state. Patriotism is a mockery. Every question, to excite a general sympathy, must become a question of profit and loss ; and it is in proportion as it resolves itself into a consideration of money that it attracts attention. For subjects of this nature a spurious enthusiasm may be excited. Those of abstract political value have no chance of deeply entering into the public mind. In support of this opinion I may state that of the various questions in dispute between America and England for the last twenty years, the only one which was called by the Americans one of national honour, was precisely that one which was not so. I mean the North Eastern Boundary question. But as I shall have to speak on that subject somewhat at large, I shall not here enter into it, but will recur to the consideration of another, of far more importance, which is closely allied to the individual object of this sketch.

The most embarrassing question of a durable nature connected with Everett's career was that of negro slavery. His opinions were, beyond doubt, like those of many New England men, hostile to its continuance, and it is probable that he would, if he dared, have become an abolitionist. But when he gave up his Professorship in Harvard University, and was sent to Congress as a member of the House of Representatives in 1826, he felt the necessity of conciliating the opinion of the Southern States. He consequently took occasion to make a speech, when, carried entirely out of his depth in the impure and troubled waters of the question, he went the length of vindicating the existing system of slavery; and in a gratuitous attempt to prove it consistent with Christianity, and his own scholastic knowledge, argued that the word used in scripture did really mean a *slave* and not a *servant*, as some ardent abolitionists had asserted in their publications. This speech was so strong and so inconsistent with his previous professions of faith, that immediately after its delivery, John Davis of Massachusetts, his colleague in Congress, went over to Everett and told him he had gone much too far; upon which he hurried to his lodgings, re-corrected his discourse, and sent it to the press in an extremely modified tone, such as it is on record in his published works. But unluckily the reporters and correspondents for the papers gave sketches of it as really spoken; and particularly dwelt on the replies and rebukes made impromptu on the spot by Cambreleng of New York, Mitchel of Tenessee, and the eccentric but powerful John Randolph, who, though a Virginian and a slave-holder, detested slavery and despised its northern apologists, as was proved by his emancipating all his servants, and by severely handling the sophistries of Everett on this occasion, sarcastically calling him "the learned professor," a title which the latter was anxious to sink altogether.

As editor of the "North American Review," Everett was the frequent apologist of "the peculiar institutions of the South"—the "filagree phrase" which is used to designate the iniquity of Negro slavery. In 1836, he was elected Governor of Massachusetts, though many of the abolitionists voted against him. In the following year, seeing the rapid increase of that party, and being no longer in Congress, and so removed from immediate contact with Southern members, he manifested a change of *public* opinion, and became by degrees a thoroughly pronounced anti-slavery man. Marcus Morton, the rival candidate at every yearly election of governor, was likely to press him harder than ever in 1839, and on occasion of the contest in that year before alluded to (and in which he in fact defeated Everett), the abolitionists brought up against the latter the celebrated pro-slavery speech, and pressed him to avow his decided opinions at this important crisis. Two letters were written to him by leaders of the abolition party, one of them a member of Congress, to which he gave answers which were published in the newspapers, apologising for, and endeavouring to explain the affair. The first of these not being considered satisfactory, he wrote the second, in which he went almost the whole length of abolitionism, declaring himself in favour of the immediate abolition of slavery in the district of Columbia, of the prohibition of slave-dealing between the several States of the Union, and against the admission of any new State into it with the privilege of holding slaves. This satisfied the anti-slavery electors of Massachusetts, whose organ, Mr. Garrison, in his paper, "The Liberator," stated that as the Whigs of that party could not "go behind" Mr. Everett's statement to find out whether or not his opinions were really sincere, they were bound to believe his assertions, and to give him their vote at last. They did so, but he failed in his election notwithstanding, the Irish votes turning the scale against him; and leaving him to lament his weaknesses and tergiversations, perhaps the more acutely from their insufficiency to carry his point ; and, soon after his defeat (in the year 1840), he went to Europe with his family.

After General Harrison's death in 1841, and the accession of John Tyler to the Presidential throne, and on the refusal of Mr. Sarjeant, one of the Whig party, to accept the post of minister to the Court of London, the Cabinet, which was still at that epoch Whig, though the President's principles had begun to waver, nominated Edward Everett for the rejected place. But strong objections were urged against him by the majority of the Senate, with whom rested the confirmation or rejection of diplomatic nominations. The members from the Slave States, forgetting or holding cheap the spoken manifesto of poor Everett in Congress, but bitterly recollecting his *quasi*-abolition disclaimers of former opinions, so much more recently inserted in the Boston papers, he was now denounced in the Southern journals as totally unfit to represent the interests of those States at a foreign court. "The National Intelligencer," the Whig organ at Washington, defended him in reference to those unfortunate letters, by stating them to have been mere (and it might have added, unsuccessful) electioneering ruses, into the writing of which he was entrapped in the heat of the contest. This was a shabby defence. But some cogent reason on the necessity of party union, the continuance of which was then threatened by the President's wavering policy, and which would have been more seriously risked by the rejection of Everett, prevailed with a sufficient number of the senators. They withdrew their opposition, and, after some weeks of suspense and much angry discussion, the absent candidate was confirmed as minister to London, where he arrived, from his residence in Italy, in November, 1841.

During the three or four years of Mr. Everett's residence in England he can be considered little more than a public nullity. No event of any importance connected with his mission gave a chance of distinction or a risk of failure. Luckily for him, perhaps, for his private objects were fulfilled, and his personal conduct unexceptionable. He had several opportunities of making set speeches, and in these he was generally very happy ; while his unassuming and urbane deportment in society made him many friends, and went far to lessen the objections to his countrymen generally inherent in the English fashionable world.

Mr. Everett returned to Boston without éclat, and sunk quietly soon afterwards into the obscurity of the village of Cambridge as President of Harvard University, for which he appeared to me some years previously to be so well fitted, and to which he was elected on the resignation of Mr. Quincy in the year 1846. I saw him occasionally after his return. He did not appear to be much affected by his European sojourn. In manner he was just the same. But I thought I could perceive a worn and somewhat dissatisfied expression of countenance, as if he felt the change from the highest circles of civilisation to what was his present lot, with more acuteness than his cold and cautious temperament would allow him to admit.

Mr. Everett was nominated Secretary of State under President Filmore. The only remarkable transaction of his official service in that capacity was his elaborate reply to the overtures of the governments of France and England to that of the United States, for the conclusion of a tripartite Treaty for the purpose of guaranteeing the possession of the Island of Cuba to Spain. In the important state paper in question, Everett gave ample proof of eloquent diction and plausible argument, professing to oppose the filibustering tendencies of the day, but really lending his indirect sanction to the principle of "Manifest destiny," which, plainly interpreted, means unscrupulous spoliation on the part of the American Union.

Everett, like several other ambitious politicians, had no doubt the alluring image of the "White House" and the Presidential dignity in perspective, in thus in a measure compromising his claim to conservative integrity. Disappointed in his political hopes, he has again fallen back upon his more congenial pursuits, delighting his fellow countrymen by the delivery of highly finished orations on varied topics of national interest.

CHAPTER IX.

MY FIRST VISIT TO WASHINGTON.

Departure from Boston—New York—Festival in honour of Queen Victoria's Marriage—Ox-roasting—Journey to Philadelphia—Rail-road Accident—Baltimore—Washington—Reflections on its present appearance in connection with its Founder, and in reference to the Outrages by the British Army in 1814.

If the main object of interest in America be the political movement of the country, and I think it is so—the seat of the Federal government, the place of meeting of Congress, the arena of party contest, is certainly the scene of paramount importance. I therefore took an early opportunity of paying a visit to Washington, and I chose the spring of the year 1840 as the most agreeable season in the capital, as well as the most convenient to myself and my family.

Accompanied by my wife and daughter, with their French maid (who soon turned out a dreadful incumbrance and torment), I left Boston on the 23rd of March, arrived at New York the next morning, and spent several days in that place very pleasantly. I made some valuable acquaintances there, and it being the period of the arrival of the news of Queen Victoria's marriage, I had an opportunity of witnessing a singular and peculiarly English celebration in honour of the event. This consisted, in the first place, of the attempted operation of roasting an ox whole; and, in the second, of the huge animal being served up and eaten (the repast being completed by due accompaniments of plum-pudding and port-wine) by some hundreds of widows and children, all British subjects and inhabitants of the city.

My warm-hearted and energetic colleague, Mr. Buchanan, had put his whole mind and strength into the management of this fête. He was seconded by a zealous committee of gentlemen, English, Scotch, and Irish; but in proportion with his exertions to have everything go off well, were the efforts of his personal dislikers (I do not like to say enemies) acting on the passions of the anti-English portion of the community, to mar the effect of the whole.

When I reached New York the day previous to the roasting, I found symptoms of considerable public hostility. Handbills were posted on the walls, couched in violent language against England, and calling on the people to destroy the preparations made on a grand scale in Niblo's gardens, a favourite place of public resort and entertainment. To counteract these attempts, Mr. Buchanan had opposition bills distributed, with a programme of the intended solemnities, a wood-cut representing a huge ox, hanging up in a temporary temple, and surrounded by the gas apparatus by which it was to be roasted entire, and winding up (to my serious dismay) with the announcement that "the celebrated author of 'Highways and Byways,' Her Majesty's consul at Boston, would (among other orators) address the meeting." It was quite too late for remonstrance; and, in the agitated state of mind of my worthy colleague and countryman, reproach would have been cruelty. I never saw a more painful picture of anxiety. He was tortured by a dread of some collision with the hostile citizens, and not only that but of the failure of the *procédé* by which a new-fangled gas company had undertaken to perform the job of cookery. Vehemently did he vow, but, like Lafontaine's crow, *un peu tard*, that he never would be caught again in so critical an undertaking, for the result of which he saw nothing in perspective but defeat and mortification. But having begun the thing, he was resolved to go through with it, for he was made of sturdy stuff. The aid of the police was requested and promptly afforded by the City authorities ; a magistrate with a sufficient force took the matter under his protection ; the anti-English faction was overawed, and the roasting began.

Mr. Buchanan reckoned, calculated, and guessed, with a truly (naturalised) Yankee imagination, relative to the probable proceeds of this novel exhibition, to which the public were invited, at the rate of half a dollar a head, to form a fund towards defraying the expenses of the fête. At his urgent request I accompanied him to the scene, two or three hours after the gas company had opened its fire on the suspended carcase. When we reached Niblo's gardens but three individuals, instead of the expected hundreds of paying visitors, were to be seen. Not a dozen presented themselves altogether. My poor compatriot was quite crest-fallen. Nothing could be more desolate than the aspect of the place. The day was cold, the garden comfortless ; and the ox swung slowly round, an ugly object, I thought, in his unpainted, wooden temple, successive ranges of gas-burners from the top to the floor warming, but being evidently insufficient for the task of roasting, him. While I peeped shiveringly through the little glass windows of the temple at this operation, pitying and sympathising with the projector by my side, a sudden crash was heard, and at the same moment I was shocked at seeing the staple from which "the entire animal" (as the *genteel* Yankees say) was suspended, give way from the roof of the temple, while the huge ox fell heavily to the floor, and against one of the six sides. The wood-work, however, stood this rude assault. It did not give way and tumble into ruins as I expected. But having witnessed too much of the disappointment of my fellow-consul, I turned away, leaving him in the midst of a clamorous crowd of workmen who hurried to the spot, while I made my escape, and hastened to my hotel, the "Globe," at the other end of Broadway.

I heard nothing from Buchanan for the rest of the day; and at a soirée for which we had an engagement, the consular discomfiture formed the main joke of the entertainment. Everybody seemed pleased at what had happened. No one expressed any sympathy with the project; many laughed at it; and all agreed that the crowning scene intended for the morrow (the roast-beef feast) must of necessity fail, from the fact of the ox not being roasted. Hearing nothing the next morning, I concluded that this prediction was verified, and that the hostile party had finally succeeded in bullying the consul, the committee, and the constables. I therefore dismissed the matter from my mind, occupied myself after breakfast until nearly one o'clock writing letters, and then sallied out with my wife on a shopping excursion. Before long we were accosted in Broadway by a gentleman unknown to me, smartly dressed, bearing a wand, and decorated with a bunch of white ribbons fastened in the lappel of his coat. He had just descended from a carriage on recognising me, and he told me he was one of the committee sent to look for me, and escort me and "my ladies" to the feasting which was going merrily on, where places were reserved for us, and where I had been for some time anxiously expected.

Completely taken by surprise, and unwilling to hurt the feelings of the worthy committee-man, I could only say, that not having received any tickets, I did not know we were expected, and I regretted that we had now other engagements. The gentleman left me, evidently much annoyed, and muttering denunciations against Her Majesty's Consul for New York, to whose blundering mismanagement he attributed the *contretemps*. As he rattled up Broadway in his "hack," my conscience smote me for having thus implicated Mr. Buchanan, whose pressing verbal invitation (often repeated on the previous day with many complimentary expressions) was worth a dozen formal summonses. Scarcely had I time for repentance, when I met Mr. Austin, the Attorney-General for Massachusetts, coming from Niblo's gardens, where he had been a spectator of the early part of the doings. He took it for granted I was going there, and recommended me to make haste, "as the last orator on the list before me was speaking, and my turn came next!"

This startling news made me take quite *another* turn. I called a coach, and was very soon ensconced in my apartment in the "Globe," enjoying my escape, and having no doubt that the feast, both of roast beef and of reason, was completely over. But very soon a short-breathing waiter rushed upstairs and into my room, announcing the arrival of a "deputation of the committee from Niblo's;" and he ushered in three gentlemen with all the well-known official insignia, who implored me in pressing terms to repair to the scene of action, describing the consul's despair as quite heart-rending, under the angry reproaches of the committee for his *gaucherie*, to which my absence was alone attributed.

"But," said I, "it must be now too late—surely all is over."

"Not at all, Sir; Dr. Hogan is speaking against time, and he'll certainly not stop till you come."

This was irresistible. Compassion, in a double sense, for the doctor and his audience, as well as for my badgered friend Buchanan, left me no further wish for refusal. Besides, I was not a little pleased at the cordial expressions of the "deputation," and I thought my hesitating longer might look like conceit, instead of real disinclination to be compromised in a failure. We therefore were quickly in the carriage provided by the gentlemen; and following them we dashed along the pavé, in a style that caused no small alarm, and no trifling amusement to the beholders of the gallop, and all who (safely) crossed our path.

My wife and daughter were conducted to the reserved places in the gallery, and I was led into the lower portion of the great room, and to the middle of the floor, where stood the committee, wanded and decorated, round a plaster figure of Queen Victoria, placed on a broad, white elevation, balanced on a pedestal, to which an Irish gentleman (to whom I was subsequently introduced as Dr. Hogan, the President of the St. Patrick's Society) was apparently addressing a strain of most impassioned eloquence, that drew down thunders of applause.

The scene around and above me was truly imposing. Having had no real notion of what was previously expected, and thoroughly convinced that the affair had after all been abortive, my astonishment was great at seeing this vast room, which can contain, I understand, 3000 persons, completely full; several long tables, at which sat some hundreds of well-dressed women and children; the remains of the feast, flowers in profusion, and an enormous sugar-covered plum cake, forming, in fact, the upper stratum of the Victoria pedestal. The remainder of the arena and the galleries were filled with fashionably-dressed people, the ladies being brilliantly conspicuous. I was very handsomely received by the committee. But poor Buchanan, though evidently delighted at my coming, held down his head — or shook it—with shame, and was clearly puzzled as to whether he should laugh or cry. But he recovered himself sufficiently to halloo out, in his own peculiar length and breadth of brogue, as soon as Dr. Hogan ceased speaking, that "Mr. Grattan, Her Majesty's Consul, was going to give them a speech."

Thus at once *in medias res,* without a chance of retreat, and warmed by the encouraging applauses which followed this announcement, I threw off as well as I could a few random sentences, which seemed to *tell.* I thought that there had probably been a great deal of serious and sensible oratory expended before my arrival. And knowing, by my Boston experience, that it must be the dullest of all possible jokes that does not make a hit at a public meeting, I ventured one or two, which my good-natured audience took in good part. I told them the Queen had proved her love for America by becoming a citizen of the oldest of the United states—the state of matrimony; that she had, moreover, settled the Boundary Question—between girlhood and womanhood; and I advised all the young ladies present to follow the good example; and having thus ended the solemnity by a laugh, I closed my "oration," when the cake was cut into pieces and distributed, and the meeting broke up to the tune of "God save the Queen."

I was really and truly rejoiced at the triumphant result of my colleague's great experiment. He had had the precaution to take down the ox soon after it was replaced on its hook before "the ineffectual fires" of the gas batteries, and had it cut up into rational-shaped joints, and cooked on spits and strings at sea-coal furnaces. The large amount of persons assembled at the feasting, in comparison with the paucity of spectators at the roasting, was easily (but not satisfactorily) accounted for by the first being invited *guests*, and the latter half-dollar paying visitors.

And great was the self-gratulation of Her Majesty's Consul for New York. I have no doubt he was quite ready to begin another roasting as soon as the party dispersed. And laborious were his attentions towards numerous individuals absent in England, America, and the British Colonies, in transmitting to them printed and manuscript accounts, and in sending them solid tokens of the celebration, in the shape of thick pieces of the *gâteau-monstre*, as the French would have called what he in homely phrase, denominated "the Big Cake."

The only thing I regretted on the occasion was my having missed the consul's speech, addressed to the youthful partakers of that very indigestible condiment. The following report of it appeared the next morning in the columns of the "New York Herald."

* * * * * *

I omit this report, which savoured too much of burlesque. I prefer inserting a sentence of regard to the memory of the speaker, to whom I was indebted for many kind and disinterested attentions, until he resigned his consulship, and retired to the enjoyment of his property in Canada, where he died in the year 1851.

After a few days spent pleasantly in New York, one of which was devoted to a dinner and dance, given on board the "British Queen," by Captain Roberts, at which some very lovely (and as I was informed, some very "fashionable") women *assisted:* and another of which was rendered interesting by a meeting with my old friend Davezac, United States Chargé d'Affaires at the Hague, where I had known and left him in 1831, we proceeded on our way to Washington.

Every league of our route, whether by road or river, afforded matter for observation, reflection, and I may truly add, for admiration. The fine broad Delaware, the passing glimpse of "Susquehanna's banks," Chesapeake Bay, as well as portions of the country traversed by the railway, all gave me new notions of the New World, or awoke recollections of what had heretofore stirred my imagination or excited my curiosity. The richly cultivated plains of Pennsylvania seemed to proclaim how the many millions of inhabitants were distributed through the land, of which my rapid passages across the meagre districts of New England had given but a poor idea. The beautiful village of Burlington and the town of Bristol on opposite sides of the river, the rich verdure, neat cottages, villas, farm-houses of painted wood or red brick, poplars, willows, and fruit-trees, spoke a quiet language of improvement and comfort. The accommodation in steam-boats was well managed, although the railroad travelling was in all points inferior to that between New York and Boston.

I have no wish to give descriptions of scenery, which has been over-described, or of manners which have been over-caricatured. The quiet and orderly demeanour of the people, the sameness and tameness of their conduct, the lack of originality, and the cautious apprehension of each other, which is common to all classes, afford small chance of adventure, and few specimens of singularity on the great thoroughfares between the Atlantic cities. The whole human family there met with seems not only cut out of the same piece, but often of the same pattern. Slight varieties of costume, dialect or accent are observable, but the beings themselves are all alike; and the different successive parties, for some hundreds of miles' travelling, are scarcely to be distinguished from each other.

We left New York on a Sunday morning at nine o'clock, crossing the Hudson in the ferry-boat to Jersey City, and thence proceeding by railway to Philadelphia, where we arrived at three in the afternoon. We remained there two days, during which we were occupied in paying and receiving visits, and seeing some of the not numerous wonders of the place and its near neighbourhood. The city altogether pleased me from its cleanliness and regularity, and the beauty of the public buildings. But the wearisome monotony would have soon worn me out, and I rejoiced in the reflection that fate had not fixed me there. The most gratifying incident which occurred to me was my meeting with the then celebrated, and since notorious, Nicholas Biddle, whose sleek appearance, courteous address, and great agreeability, gave so little indication of the reckless profligacy of his financial career. A year later brought about the final explosion of the Bank of the United States, and exposed a system of speculation and peculation on the part of its former President and his associates, which out-Biddled everything of which Biddle had been accused, and out-diddled all that diddling had ever before accomplished.

Sundry other pleasant or amusing acquaintanceships were formed during my short delay in Philadelphia; and among the latter sort was that of Mrs. Butler, formerly Miss Fanny Kemble, whose spirited conversation was quite equal to what her "Journal" led me to expect. Time was pressing — the sight-seeing of Philadelphia was over—so we started for Baltimore by steamer on the 1st of April, and it was with feelings of something akin to exultation, as though the noble river were my own, that I found myself launched on the broadly-swelling Delaware. The cramped and retail tone of New England and its inhabitants was gradually leaving my mind, which seemed to expand in proportion to the largeness of the scene. We went on our way, sometimes by land, sometimes by water, little occurring to us worth recording, with the exception of one incident of our journey, which was characteristic of the proverbial recklessness of the people.

On quitting the steamboat at Newcastle, we took the railroad for twenty-two miles to Frenchtown, which thus connects the Delaware with Chesapeake Bay. We had made about two-thirds of our journey, when, at one of the "crossings" a violent jolt, accompanied by a loud crash, made all the passengers start, and considerably alarmed some of them. The continued rapidity of our movement, however, satisfied all that no accident had occurred to the carriages; and in a quarter of an hour the train stopped close to the water-side at Frenchtown. As we stepped out, I went up to the conductor and engineer, who stood together on the platform of the locomotive, and inquired the cause of the sudden shock we had experienced.

"Well, it was in going over a chaise and horse," replied one of them, very coolly.

"There was no one in the chaise?" asked I, anxiously.

"Oh, yes, there were two ladies."

"Were they thrown out?"

"I guess they were, and pretty well smashed, too."

"Good God! and why didn't you stop the train? Can't you send back to know what state they're in?"

"Well, mister, I reckon they're in the State of Delaware; but you'd better jump into the steamer there, or you're like to lose your passage."

With these words the conductor turned to some other inquirer; and on my looking towards the steam-boat, I saw they were just letting loose from the wharf. We had not a moment to spare. We were almost instantly cutting through the waters; but, as may be supposed, absorbed for some time in the reflections which followed the shock our better feelings had received. Many of the passengers agreed with us, that it was inhuman of the conductor not to have stopped the train and looked after the injured persons. Others remarked that that wouldn't have done any good, and that the train was obliged to be up to time, or have delayed the steamer for ten minutes or more. This was unanswerable: the subject dropped. But a few days afterwards I saw in a Baltimore paper a paragraph, stating that one of the ladies had been killed, the other badly wounded, the horse "smashed," and the chaise (*Anglicè* gig) broken to pieces. The miracle was that the train was not shaken off the track. But even that had no power to excite the phlegmatic conductor or go-a-head engineer.

We reached Baltimore in a heavy fall of rain, which had for some time obscured the view on Chesapeake Bay, and was unfavourable to the aspect of the city, now seen for the first time. But many a subsequent visit made me familiar with the scenery of both, at all hours and all seasons; and left traces on my memory more lasting than the storm or sunshine in which I have alternately known that neighbourhood. On the occasion I now speak of, we found a tolerably good hotel (the Exchange), ready to receive us, our rooms having been engaged. And scarcely had we taken possession of them, when we were favoured with several visits from some of the most agreeable persons I had yet met with in America. There was a frankness and cordiality of manner about them which we had not lately been in the habit of meeting. Almost every one who called on us invited us to dine with them; and we regretted that the plan we had traced out did not then allow of our accepting their proffered hospitality. But in after years I had many opportunities of enjoying it most amply.

We just staid long enough at Baltimore to admire its commanding site, neat streets, and handsome dwelling houses; examine the columns, two in number, a hundred times described, which give it the sounding title of "the Monumental City," buy a ticket in the lottery (which, of course, turned up a blank), and make some passing observations on slavery, this being our first experience of a State cursed with that foul blot. These few objects effected, we proceeded, in bright weather and good spirits, to Washington, where we arrived and took up our quarters at Gadsby's Hotel, on the 4th of April.

I have elsewhere made some disclaimer of any desire to note down my first impressions of institutions or their working, of manners, or of social characteristics. As to towns and scenery in general the case is different; and what I object to in the first mentioned cases, I approve of in the latter. First impressions of places are at once the most vivid and most true, before local influences or the force of habit deaden one's perceptions as to faults or merits. I am, therefore, ready and glad to state that the whole appearance of Washington struck me with pleased astonishment. I had read so much of its wild and lonesome aspect, of its unfinished streets, its morasses, and "magnificent distances," sarcastically specified by disappointed or splenetic visitors, that my mind was quite prepared to realise their worst exaggerations. My admiration of its fine position, the vastness of its plan, and the progress of its filling up, was probably greater than it would have been, had I come there without any preconceived notions. To my view Washington was a grand conception, imperfectly carried out, but by no means the absurd abortion it is generally represented. I will not attempt descriptions of its edifices, or a measurement of its length and breadth. Its then population of 20,000, or thereabouts, had certainly space and verge enough; and its politicians cannot complain of want of room. The Capitol is a noble structure. I can imagine no one so fastidious as not to be delighted at the prospect from its terrace. Others of the public buildings—the Treasury, the Patent Office, the Post Office in particular—are worthy of any city in Europe.

But I am convinced that one feeling mixed with every glance of observation which I cast around me, of a nature so powerful as to imbue everything with its colouring. I could not help imagining that the place, in all its vastness, was filled with the spirit of its immortal founder. Everything in Washington was to me impressed with the image of him whose name it bears. Its whole design was as a monument to him. The unfinished plan, slowly going on towards completion, bore the impress of his large and reflective intellect. It was not a place of mushroom growth, run rapidly up, like the flimsy constructions which overspread the country, but a solid city, founded on a grand scheme, which it may require a century to carry out: a fitting illustration of the powerful and patient mind by which it was conceived and commenced, and which seems still to preside over its gradual advances.

Another impression forcibly affected me on occasion of this first visit to Washington, and in a scarcely diminished degree on every following one. This was a sentiment of shame at the recollection of the scenes acted there by the British forces under the command of General Ross, in 1814. If America should become magnanimous enough to forgive, or mean enough to forget them, England at least should remember them for ever. But with deep contrition, and as a warning against similar excesses in future.

The destruction by fire of public buildings, the plunder of private houses, are sufficiently revolting, even in a fortress taken by storm after a long resistance. But in an open and undefended town, left to the mercy of the assailants, such outrages are the disgrace not the triumph of war. Every English visitor to Washington, whether in official employment, or for passing business, or mere pleasure, should bear those deplorable transactions in mind, and let the pride of superiority over the people he mixes with be tempered, by the thought of what many of them witnessed, and what all must feel. The crimes of one generation are often visited on another; and not unjustly, if that other fails to admit, and does not endeavour to atone for them.

CHAPTER X.

WASHINGTON.

Hospitalities of the Place—General aspect of Society—Senate and House of Representatives—Parliamentary Peculiarities and Manners—The President, Martin Van Buren—Dinner at the White House—Henry Clay—Official Civilities—Mr. Fox, the British Minister—His Successor, Mr. Pakenham—Diplomatic Qualifications—Danger of a keen Correspondence—Advantage of a good Cook—John Ross the Cherokee Chief—The Grave of Washington—Alexandria—A Slave Jail—John C. Calhoun.

THE hospitalities of Washington were soon abundantly proffered to us; and we gladly availed ourselves of each opportunity to see society in the easy and pleasant style which prevails there. Independent of the several members of the *corps diplomatique* previously known to me in Europe, Mons. de Bacourt and the Chevalier d'Argaiz, the ministers from France and Spain; and Mr. Serruys, the Belgian Chargé d'Affaires, I had some other acquaintances from the Old World; among others, my quasi-countryman, Sir John Caldwell, for though born by mistake in Canada, he was an Irish baronet bred, and almost as good as born, his boyish recollections being all connected with the green island, and many of his relatives being well known to me, and some of them among my earliest friends. He was quite at home in most of the cities of the United States, and being as lively and active as any man of nearly seventy could be, and perfectly well-bred and good-tempered, his company was very agreeable to us, and he formed one in almost all of the many parties to which we were invited. The President gave us a very handsome dinner, and we also drank tea once in a quiet way with him at the White House. We dined at Mr. Forsyth's, Secretary of State; Mr. Poinsett's, Secretary of War; Mr. Clay's, Mr. Preston's, and other members of Congress, besides assisting at various evening parties; a ball at Commodore Morris's, and a grand *reception* at Mr. Bodisco's, the Russian Minister, on the occasion of his marriage, which took place while we were at Washington, and gave rise to many anecdotes, amusing or *méchantes*, some pleasantries, and *on dits* without end. We thus had sufficient specimens of the ways of life in the capital; and these, confirmed by subsequent visits, and a more extended circle of acquaintanceship, satisfied me that society is there on a most agreeable footing, and that the mixture of political excitement, private hospitality, European polish (among the *corps diplomatique*) and the rough kind of civilisation (displayed by the natives), together with the dash of savageness in the Indian deputations, and the deep shade of slavery pervading the whole, form a combination quite unique, both for amusement and instruction.

I gave a good deal of time to the Senate and House of Representatives, and heard many of their best speakers, but no question of any great interest was debated, and I had, consequently, on this occasion, no fair specimen of Congressional eloquence. I, however, heard Clay, Calhoun, Preston, Webster, and others; but none who then gave me a high idea of oratorical power. I had the misfortune to consume the better part of two mornings in listening to a rambling, rigmarole tirade by a member from Ohio, the only lesson I learned from it being one of wonder at the forbearance of the House in tolerating without a murmur such a nuisance for such a length of time. I, however, passed some hours very pleasantly, attending to sundry desultory debates, lounging with other visitors on the couches under the galleries, or chatting with the members in either House.

One of the parliamentary peculiarities of Congress is the arm chair and writing desk allowed to every member, affording considerable convenience and comfort, and forming an irresistible inducement to letter writing, and other employment, which not only diverts individual attention from what is going on, but leads to indifference to the prolix and irrelevant speeches, many of which are unheard by three-fourths of the assembly. The benches of our Houses of Parliament afford no such consolation for those forced to sit out a dull debate; and they furnish the chief cause for that impatience which cuts short a proser, and hurries on the "question." The complacency of Congress under what would be considered in England a dreadful boring operation, is, however, of easy solution. Members are paid eight dollars per diem as long as the Session lasts, and as this salary is a matter of vast importance to the great majority, the longer the Session the better for them.*

I saw many proofs of the looseness of parliamentary tactics in Congress, some instances of indecorum, fearful spittings, but no scene of actual violence. Altogether, I observed that here, where the most complete example of

* During the short *extra* Session of 1841, held in Summer, when Washington was hot and unhealthy, a rule was introduced and rigidly enforced, limiting each speaker to one hour on each question. This salutary regulation still exists. But the only sure means of permanent reform would be, to make the remuneration so much per Session or per annum instead of per day; in fact, to make the business of legislation so much task-work, and pay for it in the lump.

national characteristics might naturally be looked for, there was the least to be found in that essential distinction of discipline and order which pervades the people at large. And I am sure that whoever might be led to judge the Americans *en masse* from the conduct of their representatives in Congress, would make a serious mistake. To account for the great irregularity, and the many breaches of good manners, and of "the peace," occurring in the halls of Congress, it must be considered that men are brought there, face to face, the most fiercely opposed in politics, and in the personal interests on which all political feelings in America are based. They are also imbued with dislikes on local grounds, despising each other not only for opinion's sake, but from sectional jealousies. Then, in this field, every man feels his independence more strongly than elsewhere. He knows that he typifies a class, that he is acting a part, that the eyes of his constituents are on him, that he has an aggregate amount of passion to give vent to, and that, even if inclined to relax on his own account, he dares not do so in his representative capacity. Then, again, he holds many of his colleagues in sovereign contempt. North and south, east and west reciprocate no national courtesies, and their delegates interchange no feelings of mutual respect. They are mostly strangers to each other, coming together from immense distances, and knowing little or nothing of the private character, family connections, or other circumstances which generate good feeling between political adversaries. In Congress party confronts party and man meets man as enemies on a battlefield ; and where so many rude specimens of humanity are thus pitted against each other, it is strange that a still more "admired disorder" does not prevail.

Although thus offering such palliatives as I deem fair, I will however give, by way of note or appendix, a few instances of Congressional manners, although I cannot vouch as an eye-witness for the accuracy of the reports.

My more particular attention was given to individuals on occasions of private intercourse. In this respect I found a fund of entertainment. My first visit was, as well from inclination as in due order of etiquette, to the President, Martin Van Buren. I was well aware that, notwithstanding his elevation to the (then*) proudest elective station in the universe, he was not one of the master spirits of even the New World; yet, thinking that no very commonplace man could have attained his position, I went into his presence with a due feeling of respect. I was presented to him in his general reception room by Mr. Forsyth, the Secretary of State, having previously left for him a letter of introduction from one of his political friends. I found Mr. Van Buren as nearly as possible what I expected him to be. Most of his published portraits are good likenesses, and he has, I think, been fairly described by several writers. He was sufficiently well-mannered, with an air of mingled self-esteem and self-control, not over-candid, nor yet showing too many under-bred indications of caution. He gave no direct evidence of constraint, yet had none of the frankness that captivates at first sight. He was at his ease without cordiality, and talked freely without being fluent. Too much a man of the world to be off his guard for a moment, yet too little of one not to give the notion that he was standing in a measure on the defensive. He said many obliging things without seeming to feel them; and without anything downrightly artificial

* This allusion is in reference to the brief and abortive institution of the Republic in France in 1848.

in his bearing, he did not appear altogether natural. His urbanity seemed rather acquired than instinctive; and his tone altogether the effect of calculation rather than impulse.

But in neither my first nor in any subsequent interview with Mr. Van Buren did I trace that unpleasantly cunning and deceitful air which his enemies ascribe to him. I was in fact myself careful not to touch on any subject that might call his sensitiveness into play. I felt that it would be unbecoming to do so; and I consequently saw the President in his best aspect—that of a well-tempered and not ungentlemanlike man, who, if he had not much of the doubtful characteristic of high station, commonly called dignity, showed none of the arrogance which often disfigures those who have greatness thrust on them. Van Buren's conduct through his whole career has been calm, cold, and safe. Respectable in his dealings, consistent to the principles of democracy, the democrats have upheld him. Possessed of no brilliancy of talent, he excites no envy; with little energy, he makes no enemies. Steadily active, he loses no friends. Without strong or startling efforts, he is a good *timeist.* He regulates rather than guides opinion. Wanting in the qualities to make him the mainspring of a party, he is well fitted to be the pivot round which it turns. Owing his elevation to the favour of General Jackson rather than to his own merits, he cannot hope to maintain it in case of a contest with any powerful or popular rival. If his party should then rally round and cling to him, he will surely drag them down.*

At the dinner given to us by Mr. Van Buren at the White House, there were three or four ladies besides my wife, several members of the Cabinet (Messrs. Forsyth,

* This prediction was fully verified in the ensuing Presidential election.

Poinsett, Gilpin, and Woodbury); Messrs. Clay, Preston, Crittenden, of the Senate; General Scott, Mr. Cushing, and other members of Congress; Mr. Fox, and two or three other *diplomates*—altogether, a party of twenty-six. Nothing could be in better taste than the entertainment. Good cookery, good wines, excellent attendance, handsome plate, glass, and china, with a profusion of lights and flowers. Nothing was deficient that might be considered in keeping with the establishment of a gentleman of six or seven thousand a year in England; nor was there any ostentation, nor any vulgar attempt to do more than was requisite and fitting.

As I had previously made acquaintance with almost every one present, I found the party a very agreeable one. I sat opposite the President, beside Mr. Clay, who very soon took the lead in the talk among those occupying the centre of the table, which was too long to allow of any general conversation. There were a great many pleasant things said; but only one of an individual nature impressed itself on my memory. It was, however, sufficiently characteristic to induce me to record it.

During the dessert Mr. Clay borrowed somebody's snuff-box, the only one in the room, for scarcely any American gentleman takes tobacco in *that* form, and, plunging his finger and thumb deep into it, he attracted the President's attention.

"Why, Mr. Clay," said the latter, "I thought you had long since given up that bad habit?"

"Why, really, Mr. President," replied Clay, with his peculiarly long and measured intonation, a bantering not a sarcastic smile, and tapping the box which he had just closed, "I have been intending to give it up; but I find it impossible to abandon anything, good or bad, until we can succeed in getting rid of the present detestable administration."

To appreciate the independent *naïveté* of this somewhat hazardous sally, it should be known that party hostility was at a most furious height at that epoch, and that it was only at "the White House" that men so opposed in politics, as the members of the Cabinet and others whose names I have enumerated, could be met with together. It required a good deal of self-control to wear a friendly face to each other even there; and Van Buren's boldest and most dangerous political opponent was certainly Henry Clay. His observation was altogether a most wonderful hit. A loud burst of laughter from Whigs and Locofocos alike, the President joining as loudly as any one, answered it from one end of the table to the other. And it was the signal for a series of well-tempered sharp-shooting, that never went beyond the harmlessness of blank cartridge, on various topics of the time; a foremost one, but treated rather too jocosely, being the reported employment by the United States troops of a pack of bloodhounds in their warfare against the Indians in Florida.

The opportunity thus given of laughing down this calumny chimed in with the humour of the hour. Everything prosy or even serious seemed banished as if by preconcerted plan. We sat some time longer than usual at table. The drawing-room became the scene of some sociable grouping and lively conversation; and we took our leave rather late to go to some evening party, most favourably impressed with the courtesy of our host, and the good sense and good temper of himself and his company.

A few evenings afterwards, accompanied by Sir John Caldwell, we spent a couple of hours very agreeably at the White House, drinking tea with his democratic Majesty, quite alone in "the Blue Drawing-Room," as well known and as often described in all its details (both in and out of Congress) as the notorious Blue Chamber in the Castle of Him of the Beard of that colour.

On this occasion Mr. Van Buren was particularly pleasant. He talked a good deal of England, and of his short residence in London as Minister. India becoming incidentally the subject of conversation, he mentioned his recollection of Lord Auckland, the then Governor-General, as connected with one observation of the latter, which had made, he said, a strong impression on him. It may be remembered that Mr. Van Buren, appointed to this English mission by the then President General Jackson, was in a few months obliged to return to America, the Senate on their assembling in session, having refused by a majority of votes to confirm his nomination. It was just at this period that he met Lord Auckland in London, and on being introduced to him, his lordship somewhat surprised him by offering him his congratulations on his recall. But he quickly explained by assuring Van Buren that "he had never known an instance of a man being politically persecuted that it did not make his fortune." The instance in question was certainly a striking confirmation of the axiom; for Van Buren on his return home was adopted by Jackson as his second self, elected Vice President of the Union by his influence, and became the successor of that extraordinary man as President, merely by having stuck close to his mantle—only the skirts of which, however, fell on him, when the owner left his seat of public turmoil for the quiet dignity of private life.

All these circumstances were freely talked over and commented on by Mr. Van Buren that evening, with many others, which not being of a public nature may not be touched on here. The honours of the White House were ordinarily done by the President's daughter-in-law; but at this period she was recovering from a recent confinement, and we did not see her. His sons, one of whom I had met in London, were unassuming young men I thought, and the Van Buren family altogether, as far as I saw of them, were a very favourable specimen of Locofoco gentility.

Mr. Forsyth and Mr. Poinsett performed the courtesies of official station unexceptionably. Their ladies were very attentive and polite to mine, and we were particularly pleased with the four generations of female Forsyths, his mother, wife, daughter, and daughter's infant child. They were then a happy family, with all the enjoyment of political position and social comfort. My next visit to Washington, a year later, showed me a serious contrast.

I met with many civilities from other official persons, and more hospitalities were cordially tendered than our limited stay enabled us to accept. Social intercourse among the families of members of Congress is on an easy footing. They almost all occupy hotels, or board and lodge several together in private houses, in what are technically called "messes." Their whole business at Washington is pleasure. Having no housekeeping cares to occupy their time or sour their tempers (supposing the latter a possible contingency), the ladies can give full scope to their *talents de société*, and these are considerable. I could specify names of those among them possessing accomplishments and conversational powers of no mean order.

Among the members themselves are of course to be found many of the *élite* of American gentlemen; while the mingling of vulgarity and occasional coarseness, gives a certain zest not quite out of keeping with the whole. The *corps diplomatique* constitutes a pleasant element of society everywhere. The greatest curiosity in that particular circle then at Washington was beyond doubt Mr. Fox, the British Minister. His eccentric habits of life formed a standing subject of gossip and conjecture. I met him three or four times at dinner, invitations to which, I understood, he rarely refused, and never returned. Inverting all the usual regulations of time, sitting up all night and lying in bed all day, his cadaverous looks made a most painful impression, which his lively and sarcastic conversation after awhile dispelled. Abundant anecdotes were related to me illustrative of his character and conduct. They were rather amusing, and would have been interesting enough for repetition here had their object been a person of any great note. But he was chiefly remarkable for the poor ambition of living unlike other men, and for being little fitted for the position he held; and he died obscurely soon after his retirement from the diplomatic service, and in the very house in Washington which he had for several years occupied in single loneliness. Mr. Fox possessed considerable talent. He wrote tersely, and was a sharp controversialist. Some of his published despatches gave cutting proofs of this; but it forms a very inferior portion of the diplomatic qualifications required for a minister at Washington. His successor, a dull man, with infinitely less ability, was a far better negotiator. Mr. Fox went near to embroil the two countries on the North Eastern Boundary dispute, by the keenness of his correspondence. Mr. Pakenham kept the peace and settled the Oregon question, by the cleverness of his cook.

Among the persons more or less remarkable then at Washington was John Ross, the chief of the Cherokee tribe of Indians, who, with a few of the principal men of that nation, was following up some claims against the government, I believe with no satisfactory result. I was introduced to him by Mr. Howard Payne, formerly of some celebrity as "the American Roscius," but who had long subsided from that exaggerated *sobriquet*, into an adapter of small pieces for the stage in London, where I had met him with Washington Irving many years before, and who had for some time been attached in some capacity, I know not exactly what, to the Cherokee Indians, with whose deputation he was now identified. John Ross, who inherited his station in the tribe from his father, a Scotchman, who had gained his rank by marriage with the daughter of the former chief, was so completely European in appearance, manner, and dress, as to destroy in a great measure the illusion one wishes to attach to the peculiarities of Indian character. He spoke English without any Indian or even American accent. I had several interviews with him, and some conversations, which, had I been disposed to encourage certain views thrown out rather than actually proposed, might have led to serious, perhaps embarrassing, consequences. But I felt no inclination, then or at any other time in America, to go farther than the duties of my position required, or to mix in matters foreign to my jurisdiction; and I confess that nothing, either from personal experience or from acquired information, gave me any particular interest in Indian concerns.

We made a few excursions in the neighbourhood, the one of most interest being to the grave of Washington, at Mount Vernon—that little spot of earth, more suggestive and memorable than whole districts of prairie land; and to Alexandria in Virginia, a desolate, ragged-looking old town, remarkable in my memory as being the first place where I visited one of those strongholds of iniquity, a negro "jail." This word does not in this sense apply to a prison for criminals, but to a place of confinement for the wretched slaves bought by its ruffian owner to be sold again for profit. These places have been often described, and as often held up to execration by travellers. I shall not trust myself on this theme. There were but few of the poor wretches, of whom it could accommodate some scores, a large batch having a day or two previously been purchased, "cleared out," and carried off to the more southern states, from their parents, their relatives and friends, from every object of local attachment in the place where they were "raised," to a hopeless banishment they knew not and cared not where. And yet the people and government who practise this atrocious traffic openly in the face of the world, have the effrontery to brand the *African* slave-trade as piracy, and to boast of their efforts for its suppression—finding it less costly to breed than to import the stock for this domestic infamy.

CHAPTER XI.

JOHN CALDWELL CALHOUN.

Among the most prominent of those to whom I brought letters of introduction was John Caldwell Calhoun, whose name is pronounced Caloon. I soon called on and presented my credentials to him. He was at once very cordial, and consequently agreeable. His manner was more prepossessing than his appearance, which was harsh without being exactly coarse, and gave an idea of stiffness without actual severity. He had a military, erect, drill-serjeant air. His very hair stood on end; and one could not imagine any graceful curvatures of mind in a body and countenance so unbending. The familiarity of his address took me therefore by surprise; and I thought I soon discovered a sincerity of tone in him, which further intercourse satisfied me was natural to the man.

We exchanged several visits during my stay at Washington, and I had opportunities of meeting Mr. Calhoun at some of the dinner parties, where I found many occasions for conversation with him. The tenor of these, added to my observation of his public conduct, enabled me to form a tolerably fair judgment of him; and the freedom and ardour with which he discussed the main subject of his political sentiments, and of difference between us—I mean the subject of slavery,—gave a wider opening through which to take a view of his character and the compass of his mind.

Calhoun was unquestionably a remarkable man, and he gained a high place among the leading politicians of his country. No one of merely ordinary talents could have done this. But it has in his case been more owing to his prompt temperament and the flexibility of his opinions than to the depth or solidity of his understanding. The shiftings and changings of public men throughout the Union form the most remarkable features of their career; so remarkable, indeed, as to make me believe that a steady and consistent course is incompatible with an admission of a man's eminence. There is scarcely one among them who has not been recreant to some one or other of his early professions, or converted from some political creed into one directly opposed to it. Convictions to this effect are constantly recorded, and proofs afforded out of their own mouths, against all the leading men. But, as far as I can observe, but little disgrace attaches to this common offence. The truth is, that the main questions of domestic policy in the United States are constantly undergoing fluctuations which make it hard to keep them within fixed bounds. They are almost all experiments. Few of them can be called principles; and those who follow them as theories may be pardoned for abandoning them when it becomes clear that they cannot be made facts. This is discovered sooner or later; and so surely does the discoverer lay himself open to the charges which have been so truly urged against Calhoun.

This statesman has been at the very pinnacle of that one-sided popularity which party men may attain in this country. No one that I have ever heard or read of, with the exception of Washington and Franklin, has had more than that. To rally the opinions and gain the hearts of the whole people is not given to the men of the present day, and least of all to such a man as Calhoun. He was a striking instance of the danger of individuals "missing their vocation." He had qualities well suited to the management of details. I am assured that he made an excellent Secretary of War, and later still an efficient Secretary of State, doing the routine business of his offices with scrupulous industry. But a "too vaulting ambition" forced him into the wholesale line in politics. A subordinate station would not satisfy him. Nothing short of the Presidential throne seemed a fitting seat for his self-esteem. He was consequently forced to grapple with all the great questions of state policy; and every one of them proved too strong for him. Without having studied metaphysics he gave himself up to abstractions; and, with a remarkable mental shortsightedness, he ventured to throw a glance across the whole extent of human affairs. His mistakes were numberless. He continually confounded matters, persevering in his blunders with an obstinacy which ruined him with all the parties to which he had in turns belonged.

Born of Irish parents in an humble walk of life, he was almost entirely uneducated at the age of nineteen. At that period his mind awoke to the consciousness of its powers, and he commenced a career of self-culture the results of which were so honourable to him. He entered on the usual course for ambitious men of talent in the United States: became an attorney's clerk; practised as a lawyer; was elected to the legislature of his native state, and chosen a member of Congress.

Of a vivid fancy and active temperament, and a fluent speaker, his election as Vice-President of the United States, and *ex officio* President of the Senate, forced him into a post of dignified inaction, where he was obliged to hear everything, reply to nothing, and turn into mental speculation all the reasonings that would have willingly broken forth in argument and declamation. Hence probably arose his habit of theorising on all subjects, of pushing a principle to what he considered its ultimate consequences; and hence it is that his doctrines of Democracy appear to be rather metaphysical shadows than matters of fact.

In Mr. Calhoun's conversation there was a terseness and a decision that passed with some persons for logic. He seemed labouring to maintain his character as a great dialectician. He was no doubt at times right in certain opinions, for he to all appearance changed his own on almost all subjects of importance; though, like all public men, he asserted his consistency on all, in the face of fact and in defiance of proof. But on the only point relative to which I talked very seriously with him he exhibited a doggedness, that would have been disagreeable had it not had a stamp of sincerity about it which made it quite amusing.

That point was the question of Negro Slavery in all its bearings. There was to me great originality in Mr. Calhoun's way of treating it; but I have since learned that to General Mc Duffie, whilom of South Carolina, is due the merit or demerit of having first promulgated in print the astounding doctrines advocated so enthusiastically by his more celebrated colleague.

Mr. Calhoun maintained seriously that slavery is a necessity for the purposes of civilisation; that the coloured race has been made black to place the badge of inferiority in manifest traces upon it; that both races, the white and the black, are bettered by the institution of slavery; that the slave owner, being the representative of both labour and capital, combines in himself the most important attributes of humanity; and in short, that slavery (like charity) is "twice blest," in the person of the enslaver and the enslaved.

"Liberty," argued Mr. Calhoun, "is a great reward for virtuous and noble deeds. No people is entitled to it who have not earned it at that price. Neither can any people become truly humanized or great who have not possessed slaves, that they (the masters) may know the value of freedom, and also have the opportunity of practising benevolence towards their dependants. There must be a superior and inferior rank," quoth he; "Servitude is a necessity of civilisation. Those who perform its offices are virtually degraded. Better that it should be a coloured and inferior race than a portion of the white one, our equals. The higher feelings of honour and chivalry can be fostered but by feudal institutions. In the actual state of civilisation they can now exist only in a country that possesses two distinct races, brought together by Providence for that special object. That is the case in the Southern States of the Union."

Ergo (he might have continued), the southern states of North America are the soil where honour, independence, and chivalry best flourish; and I, John C. Calhoun, as the most distinguished of the inhabitants, proprietors, and slave-owners of that paradise, am the fitting representative of those glorious qualities, and consequently

The foremost man of all this world.

There is really no exaggeration in this statement. The

premises were broadly and plainly stated by Mr. Calhoun; and the conclusion is very natural without his having to jump to it. During one of our discussions, and while he was freely pouring out a stream of sophisms, and working himself up to unusual fervour while arguing that slavery was a blessing to the African Negro, forced into the comparative heaven of American bondage, and that the evils of emancipation were greater than its promises were good, I observed that I had no doubt the slaves themselves would, like all other men, prefer liberty to bondage.

"Now let me ask you," said I, "what, for instance, was the feeling of the very last slave you liberated?"

"I!" exclaimed he, in surprise, and with somewhat of indignation in his tone—"I liberate a slave! God forbid that I should ever be guilty of such a crime. Ah, you know little of my character, if you believe me capable of doing so much wrong to a fellow-creature."

"Are you really serious?" asked I.

"Indeed I am, and I know you will pardon my saying, that in fancying emancipation to be in any case desirable for a slave, you take a very narrow view of the question."

This was too much for my gravity, or even for my sense of decorum. I laughed outright; and telling him that I believed after all he was mystifying me, after the fashion in which English travellers were sometimes treated in the United States (though I saw with painful conviction that he was most soberly serious), I changed the conversation, and never renewed the subject with him.

A day or two afterwards I was present in the senate when Calhoun brought forward his somewhat celebrated resolutions on the subject of the American slave ships, the "Encomium," "Comet," and "Enterprise," which were forced by stress of weather on the coast of Bermuda in the year 1838, their cargoes of human merchandise being all saved, and immediately set at liberty by the British authorities. It may be remembered that, as regards the two first of these vessels, the British Government allowed a compensation to the American owners of the slaves; but that in the last instance, Lord Palmerston peremptorily refused any, on the plea that at the epoch of the shipwreck, slavery having been totally abolished in the British possessions, he would not grant pecuniary remuneration for men who by touching the soil of an English colony were absolutely enfranchised. Considerable negotiation and a long correspondence followed this decision. And at length Mr. Calhoun, despairing of producing any effect on England, determined to commit the whole of the United States senate to his own principles, and introduced the resolutions in question, which formed a decided and somewhat violent protest against the conduct of the British Government, on grounds of international rights assumed to have been infringed.

There was no debate on this occasion. Mr. Clay alone offered a few words in the shape of remonstrance, rather than opposition, resting his disapproval of the resolutions on a mere *cui bono*. I asked Mr. Calhoun in the Senate Chamber if he meant to follow up the resolutions by a declaration of war against England? He laughed at my question, but he certainly had no satisfactory answer to make to it. Nothing, in fact, could be more inconsequent than to let resolutions of so formidable a nature, containing an accusation against England of having violated the laws of nations, lie a dead letter in the records of the very senate which had unanimously concurred in them. Perhaps Mr. Calhoun only wanted to establish a precedent (of opinion) on which he might be able to fall back on some future occasion, when the question might be riper for discussion on general grounds.

Mr. Calhoun was, I believe, a man of real purity of character. Ambitious, but not sordid. Of small fortune, but maintaining a deportment that made you forget whether he was rich or poor. Sacrificing the nomination for the Presidency, rather than swerve from what might have been by chance his opinion at the moment. George Bancroft was to my knowledge deputed by his party in the winter of 1840—1841, to propose to Calhoun a certain compromise of his declared convictions on slavery, as the means of reconciling the democrats of the North to his nomination. But Calhoun, after listening to Bancroft's views, and reading the memoir in which he had embodied them, resisted the proposition, remained firm in his conscientious bigotry, and so lost his last chance of obtaining the distinction which had been the great object of his life.

Much of Calhoun's failure as a public man was due to his struggling against destiny. The chosen champion of a system which is fated, sooner or later, to destruction, he shut his eyes against the inevitable doom, hoped against hope, and, more desperate than Curtius, leaped into the gulph although convinced that the state could not be saved by his immolation. The policy of Carolina cannot finally prevail. Impoverishment and the rapid increase of the slave population go hand in hand for the ruin of the system, the influence of which has been long on the wane. And the fiery temper of the south, unbending in reverse, and furious from opposition, rushes to extremes, and adopts "nullification" in despair. This temper found its ready embodiment in Calhoun, and he seemed resolved to perish politically rather than yield to the force of things, and flourish under a change whose progress is irresistible. I had several opportunities in after years of meeting Mr. Calhoun in Washington. On one of those he expressed his positive determination to retire from public life for ever at the close of the then session of Congress. In the following winter he was filling the office of Secretary of State. His resolutions, like most of his political opinions, were not immutable. On one subject, however, he maintained his consistency to the end of his career. The last time I saw him was during the delivery of his great speech in the Senate in 1846. Still later he made a last desperate display of his powers of sophistical dispute, in a written essay, which physical weakness forced him to entrust to the reading of a brother senator. And with that farewell oration ended his political and his mortal career. He died almost immediately afterwards, having exhausted his constitution without adding to his fame, and giving by his death a relief to his party and his native state, proportioned to the damage caused by his long-lived obstinacy.

CHAPTER XII.

AMERICAN ARISTOCRACY.

The word "Aristocracy" a misnomer in America—Real American Gentlemen, where to find them—Well-washed Presidents, Jefferson and Buchanan—Merchant Lords, Grocers, and Linen-drapers—Every essential of Aristocracy wanting—The English Nobility, its Merits and Defects—English Gentry—English Reformers—The true method for Europeans to look on America, and the Americans on Europe—Social Malcontents, their unhappy position.

Among the many words misunderstood or misapplied throughout the United States, there is not one more frequently used, or in its application more thoroughly abused, than the word "Aristocracy." It is one of those which are in common usage in England, with a distinct and specific meaning, but which, when they enter into American discourse, seem totally devoid of the sense an Englishman gives them. I cannot here attempt to enumerate all those which are applied so differently in the two countries, expressing qualities in individuals or in things. But I may mention, as an example, another word of the same genus as that now in question: that is, "gentlemanly," and it shares the same fate, of being, as I have elsewhere remarked, quite misunderstood on the American side of the Atlantic. This latter word is almost invariably employed there to designate the manners of hotel keepers, the persons serving at the bar of a public-house, the box-keeper at a theatre, conductors of railroad cars, or other individuals of that class, who have opportunities of being civil and accommodating to customers. The meaning which we attach to it, as implying well-bred, or courtly demeanour, is quite unknown. Any one possessing this engaging quality is distinguished in America by some other epithet, as "a fine man," "one of the upper crust," &c., while the newspapers teem with compliments to the "gentlemanly" mixers and vendors of mint juleps, gin slings, or snake-root bitters. The profuse repetitions of the word in this way naturally make an Englishman smile, merely because they are to him indicative of vulgarity.

To meet anything quite coming up to English notions of a finished gentleman is scarcely to be expected. The difficulty can be proved on a perfectly (popular) heraldic principle. Every one knows that it takes three generations to make a gentleman. And as that implies three generations of liberal education and all the appliances of gentility, ergo, it is very rare, if to be found at all among Americans; for such a thing as grandfather, father, and son in one family preserving their fortune and station is almost unheard of. The fluctuations of property are sure to reduce one generation out of three to a low level; and thus it is that we see so many persons of respectable manners just bordering on good-breeding, and so few that are thoroughly well-bred.

This subject of American gentlemen is one of so much difficulty—I might say delicacy, in as far as the feelings of many are concerned—and it rises up in so many forms, that I must revert to it in a desultory way, instead of having made it a topic to be treated under one distinct head, and standing, like any abstract question, by itself.

Laws, institutions, and principles are independent facts, established and, comparatively speaking, of fixed tenure in the country. They are things to be referred to as precedents, apart from the every-day pursuits of the population. But manners are mixed up with every movement of the social system. We are in unceasing contact with them, in every situation of life. Their varieties surround us ; we meet them at every turn, and see them in ever-shifting aspects. It is, therefore, that we may be deceived by impressions strictly just in themselves, but which some new position may throw into totally opposing combinations, as a shake of the kaleidoscope changes its commingled atoms into forms directly different, though the materials are always the same.

Manners in the United States are of this nature. There is no standard for them, from the want of a permanent class in society to be looked up to and imitated. As the whole of its ingredients are mixed and incongruous, almost each individual follows his natural bent ; and we find in the same circles most striking contrasts of style, "every one" being, as might be said, "his own gentleman." Persons are to be found in America of really good *ton*, even according to the European estimate, but they are infrequently met with in the business or political world. You must look for them on the banks of the Hudson, the Delaware, or the Ohio, in villas with the appurtenances of refinement ; in the remote valleys of New England ; or on the plantations of the Southern States—and *there* surrounded by the repulsive associations of slavery, which neutralise the graces to whose culture they administer. All the men of that superior stamp, to mix with whom it was occasionally my good fortune, were (with rare exceptions) out of the whirl of politics, and what is called in the phraseology of the cities "high life." They do not come into contact with the pushing inelegancy of the mass from which the leading party-men and the highest functionaries, whether state or federal, are chosen. Many of the secluded gentry of whom I speak have been partly educated in Europe, or have extended their adult experience there long enough to appreciate the tastes and habits of the Old World; and they do not hesitate to choose between the obscure enjoyments of their country homes and the ambitious vulgarity of public life. It was most gratifying to join those delightful circles. But it was not in them that I was to find materials for a book on the general characteristics of civilised America. It was among the motley crowd of the millions that I had to make my way, and among whom my temporary lot was cast.

Admitting, then, that those millions have no available resource in which to find models of refined behaviour, it is no blame to them if the system under which they live and thrive should be the foundation of a somewhat inelegant superstructure. It is, on the contrary, in my opinion, well adapted to their whole scheme of polity; and it is much to be lamented that they are not satisfied to conform to it. I might accumulate proofs, extracted from the public papers, of the generally ignoble notions they form of "high" and "fashionable" life, as well as the meaning they attach to the word "gentlemanly"; but I will confine myself to a few.

In the columns of a New York paper, I find the following obituary notice of a gentleman whom I had frequently met in that city and elsewhere, without being at all aware of his antecedents or pretensions:—

Mr. Hone has long occupied a prominent position in our social, commercial, and political circles. He was of humble origin, being the son of a baker. In early life, he entered into the mercantile profession in Maiden Lane, and afterwards engaged in the auction and commission business in Pearl Street, always standing at the head of the auctioneers. In the fashionable world Mr. Hone always held a high rank, being always considered a leader of the *ton*. Indeed, it has been said, that if an order of nobility had existed in this country, Mr. Hone would have claimed the right of being numbered in their ranks. His bearing, though courteous towards his fellow-citizens, was aristocratic and self-confident; and when any of the foreign nobility visited our shores they received his hospitality, while he was personally but little known to the mechanics and other middle classes of American society.

This fluent and clever auctioneer might possibly have had the patrician contempt for the class he sprang from which is here ascribed to him; and he was perhaps a Coriolanus in pride, though not in bearing; but the thing to remark in relation to him is, that he is here held up as a model aristocrat and a ready-made nobleman.

Flying to a higher altitude, that of the White House itself, and without reverting to its past distinguished occupants, *The Baltimore Sun*, of the month of August, 1858, gives the following anecdote of the present incumbent, Mr. James Buchanan. It has nothing to do with his political position. It is given merely as an illustration of manners among the highest politicians and statesmen of the United States, whose habits are, no doubt, formed from those of early youth, the boy being, more particularly in such matters, the father of the man. The Presidents have not been uniformly models of good breeding or good taste. Readers may remember the mention of Sir Augustus Foster, of Mr. Jefferson having told him rather exultingly that "he was in the habit of washing his feet every morning," implying that it was an unusual thing even with persons of his station. I myself can truly record that on being presented to another occupant of the White House, he, previously to shaking hands and giving me welcome, took a quid of tobacco from his mouth, and threw it behind one of the gilded and satin-covered sofas; and a good deal of notoriety was about the same time given to the fact of the same gentleman having, not merely "roomed" with, but actually slept with a member of the Federal Senate, who proved himself to have been a very "strange bed-fellow" indeed. With these homely examples before him, Mr. Buchanan may be fairly cited as another, in the following free and easy sketch, which I give in its entirety:—

Familiar as our people are generally with the unostentatious habits of the chief officers of our government, one cannot witness them, with the knowledge of the pomp and show of royalty to invite the contrast, without involuntarily indulging it. On Saturday last President Buchanan arrived at the Relay House, or Washington Junction, as it is more properly called, *en route* for Washington city. There was a rumour abroad that he was to arrive, and the visitors had consequently grouped about the house when the train came along. We soon perceived the President coming from the cars to the platform, looking heartily, but thoroughly travel-soiled, smiling and cheerful. By his side, and evidently offering with gentlemanly deference the courtesy of attention, was a rather rough-looking individual, whom we took for a conductor or brakesman. The gentleman will excuse our blundering in such a matter; but, upon inquiry, we were informed he was Sir William Gore Ouseley. On passing into the bar-room the President threw off his coat and his white neckcloth, carelessly pitching them over a chair, opened his shirt-collar, and tucked up his sleeves for a wash, conveniences for this purpose being in the apartment. At the time, however, both basins were occupied by two young men, neither of whom seemed to be aware that the President was about. He waited patiently some time, when some one spoke and invited him upstairs. He declined, however, quietly remarking that he would wait for his turn. And as soon as the basins were vacated he "took his turn" in a jolly good wash in the public bar-room. This done, he seemed rather perplexed about the arrangement of his neckcloth, and seemed likely to tie his nose and mouth up in it. Somebody just then offered assistance, and the President was briefly equipped. At about this time, a person who had come into the room sang out pretty near to him, "Look here, I thought the old Pres. was to be here to-day ——" The speech was cut short by a nudge, while a momentary comical expression passed across the face of that same "old Pres." A cigar was handed to him by a friend; he took a good satisfying drink of—not "old rye," which he is said to affect, when prime—but ice-water, had barely fired up his cigar, when the bell rang, and "all aboard" summoned the chief magistrate of the United States to his seat in the cars, and away they went to Washington. We took our admiration of this scene of republican simplicity quietly with us into the cars for Baltimore, and mused with some complacency *over the sterling honour of being an American citizen.*

I record these small matters to show that I have good reasons for saying that American ideas about gentleman-like manners and habits are different from ours. No one more despises instances of over-fastidious coxcombry. All who, like me, have seen a good deal of the rough work of life in various countries, have often been reduced to far greater straits than that which the President of the United States here voluntarily chose for himself. In his case it was matter of taste, not necessity, and he had a perfect right to indulge it. But the striking moral of the story is contained in the concluding words of the foregoing article. Here we find the Editor of an American newspaper of well-established credit, and to a certain degree (like all persons of his profession) a censor, or at least a critic of manners as well as morals, glorifying himself for "the sterling honour of being an American citizen,"—not from pride in the greatness of his country or the virtue of its people; not from the contemplation of any deed of heroism, piety, or benevolence, on the part of a compatriot; but simply because President Buchanan, in preference to decently performing his ablutions in a private room, chose to take "a jolly good wash" in a public bar, out of a basin recently used, and in all probability imperfectly rinsed.

Can any American of any grade, who knows anything of English habits, complain after this so recent instance, of my saying that their general notions of gentlemanly bearing are different from ours? I was glad to find on reading the anecdote that there was no intimation of Sir William Ouseley, our special Minister to Central America, having followed the President's example (much as his appearance seemed to require it) in making use of the other utensil in a similar manner; though it might have increased his popularity, and given him some advantage in conducting his negotiations.

Such being shown, on the authority of one editor, to be the act of the President, and his own feelings on witnessing it, I will subjoin an extract from the letter of another (the Editor of the *Boston Courier*), dated from the same town of Baltimore, and showing *his* idea of what is "gentlemanly," and with whom its exercise is to be found.

I write this at Barnum's Hotel, in Baltimore (August 15), which it is my purpose to leave to-morrow, but where, if I were to consult only the pleasure of enjoying good breakfasts and dinners, and the pleasant company of the good old landlord, I would stay till next Thanksgiving. Such a spacious house—such neat and comfortable beds—such polite and affable courtesies, without any affected or obsequious civilities on the part of the hosts (there are three or four of them), and *such gentlemanly attentions on the part of the servants,* surely none but a downright professional fault-finder could be otherwise than at his ease in his inn.

In further illustration of the different sense attached to certain words in America from their meaning in England, particularly as applied to social gradation, the following article from the New York *Times*, a leading newspaper, will be found instructive. It is a commentary on a reference by Lord Ellenborough to "the sons of grocers and linendrapers," in a speech on Indian affairs, in July, 1858. It shows that public writers at the other side of the Atlantic do not comprehend the distinctions established among us between the pursuits of wholesale commerce, banking, or manufacturing, and the retail trades, which, however respectably carried on, do not confer the same status on their followers. It is certain that none of Lord Ellenborough's noble audience had reason to wince, from any personal sensitiveness as to his remarks. The "Merchant Lords" alluded to, or their descendants, might, however, be amused at the strange want of classification in regard to social grades in the very centre of American civilisation.

New York Times, August 26, 1858.

MERCHANT LORDS.—There are many noble families in England which are indebted for their patents of nobility to their founders' success in trade. It was a singular circumstance, therefore, that a member of the House of Lords, of so recent a creation as the Earl of Ellenborough, should utter such disparaging remarks, in reference to the mercantile classes, as he did in a speech lately on the Indian bill, when referring to the admission of cadets to the military service. He advocated the exclusion of the sons of merchants, and for the following most remarkable reasons:—

"The education," said his Lordship, "obtained in these cramming colleges is not the highest species of education;—that which is attained at *home, by the example and conversation of good parents, is by far the highest. You cannot compare for a moment the education which the sons of clergymen and officers get with the education obtained by the sons of rich grocers and linendrapers*, who will be successful in these competitive examinations. Depend upon it, this is a great and most injurious social revolution."

This allusion to the good parentage of boys who have the fortune not to belong to the commercial classes, sounds sufficiently whimsical in this country where merchants form the upper-crust of society. As the speech of Lord Ellenborough did not even elicit a "hear," according to the reports, it must have been considered as altogether proper by their lordships to whom it was addressed. And yet there are in the House of Lords several merchants and sons of merchants, who must have experienced a very queer sensation if they listened to the disparaging remarks of Lord Ellenborough. There are, for example: Baron Belper, formerly Mr. Strutt, the manufacturer, who has but just been admitted to the House of Lords; and Baron Overstone, formerly Jones Loyd, the Manchester banker; and Baron Macaulay, the son of a merchant; and Baron Ashburton, the son of a London merchant, and whose mother was the daughter of a Philadelphia merchant; and there, too, is the Governor-General of India himself, Lord Canning, who came from a mercantile family, and whose father, the great statesman, was educated by his uncle, a banker, who was raised to an Irish peerage; and then there was Sir Robert Peel, whose father sold calicoes, and many similar cases that might be mentioned. It was a most strange circumstance that a member of the House of Lords should make such insulting and disparaging remarks about a class of men whose representatives must have sat within the sound of his voice. It was like Governor Hammond, of South Carolina, the son of a wagon-maker, denouncing Northern mechanics as white slaves.

But, however we may smile at the way in which gentlemen, servants, lords, merchants, bankers, inn-keepers, and grocers are jumbled together in the American nomenclature, the misapplication of the important word which furnishes the heading for this chapter must excite most unpleasant feelings in all who observe the source from which the fondness for it springs.

I need scarcely state that the word "Aristocracy" means that form of government which places the supreme power in a privileged class, in fact, in *the nobles* of a country, and that it is consequently a word which designates a political, not a social grade. Now the United States not being yet graced, or cursed, with any orders of nobility, and not possessing any class that can be entitled to be called the best or greatest, it is manifestly impossible that they can contain an aristocracy. Even if any particular section of the people could get the government into its own hands for awhile, that section would not be an aristocracy, unless it were dignified by some titles of hereditary honour, or possessed certain exclusive privileges which might bring it under the meaning of the term. To call the wealthy citizens, who live in better houses and give better dinners than the people at large, the "aristocracy of America" is to give them a mere *sobriquet*, which carries no meaning beyond an absurd adaptation of a phrase that has with them no "local habitation."

It is not sufficient to entitle any set of merchants, manufacturers, or lawyers, to be called the aristocrats of a place, that they are the wealthiest men in it. The distinction due to either rank or birth, with some exclusive political privilege, is quite essential to constitute an aristocrat. Rank there is none in America, beyond that accorded to the temporary possession of some elective post, and birth entails no certain respect or regard. It is only valued while it is allied with money. Let but a family, however respectable its origin or connections, be deprived of its property, and it retains none of the public consideration. The individual who loses his fortune is despised, and in a generation or two the family name becomes a bye-word of contempt. A "poor gentleman" is a thing altogether unknown, in our acceptation of the term, even though the individual might have once kept a flourishing tavern or concocted sherry cobblers at its bar. Many persons have been pointed out to me who had formerly been in good circumstances, and admitted as a part of "the fashionable society," but for whom or their sons not a symptom of regard was shown, as soon as some unlucky speculation, or unlooked-for misfortune laid them low in worldly esteem.

This general callousness towards the unfortunate does not, however, always go the length of leaving them in destitution. I have known instances of contributions being raised among the mercantile classes for the wife and children of a man who was accidentally killed, or for one who had failed in trade. But the feeling that led to these donations was, I believe, an ostentatious, or at least a narrow one. Men of large means are proud to prove their wealth on such occasions ; but the public sympathy for a respectably born, but reduced family, is never shown, as far as I could learn, by spontaneous public subscriptions, or by conferring places of emolument or honour on its sons, even when they are qualified for such. They are, on the contrary, left to work their own way through life, and their name is rather a disadvantage to them, as it is coupled with the greatest stigma that can be attached to anyone in the United States—that of having been outwitted by the world.

All this proceeds from a total want of the pride of birth, a virtue (when not pushed to excess) that, on the one hand, sustains a man through a thousand trials and reverses, and, on the other, secures to him the generous respect of his fellow-citizens. Without this main impulse of chivalric feeling, there can assuredly be no sense of "aristocracy." Yet these people, who are utterly deficient in it, "prate of its whereabout," as the denizens of cities who never saw a paddock "babble of green fields."

But the yearnings in the United States for the vague aristocracy thus dreamt of is not unnatural, nor inconsistent with republican ideas. Almost all the great writers of antiquity, expressing no doubt the prevalent feeling of their times, were more inclined to aristocracy than democracy; and even Harrington, in (comparatively speaking) our own days, says, that "if any man founded a commonwealth, he was first a gentleman," which, he adds, that Oliver Cromwell was; showing, at any rate, his own fitness (or unfitness) for judging what constitutes a gentleman according to a high standard.

No family, as far as I can learn, has yet taken root in the public heart of America. No descendants of the heroes or sages of the Revolution, of the various presidents, or other leading men are now looked up to in honour of their name; nor are the sons or brothers of living *notabilities* considered as entitled, as a matter of course, to a preference for official station, or treated with any peculiar distinction. There is rather a prejudice against such nominations and such indications, and they are rarely heard of. A needy adventurer, in power himself, may now and then venture to give a post to one of his family, but his doing so rather tells against both the patron and the nominee.

It must be, on the other hand, remarked, that the children of a disreputable parent do not suffer in the public estimation from that cause. It is no bar to a man's preferment that his father was unworthy. This would seem to argue a generous forbearance in the public mind; but I regret to say I cannot trace it to that cause. I am rather inclined to attribute it to an indifference to disrepute, parallel to the evident want of appreciation of virtue. The natural repugnance to dishonour, any more than the instinctive veneration for respectability, which leads European minds to give credit for the merits, as well as to visit the sins of the fathers on the children, are no part of the good or the evil of American character. They seem to me essentially results of the spirit of feudalism; and they must, therefore, be co-existent with aristocratic tendencies. I am not, in stating these particulars, giving either blame or praise to the strong anti-aristocratic leaning which prevails, even in the minds of those who are very glad to consider themselves "American aristocrats." They are, in fact, altogether unaware that the pride of birth is the fundamental basis of an aristocracy; and if they hope to establish such an institution, at however remote an epoch, they must begin by encouraging feelings of liberal respect for the inheritor of an honourable name, and proving them by according him more consideration than they show for the tradesmen whose wealth places them in the front ranks of their "first men."*

Large landed possessions, with a train of dependent serfs or tenants, another absolute element of stability in the formation of an aristocracy, exist not at all in the northern or eastern portions of the United States; and are, in the west, coupled with certain drawbacks of inelegance in the possessors, that neutralise this effect. The rough-work of forest-clearing, or prairie-planting, brings all those western men to a level, which their particular number of acres does not at all affect. The coarse-clad settler who oversees his workmen, differs little in the eyes of the latter from themselves. And the squatter who claims a patch of land, considers himself as well worthy of regard as the purchaser of a district. Aristocratical institutions are

* A gentleman now living in Boston yearning for some distinctive claim to be considered aristocratical, went the length, as I was credibly informed, of petitioning the Legislature for permission to build a villa in the centre of the Common, and also for a bill to allow of his entailing some of his large property on his eldest son. I need scarcely add that neither project succeeded, but the individual contented himself with erecting a mansion fronting the Common, and which may be considered the finest house in Boston.

altogether incompatible with such a state of feeling in the majority of the community, and the mere ambition of a few wealthy individuals, who wish to consider themselves better than their fellows, is the only approach that can be found to the much envied gradation of rank which that minority longs for.

The slave-owners of the Southern States are certainly possessed of land and of human stock sufficient to give a *primâ facie* claim to aristocratic distinctions. But let that claim be tested by an examination of what constitutes an aristocracy, either in the modern European sense, or in that of the days of chivalry, and its pretensions are not tenable. The large proprietors of England and the nations of the Continent, with titles of nobility, broad domains, and a dependent peasantry, are not farmers of their own lands, except on a contracted scale for domestic wants, or for purposes of example and encouragement to their tenantry. Few if any of them make a profit, except in the receipt of rents; and their influence over those who cultivate their lands is of a purely political or moral nature, quite uncontaminated by physical power. An English nobleman of to-day can control the votes of his yeomanry, nothing more. A feudal baron of old could command the services of his vassals in war; and he had the power of life and death, with several revolting personal privileges. But coupled with the influence of the modern lord, or the by-gone *suzerain*, there is and was a sympathy between superior and dependent; a mutual reliance, a confidence on the one hand and a veneration on the other, forming the brightest colours in the arch of aristocratic institutions. There is something touching and elevating in the picture of a hero of chivalry arming his serfs to fight out his quarrel, leading them to battle, and feeling that his honours, his estates, his life, his all, are in the keeping of their courage. Even in the degenerate subserviency of the agricultural classes of the present time, the respect and affection which makes them the blind followers of their titled landlord's political creed, has something in it that comes home to the heart. But when we look at an American cotton-planter, or tobacco-grower, in the midst of his brutified and trembling slaves, how repugnant is the picture to our sense of all that is ennobling or affecting! Terrified for the results of the vile system of which he unfortunately forms a part, he dares not arm his creatures; no, nor even allow them to learn the meanest rudiments of knowledge. The dread of moral improvement is as great as that of physical force. No condition can be more humiliating than that of those slave owners, who cultivate their plantations by the double degradation of their slaves and of themselves; and who, declaring that the beings they breed, hire, and sell, are animals of an inferior race (the apology for their inhuman trade), become mere cattle-dealers, without any of the attributes of the nobility they would emulate.

And where—north, east, west, or south—may we look for that proud peculiarity of aristocracy, the large encouragement given to literature, art, and science? What individual in the whole Union fosters talent for its own sake, and is prodigal of his money in the purchase of its *chefs-d'œuvre?* A wealthy banker or broker may order his portrait or his bust, but which of them subscribes for a great national picture, or sends a promising artist at their expense to Rome, or pays a liberal price for a group of statuary? If those persons exist, I know them not; and if individual exceptions to the general ignorance of art, and niggard indifference to artists, are to be here and there found, most assuredly they would not, if united in any one American city, be enough to form a class.

Wanting, then, everything that really constitutes an aristocracy, how absurd is the application of the epithet to any portion of the citizens of America! Such an institution is essentially permanent, privileged, and powerful. No individual portion of the American institutions possesses *per se* permanency, privilege, or power. Their force and their stability exist only in union. Not one of the component parts of their constitution taken singly could stand alone for a day. An oligarchy might be claimed as their birthright by a clique, with just as much justice as an "aristocracy," founded merely on purse-right, can be asserted to exist in any country on earth. Let the citizens of the United States mark it specially in their vocabulary, as being a term that cannot bear any possible application to themselves. And, for the happiness of the masses which are spreading so fast over the immense Republic, let it be hoped that the thing which the word really designates may never be transplanted thither from Europe, where it is indigenous and congenial.

The nobility of England, which is really the class to which those ambitious Americans would claim a similitude, forms a picture at once the most graceful and dazzling that civilisation can present. The elegance of style and suavity of manner, the intellectual culture, the patronage of talent, the profuse expenditure, the self-confidence arising from security of social position, and the air of superiority in those who have great power as their inheritance, are but items in a combination nowhere to be paralleled. To be born an integral part of this system is, perhaps, the most fortunate accident that could befall a man. To be admitted to it by the monarch's creation is a just object of ambition. To look upon the very large majority of its members with involuntary respect, is natural. But for those who do not possess one of its distinguishing traits — jackdaws with a mere mockery of peacock's plumage—to assume a tone which they fancy an imitation of it, is indeed a painful, yet a ludicrous spectacle. Often and often have we to smile, albeit with a dash of sadness in our hearts, at the servile tricks of some of what are emphatically called the English "gentry," in their frog-in-the-fable attempts to vie with the "nobility," and to prove themselves distinct from the "public in general." Manifold are the instances of self-prostration, of wriggling like human eels through the social slime, to gain admission into that pure stream of *haut ton*, where the titled aristocrat disports. But viewing the real elegance of high life in England, and knowing that it is endowed with almost every attribute that entitles men to distinction, some excuse may be made for those who, being its worshippers, would become if they could themselves a portion of it. We at once pity, and almost pardon them. And if the evils of an aristocracy were confined merely to such humiliations to the class immediately below it in the social scale, we should not only be satisfied to retain the institution intact, but we should be glad to promote its establishment elsewhere. But when we see the cruel consequences that have followed in its train, the misery of the millions over whom it exercises its influence, and the corruption which is the very essence of its existence, we would gladly dispense with all its glories to escape from the ills with which they are coupled. We, however, admit that the social system of England being established, and nobility being one of its firmest pillars, the attempt to remove it would assuredly imperil the whole structure of society. The hardiest hater of our nobility will not venture to stigmatise it as wholly bad. Its splendid redeeming qualities are too evident to admit of cavil. And the true philanthropist and patriot, who strikes boldly at abuse, will nevertheless be cautious not to drag down the stem, whose roots he would disentangle and whose branches he would prune. Aristocracy is an integral part of the genius of English character, and if the whole is to be preserved, the parts must rest uninjured.

Let Reformers, then, true to the meaning of their appellation, their mission, and their creed, be satisfied to alter what they could not, if they would, destroy. Let them take the real road towards improvement, and begin at the right end. Let them cultivate the inferior classes of society, by throwing education broadcast across the land, by teaching just and wholesome lessons to the masses, and, in giving them instruction, give them its inseparable concomitant, power. And as surely as that great plan of enlightenment goes on, so surely will the work of aristocratical reforms come into simultaneous play. Action and re-action will take place successively by the laws of morals as certainly as by those of physics. While the middle-class Reformers are teaching the lower orders to *think*, the upper ranks will inevitably begin to *feel*. The truth which is gradually penetrating into one portion of the social structure, will suddenly flash its light into the other. While it glimmers in the cellars it will illuminate the dome, and then and then only the real and rational progress of improvement will commence. While the heretofore ignorant boor, or half-taught artisan, is slowly learning lessons of political wisdom, and gaining a gradual knowledge of what are truly the rights of man in society, the arrogant noble will see the same truth with the instinctive perspicacity of an awakened intellect. The privileged few will rush onwards to meet the enfranchised many, until both extremes shall touch in the just medium of demands and concessions, which, without unwisely destroying or unduly elevating, will in all human probability conduce to the common happiness of all. To this domestic balance of power we may look forward as the result of English good sense and good feeling ; but the state of things which has led me to this train of thought has no existence in America, and most cordially do I trust that it may never be established there.

The error most manifest at both sides of the Atlantic with respect to America, is that of viewing its institutions in comparison with those of England. None of the hasty travellers from the Old World seem capable of looking at the New in an aspect of separate existence. They seem to consider both as parts of the same system, political and social. This would be all very well if they bent their thoughts to the examination of mere character—for human nature everywhere presents certain characteristics in common. But although the same kind of human beings are to be found in the Old and New World, the systems which they have formed for themselves, and which in their turn tend to fix, if not actually to form, their characters, are totally different. Yet the American seems at times as much at fault as the European in this respect. If the latter sees in American civilisation only its discrepancies compared with that which he left at the other side of the ocean, the former too often considers it as susceptible of the same regulations, while in fact it is utterly distinct, and as opposite as it is distinct. A totally different order of things is produced from two separate stocks having many resemblances, but not more than varieties of fruits or flowers of a different species, agreeing in certain generic elements with those on which they are artificially grafted.

Europeans who would rightly judge the working of things in America should look at it as though they had never seen Europe, and Americans should manage their country as though Europeans never could come to look at it. Invidious comparisons on the one hand, and a servile emulation on the other, are the consequences of an impracticable standard being set up. But, erroneous as this general method of judging undoubtedly is, it is more pardonable in the man born and bred in European habits of thought and feeling than in him who knows nothing of those habits but from reading or hearsay, and who ought to be superior to a paltry imitation. The great mass of the American people are, no doubt, free from the reproach I would convey to still a large minority, and one unluckily formed of individuals filling the foremost ranks among the intellect and influence of the country. That the leading classes in social position, as well as the chief leaders in political life, are infected deeply with this disease of European tendencies is a truism established and admitted. Very lamentable is it that it should be so ; for, by setting up a model they can so poorly imitate, and measuring themselves by a standard disproportioned to their growth, they make the most awkward mistakes, and cut the most *outré* figure. This argues a great want of independence ; and it proves the scarcity of original minds in the wealthier orders throughout the country.

Were a well established national self-reliance felt among the leading men in the United States, there would be none of the melancholy parodies of "High Life," none of the yearnings after aristocratical distinctions, which are now so flagrant. Men would then strike out some new plan of social organisation, and act up to it, even though it clashed with the scheme of polity in force elsewhere. However defective that plan might be, it would be, if it were only consistent with existing institutions, better for the country than the best of any other country which was adopted at second hand, and forced into a system with which it had no fitness.

Were I disposed to follow up the subject of these general remarks with minute details of personal observation, I might make a very amusing chapter; but I have no wish to trace invidious instances, or to give offence to individuals. These pages may possibly some day meet the eyes of many of those members of "fashionable society," those pseudo-aristocrats, at whose pretensions I have often smiled. And small as the annoyance might be of seeing themselves held up individually to censure, I do not wish to add that item to the mass of troubles created by their efforts to make themselves more than circumstances allow them to become. The struggle to maintain their mock dignity is in itself painful enough. And the worst part of it is the incapacity it produces for the enjoyment of the many advantages they possess. If they could be reasonably satisfied with their position and liberally expend their wealth, and if the honest respect of their fellow-citizens were enough for them, there is nowhere a class of people having truer elements of happiness than the rich inhabitants of the American cities. No real good of life, suited to their condition, is beyond their reach. They may have education, accomplishments, luxuries, and refinement. They may relieve distress, foster talent, encourage the arts, ornament their native places, and perform enduring acts of beneficence. But these nobler paths of emulation are too wide for them to walk in. They require the narrower ways of a niggard ostentation, in which they may meet no obstruction from the vulgar herd. They must, forsooth, be exclusive to become happy. They must stand aloof or move apart. Their small clique must have an orbit of its own, round which the meaner beings of the social system ought, they think, to circulate, looking for light and warmth to *their* great brilliancy. Nor are they content with mere social distinction, which is on all hands liberally allowed to them. They pant for political privileges, for corrupt influence, for domination, for all, in a word, that ages and the force of things have gradually conferred on the nobility of England. But in one respect they quite misunderstand the home influence of English aristocracy. They think it is accorded to their *titles*, while it is, in fact, founded on their power. Mere nobility without landed property is of small weight. There are, of course, some little minds which shrink into a still lesser compass at the mere title or the look of a lord. But the community in general measure a peer by his possessions and his patronage, and are prone to lean heavily upon one whose poverty places him in the falsest of false positions. No class of Americans being possessed *per se* of political or territorial power, it is sheer absurdity for them to suppose that any creation of titles, any more than their widely lavished one of "Honourable," could of itself confer any real influence.

They are, however, shrewd enough to know that it is at any rate impossible to obtain the object of ambition suddenly. They are aware that it must, if attainable at all, be the work of time; that generations must pass over first. But they make a compromise, as it were, with the future ; and, in the hope of their visions being some day or other realised, they sacrifice a thousand attainable delights, some of which I have just enumerated, for the untenable assumption of a species of superiority which the people at large will not concede to them. Social distinction is a matter of convention. The consent of all the various portions of society is required for its establishment. It is not enough for an individual or a class to say I am, or we are, superior to the rest, if the rest refuse to confirm the dictum. The natural good sense of mankind acknowledges the necessity of distinctions in society suited to the circumstances which should regulate its existence. The labourer, the mechanic, the shop-keeper, and the more elevated gradations of the scale adapted to a republic, readily admit the propriety of each class, generally speaking, associating among itself. And the spread of education teaches that self-respect which makes each one satisfied with its own position, even while the individuals who compose it use all their energy to raise themselves into that immediately above them. Even if the less wealthy, and consequently less refined grades, were dissatisfied with the superior influence of the more elevated, they could not prevent its existence. An inherent sentiment tells all men of common sense that social equality cannot exist in a high state of civilisation and in a large community. Small companies composed of enthusiastic persons may try the question on a narrow scale, and conform themselves, for singularity's sake, to the inconveniences of a temporary equality. There was one of those little bands of theorists established for a short time within a few miles of Boston ; it soon failed, and the wildest speculators have, I believe, given up the notion of any wholesale working of such experiments, which must not be confounded with the broad and philosophical, but still untried schemes of Fourier.* Therefore it is that the mass of the American people do not grudge to their foremost men all those reasonable distinctions which the hindermost have themselves the hope of reaching, at least in a graduated scale of chances.

It is, then, only when the class which assumes to itself the title "aristocracy" infringes on the sound doctrines of practical republicanism, and either openly or covertly attempts to undermine them, that the people at large may be considered at variance with their pretensions. And the events of late years have clearly established the faint chance of those pretenders to a triumph in the contest they have provoked.

Certain people are constantly complaining in America of the hardness of their fate in not being able to enjoy themselves becomingly, of a sense of social thraldom, and the like grievances. On inquiring into the situation and circumstances of these grumblers, I always found that they are the children of men who have made large fortunes by trade or speculation, and that they themselves are without any fixed profession or given object. They have all ample means for the enjoyments of life on a scale of reasonable comfort, and many of them are rich. Wherefore, then, this dissatisfaction? Why this morbid imagining of ill? It is nothing more nor less than the longing for an impossibility, on the part of these miscalculating persons. Conscious that they never can obtain the privileges of British nobility, they yet fancy themselves entitled to an analogous station in their own country, and

* If I recollect rightly, Fourier made it an especial request, or at least expressed the hope that the American community might not be that which brought his theories into practice.

think that, by professing a contempt for all classes but their own, they acquire a sort of spurious distinction.

One scarcely knows whether to be angry or grieved at this painful perversion of the reasoning faculty, in beings well educated, and possessing all the advantages of a respectable position. There is probably no misfortune of life greater than that of fixing for oneself an unattainable standard. If a man enters upon a particular profession, its highest honours ought to be the object of his energies. In his struggle he gains at every step a new accession of honour, as the eagle's plumage becomes brighter the higher he flies. And even falling far short of the goal, he sinks with dignity, sustained in his descent by the force of the emulation which bore him up. But when an American strains through the long vista of conventional distinctions which form the social system of England, and for none of which he is qualified while he yearns for all, he presents a pitiful picture of mean ambition.

The individuals in question have seen entertained in their father's houses some English gentlemen, and a stray Lord now and then. Knowing their fathers to be the wealthiest, and consequently the "first men" in their locality, to use the national phraseology, they are satisfied that they are in all ways entitled to rank with the "first men" of other countries; and forgetting the value of their own institutions, they think but of the privileges or the titles of the foreigner, and ascribe to their want of those distinctions the self-inferiority of which they have a painful consciousness. "Did we but live in a country," argue they, "where a man's merits, industry, and talent give him a chance of rising above the vulgar mass, where honours follow wealth, and public services lead to privilege, then indeed we might be happy—but here we are nothings, nobodies. We cannot herd with the rabble, we will not submit to their control. What then is left for us? a perpetual struggle against mob influence, or a hopeless obscurity for the sake of peace!"

It would be impossible to convince these *reasoners* that they have no "discourse of reason;" that they make all their sufferings for themselves; and that they have a thousand blessings in their reach which they will not condescend to enjoy. It is unlucky for them, indeed, that they know anything of England, except her language and literature. If they have happened to cross the Atlantic, and have seen the outside glitter and pomp of English high life, or have made acquaintanceship with the middle classes, they know nothing of the grovelling vanity which, alas! so often degrades a portion of the one into a servile mimicry of the other. As to the misery of the inferior orders, their eyes cannot view it aright, nor their minds duly reflect on it. They only look upwards as they walk along, and their sight is consequently dazzled by the blaze. If they have hurriedly travelled on the continent of Europe, they are mostly ignorant of the languages and the social economy of the different nations; and they come back to America without any wholesome acquisition of knowledge, and filled with a vague admiration of the very peculiarities in the "mother country" which, though in keeping with its institutions, are of all others those which are most unfitted to their own. Knowing the hopelessness of expecting to establish such an order of things as they so vainly sigh for, these persons would remove to Europe, and there be content to gaze on what they cannot belong to, were it not from their ostentatious delight in telling over what they have seen in the Old World, and in making disparaging comparisons with what they find at home. The false importance arising from this is their only consolation. But that falls far short of gratifying their pretensions; and they are in the midst of many sources of mortification.

The main defect of this unhappy class is that lack of independence of mind, which I have so often noticed in individuals, and the want of originality of thought so palpable in the people at large. If, instead of fixing on the higher orders of England as a standard of imitation, they had the courage to establish a style of their own—if, instead of desiring to engraft the usages of a Monarchy and the manners of a Court on the rough stem of Republican forms, they would foster a frank and generous simplicity in word and deed, they might be very happy, softening by their example the manners of the people, and soothing them into a gradual refinement. But by their present course they do nothing but mischief. They excite for themselves contempt and enmity; and they become the medium through which the unkind or angry feeling of the mass towards England is in a certain degree justified. These pretenders are looked upon as so many personifications of British arrogance and conceit. They are considered as having imbibed all their faults abroad; and home-merits are proudly contrasted with them. England is sure to sink in this scale of comparison; and the inflated pride of those who adopt it puffs them up into a vain and prejudiced population.

There are two facts to which the wealthier portion of the wealthy class of America seems to be blind. First, that there exists a high order of civilisation and even "fashion" (their darling word) easier of adoption than the fastidious elegance of English high life; and that this is to be found in the manners and habits of the upper circles in France, Germany, and the other countries of Europe. Secondly, that even if it were possible to establish an aristocracy in America, it would be incompatible with the existence of the Republic. Exotic plants can grow only in a hot-house. A Lord could not live long without a congenial atmosphere. And to enable an order of nobility to exist, there must be not only an ambient air of popular homage, but a vivifying source of light and heat above, to draw up the dews, that come down again in fertilising showers of dignity and honour.

If some of the American aspirants for aristocratic station would strip this metaphor into plain sense, and ponder over the truth it is meant to illustrate, their yearnings might be modified into simple regret. Admitting their hopes to be impossibilities, they might in time become satisfied that what is must be. And viewing the state of things in England rather as warnings than examples, be content to enjoy in their own country a system of equalised well-being that has no parallel on earth.

CHAPTER XIII.

POLITICAL ULTRAS.

False teaching of the People by Public Men—Truths which they should teach—Great Happiness of the Country—The Paradise of Mediocrity—Democracy best suited to the American People—Its Defects in Practice.

IN the preceding chapter I pointed out the mistaken ambition of a class of social malcontents. I must now advert to the fatal obstinacy of a band of political Ultras, who, instead of bending to the general principles of democracy, wage a constant and hopeless war against them. They resemble those uprooted trees which struggle in the waves of some great river, with just force enough to trouble the waters that sweep them onwards. Were those men endowed with an enlarged conception of their own institutions, were they satisfied to be of the people from whom they stand apart, to give them good counsel, to guide, and to inform them, they would become the benefactors of their country instead of being its bane.

I maintain that the people of America are the most clear-sighted and intelligent in the world; the easiest to be reasoned with, the readiest to comprehend the truth; simply because they are the most independent, and the least warped by the conflicts of classes. With those qualifications, they must be the most likely to adopt the right, if it were rightly explained to them. But a rabid opposition to the rational tenets of republicanism, and constant efforts to raise a structure of aristocratical distinctions, on a foundation with which they do not harmonise, inflame the masses into a more exaggerated democracy than their sober sense would warrant.

Such a people, knowing their power, but ignorant of its proper uses—for no great mass of men can be instinctively imbued with the philosophy of self-government—requires instruction, and are entitled to it, at the hands of the more educated portions of the community. If these portions would talk the true language of enlightenment, plain, straightforward and manly, the people would be sure to understand and listen to their advice. If their example instilled honour, integrity, and truth into the public mind, I am satisfied that a rich soil is there ready to receive it, and to give back a tenfold return. A just knowledge of the advantages of America, and a fair appreciation of those of other countries, would at once expand and strengthen the national understanding. But overstrained comparisons of their own merits with the defects of foreign nations, lead to a very mistaken estimate of both. Were the people taught that their peculiar form of government is good as adapted to them, but would be full of mischief if forced on other communities, they would respect it for its true value, and give a due consideration to that existing elsewhere. It is the false representations of writers, lecturers, and demagogues, that keep their readers and listeners ignorant. When the people are told, by their loudest and loftiest authorities, that republicanism is alone worthy of mankind; that all monarchs are tyrants, and all subjects slaves; that the adoption of Democracy, immediate and unqualified, is essential to the well-being of the world at large;

that they who enjoy it now are alone "great, glorious, and free," and that "their principles are making the conquest of the world,"* can we be surprised at their prejudices in favour of their own institutions, and against ours?

Let it be considered how very few of the American community have the opportunity of travelling in Europe, how short a time those who go there remain, how insufficient are their means for scanning its political and social state, how strong the force of their early impressions, how feeble the lights that fall on, but cannot penetrate them—and we shall not be astonished at the prevalence of false opinions, even on what they have seen and heard, but cannot be said to have *known.* And of course these opinions, which I am now supposing to be candid and conscientious, are still more erroneously adopted by those who receive them at second-hand, and who, making a virtue of an impossibility, pride themselves on not having mixed with the errors and crimes of those foreign lands which circumstances have debarred them from visiting. Such persons have a pious conviction that their home morality is good, in a direct ratio with their exaggerated idea of the vices they believe to abound abroad; and thus, fair-minded individuals—and of them the mass is formed—acquire the most mistaken notions of other countries and of their own. They look at both through a magnifying lens, instead of the naked eye.

An influential body of men, chosen from among those of superior attainments throughout the Union, furnish the different grades of the diplomatic service in Europe; and their opinions have naturally great weight in America. I must, however, remark, that the private communications

* Speech of Mr. Dallas, the American Minister, at the dinner given, July 5, 1858, by the AMERICAN ASSOCIATION, at the London Tavern.

sent home by those persons are confined to a close circle of relatives and friends ; and even to them are generally most guarded and cautious. The universal awe of public opinion, the fear that a liberal word in praise of foreign manners might be converted, by too ready enemies or over-sensitive partisans, into a sentence of disparagement against their contrasts at home, blunt the points of their pens while they are absent, and more than half close their lips when they return. The private correspondence and conversation of the most talented American diplomatists offer less of true information on what they have learned during their mission, than can be well believed by those who have not seen their letters or listened to their discourse.

Not one in a hundred of this class has the boldness and the energy to tell the truth to the people. Subserviency to their passions, instead of appeals to their intelligence, is certainly the characteristic of the large majority of public men, and of all political parties. They have no reliance on their own power ; no faith in the virtue of the mass. They therefore labour to make the latter what they are themselves ; and having moulded an idol in their own image, they see in its unworthiness a conscience-whispered illustration of their own.

The harsh and virulent tone of the newspapers respecting Europe in general, and particularly as regards England, is calculated to produce intense error in the great body of the population, who are too prone to take all they read for granted, and who have no means of sifting the unfair statements of the press. It may therefore be safely said, that almost all public men in America —speakers, writers, legislators, ministers—are engaged in a negative, but wide-spread conspiracy, to foster the prejudices, warp the minds, and blind the judgments of the people at large.

The truths that should be told to the people of America by their men of authority and influence are what I here tell them, without any claim of authority or any hope of influence—that to be great, they must frame a model of greatness adapted to themselves alone; and that they must discard from their mind altogether the wish to rival other nations, in forms unsuited to their own political institutions, their social habits, wants, and capabilities.

They should be taught that their geographical position, the immense extent of their territory, their unbounded means of support for a numerous population, the spread of education, the political equality, the pride of independence, the spirit of that liberty which they fought for and won; make them, by instinct as well as by institutions, entirely unfitted for those forms which suit the cramped but refined communities of the old world. They should learn that Providence has given them a country and a constitution, in which physical and moral combinations are beautifully blended, for the welfare of many millions of human beings, provided they will understand, in a spirit of humble gratitude, the goods which God has showered on them. They should know that the concurrent testimonies of the wisest men pronounce the state of midway enjoyment, between the voluptuousness of high station and the miseries of low life, as the best and happiest for mankind; that they themselves are in possession of that very state, without excessive wealth, and free from pinching want; untrammeled by the gorgeousness of monarchy, untempted by feudal pomp, uncursed by pauperism; and that thus the free population of the United States is the wholesale realisation of that desideratum, so longed for by the ardent philanthropists of Europe.

With thankfulness to Heaven the people of America should understand all this. But they should also know, that if to possess these advantages be a blessing, if it be a duty to preserve them, their permanent security must arise, not merely from the conviction that a loftier order of civilisation is not in keeping with their institutions, but that it is incompatible with their own nature, that it is, in fact, beyond their reach.

A thousand illustrations might be given, to impress these truths upon the American people. Many arguments might be urged—and some may be found scattered through this book—to prove them. They rise up on every hand. The United States is designed by God's destiny for the greatest well-being of the greatest number; but that well-being is to be found in a simple, economical existence, which makes the country a paradise of mediocrity, but of nothing more. Genuine Democracy can produce nothing more. To be consistent with itself, it wants nothing more for its disciples than a medium quality in mind and manners, respectability of talent, moderate acquirements, unpresuming tastes ; no meretricious ornaments nor luxurious displays ; homely living, plain attire, industry, integrity, and truth. These are, as I understand the question, the component parts of the social and political system alone suited to the United States of America. Let Democracy, then, stand rooted there and flourish, like the tree of life. Let no offshoot of Royalty, or its associate honors, be grafted on its stem ; no shields of pretence be hung upon its branches. Let its blossoms and fruits be unmixed with foreign flowers or artificial essences. Let those who bask under its broad canopy be content with its protecting shade, nor seek the glare of distinctions which would but bring their unfitness into grotesque and disparaging relief.

If the wealthy classes of the American people would do great service to the country, they must renounce their ambitious aspirations, and gradually sink into that state of decent distinction, which is sure to be accorded to the possessors of education and the moderate elegancies of life. If, instead of rolling up the hill the huge and still-returning stone of hopeless pretension, they would remove the few pebbles that obstruct their path, they would become ten times happier, and a thousand times more respectable than they are. It is really pitiable to witness their present course of self-inflicted torment, and of desperate public mischief. Individual instances illustrate, and very often explain, great public principles. I will therefore mention, that within a stone's-throw of each other in the city of Boston, (perhaps it would require a sling to reach the utmost extent of the circle involved) there live the sons of three grocers—all of different names—two brothers who themselves kept retail tape and thread-shops, two others who were working farmer's boys ; a man who was a journeyman printer ; another the cabin boy of a ship, and several others of like origin, who, not content with their present position of great wealth and respectability, are imbued with the most ludicrous spirit of what they call "aristocratical distinction." These mistaken individuals, and others of their kind, despise the people from whom they are sprung, loath democratic principles which have fostered their fortunes, and sigh for the enjoyment of lordly associations. If a foreigner of title visits America, they are ready to lay themselves at his feet. They boast of their intimacy, and they at times strive to prove it by a familiarity, vulgar in this case, but which they rarely use towards each other where it would be becoming. I have heard a couple of attorneys, call by his name, but without his title of courtesy, (as one might say, "How d'ye do, Smith? Jones, will you drink wine with me?") the eldest son of an Earl, himself an ex-cabinet minister of England. And, in another instance, I knew one of the quondam tape-sellers above alluded to, boast that, "he and (Lord) A. sat together and talked matters over, man to man, as equals ought to do." This deplorable presumption is wide-spread among the "fashionable society" of the American cities. Tainted with this longing after nobility, and with a belief in their own fitness to mix on equal terms with its highest ranks, they have no sympathy with their fellow plebeians, to stand aloof from whose companionship is their greatest pride.* Yet these persons, as I have elsewhere remarked, are conscious of the fruitlessness of the struggle which consumes them. But I verily believe they are not aware of its being the great primary cause of the evils it is opposed to. For that there are serious evils existing in the administration of democratic principles is too true: and I proceed to point out some of them.

Being firmly convinced that Democracy, as purely

* I once asked an American lady who had been in England, and had formed a chance acquaintanceship with a few persons of title, if she ever gave them in her correspondence sketches of the different ways of life in America, as compared with those of Europe? "Oh, no," replied she, "it would be of no use. The manners of persons of refinement are the same in all countries." "Very true, said I. But I could not help remarking (to myself) that we were at the moment sitting on the bench before a country ale-house where the lady was lodging for the summer, three or four coarse men drinking, chewing tobacco, *et cetera*, within a few feet of us; and the lady's sister, a great ornament of American "fashionable society," walking towards us with some "beaux" and "belles"—all reeking from the effects of an August match at nine-pins, in a bowling alley hard by.

administered as may be consistent with human imperfection, is the form of government best suited to the American people, I am satisfied that its excesses are in a great measure the consequence of the undue opposition it meets from the Whig party, under whatever designation that disjointed party may assume.

The Democrats, incensed at its inconsiderate efforts to create a separate political class, instead of being satisfied with the gradations of social life in one great and united community, are provoked into a furious disregard of *all* the measures of their opponents. Many of these would be, if wisely worked out, great blessings to the country. But turned as they have been into instruments of misrule, injuring the people at large, and benefiting only individual capitalists and corporate bodies, they have become odious to the Democrats, who confound the action of the machine with the principles on which it is formed, and reject a whole system from disgust at its abuses.

This may be called a primary symptom of disease in the body politic of American democracy. And this having been checked, by the failure of their opponents' plans, the secondary symptoms break out, in the shape of an inveterate determination to frame measures of deep mischief, merely because they are violent contrasts to those they have succeeded in defeating. *Medio tutissimus ibis* is a maxim they will not understand. Escaping Scylla, they are swallowed by Charybdis. I wish I had less hackneyed illustrations at hand; and still more, that the cases were less frequent to which they may be applied. But they are so abundant, that in enumerating some, I run the risk of being thought to exclude the rest, although all are equally palpable.

I must here remark, that many questions of vital importance are not exclusively party questions. The leaders on either side often agree on some of those, when their followers are much divided in opinion. Personal interests have naturally great influence on these "open questions." And the wild fluctuations in individual opinions make it difficult to fix on what are, or are not, steady points of agreement with the separate parties.

As examples of the open questions alluded to, I may mention the veto power possessed by the President of the Union, in common with the Governors of the Several States; and the right of re-election to his high office, for a second term, on the expiration of the first, of four years' duration.

Passing by all consideration of the Veto Power, that most important, complicated, and questionable privilege, I can speak with more confidence on the subject of the re-election of the President, and say without hesitation, that it is one of the most positive evils that afflict the country. From the very first day a President enters on his duties, ay even before his inaugural address is delivered, he begins a system of electioneering, designed and deliberate, and even if he has the tact to conceal it, nothing restrains his partisans from openly proceeding to the work. The President, therefore, elected by a party, is a party leader; and when its conduct degenerates into factious proceedings he becomes the head of a faction. This is, indeed, the inevitable condition of his lot. No man placed in that elevated position could venture to indulge in any feeling of magnanimity, if peradventure he possessed any such, or a generous forbearance towards a political opponent, or a sense of justice as between political sects. The President cannot afford to forget the wrongs done to him as an individual. His personal prejudices do not become merged in his official duties. If even his own ambition be satisfied by the one election which has gained him his four years' tenure of power, the honour of his party, to say nothing of their interests, is at stake; and for their sake, if not for his own, he is pledged to labour for his re-election. Scarcely any man, however, can resist on his own account alone the temptation of retaining as long as possible the rank that places him on a level with crowned heads, that gives his family precedence by courtesy in the European courts, that fills his hands with home patronage, makes him the free tenant of the finest house, and gives him the enjoyment of the largest income in the country; for scarcely any other man could venture, in the teeth of public watchfulness and envy, to spend on his mere living 5000*l.* a-year. It is true that Harrison avowed, and that Tyler pretended to, an objection to re-election. But had the first lived long enough, his party would no doubt have induced him to withdraw his avowal; while the latter within two years of his expressed determination to serve but for one term, was notoriously labouring, through every imaginable means, to create a party, in opposition to the Whigs whom he betrayed, and the Democrats who rejected him, for the purpose of securing his second nomination.

This attempt on the part of Mr. Tyler and his few friends forms a curious episode in the political history of the country. It produced instances of the most flagrant abandonment of party by certain public men, and a defiance of principle by the party they seceded from. The Whigs *en masse* at this epoch (1843) cut a most deplorable figure, split up, divided, disjointed; their majority in the Congress dissolved in April of that year, having effected nothing good for the country or creditable to themselves during a long session; and several of their foremost men, such as Webster, Spencer, Wise, and Cushing, having altogether abjured their political creed, either from views of personal preferment, or jealousy of the master spirit of their old party, Henry Clay.

Tyler by his vetos of the several bills for the re-establishment of a National Bank, sent up to him by rather large majorities of the Whig Congress, under Clay's dictation, no doubt saved the Union from a great convulsion. But in this he gained little personal credit, and lost the confidence of all parties. He had the misfortune to do a really great thing without acquiring the reputation of a great man.

The right of re-election for a second term, objectionable as it is, can be defended on some plausible grounds, one of which, mentioned by De Tocqueville, is that "it may inspire the President with the hope of carrying into execution, undertakings for the public good." But the strongest point in its favour is that Washington, having established the practice of declining a *third* election, and all his successors having followed his example, a compromise of the question seems to be admitted; and the chances of one re-election are increased, as it is a measure which would practically exclude the individual from ever again entering the lists.

The result of President Buchanan's professed reluctance to being elected for even a second term is yet to be seen. Those who know him, and have observed his political career, will be scarcely surprised to see him again in the field in 1860. The Ultras of his party are already, in 1858, preparing the public for such a movement.

CHAPTER XIV.

DANIEL WEBSTER.

Public meeting of Welcome—Mr. Webster's Speech—Concealment of truth by Public men—Dinner given to Mr. Webster—Explanatory Speech at the Dinner—General view of his Career—Comparison with O'Connell—The Harrisburg Convention—Death of Mr. Webster.

My first meeting with Mr. Webster was in London, in June 1839. Having received a letter of introduction for him, addressed to Boston, where I had hoped to deliver it, but finding that he had reached England when I was on the point of sailing, I called upon him at his hotel. The impression this interview made on me was, that I had never seen a man whose physical appearance conveyed such evidence of intellectual power. Besides, I was greatly pleased with his manner. Without being polished, there was an air in it that seemed derived from a consciousness of superiority, rather than from any training in a school of good-breeding. Webster's whole look and tone were massive, but not heavy. His personal bulk was relieved by the fine expression of his countenance. His brilliant eyes, deep set, and overhung by large brows and a lofty forehead, shone like the signal lights of genius.

When I called on him a dignitary of the church was sitting with him, and had he desired a contrast to bring out his own fine bearing into effective relief he could not have better chosen; the patronising, yet somewhat sycophantic tone of his reverend visitor being the very antithesis of his own.

Half an hour's conversation, chiefly on America, gave me a good deal of information for my guidance on my arrival there. Mr. Webster offered me some letters for Boston (which he however forgot to send to me), and in all he said he impressed me with a conviction in his good sense, the only quality he had then any opportunity of displaying. I asked him if he meant to visit Ireland? He replied that it had not at all entered into his plan; that he greatly regretted being obliged to go even to Paris, for his wish was to devote himself entirely to England, the great, indeed the sole object of interest to him in Europe. I was asked to meet him at a party the following day, but I was obliged to leave town; and, sailing for New York within a week, my next meeting with him was in Boston, in November of the same year.

On his return from his voyage his fellow-citizens were naturally very anxious to hear what he thought of Europe, and of England in particular; besides which, they wished to have his opinion on the subject of the recent election in Massachusetts, the results of which were not just then definitively known, but which were pretty generally conjectured by the Whig party to have been unfavourable to their candidate, Edward Everett. He was, however, still in his place as Governor, which he had held for four or five years, until the votes should undergo the strict scrutiny of a committee of the legislature. It was decided to call a meeting of the Whig members and citizens at large to welcome Mr. Webster and hear his sentiments on Old and New England. The hall in which the House of Representatives holds its sittings was chosen, and a due announcement was made of the projected meeting.

Governor Everett, with his usual kindness, gave me notice of it, and took me with him on the evening appointed. We found Mr. Webster in one of the ante-rooms surrounded by political friends. He received me very cordially. I spoke but a few words to him, just to welcome him and introduce my son; but I thought his whole air and manner to those who pressed round and conversed with him was as different as was possible from the unembarrassed frankness which had struck me so much in London. He seemed ponderous, consequential, and constrained. He gave me the notion of an actor studying one part while he was playing another. His mind seemed absorbed in the consideration of what he was about to say to the public, while he spoke to his friends as though he was giving them merely words, not thoughts. In a very short time the hour for opening the meeting arrived, and Mr. Webster, preceded by the Speaker of the House of Representatives, Robert C. Winthrop, and followed by Governor Everett, and a large group of personal friends, advanced into the hall.

The scene was impressive from its strange mixture of gloom and animation. The room is a handsome and convenient one. The member's benches are raised one above the other in a semicircular form. There are two galleries, and the chair of the Speaker is on a raised platform, with seats at either side for clerks and secretaries. Every place was full, and all the standing room occupied. I dare say there were altogether 1500 persons. In the chair was Mr. King, the President of the Senate, all the members of that body and of the House of Representatives, which was then in session at Boston, being present, and the rest of the auditory was composed of the citizens at large. Immense applause hailed Mr. Winthrop's announcement of Webster's approach; and when I got within the body of the house, all this boisterous enthusiasm seemed at first as though it proceeded from a hidden audience; so wretchedly was the place lighted by a few scattered lamps stuck here and there against the walls, that it was impossible to distinguish a face at ten yards distance. While the cheering went on this was rather exciting than depressing, from the wild solemnity it threw on the scene. But when that ceased it was inconceivably unpleasant.

Mr. King opened the proceedings in a short, animated, and appropriate address of welcome to the returned traveller; and, among other things, said truly that "No private individual had ever met a more distinguished reception in a foreign land than Mr. Webster had been honoured with in the mother country." This preface being over, the hero of the scene took his station on the platform close beside the President's chair, and commenced his speech.

He began heavily and coldly. His voice was loud and sonorous, but neither deep nor musical. Its tone bore no proportion to the appearance or the gestures of the man: it was like an insufficient sound proceeding from a splendid looking instrument. It filled the hall, but did not sink into the heart. I was disappointed; but I said to myself, "Wait, wait awhile for the sense, never mind the sound. What a fine opportunity is there now for a just picture of English generosity, hospitality, and appreciation of merit. With what gratitude will he speak of the kindness he received—how skilfully he will disclaim its being shown out of consideration for him—how soothingly will he say that it was from respect for the country of which he was considered the representative—how beautifully will he improve this opportunity of drawing closer the ties which bind the people together—what a link will he this night show himself to be in the chain of social and political sympathies, which, in spite of every discrepancy, joins the two great members of the Anglo-Saxon family!"

I did wait awhile—a short while. I was not kept long in suspense. After a few phrases of acknowledgment for his warm reception that evening, he said, turning to the President, with cold and callous utterance; "Yes, sir, I met with attention and civility in England. I observed closely various points in which there was a resemblance between that country and ours, particularly the system of agriculture, which you, sir, as a farmer, would appreciate." He then proceeded to assure the meeting that in some things English farming was equal to American, in some things inferior; and with that ended every allusion to his voyage, to his visit, or to the great country which had literally showered its hospitalities on him for four or five consecutive months. He turned to local politics, and talked about currency, banking, and electioneering, for an hour or more. I can truly say that I never was more disappointed in a public display. Webster was, all through, like a great bird whose body was too big for its feathers; which strove in vain to rise, but which could never get on the wing. During full three-fourths of his speech the listeners were completely dissatisfied and tired out. Here and there a political axiom or a party allusion familiar and agreeable to the Whigs, excited some small applause. But altogether, the address was as dull, and fell as heavily, as a common-place sermon on a drowsy congregation. When we broke up, not one person, out of the hundreds to whom I was more or less known, asked me, with their usual familiar curiosity, "Well, how did you like him?" Every one seemed anxious to get away, and to say as little as possible about what was spoken or what was unsaid. Two or three Englishmen who were there were, like myself, surprised at the absence of that latter portion (that ought to have been) of the speech. One gentleman, long accustomed to hear the best specimens of English oratory, parliamentary and other, made no secret of his disgust at Mr. Webster's apparent ingratitude, and pronounced him to be a speaker far below mediocrity. I think I should have agreed with this opinion had it not been from the force of first impressions. But I could not divest myself of the feeling that Webster was a man of great powers, and I strove to account for, though I could not possibly excuse, his failure on such a fine occasion for a most effective speech. After some inquiry into the opinions of others, and a due balancing of my own notions, I came to the conclusion that the double action of personal conceit and political sycophancy was at the bottom of the secret. He was, in the first place, resolved to give the impression, that he considered the reception he met in England as neither more nor less than what he was entitled to, and not deserving of any particular acknowledgment. In the second, he was afraid of expressing his admiration and wonder at the great superiority of England over America, in those very points which to an ambitious haughty, and "aristocratical" *parvenu* must have appeared the most important. Wanting the candour to tell the truth, the tact to conceal it skilfully, and the courage to enter on a subject which was so difficult of management, he shirked it altogether; offering another instance of a leading political character sacrificing to time-servingness his private opinions, and a new feature in that system of concealment of the truth relative to other countries, which is a main source of American self-sufficiency. Their speakers and writers have very rarely the manliness to call the attention of the people to the immense superiority in science, literature, and the arts, of the liberal countries in Europe over their own. This has its source in the extreme cautiousness of the national character, degenerating into cunning and timidity, and acting on a vanity, which, if properly managed, might form a fine element in it, but which, thus pandered to, appears one of its worst traits. Having long kept the people ignorant of their relative position, in regard to moral characteristics, with the other inhabitants of the civilised world ; and having left all standards of comparison unknown to them except the negroes and the Indians ; having thus fostered the growth of a presumptuous pride, they are now obliged to bow down before the idol they have raised ; and the subserviency which is really and truly a cause, is taken for a consequence.

This is doing a great injustice to the people of this great country, and to its institutions. Had public men of talent a proportionate share of integrity, and did they firmly but gently display the popular errors, and show the points to be improved and the means of improvement, I am convinced the people would listen to, learn, and practise every such lesson. But as it is, they have certainly acquired a false estimate of themselves in the mass, while they have nevertheless not failed to discover the motives of their truckling leaders. They hear their discourses, they elect them to offices, they are proud of their talents ; but they have no respect, no love, no gratitude towards them. They like to be flattered, as who does not ? but they hold the flatterers cheap. They are aware that the adventurers whom they elevate to place value them only as the steps that lead to eminence; and having placed those persons there, for the purposes of state necessity, as they would put piece upon piece to complete a combination of machinery, they make them work as long as they are wanted; and when the turn is served they cast them aside to rot and rust, knowing that however either one party or the other, the public or the individual, might have suffered during the connection, there could not at any rate be any *love* lost between them.

This question of the indifference shown to public men after their time of service, as peculiar to the United States of America, is well worthy of examination. It is very easy to say, in reference to ancient and mediæval history, that republics are ungrateful, and thus settle the question. But then another suggests itself—why should ingratitude be in the nature of republicans more than in that of people living under another form of government? Ingratitude is certainly not a popular vice inherent in mankind. It is rather an individual failure than a public fault. The vices of the people are positive. Ingratitude is merely negative. Profusion of reward for public services is more congenial to general feeling than a stingy indifference. But whatever may be the popular turn, whether for parsimony or prodigality, it in a great degree depends on those who influence the public mind. The masses are always led. However the many may speak or act, their tone is derived from the few. And I have no doubt that did the people of America see broad instances of manliness, independence, and honour, in their public men, they would treat them with a corresponding measure of recompense. This is in seeming a digression from the matter of this sketch; but I think the sequel will prove it to be germane to it.

The whole Whig party of Boston being dissatisfied with

Daniel Webster's appearance in his single individual character, resolved on giving him another opportunity in a more exciting atmosphere than that of the dimly-lighted hall of Representative legislation. A day was fixed on for a public dinner; the great room at the United States Hotel, which can accommodate between 300 and 400 persons, was engaged; a subscription list was opened and at once filled up, hundreds who were anxious to attend being unable to obtain tickets. An invitation was sent to me by the committee; and I was not sorry at an opportunity of letting the people of Boston, and through them, those of the whole Union, know the manner in which Mr. Webster had been treated in England, the account of which he ought not, in my opinion, to have allowed his countrymen to learn at second hand.

The entertainment on this occasion was of high interest. Governor Everett presided; the principal functionaries of the state were present; and several guests from other parts of the Union with a sprinkling of foreigners, English, and others, took from it the appearance of a mere local party feast. Everett was, as usual, fluent and eloquent in his prefaces to the various prepared toasts, particularly that which ushered the main one of the evening, "the health of Daniel Webster," and which called on him in plain terms to enter more at large into a detail of his recent visit to Europe.

Webster rose, somewhat more animated than on the former occasion, but still without any of the buoyancy or ease, which a scene of festivity and a willing audience naturally excite in the person so honoured. The fact was, his subject weighed him down. There was no inward feeling to lift him upwards. He dragged on for a while, telling what he felt and thought, that is as much of it as he dared to tell. He did not confess his admiration for the Tory nobility and their principles ; his contempt for the liberal ministers, and his abhorrence of the radicals; nor did he venture to speak of "the dear Duke," whom he afterwards publicly wrote to with such familiarity. He said nothing disparaging of the Queen. But every one of those topics I knew afterwards to be favourite ones with him in private society. On this occasion, he declared that the objects which chiefly struck him with admiration in England were,—what does the reader think? The splendid evidences of commerce, wealth, and munificence? The vast amount of shipping? The great manufacturing establishments? The magnitude of London, or the grandeur of the country residences?—not at all. But "the picturesqueness of some old ruins, and the deep verdure of the meadows and pasture-land." He really and truly said little more than that about old England. But when he passed on to France, his wonderment at Louis Philippe's greatness and his attachment to America knew no bounds. Of France, where he certainly dined with the King, but where he lived in the comparative obscurity of a mere bird of passage, he spoke warmly. Of England, he had literally nothing at all to say. I was more and more anxious to say something for him; and when in the course of the evening Governor Everett proposed my health, introduced by some very kind remarks, I rose, and after making some brief allusions to the subject of the toast, I turned to that which was uppermost in my mind, and I trust that the circumstances of the case will excuse my introducing here a portion of what I said:—

"The newspapers of England and America have for six months

past been the record of that visit, which is now matter of Mr. Webster's private history; but it has been obvious to me that he labours under what will probably be always a difficulty to him when he makes any allusion to the honours he so justly received. For the mingled dignity and modesty of a superior mind, always makes its possessor shrink from enlarging on the triumphs of which he has been himself the hero. But, Mr. President, I cannot abstain from stating here, that the terms to which the dignified reserve of your distinguished guest restrained him in speaking of his receptions in the country where I first had the pleasure of meeting him, were as far short of what was due to him as they were of the warmth, the cordiality, the enthusiasm, which were felt towards him in every circle of society, and by all those who hurried to receive him.

"The name of Webster was well known in England.—But it is no disparagement to the greatest possessor of the name, that he was confounded by some of the people of London with other distinguished men who bear it. I was applied to by several, for information on the subject; for its being known that I was coming to America, some (particularly among my Irish friends) thought I should know everything that was passing there. One gentleman asked me if Mr. Webster was coming to England to bring out a new edition of his dictionary, another if he proposed giving a series of lectures on chemistry—and so on. But the world of London was soon set right as to who *was* coming, by several Americans, who hailed with generous pride the arrival of a great compatriot in a foreign land, and if Mr. Webster obtained, as I think will be admitted, the honours of a social triumph in England, no one certainly was more forward or more zealous than Mr. Stevenson, the American minister, in hanging up the garlands and strewing the flowers on his path.

"Mr. Webster at length arrived; and then, sir, the most eminent in title, rank, and intellect, hastened to offer him their welcome. The mansions of the great, and the palace of the sovereign were thrown open to him. Visiting cards and cards of invitation, might be gathered in packs from the table of his ante-room; and I may say, almost without hyperbole, that the pages of the red book—that record of the power, the pride, and the privileges of the British nobility—were strewn as offerings at the threshold of his hotel.

"I speak, sir, as an eye-witness; for I was in London at the time; and when I myself went to tender him my respects, I was on two occasions unable to make my way through the crowd of carriages and visitors, and, on a third attempt, was assured by his servant that, worn out by those visits—those acts of homage, I might call them, to his reputation and his talents—he had lain him down on his bed, to dream, no doubt, of his happy home, to which he has so happily returned.

"Such, gentlemen, is a faint sketch of a small portion of the honours paid to Mr. Webster in England, in conferring which she did honour to herself; and the best atonement I can now make you for this long but true narration, is to make the moral shorter than the story.

"And what is the moral to be learned, the inference to be drawn, the principle to be inculcated, by this interesting and eventful visit? It is that the people of England are anxious and ardent to hail and to receive every citizen of the United States with that graduated scale of attention due to public reputation or to private respectability. Few are entitled to such abundant marks of honour as were lavished on Mr. Webster, for he was considered as the admitted personification of the industry, the energy, and genius of a great and powerful people; nor will I go the extravagant length of saying that every American is received in England as if he were a brother; but I do say, that he will be sure of meeting the cordial reception due to what Mr. Webster himself has designated as 'our distant relations, our kith and kin of the Anglo-Saxon race.'"

This was well received; but I was happy to find that of all the Americans present no one seemed to perceive any lurking satire in some of the passages, which the few Englishmen present might have suspected. My purpose was completely answered. While Webster himself was so well pleased that he thanked me with evident satisfaction; and on his return at night to the house of the friends with whom he was staying, he repeated almost all I said, word for word, walking up and down the drawing-room, as his handsome and agreeable hostess assured me some time afterwards, when I was myself admitted to terms of intimacy, I may say of friendship, with the family.

I had many opportunities of subsequently seeing and

knowing Mr. Webster, both in private and public life ; in his home at Washington, in the hotel at Boston in which we lived at the same time ; at my own house subsequently, and in the houses of his friends, where he was sometimes pleasant, but mostly dull, and more than once nearly morose. I have seen him preside in the Senate *pro tempore*, and officiate at the White House as prime minister (secretary of state) ; I have heard him plead before the Supreme Court as an advocate ; I have listened to him at great meetings in the open air ; and sat beside him at public dinners under canvas, and literally *sub tegmine fagi*. But often as I have heard him, anxiously as I have listened to him, and willing as I was that his performances should come up to his reputation, his appearance, and his undoubted talents, I may truly say, that he never, to my notion, reached to anything like the height I expected. In public he was ponderous rather than powerful. In society he had none of the lightness of a man of the world, nor the weight of a man of genius. He declaimed, debated, argued, or conversed, according to the occasions. But in all the frequent times I have enumerated, I never once saw him put his audience at ease with, or transport them beyond, themselves. Judging him by those displays, or by comparison with his contemporaries and countrymen, I should have come to the conclusion that no man was ever so bepraised beyond his merits. As to the statesmen, lawyers, and orators of Europe—O'Connell, Brougham, Peel, Macaulay, Sheil, Guizot, Thiers, Berryer, he cannot be ranked with them at all. In elegance of style and diction he was inferior to Everett ; in fluency and quickness, to Judge Story ; in bold persuasiveness, to Clay ; in sententious and antithetical terseness, to Calhoun ; in fervour and command of language, to Preston. In his cause before the Supreme Court (the Massachusetts and Rhode Island Boundary Question) he failed. I cannot, in fine, believe that I saw Webster in his best days, either as an orator, a lawyer, or a man of society; yet the time of my acquaintanceship with him was the period of his greatest exertion and greatest triumph. He, in common with all the leaders of his party in the year 1839, worked with a zeal never exceeded for the overthrow of the Democrats, and the election of Harrison to the Presidency. Their success was complete. The most urgent stimulants existed to call forth their highest powers, and particularly in the case of Webster; for, independent of the political interests at stake, the question was considered as one of social existence to him individually. It was made no secret, either by his friends or enemies, that his finances were in a state of serious derangement. The large sums of money received for professional services during a long life were all spent; and it was notorious that he had for years chiefly subsisted on contributions from his Whig partisans. They could not dispense with the aid of his talents, in advocating their cause against their Loco-foco adversaries. They wanted him in Congress, at the *caucus*, on the *stump*. To attend to all the political duty required of him he was obliged to give up almost all the profits of his profession, as an attorney and counsellor at law. When his Whig friends called on him to do so, had he replied "*Il faut vivre,*" they could not retort, "*Nous n'en voyons pas la nécessité;*" for his life was the vital spark of the federal cause—his death would have been its downfal. Money, therefore, was necessary for his support, and the party supplied it freely. His connection with Nicholas Biddle and the United States Bank was not mere whispered insinuation; and when the explosion of that concern, and the imperfect disclosures of Biddle and his associates so much agitated the public mind, every one awaited, but in vain, for the explanation of large sums unaccounted for, either with anticipated exultation or shame, as the list of the spoilers might or might not have disclosed the name of Daniel Webster.

His whole career has proved him to have possessed that ambition which seeks power for the sake of display, which yields to the supremacy of prejudices, and which barters for vain show the solid independence of the mind. Webster was the son of a farmer in the state of New Hampshire. A scrambling education prepared him for the struggles of life. He first tried his hand as a schoolmaster in a neighbouring village; but soon abandoning that line, the profession of the law, studied at small expense, threw him on the readiest road to fortune in the United States. His talent and energy soon became remarkable in the narrow sphere of action of a country town, which he wisely changed for the more extended one afforded by the city of Boston. There he began to practise with a considerable reputation, and found a fair field with few competitors. He quickly gained the first place in public favour; and had he been as prudent as he was successful, he must soon have made a handsome fortune. But his turn for expense was, to say the least, as great as his thirst for distinction. He chose to vie with the wealthy merchants of the city, in entertainments that had no heart in them, and in an ostentation which gained him abundance of envy and unpopularity, but neither admirers nor friends.

The popular feeling in Boston is decidedly adverse to expensive display, even from those who can afford it. Money is held in high honour; but it is an abstract adoration for the thing itself that prevails, without a due appreciation of the uses to which it may be advantageously turned. The Bostonians worship wealth in the mass, in solid ingots, in wholesale existence ; but they do not like to see it distributed, even in usefulness. They would never countenance the cutting up of an old moon into little stars, even if a more advantageous radiation of light were to be the result. They venerate the individual grocer, linen draper, or cotton spinner, who has realised a fortune, bought or built a fine house, and who lives in it parsimoniously, hoarding his dollars, and merely paying his income tax when called on by the assessors. They will elect him to public offices, invite him to the city entertainments, treat him with respect, and call him one of their "first men." But when he dies and his property is shared among his children, and by them disbursed in channels of general utility, neither the comparatively poor successors to the one overgrown capitalist, nor the beyond-comparison more valuable uses to which the wealth is turned, are considered with much favour. The tangible mass of money is no more. He who identified himself with it is gone. The altar is shattered, and the high priest out of sight ; and no veneration remains—because *the spirit* of a religious feeling does not exist, in the worship which the Bostonians pay to wealth.

But if they disapprove of expensive habits, even in those who can afford them, much less leniently do they consider a profuse expenditure in a man who lives as may be said from hand to mouth, and who wilfully lays himself open to inconvenience, and it may be to distress. Webster's extravagance was, therefore, a serious obstacle to his political success. His talents must have been great to have enabled him to overcome the prejudices of his party ; and their greatest proof is in the fact, that the party so long continued to be self-mulcted for his support. Most fortunate for him was his elevation to office as secretary of state, to which post he was appointed by General Harrison, immediately on the latter taking possession of the Presidency, in March, 1841. He had great influence. His patronage gave him the power to name or recommend others for employment; and as long as he had strength of limbs and lungs to battle for his party in the political arena, so long could he reckon on a continuation, in one shape or other, of the support which enabled him to maintain his position. But had he, by some caprice of faction prematurely lost his place; or, by some failure of health, his voice; or had he lived to be very old; woe to him! America is not the country where a public and a poor man may meet any of these misfortunes with impunity. There is no gratitude for past service, no compassion for present want, no protection against future suffering. Down goes the individual to his grave. And the best wish of the country—or, indeed, of his friends—is, that his descent may be as rapid as his rise was rough, and his elevation insecure.

A parallel and a contrast, both very remarkable, might be traced between Daniel Webster and Daniel O'Connell, two men of singular contemporary eminence. Both were of obscure origin; and the manner in which each considered that chance circumstance shows the occasional influence of political institutions on the highest order of intellect. Webster, so far imbued with an intuitive republicanism, looked on his low birth with pride, as the proof of his individual merit, and rose in his own esteem in proportion to the height of his public elevation. He boasted of his early struggles, and spoke affectionately of the log-cabin in which he was "raised." O'Connell, under the infection of aristocratical yearnings, laboured to prove himself of gentle blood, sunk all allusion to his plebeian source, and felt no offence so deeply as the assertion that he sprang from such. Yet he was most emphatically the man of the people, with whom he denied his inborn fellowship ; while all the tendencies of Webster were towards the would-be upper classes, to a share in whose sympathies he disclaimed all birthright. These startling discrepancies may be accounted for on a principle common to both individuals. They were equally of lavish habits of expense, and they had an instinctive sagacity that taught them where the supplies were surest to be found. In free America the rich merchants, manufacturers, and other corporate monopolies, form the well in which the truth (as it seemed to Webster's vision) was to be found. He accordingly drained it to the bottom. Ireland, where rank and wealth require no champion, presents an ocean of political excitements, through whose waves O'Connell saw the pearl of popular reward. And down to its troubled depths he dived, and boldly he secured the hard-earned prize. Had the position of the adventurers been reversed, their "principles" would most probably have been so too. But their efforts to uphold distinctly opposite interests brought them again upon a level. They mutually gave up the pursuit of their common profession, the law, in which each held a high place, for the parliamentary career, in which they were equally successful; and they both accepted without scruple the large remuneration afforded by the classes whose political advocates they were. But here the superiority of O'Connell—rather of chance than choice, as I before intimated—is unquestionable. While Webster was but a hireling, toiling to promote the selfish objects of a small moneyed minority, O'Connell was the paid representative of a suffering people. If paid, he was paid openly—honourably—by public subscription, from a national impulse contributing in broad daylight, in the temples of his sect, under the sanction of its priests, of which his enemies would make a reproach, but which were, in truth, so many tributes of generous gratitude. While Webster received his reward in ignominious dribblets—notorious, but not avowed—wrung from party necessities, sordidly acquired and grudgingly given.

The parallel and the contrast might be carried farther. But enough has been said to show the striking similarity that existed, and which is more striking when we recal the large and portly persons, and the commanding demeanour of each individual, and the great influence exercised by both over their political adherents.

In manners, as in features, they were, however, widely different. The swaggering air and vulgar countenance of O'Connell were strongly contrasted by the heavy gait and dignified lineaments of Webster. But still power was in both displayed, with equally distinctive marks, and the differences were more national than individual; the loose and off-hand bearing of the Irishman being as completely generic as was the cautious and uncordial carriage of the Yankee.

The most marked distinction between the objects of the two men, arising from the difference of political institutions, was the importance of obtaining office to the one, and the value of not accepting it to the other. The cogent motives prevailing with O'Connell, even to the refusal of official dignity, were obvious. But a distinguished place is of paramount necessity to a statesman in the United

States, particularly to a needy one; therefore were Webster's exertions long directed to that point. The post of senator to Congress is a high honour; but he of course always looked to the chief prize of talent and ambition—the Presidency. The two next places in gradation are those of Vice-President and Secretary of State. With no possible chance of being nominated for President of the United States by a majority of his party, in opposition to Clay, Harrison, or Scott, he was nevertheless put upon the list by some of his adherents, when a general union of the Whigs agreed to send delegates to a convention, in the year 1839, to choose between their four rival candidates, and fix on him who should be pronounced as most "available," to rally all shades of opinion, overthrow the Democrats, and oust their man, Van Buren. When this convention assembled at Harrisburg, in Pennsylvania, in the month of December in that year, it was soon found that there was no chance for Webster, and his name was not brought forward. His popularity was evidently confined to a small circle of associates, and the men under their influence, in Massachusetts, and specially in Boston. Clay and Scott were also obliged to yield their pretensions; and Harrison was unanimously fixed on, and ultimately elected, to the great triumph of the Whig party, and under circumstances which I shall have occasion to allude to elsewhere.

Mr. Webster was in England during the proceedings of the Harrisburg convention; and well aware of his political position, he wrote a letter from London, addressed to I do not exactly remember whom, begging to withdraw his name from among those offered for the suffrages of the delegates. In one respect he made an unlucky calculation at this crisis. He had his choice of being nominated for the Vice-Presidency of the Union by this convention,* or of being appointed Secretary of State in the event of General Harrison being elected President. In an evil hour he rejected the first of these proposals and accepted the latter. The rejection was made through the medium of Mr. Peleg Sprague, the delegate from Massachusetts to the convention. But this was rather ill-luck than bad management. The office of Vice-President was almost ever since the days of Jefferson, considered of small comparative importance. No man of eminence was now proposed for it, or would be likely to accept it; for no one ever reckoned on that contingency, the death of the President, in the event of which the constitution provides that the Vice-President should fill the place, for whatever portion of the term might be unexpired at the chief magistrate's decease. The Secretaryship of State was, however, a post of great importance. The person who fills it may be considered in a certain degree prime minister of the country; although with a man of talent in the Presidential chair, the various Secretaries of State are little more than head clerks—*chefs de Bureaux*—of their several departments. But Mr. Webster, in gaining that position, no doubt reckoned on being able to act pretty much as he might choose to do, with a man of the mediocre calibre which he unquestionably ascribed to "the Hero of Tippecanoe."

But here was one of the instances which prove some men to be born under a lucky, and others under an unlucky star. On Webster's refusal, John Tyler was

* I do not believe that this fact was ever made generally public; but it was still no secret, and was communicated to me by Mr. R. C. Winthrop, a Member of Congress, much in the confidence of Mr. Webster, and confirmed by Mr. J. W. Paige, of Boston, his brother-in-law.

named by the Harrisburg Convention as the Whig candidate for the Vice-Presidency; and in one short month from his election jointly with General Harrison, the death of the latter placed him in that highest dignity, which he had not the remotest idea of seeking by the suffrages of the nation, and for the possession of which Webster had been toiling for years, and now was doomed to be debarred of for ever! For in addition to Clay, generally considered as next entitled to the choice of the Whig party, and Scott, who but for his own impatience was quite as likely to be elected in 1844, Tyler became now a formidable rival, with great probabilities in his favour, had he managed matters well during the unexpired term of those honors, which he dropped into, in the first instance by chance, but which he might have been confirmed in for another four years by election.

The events of Mr. Tyler's administration and of his political fate may find a place in another portion of these volumes. But I shall here, after a long interval, resume my sketch of Daniel Webster's career.

The cabinet which Harrison left as a legacy to his accidental successor, Mr. Tyler, very soon resigned their offices *en masse* on the question of his veto of the first Bank bill, with the exception of Daniel Webster, the Secretary of State. He, beyond any doubt, did himself great dishonour by the retention of place while his colleagues gave up theirs, if high sentiment instead of personal interest ought to be the ruling principle of political as well as private life. But Webster, not content with clinging to office, published a letter, in which he said that he saw no good reason for the retirement of his colleagues.

This gratuitous attack upon men with whom he had all

along acted, who were chosen with his consent, if not actually at his suggestion, with whom he was entirely committed in the measure that forced them from their posts, completely severed Webster for a time from his previous hold on the regard of the Whig party. His talents were so considerable, that this party long abstained from denouncing his conduct, in hopes that he would redeem the false step, and, like a strayed sheep, return again to the fold. But month after month he "held fast;" and he never yielded to the combined voices of both the great parties, to his new associates in office whom Mr. Tyler picked up here and there, or to the strong wishes of the President himself, until the increasing ascendancy in the state councils of his fellow apostate, J. C. Spencer, the Secretary of the Treasury, became too strong for him, and he reluctantly let slip his last grasp of office in the month of May, 1843.

During his tenure of office as Secretary of State, Webster had two important transactions to conduct relative to the foreign policy of the country; namely, the dispute with the Government of Mexico, respecting the assistance afforded to Texas by armed citizens of the United States; and the treaty with Great Britain negociated at Washington with Lord Ashburton, in the year 1842.

During both of these transactions he wrote several state papers, in the form of despatches and diplomatic notes. They were almost all studied, pompous, and tedious; saying, as the papers of lawyers generally say, much more than was necessary; mere specimens of special pleading where there was a question of dispute; arrogant where there was a feeble opponent to bully, as in the case of the complaint of Mexico against American aid to Texan invaders; and uncandid when there was a point to carry against a strong one, as on the Boundary question with England.

Webster acquired no honour, nor any solid advantage, as far as the world knows, from his forced retention of office in the teeth of general opinion. Both parties rejoiced when he was obliged to resign. A few adherents endeavoured to get up a public dinner for him in his passage through Baltimore from Washington to Boston. Not 100 individuals could be brought together on the occasion. And Webster, completely disheartened, wanting both frankness and nerve to meet the country, by a bold avowal of his personal views on the stirring questions which agitated it, avoided them all, and delivered a speech on the theoretic abortion of commercial treaties, to an audience half asleep and wholly disappointed. He passed unnoticed through Philadelphia and New York, arrived at Boston, and spent some weeks preparing the oration which he had to deliver on the 17th of June, 1843, at Bunker's Hill, to commemorate the completion of the noble granite monument erected there in honour of the celebrated battle fought upon it. This task he performed. His speech was a laboured and heavy composition. The multitude of listeners who attended the ceremony were cruelly fatigued by standing nearly two hours under a broiling sun; and the comparatively few who heard the oration thought its concluding sentence was the best.

Immediately after this exhibition Webster returned to the practice of his profession as an attorney and advocate. His first client was the delinquent President of a Boston bank, tried on a prosecution for embezzlement of the entire funds, by which hundreds of victims were utterly ruined. Webster worked hard for his acquittal. But the jury not agreeing, the culprit was remanded for another trial, which took place a few months afterwards, and a better jury being found, all Webster's strenuous efforts were defeated, and a verdict of guilty was the result.

During this trial Webster tauntingly enquired, "What has become of the money if Wyman embezzled it ?"

Mr. Huntington, the prosecuting counsel, replied that one of the items was the large fee paid to the counsel for the defence.

"That is vulgar," exclaimed Webster.

"It may be vulgar, but it is true," retorted Huntington. "The large fee paid to the eminent counsel is paid out of the plunder of the bank."

This sting sank deep, and it remained festering to the day of Webster's death.

Webster never recovered his footing in public affairs. He sank by quick degrees from his high eminence, forfeiting his old claims on the Whig connection, and receding from his proud position as the leader of the great party it embodied. Bombastic eulogies pronounced on his character and career have slurred over his backslidings from the cause of philanthropy and freedom. Sophistry has sought to screen his too manifest conversion to the interests of slavery. His motives or inducements to this grievous change are buried with him. The results of it were not of much moment. All his eloquent tergiversation could not injure the immutable truth, that slavery is a crime. Compromises, equivalents, peculiar institutions, vested interests, and all the usual vocabulary of slave orators or slave apologists are as mere puffs of wind against a mountain side when directed to the overthrow of liberty. Manly, bold, unscrupulous action is required in such a conflict. Webster's mind was not cast in that mould. He dared not openly assail the principles of abolition or free soil, but he attacked them by many a side-wind; and the most burlesque excuses have been made for him, on the score of some mysterious, inward revelations, "the dialectics of conscience," and such trash, which told him that the protection of a fugitive slave was not an obligation of Justice, but only of benevolence, and that its violation in short was prescribed by humanity itself in consideration for the constitution of the United States!

The inferior mind which ventured on this apology had much better have allowed the reputation of Daniel Webster to rest with him in his grave, and trust to the wings of time for fanning away the mists that shroud it.

The chief glory of Webster's career was, on the same authority, the negotiation and conclusion of the Treaty of Washington, executed between him and Lord Ashburton in 1842; the settlement of a claim on the part of the United States, "made in pure good faith." Of the value of this attribute, applied so tersely to that claim and its management by Daniel Webster, I shall be able to give my readers a true estimate in the chapter which will treat of the settlement of the NORTH-EASTERN BOUNDARY QUESTION.

Daniel Webster died at Marshfield in the state of Massachusetts, in the year 1853, and is, I believe, buried in that place.

Many portraits of him exist, and his splendid head has been often done in marble. A dignified presence, powerful intellect, long public service, are not in themselves sufficient to deserve a national monument. But the Americans will, no doubt, in after time place Webster's statue high on some proud pedestal; and thus give to his memory the elevation denied by his cotemporaries to the man.

CHAPTER XV.

SERVANTS.

Inefficiency of American "Help"—In the West—South and North-eastern parts of the Union—Slave Attendance—Domestic Servitude in general—General Advantages of the Native Americans in comparison with the Irish Help—Want of Attachment in the Former—Appellations of House Servants—Many of those used in Europe unknown in the United States—Rates of Wages—Unscrupulous Seductions of Servants by American ladies—Probable deterioration in Domestic Attendance.

One of the subjects on which the minds of men and women in the United States seem to be unanimously made up, is the admitted deficiency of *help*—the word which describes menial attendance in the aggregate—and the very little assistance which the "help" affords to the employers.

I cannot, of my own knowledge, speak as to the truth, falsehood, or exaggeration of the descriptions of this grievance, as regards the far-off portions of the country. It is, no doubt, a very serious nuisance to such persons as may have quitted the ways of civilised life, to grub their path through those barbarous districts. In the half-settled regions of the New World, the inconvenience in question is a matter of course. Every one who braves the hardships of "life in the West," must go there prepared to do a great deal of rough and dirty work, with his or her own hands.

As to the south, in all the slave states in fact, there

ought to be no ground for complaint on the score of domestic servitude. As long as "help" may be raised on every proprietor's estate, bought in a public mart, and whipped into discipline, the unfortunate beings may be made so tractable, and there is so large a number to choose from, that their owners might be supposed to have everything their own way. Indeed I can vouch, from personal observation, for the excellence of slave attendance.

But, even with all the facilities just mentioned, considerable dissatisfaction is expressed by planters and other slave-holders, at the laziness, unwillingness, and insolence of their house servants.

There may be some justice in their complaints ; for these poor slaves may find themselves to a certain degree a privileged class, in comparison with their wretched brethren doomed to toil in the fields, under the burning sun and the overseer's lash. Taking advantage of the indulgence granted within doors, of their familiarity with the children of the family, with whom they have been reared, and the species of regard they receive from the heads of the house, in common with the domestic animals, these in-door unfortunates may now and then take petty liberties which their owners magnify into great ones. But it would appear strange that these human machines, trained to obey the will of their master, like the spaniel who follows in his track, and with the everlasting fear of the scourge before them, should deviate from the strict line of duty, or dare to give a hasty word or a reproachful look to their tyrants. Nor would they, I am well convinced, were it not from that instinct of self contempt implanted in every human being who, from any cause whatever, is doomed to do menial service, and which breaks out at times in a spirit of irresistible revolt, that the dread of punishment in the slave, or the loss of place to the freeman, cannot entirely check.

Disguise it as we may, under all the specious forms of reasoning, there is something in the mind of every man which tells him he is humiliated in doing personal service to another; no matter though necessity may force him to its adoption, or avarice reconcile him to its continuance, he must often feel a throb and a blush, as the recollection of the truth flashes across him. And in the mood which follows, in the very teeth of distress or danger, he will give involuntary vent to his feelings, often unjustly, to the injury of the employer, who is guiltless of the cause, and unconscious of its existence. How few masters in a thousand have a notion that, do what they can for their domestics, those persons labour under an inward sense of degradation, that at times disqualifies them for the duty they are perhaps well disposed to perform!

This observation, and the considerations connected with it, are infinitely more applicable to the Old World than the New. The servile nature of domestic duties in Europe, and more particularly in England, is much more likely to generate the feeling I allude to, and consequently to make servants more liable to the discontent which mars their merits, than the common understanding in America, which makes the compact between "employer" and "help" a mere matter of business, entailing no mean submission on the one hand, and giving no right to any undue assumption of power on the other.

Inconsistent as it may appear to be with the pride of personal independence, inherent in the republican, it is certainly true that domestic service is not considered so disgraceful in the United States, as it is felt to be in the United Kingdom. I have often seen a contrary remark made by travellers; but I know them to be mistaken. An American youth or "young lady" will go to service willingly, if they can be better paid for it than for teaching in a village school, or working on a farm or in a factory. Many girls prefer the latter occupation, because the high rate of wages soon enables them to lay by a larger sum than they could possibly save in the same space of time as "chamber girls" or "sempstresses." But those who do prefer going to service, and the observation applies to both sexes, assuredly feel less degraded by it than persons in a similar condition in any other part of the world.

There are several causes for this. In the first place they satisfy themselves that they are *helps*, not servants—that they are going to work with (not for) Mr. so and so, not going to service—they call him and his wife their *employers*, not their master and mistress—they bargain for great privileges as to receiving their friends, going out, and coming in—they consider themselves entitled to, and will insist on, sharing all the delicacies consumed in the family, and, above all things, they have their conviction that the persons they serve, or their parents, or some of their immediate connections, have been themselves in the very position *they* now occupy; and the male or female servant, whose father is an independent farmer and proprietor of his land, is quite satisfied that such a position entitles him and them to a perfect feeling of political equality with any other person in the country. This innate sentiment of independence, when modified by good sense and a fair share of education, which is common to most persons of that class, qualifies them, in my opinion, to make very good servants, when properly managed.

I have had ample opportunities for observation, in families with whom we were intimate, in hotels innumerable, and in our own actual service; and everything has satisfied me that, if well treated, the native Americans are the best servants in the country, and according to my experience the best I have ever known, in the qualities which I consider among the most essential. They are regular, quiet, good-tempered, sober; all knowing how to read and write, and every one looking forward to some better condition in life, for which they seem to prepare themselves by economy and good conduct. They are not conscious of having forfeited their self-respect, from the manner in which they choose to view their condition, in comparison with that of their employers. They can consequently afford, without any sacrifice of self-importance, to be respectful to those whom they serve. It is only those who wince under the sensitiveness I have before described, and sensitiveness is rare in the Yankee temperament, who give themselves relief by insolence to others. Native American servants undoubtedly take great liberties in comparison with those of Europe, as to the distribution of their time. Engaged to do a certain quantity of work, it is always understood that when it is done they are free to do with themselves what they like. They do not hold themselves obliged to ask leave for the disposal of their extra time, which they frequently employ (the females I mean) in needlework of various kinds, for their own benefit. It is very common to see a cook or a chamber-girl at work, making a set of shirts, or the like, for persons not in their employer's family. They do not stand on much ceremony as to giving warning, if it suits them to quit. They do not in general form attachments to their employers, any more than a labourer or mechanic who hires himself for a certain piece of task work or to complete a job. A servant who will make herself useful, which implies in England a disposition to turn her hand to all things from regard to the family, is almost unknown in Yankee-land. The affections are not strong there, and they are certainly less so between employer and helps, than between any other classes of individuals in the community—except, perhaps, between parents and children.*

And here is the true source of the never-ending lamentations about the badness of servants and the miseries of housekeeping, which form the chief staple of complaint on the part of the ladies and gentlemen of America. The employers having no confidence in persons whom they hire for a temporary purpose, treat them with extreme distrust. They have nothing in common. The interests of each are altogether matters of a separate feeling. The employer does not inquire into those of the helps, and the help takes no care of those of the employer. The greatest apprehension of the latter is that the former may not have a fitting sense of the difference between them—may not treat them with sufficient deference—may take undue liberties with them. There is consequently no ease of manner, no security of position on the part of the employer; and there is nothing so easily detected as a forced reserve. Its natural effect on those towards whom it is assumed is to create an antagonist influence, which soon amounts to dislike. So that the help who discovers in his employer an air of false importance, is sure to pay it back with an assumption of equality.

* A man who had lived a couple of years in a family suddenly gave notice to quit, without any apparent cause. His employer asked him if he had anything to complain of? "No." Was he going to work with another? "None in particular." What then was the reason for this unexpected conduct? He felt that "he was becoming attached to the family, and thought it best to clear away in good time."

To escape as much as possible from this evil, the majority of persons prefer Irish servants to native helps. With those they are under less restraint; they can treat them with greater kindness with less risk of compromising their dignity; they have a chance of meeting gratitude in return for good treatment, and fidelity for trustingness. These uneducated immigrants readily admit the superiority of those they serve, without inquiring into their origin or their earlier occupations. In fact, the grand desideratum of the wealthier class is thus in a certain degree realised. They establish, at least in their own household, an acknowledged gradation of ranks, which they so vainly sigh for on a more extended scale.

But these Irish servants, so agreeable in this regard, are, with some exceptions, of a very indifferent order as attendants. They have rarely lived in the same capacity in Europe, the great majority having adopted this line on arriving in America, without any previous training. Many of the men are deserters from the British army in Canada, and the other British provinces, and these, from their former habits of discipline, are not badly adapted to the great hotels, where a regular system of drill and duty is strictly preserved; but as they are generally volatile and fond of variety, they change about from one place to another, and, as private and public houses employ them alike, they have all the air and manner of waiters, and you rarely see in a family a domestic that gives the notion of his belonging to a fixed and reputable service. The Irish women, on the other hand, who have learnt their little knowledge in the United States, are rarely anything but very indifferent. The cooks particularly know little or nothing of their art; they adopt the thick, greasy, salt sauces common to the country; they roast or boil a joint in the ordinary fashion, but are altogether ignorant of the lighter and more graceful appurtenances of a repast.

The applications which designate house servants with us are not used in America. There are none such, for instance, as those of butler, valet, own man, footman, page. Steward, or groom of the chambers, are of course not to be expected, belonging, even in England, only to a scale of establishments which has no existence in the New World.* A man servant in America is in the best houses called a waiter, and it gives great offence to a European ear to hear a gentleman at a dinner-table call to the servant of a host, "Waiter, get me a piece of the beef," "Waiter, hand me the castors." A most ludicrous, yet unmeant sarcasm on the abuse of military titles exists in the appellation of "kitchen colonels," given by servants in America to men servants in families.

Coloured men are not much employed as permanent house servants in the northern and eastern parts of the Union. But extra attendants for both private and public parties are almost entirely chosen from them. They are a very respectable class, and excellent for such employment, being not so independent and indifferent in manner as the native white men, nor so bustling and fidgetty as the Irish. The greatest annoyance from the latter class arises from their over anxiety to serve and oblige. They give one no rest at table, but in accordance with the usual taste of the native Americans of all classes, are constantly putting every possible incongruity before or beside you; offering you, for instance, cranberry sauce

* "By his black dress I at first took him for a brother physician; but his obsequious manner soon undeceived me. He was in fact a *Gentleman Housekeeper*" (steward).—*Atlas*, Dec. 9, 1845. Translation of a French tale called "Geneviève." The original must have been Maître d'Hôtel.

with your fish, maccaroni with mutton chops, vegetables of any and every kind with stewed oysters, and so on. On one of my earliest days of dining at a public table in America, a good-natured fellow was thus over-loading me with civility, and on my declining offer after offer, and telling him I would take some roast duck (which was marked in the bill of fare) he replied, " The ducks isn't up, sir, would you choose some butther ?" at the same time placing a plate of salt butter beside me. Attentions of this nature (but not quite so delicate) are common at every private table.

With respect to female servants, they are on the most limited plan. There are no housekeepers or ladies' maids. The lady herself does all the duties of the former, those of the latter are performed, jointly and severally, by the "sempstress" and the chamber girl, the regular employment of the first of whom is to do the "sewing," the latter to attend to the bedrooms, or, in American phrase, to "fix the chambers." Needlework of all kinds is, I believe, technically called "sewing" throughout the United States. Ladies do very much to assist their female servants in their ordinary duty, making beds, "fixing" the rooms, making puddings, ironing, making up linen, &c. Servants are thus really justified in giving to themselves the favourite designation of "helps." Even in the Atlantic cities they frequently make it a point, on entering into a service, that the ladies of the family share with them such kind of work as I have specified. I dare say that condition will be more rigidly enforced by the native domestics in proportion as democratic principles spread and become permanent. Nursery governesses are unknown, the mothers performing some of the multifarious business expected from that over-worked class of young women in

England ; but teaching the young idea how to spell or write does not enter into the list of maternal duties. Ladies keeping houses in America are indeed little better than upper servants. The whole superintendence of the indoor work depends on them. And very often do they assist in all that is going on, in laundry, pantry, nursery, and kitchen. The husbands invariably go to market. No woman does any of that essential business beyond giving an order at the " Grocery," or the " Provision store." It is not easy to know the secrets of the scheme of domestic economy, followed by so very close and cautious a community. But a strict avoidance of needless expense, a great distrust of servants, and a mean system of locking up and doling out, are, I am inclined to believe, its general characteristics, though there, I am satisfied, many exceptions exist. The cook is a very independent and irresponsible person. She has none of the importance of housekeeping, but she is without its cares ; little being required from her she has little to look after ; the meals of the family prepared, her time is her own. Between the regular hours she goes where she chooses, and if she be a person of the least pretensions in her profession, she fixes her own time for everything, and upon the slightest deviation from the arrangement, which might interfere with her plans for going to meeting on Sunday, or to lectures on week days, she quits her place without notice, frequently while the dinner is half dressed, and the company waiting for it in vain. In general, these cooks are wretchedly bad ; chiefly Irishwomen, who knew little at home beyond boiling potatoes, they learn their art in America, and nothing can be worse than the Yankee taste in all that concerns the *cuisine*. They have in eating, as in speaking or dressing, a great love of finery. A simple gravy is distasteful to them; thick sauces, and highly salted and over-spiced dishes, with quantities of pickles, are the common style. The cook catches the taste of the employer, and the unfortunate foreigner who would model his *cuisine* on that of France or even of England, suffers constant annoyance and disappointment.

The wages of house servants are high in America in comparison with those of Europe. A man servant or "waiter," not by any means of high qualifications, receives from twenty to twenty-five dollars per month; a cook, three to four dollars per week; a sempstress or chamber-girl, two to two and a-half dollars per week. Wages of female servants are always calculated by the week, and whether it be a cause or a consequence I know not, but it is in perfect harmony with the loose tenure of place, and the perpetual changes on the shortest possible notice. Being strongly infected with the national bad taste for being over-dressed, they are, when walking the streets, scarcely to be distinguished from their employers, and when going to a party, the free use of their mistresses' finery, always "loaned" to them without reserve, brings them as nearly as possible to an equality in appearance. I know ladies in some of the cities who carry this accommodation still further, in allowing their servants to give parties in the best rooms in the house (which the owners vacate for the occasion), those *domestic soirées* showing, no doubt, amusing specimens of low life above stairs.

Very curious instances of equality and familiarity have come to my knowledge. The lady of the house and her cook call each other reciprocally Mrs. A. and Mrs. B., the appellative "Ma'am" being unused by the help, and the christian name not known perhaps to the "employer." The maid and man servants invariably address the younger branches of the family by their christian names, omitting the "Miss" or "Master." A gentleman and his servant may belong to the same volunteer company, the latter being an officer, the former a private, and the servant (I have known instances of it) sitting at the head of the public dinner as chairman one day (the master at the foot), and waiting at table the next, on the very man over whom he had precedence twenty-four hours before.

All well-conducted white native American servants in America are sure to realise money during their time of service, and they invariably quit that station after some years, to establish themselves in business, or as farmers, and many reach a high standing as regards fortune and local consideration. Once discharged, they are looked on as friends of the family. I have known instances of their being made welcome to come and dine at the same board, and to receive at their own more homely one, the individuals whose orders they whilom obeyed, without any feeling of condescension on the one hand, or undue familiarity on the other.

There is no consideration whatever, as far as I have been able to judge, on the part of persons anxious to engage a particular servant, towards the individual in whose employ he or she may be. Open visits to the cook, sempstress, or chamber girl, by the lady who wishes to hire her, are very common, at the very door of the house in which she may be doing service. Irresistible offers of higher wages, or greater indulgence, are made without reserve, and the "help" is thus seduced, without ceremony or remorse. I have been told that families arriving from Europe have had the servants whom they brought out with them at great expense thus spirited away from their duty before they have well quitted the ship that bore them across the Atlantic. Such a system is entirely destructive of confidence or regard, besides giving to the servile classes of the community an odious example of indelicacy and bad faith. Servants seem proud of being able to exercise their caprice and show their independence. They often make an engagement to enter into a service, name the day, and thus induce the expectant employer to reject other offers, yet, when the time comes, break their promise, and coolly send a message that they have changed their mind, without the least compunction or sense of impropriety. They constantly insist on fixing the hours for the family's meals, particularly on Sundays, so as to suit their own wishes. I knew one instance of one of those dictators declaring that if she entered into the service of the family, the lady of the house must see but little company, and she (the cook) be permitted to see a great deal. And this system of bidding high for servants already in place destroys all feelings in them but those of sordid love of gain. Bad as all this is in the populous cities, where housekeepers have some chance of redress, in the remoter districts of the country it must be almost intolerable, where the help insists on entire equality, sits at the same table with the employer, and will not consent to answer a bell which communicates with the kitchen, unless they have the privilege of ringing another that is hung in the parlour, whenever they in their turn may require to "have speech" of the lady who is mistress of the house, but not of the household.

On the whole, I believe this subject to be greatly influenced by that inevitable tendency towards a lower level which pervades all things throughout the country. I see no chance of a more servile and subservient feeling becoming prevalent among the domestics ; and as the political power of the wealthy class is more circumscribed, their struggle to sustain a higher social position will grow more evident and more offensive. They will, by degrees, give up the employment of native servants, who will be in future less likely than even now to submit to their pretensions, and confine themselves to the fast-increasing tribes of Irish immigrants, who, having no good models on which to form themselves, will rapidly deteriorate from even their present insufficiency, until the gentlemen of America will be served after the fashion which prevails in a low order of country inn or town tavern in the old country.

CHAPTER XVI.

THE LAW AND ITS PRACTICE.

Insecurity of the Law—The Common Law—Great number of Tribunals—Juries, their Contempt for and Defiance of the Law—Want of Respect for the Judges—Their Paltry Salaries, and Insecure Tenure of Office—Tools of Party—Materials out of which they are formed—American Lawyers—Their Practice and Progress—Superior Men—Marshall—Kent—Story—General Mediocrity.

THE most glaring and most dangerous evil in the United States is the insecurity of the law. Abundance of others exist; but, in comparison with it, they are trifling; and means of amelioration, if not of cure, seem to be within reach for them. But this greatest of ills to which a civilised country can be exposed, seems to increase in magnitude, and grow beyond remedy.

The common law of England was, at the period of the American Revolution, in all its integrity the law of the land, and nominally it is so still. But the establishment of Independence leading to the successive creation of thirty-four confederated states, each with a separate constitution of its own, necessitated various modifications in the common law in conformity with the spirit of the federal pact, and with the new-born sentiment of nationality, which required, if not a code, at least an adaptation of the traditionary system congenial to the American mind.

To escape clearly from the web of English precedent

was impossible. It was consequently only broken through here and there, and its shreds have in many instances become obstructions to the innovations entangled in its meshes.

Every legislature of every state has the power of making its own laws, which the supreme court of each is entitled to annul if it considers them inconsistent with the state constitution ; the Supreme Court of the United States, the highest court of appeal, having again a paramount jurisdiction over the decisions of all the state courts. This multitude of tribunals, filled by "many men of many minds," throws the interpretation of the law into a chaos of doubt and contradiction. Juries imbued with the absurd and fatal doctrine that they are competent to decide not only the fact but the law, frequently set themselves above what they cannot comprehend, and are influenced generally by party or personal feelings, finding guilty, or acquitting, or agreeing to disagree in a way that sets at defiance all calculation on results. Convictions in certain cases are not to be obtained, let evidence be ever so direct, or the judge's charge ever so decisive. The finding of a jury is often in defiance of law ; and even when in accordance with, is rarely influenced by reverence for it.

The want of dignity in the judges, and of respect for them in the people, are undoubtedly at the bottom of all this. The law, as an abstract idea, meets small consideration from the practical millions who have its operations under their control. They look at its tangible representatives in the "judiciary"—they have coined a word to suit the thing—and they see little there to command their obedience. The wretched salaries allowed to the legal functionaries, exclude all practitioners of talent until nearly worn out by work. The frequent reductions in this pittance, depending on the caprice of the state legislatures, and the uncertain tenure of an office subject in many cases to an annual vote, tend to make the judicial bench a mere "anxious seat" for its incumbents, a "stool of repentance" for any act which may peril their election. But the strongest reason for the want of public reverence for a station which ought to be so sacred, is that almost every judge in the United States is more or less a political character, too often the tool of a party, ready to do the higher order of dirty work for which all parties find an excuse. For this reason, much more than from his poverty, the judge has no real dignity to hedge him in; and he is treated as unceremoniously as any other political hack, when the party he is opposed to comes into power. This was forcibly exemplified in the State of Massachusetts in 1843, when, as if for the mere purpose of marking the disrespect of the democratic majority, they reduced the judicial salaries in the paltry amounts of from 500 to 100 dollars; sums which were really no saving to the treasury, the time consumed in the legislative debate on the question costing more money for the payment of members than the whole amount curtailed.

But the radical error is deeply seated in the great federal pact itself, which permits the judges to decide on the construction of the constitution, instead of confining their privilege and their duty to expounding the law. They are thus, of necessity, and *ex officiis* politicians; and while they bear the badge they must share the fate of their tribe. The true principle applied to the judges seems manifestly this: if it be considered expedient, in defiance of the opinion of Lord Bacon, that their office is *jus dicere*, to interpret law, and not *jus dare*, to make or give law—that they have the power of expounding the CONSTITUTION, they should be greatly elevated above their present condition, by being invariably named to their offices for life, and receiving such large salaries as to ensure the accession of men of standing, and their independence of party influence and popular control.

The Democratic party view this important subject with what appears to me a very narrow policy. The Federalists and their successors, the Whigs, took the enlarged and just measure of it. They have always maintained the privileges and dignity of the "judiciary," as the greatest safeguard against popular excess. In this they are decidedly right, even although it is probable that a leaning towards aristocratic institutions weighed as much with them as any higher principle.

The tendencies of judges, like those of all other magistrates, are no doubt rather arbitrary. But in the appointment to all places of trust, whether civil or military, risks must be run, and individual honesty must be reckoned on. The election of judges to the bench being wholly dependent on the people, there is small chance of seeing the judiciary composed of men inimical to public liberty. If the judges of a Democratic state, chosen under liberal appearances, should lapse into arbitrary decision, the people have sure means, through their representatives, of bringing the backsliders to their duty, by reducing the salaries, or of forcing them from the bench altogether by cutting them down below the amount of fair remuneration.

This is a fearfully degrading remedy, according to English notions. But it is in keeping with the money-standard principle of the United States. It is less troublesome and less dubious than an act of impeachment, in which;

after all, the representative body would be the tribunal. It is, moreover, frequently put into effect—the country is used to it. Judges often descend from the bench to practise again at the bar, to fill the office of clerk in the very court over which they had presided, to become collectors, or postmasters, or even to accept situations in factories or on railroads, or other such employments—all such changes tending to degrade in the public estimation the solemn character of the judgment-seat, and to create contempt for its incumbents.

The judges of the Supreme Court of the United States form the only branch of the judiciary throughout the Union that possesses any true security. They are guaranteed by the Federal constitution, of which they are the real guardians, in the possession of their office for life, and of a competent, but barely a competent, salary. The Chief Justice, who is president of the court, is allowed 5000 dollars (1000*l.*) per annum, and the assistant judges 4500 dollars (900*l.*) each. There is no appeal from their decisions. They are, in fact, as well as in name, supreme as to all questions of constitutional law.

The general body of the judiciary under the States' constitutions are under a far inferior organisation. Elected by the people, in many of the states for only a term of years, in some for but one year, and subject to removal at every change of party domination, they are, as before stated, even when elected for life, as in Massachusetts, liable to have their salaries reduced to an indefinite pittance.

The Democratic party throughout the Union, in their excess of idolatry for the sovereign power of the people, assume for them the possession of sovereign knowledge as well. They deny that any tribunal should become irresponsible to the popular will; which is, they maintain, the only security against a judicial despotism; and that the independence and integrity of the judiciary are not affected by limiting their commissions to a certain number of years, and allowing them a mere sufficiency for decent maintenance. "To give them their offices for life," say the Democracy, "and amply-sufficient salaries, will only make them arbitrary instruments of aristocratic misrule." In this, I confess, they appear to me to go wide of the mark. The true check required for the fitting regulation of the judiciary is a check upon their powers of action, not on their continuance in office, or on their means of support. While such judges as are now on the bench have the power of changing the construction of the several constitutions, as well as of expounding the laws, they will often expound the latter wrongfully, as an excuse for arbitrarily changing the former. Take from them this privilege, make them like other citizens amenable to the law, instead of being its masters, and they will take pride in improving and strengthening it. Judges, like other men, are liable to fall into temptation. It is unfair to lead them into it; it would be wise to put them out of its reach. The judges, above all public men, should be generously and largely paid. Their wealth would be the country's safeguard. In their poverty there is both disgrace and danger. Take from the people their reliance in the law, and there is no sure guarantee for the safety of the state. Better have bad laws firmly administered than good ones despised. A thousand indications show the popular contempt for the law in the United States. The people pervert it wilfully into whatever sense they choose it to bear, or they set it altogether at naught. This evil is full of peril to the state at large.

I can perceive greater danger of demoralisation in the whole frame of society than of disruption of the parts. The looser the social elements, the more obvious is the necessity for political connection. To destroy the reverence for the law is to sap the foundation of order. Indeed it is much better to do violence to legality under the fiction of law, than to obtain justice in contempt of its forms. The whole frame of society being artificial, it is futile to attempt its governance on the naked principles of nature. Her charms are made more exciting by the drapery we hang around them.

The materials out of which the "judiciary" of the United States is formed gives it but little chance of eminence. There is no country, according to De Tocqueville, where there are so few ignorant men and so few learned ones. Burke, in his day even, remarked the general study of works of law in America, and the number of lawyers sent to Congress. The diffusion of legal knowledge is immense, its accumulation is restricted. Hence, there are few great lawyers, and those few were miracles of legal lore. The practice of jurisprudence is at best but an exercise of ingenuity. The preparation for it is of a low order. Three years' attendance in some law school entitles a young man to be enrolled as an attorney, and at the same time called to the bar. There is not any distinction in the two branches of the legal profession. Barrister and solicitor are titles not used. The same man is counsellor-at-law and attorney-at-law; and he starts, after his three years' preparation, into the entire mismanagement of any suit which may, for experiment sake, be entrusted to him.

The first steps of the youthful lawyer must be among the dirty work of his craft. Trifling suits in the minor courts, mean fees wrung from low clients, small points argued before ignorant judges, are poor preparations for his career. He is an attorney for all the details, and a special pleader for the trickery of his suit. He drafts his own brief, and prepares all the winding ways of cunning which leads to his argument in court. Beginning with pettifogging to end in chicanery, he must have but a narrow view of his subject. Accustomed to its minutest bearings, he reaches no elevation high enough to let him lose sight of them. If his mind soars for awhile into the upper regions and is dazzled by the philosophy of law, it is pulled quickly down by the little threads which connect it with the little things below. He has no possible opportunity for the profound study of equity practice. Chancery suits on complicated questions of property, hereditary rights, confiscations, entails, and all those intricacies which excite and strengthen the legal mind in Europe, are altogether unknown in the practice of America. Nor can there be any of those instances which abound in the Old World, of great contests between the crown and the subject, the church and the state, the nobility and the people. All this is very fortunate for Americans in general, but fatal to the chance of eminence for American practitioners. They are obliged to work in a narrow field, and their ways are consequently contracted. There are many skilful attorneys and eloquent advocates in the United States, but few great lawyers. Among those who have done most honour to the profession were John Jay, Chief Justice Marshall, Chancellor Kent, and Judge Story. The published works of the two latter are standard books. There are many other men of great merit, and several who, if they had the advantages of English education and practice, might have become distinguished members of the Bar and Bench. But every candid American who has visited London and mixed in the legal circles, admits the immeasurable inferiority, and never dreams of making a comparison.

Nor is this confined scale of practice in America surprising, when we reflect that it is bounded by the limits of their insignificant cities. These are but what our provincial towns are in size and population, but far inferior to them in opportunity. The magnificent capital of England is within the reach of all, and its influence is felt throughout the land. There is nothing in America to give a metropolitan tone to the fragmental sections of the country. And the cities are so unprovided with great and liberal institutions, so deficient in objects of art and science, and in literary incitement, that there are no means of greatly enlarging the general intellect. A rare exception is seen bursting these trammels. But the great mass are but "haberdashers of small wares," by which Bacon meant retail dealers in all the occupations of mankind. Superiority of intellect is, in fact, a curse, not a blessing to its possessor. He sees afar off the paradise to which it ought to give him the entry. But he shrinks from the doubtful experiment of seeking a foreign home. In submitting to his cramped destiny he is tormented with a sense of superiority to his associates. He often shuns, instead of striving to improve them, or he yields himself up to a clique of flatterers and toadies, and drops down to the level of those about him, becoming a part of the general mediocrity to which nature meant him to be an exception.

The consideration of this question of law, its attributes and its anomalies, in the United States, leads to a wide range of reflection on the peculiarities of human nature, in which they have their origin. In endeavouring to reconcile the submission to social trammels so common among this people with what seems to be their inborn resistance to authority, I am led to admit that man is by instinct a tyrant. When he has no means of exercising his power over others, he often makes himself the victim; and he will bear extreme restraint, privation, and even torture, when the infliction is voluntary. The American people rebelled against a slight taxation by a parliament, but they cheerfully submit to the arbitrary assessment of their "select men." There is a wide difference between the effects of the despotism of a government and that of the people, even where the immediate result is the same. The victim of a single despot, or even of a constitutional executive, is upheld by the popular sympathy in all cases of political offence. Right or wrong, the crowd makes common cause with him, and even when they tacitly support the law there is too often a re-action against it sullenly at work. But the sufferers from popular tyranny have none to feel for them. No one persecuted by the sovereign people is considered a martyr. And an infinite increase of harshness in the public mind is the consequence of every punishment by the popular will. The masses are not usually merciful. They generally act from impulse—often from interest. They punish for vengeance-sake. They seldom reward. This is one main cause of the selfishness of republics. The people know themselves to be the law, and the sternness superinduced by that knowledge deadens the public feeling. Each man considers himself injured by the crime, and is identified with both prosecution and punishment—with the judge who tries, the witnesses who testify, the jury that convicts, and the executioner who strikes. No class compassionates the culprit, or asks for mercy. A multitude ot arms are raised against him, none in his behalf. Under a regal despotism the misgoverned have at least the consolation that the tyrant must die. But the people is eternal, and from its persecutions there is no appeal.

CHAPTER XVII.

THE FEDERAL UNION.

The Americans not a New People—Value of the Union—Little Present Danger of its Dissolution—Federal Government—States' Rights—Manufacturing Interests—Abolitionists.

Before treating of the Union in the aggregate, and examining the probabilities of its continuance, let us see of what materials it is composed.

I differ altogether from those who measure out praise or blame to the United States with the saving qualification that they are a new country; by which is meant that their population composes a new people. Under that now familiar delusion every step towards improvement is overlauded, every fault excused, and every crime palliated.

The American people, paradoxical as it may seem, are, in the fullest sense of the word, an older people than those of many of the countries from which they are derived. As individuals are better informed than the ancestors whose experience they inherit, so is the population of the New World in comparison with their progenitors of the Old. Therefore, although America is the New World, it is absurd to call the descendants of the original stock, any more than the fully civilised immigrants for the last two centuries, a new people. Were the aboriginal savages the sole inhabitants, they indeed would have been entitled to that epithet ; and in all their advancement towards refinement, or their aberrations from it, a proportionate degree of credit or of excuse should have been granted to them. But the newly found land was discovered by civilised men, who entered on its possession in the prime of knowledge, bringing traditions of wisdom as a foundation on which to build. Being generally well-educated, they were subject to none of the demoralising checks which attend the struggles between ignorance and power. They were rich in both theories and practical results. They had minds full-grown in the study of government. They had religion for their guide, liberty for their inspiration, and independence for their aim. They had to clear and cultivate a foreign land ; but they themselves, like trees new planted in a strange yet sympathetic soil, took root and flourished as freely as in that to which they were indigenous. They had to organise society on a plan of their own ; but its elements were already fashioned in the practice of worldly experience. Realising the fiction of the mythology, they started into their new existence fully formed. They well understood the capabilities of mankind. They had to hew their road through the forest ; but the paths of social life were ready made. Their only task was to improve their condition, and there was no restraint to counteract them.

The consequence was, that the features of civilisation were all at once developed. The proportions of society were complete. The new scheme of polity was immediately put into action. Strange discrepancies at times arose among the discordant varieties of the social amalgam. But the purposes of destiny steadily advanced. The possession of the vast territory was secured. The original owners were defrauded and despoiled. Population increased. Commerce and agriculture made rapid progress. Literature and science had been imported with the first adventurers, and every ship added to the store. These crowning glories of refinement came in supplies proportioned to the wants of the community ; and within two centuries a great and prosperous nation was established, in fulfilment of the mission which sent successive generations to organise another world.

Eighty years and upwards have passed over since the fiat of freedom was pronounced upon the greater portion of this immense extent of habitable soil. The thirty millions of souls now comprised within the limits of the United States have inherited, or brought with them from Europe, their vices as well as their experience. They should in all things be judged by the same rules of right and wrong as those by which the Old World is governed. Their merits and defects are those of the various nations from which they emanate. The children born on the soil are as much the offspring of its distinctive civilisation as the adults who come in their maturity to mix with the native or naturalised mass. All the evil which society presents in the United States is but the natural progress to corruption of a people old in the world's ways, and following the universal law.

Nothing, therefore, appears to me more fallacious than the expectation of finding in the long-settled portions of the United States the primitive virtues of a young and ignorant people, or more unjust than the disappointment which follows the discovery of the same imperfections usually found elsewhere. The wholesale robberies and individual murders, the tricks and cheateries every day recorded, instead of being the outrages of semi-savages, are those of a fully formed community. The isolated position of this vast territory long saved it from the wars which are the curse of other countries; while the free scope afforded to its institutions obviates the domestic struggles inseparable from more restricted forms of government. The day must no doubt come when clashing objects will break the ties of a common interest which now preserve the Union. The districts of south and north and west are joined like some wall of incongruous materials, with a cement insufficient to secure perpetual adhesion. They will inevitably crumble into confusion. But no man may foretell the period of dissolution.

To distant observers this catastrophe has frequently seemed close at hand. Every new acquisition of territory, political convulsion, or party dispute seems to herald its approach. Conflicting claims, local jealousies, sectional rivalries, all threaten disruption. But the many restraining causes are out of sight of foreign observation. The liliputian threads binding the man-mountain are invisible; and it seems wondrous that each limb does not act for itself independent of its fellows. A closer examination shows the nature of the net-work which keeps the members of this great association so tightly bound. An attempt to disentangle the ties, more firmly fastens them. When any one state talks of separation, the others become spontaneously knotted together. When a section blusters about its particular rights, the rest feel each of theirs to be common to all. If a foreign nation hint at hostility, the whole Union becomes in reality united. And thus in every contingency from which there can be danger, there are also found the elements of safety.

I cannot yet discover anything which indicates a sure and serious change. Causes no doubt exist which might hurry on the catastrophe, if the bulwarks of popular good sense could be promptly overthrown. But there are certain instincts common to nations as to individuals; and that of self-preservation is so important as to be called "the first law of nature." The American people are well aware that the strength of the various states consists in the union of all; and there is no chance of any section of them lightly acting to the injury of their self-interest.

For the Americans are not a passionate or impulsive people. In the different sections of the country they have some prejudices against each other, but not many dislikes, and no hatreds. Even against foreign nations there is no virulent animosity, such as exists between French and Prussians, Spaniards and Portuguese, Italians and Austrians, Turks and Greeks. They envy the political and commercial eminence of England. They are mortified by their own sense of social inferiority. These feelings are, however, modified by their pride in a common ancestry, language, and literature. So that even against England there is no spirit of national hatred strong enough to overbalance considerations of pecuniary advantage. And as long as those advantages depend on a state of peace, and that England avoids any open outrage against national rights, so long will there be peace between the two countries. It is with England alone that there is any chance of a hostile collision. England comprises the whole of the foreign world in the general feelings of the American people. They have little knowledge and no fears of any other country. The political news from England is alone cared for in the United States; her commercial progress alone watched; her social system alone understood. Any quarrel with the United States must be a money quarrel. They were ready to go to war with

France on a question of money. They shrank from one with England on a question of principle. A war of sentiment they will never wage. The quarrels between neighbouring states in the Old World have chiefly arisen from small causes acting on great passions. The Americans have no great passions. Therefore, such causes are to them without a consequence. National honour in America is inseparable from public interest, as private honour is from personal interest. No other motive is strong enough to rouse the national mind. This is the sure safeguard against foreign war and domestic broil.

As there does not exist any violent antagonism between the states, there is abundant reason for mutual forbearance, if not for reciprocal regard. The Federal Union, established in 1789, after violent contentions, having been found a sure bond of safety, and all the fears as to its possible injurious effects being dissipated, the states have come to a cordial concurrence for its preservation. "Union for the sake of the Union" is the by-word of all parties. And the federal government, created for the purpose of giving form and action to the union of the states, is but as a piece of machinery under the control of its makers. Arguments and disputes are very common as to the distinction between state rights and federal rights. But I cannot see any object in the latter beyond that of carrying out the purposes of the several States. The Federal Government is not an *imperium in imperio.* Neither is it a distinct establishment, beyond or above the states, with separate interests and divided objects. Viewed in that light it is, in fact, a political fiction. It is merely an instrument for executing the will of the country at large. Its functions are not performed by men unconnected with the various portions of the Union.

Every one of them is bound by local interests to his individual state, to which he returns after a temporary residence at Washington, and a brief tenure of power. It has no hereditary officers. It is not, in fact, a thing of itself, with attributes apart from, or anomalous to, those of the states in general. Therefore, it has been, and ever must be, the object of the states to confine its power to the narrowest limits, and to keep it as weak as may be consistent with its safe working for the common good. All attempts to strengthen this federal government at the expense of the states' governments must be futile. The occupants of its offices have no attachment to it; and when any question between federal claims and "states' rights" is started in Congress, the former has no chance of finding favour.

The federal government exists on sufferance only. Any state may at any time constitutionally withdraw from the Union, and thus virtually dissolve it. It was not certainly created with the idea that the states, or several of them, would desire a separation. But whenever they choose to do it they have no obstacle in the constitution. In the war of 1812 with England, four of the New England states, opposed to the war, were to all intents and purposes temporarily separated from the rest; or, in the words of Jefferson (though the simile is an old one, and the phrase a seeming contradiction), "Like dead bodies tied to living men." The federal government has no real power to enforce its will against a state that might choose to separate. Without a strong standing army, its threat would be a mere *brutum fulmen*—its 15,000 men a practical joke. When South Carolina, in 1832, refused its consent to the tariff established by Congress, and broached the doctrine of "nullification," the bold attitude of the federal government, backed by Congress and upheld by General Jackson the President, was abandoned as soon as the recusant state prepared for war. And the celebrated compromise act, introduced by Henry Clay, passed rapidly in 1833, modifying the tariff law so as to give a complete triumph to South Carolina, and to form an additional precedent for state resistance to federal pretensions. Thus, Texas in 1850, in defiance of Presidential message and menace, blustered for a monstrous boundary, and obtained a most unjust one, and ten millions of dollars of undeserved indemnity for the rest.

Had any serious sectional antipathies existed, they would have led to a rupture on these occasions, or on others which preceded them, and which showed individual states in opposition to the federal government, and always successful in their contests with it; such as the question of "Internal Improvements," and that of the "Indian Reserves." The advocates for centralisation and a strong national government have therefore little chance of success, unless in the improbable event of a war with some European power, or the less likely one of a home convulsion.

There is, in fact, a sense of general interest between all portions of the Union, more powerful than differences of opinion on abstract questions. The subject most likely to endanger the continuance of the federal pact is universally admitted to be that of slavery. It is no doubt the touchstone that will try the strength of the confederation; but the time for the trial is, in my opinion, yet far off, unless the policy of England may produce an interference that would hurry on a crisis. I see no chance of a speedy collision between the north and south on the mere merits of the question. The slave-holding states and the free states have many feelings in common. They are, with the exception of part of the population of Louisiana, Florida, and New Mexico, of the same race, speak the same language, and possess the same literature. Religious belief and sectarian forms are potent points of sympathy between them, and as to the fact of slavery itself, there is no abhorrence of it as a principle, and no sympathy with the coloured race *per se*, except among the "abolition" party—a still small minority in the northern and western states. The people of New England and New York cannot certainly be said to approve of slavery; but they love cotton, and as long as their factories are supplied with the raw material from southern plantations, they will assuredly do nothing *en masse* to check the growth or raise the price of this staple of their own prosperity. "Let us have cotton," cry the Yankee mill owners, like their brethren of Manchester; "by free labour if it can be, but at any rate let us have cotton." It is not that they love justice less, but that they love cotton more.

This is the secret of the support which the institutions of the south receive from the free states. The latter will not espouse the cause of the negroes against the common interest; nor do they hate them sufficiently to oppose their enfranchisement should the south find it practicable to attempt it. Those free states, as they are called, abolished slavery, merely to get rid of a system which they found less profitable than free labour; and because their climate presented no obstacle to the cultivation of the soil by white men. They made no pecuniary sacrifice. They were urged by no religious scruples; for, going farther back than Christianity, they found Scripture authority for slavery; and, with a text from the Bible in one hand, the Yankee believes himself justified in doing anything it sanctions with the other. Neither is he over-scrupulous in twisting a dubious quotation to suit his purpose. No counter-text has any weight in such a case. His right eye is blind when he wishes to see only with his left. Even his prejudices can be lulled to sleep by the murmur of self-interest. The repugnance of the white Yankees to their black brethren would be soon overcome, and they would soon admit them to their fellowship were money to be made by it. The abolition party have as yet but small influence in the question of sympathy or antipathy between the north and south. And I can, therefore, discover nothing imminently threatening to their Union, while every day strengthens the bonds which holds them together.

The enormous increase in the consumption of cotton by the northern manufacturing states, and in the use of tobacco everywhere, produces great prosperity to the south. The doctrines of free trade and hostility to a high protective tariff have, no doubt, their champions in the slave-holding states. But the subject is really now more a theme for declamation than of hearty practical argument. The establishment of cotton factories is spreading with great rapidity in the south. The pride of forming a vast system of home manufactures has immense influence on the American mind. The benefits of those establishments are widely felt among the working class, who receive large wages in them. Enriching a great portion of the New England states, not well adapted to agriculture ; gradually increasing in those of the south, where bad farming and want of capital is already exhausting the soil ; and offering large profits for moneyed men in all parts of the Union ; "the manufacturing interest" does not consist merely of those persons who manage the factories, and who nominally own them, but of thousands of families whose sons and daughters work in the various mills, and of the more numerous shareholders among the wealthy classes, who make investments in their stock. Speeches, pamphlets, and newspaper articles may be profusely poured forth against a protective tariff; but their temporary effect is at once destroyed by a Liverpool price-current announcing a rise of half-a-cent a pound on American cotton. Politicians may speak, and churchmen preach against slavery, another half-cent advance in the next quotation effaces the impression from forum or pulpit, and silences that "still small voice" which might have begun to mingle with the eloquence of the statesman or divine.

The abolition party is undoubtedly augmenting, but the ratio of increase is perhaps not much disproportioned to that of the population at large; and assuredly the general hostility to abolitionism grows as fast as the party which advocates it. Were the abolitionists to double their numbers in the next five years, the animosity of their opponents would show the same result, and the passions thus excited would more than counterbalance the diminution of numbers in the people at large.

The abolitionists are the only portion of the community who desire a dissolution of the Union on grounds of religious principle or moral justice. No others even hint at it, except in some crisis of local ebullition on a question of mere money. But the balance is soon struck in the counsels of those who prate about "nullification;" and the dread of pecuniary ruin, inevitable on such a result, neutralises every boast of sectional dignity.

I look in vain, then, in the domestic affairs of the Union for the probable causes of its dissolution. But I see no influence preserving its integrity in any motives of a high and ennobling nature. Abstract veneration for the constitution or the law does not form the basis of the Union. The Americans as a nation have no abstract veneration for anything but money and money's worth ; gain is their impulse and their object in all things. If the south could get a sufficient market for their cotton, or the north find a cheap supply of it out of the United States, the Union would be in serious danger.* No innate love of country or of fellow-countrymen cements the national compact. This people have no local or personal attachments. They abandon their native soil or their natural connections without a sigh. As the sentiment of permanency never enters into their calculations, they would as lief try the experiment of a dissolution of the Union as not, were it not evident that such an event would entail upon them great and general pecuniary loss. I therefore come to the conclusion, that the chief risk to the present connection between the states is the love of change, so inherent in the national character. When that passion—their only one—becomes inflamed to a proper pitch, and the sources of minor speculation are exhausted, the states may break away, and finally separate ; and it is in such a catastrophe alone that the aspirants for aristocratical forms and the advocates of a higher civilisation can expect to realise their visions and their hopes.

* An extract from a Review in the *Times* newspaper of Oct. 7, 1858, of *Ellison's Hand Book of the Cotton Trade*, containing some valuable statistics, will be found in the Appendix to this volume.

CHAPTER XVIII.

POLITICAL PARTIES.

Defects of the Constitution—Invoked by all Parties, venerated by None—Sketch of Political Parties—Whigs—Democrats—Differences between them, and Discrepancies—Want of Analogy between them and the Political Parties of England—Political Nicknames—Real Subjects of Difference between the two Great Parties.

THE Constitution of the United States, although it is undoubtedly a document of eminent wisdom and ability, has yet some weak points and some ambiguous clauses. The men who framed it, conscious of its defects, were also convinced that future circumstances must inevitably affect, and public necessities modify, the best-considered schemes of human government. The Medes and Persians are bad models for lawgivers. They who believe themselves fit to legislate for all time, are unfit to legislate for any time. The framers of the declaration of American independence, while commencing their immortal manifesto with a great and striking truth, were well aware that the institutions they were establishing violated that very fundamental axiom. Declaring "that all men are born free and equal, and entitled to the enjoyment of liberty and the pursuit of happiness," they yet knew that the canker of slavery was eating into the heart of their country; and while in one passage obliged to allude to it, they dared not name it. So, in the wording of many of the clauses of the Constitution, regulating the powers of the Federal Congress, and endeavouring to secure a due balance of power between the general government and the separate states, a vagueness of expression was unavoidable, and has led to most conflicting opinions on many important subjects. Therefore it was, in the full admission of their own incompetency to legislate for remote, or even for close-coming, generations, they inserted a clause which provided for the alteration of the Constitution at any future time, in accordance with expediency and experience.

All the great political parties since the establishment of the national independence, whether avowing or concealing the real motives on which they act, severally assert that they base their respective systems on the principles established by the Constitution. But each acknowledging that those principles are liable to different constructions, and that the powers conferred by the Constitution are of questionable extent, they virtually admit that their theories are founded on shifting sand, instead of solid granite, the favourite figure of American rhetoricians. Hence, in the abounding conflicts between federal and states' rights, objects of national or sectional concern, fiscal regulations and financial schemes, never-dying differences arise between the various parties, in their respective views of foreign and domestic policy.

Were the Constitution considered as an oracle, to whose wisdom all men appealed, and before whose judgment they bowed, this state of things would not exist; but though continually invoked, it meets with no veneration. It is a general pass-word of every party, but not the Shibboleth of any. It was largely and fiercely opposed at the very period of its establishment. Its friends were called

Federalists, its opponents Anti-Federalists. Before its adoption, and during the discussions to which it gave rise, these parties were nearly equally balanced. In the Convention held in Massachusetts to decide the question of adopting the Constitution, the votes stood 187 yeas, and 169 nays. In the Convention of Virginia, the division was 89 yeas, and 79 nays ; and these proportions perhaps obtained throughout the country. Within five or six years after the adoption of the Constitution, it was found necessary to amend it in one very essential point, arising from the opinion of John Jay (one of its framers), then Chief Justice of the Supreme Court, that the different states were liable to be sued for debt by individuals, although the federal government of the United States was exempt from such liability. Another most striking instance of the defects of the Constitution was the means it devised for limiting the power of the President, which were lauded by its framers as nearly, if not absolutely perfect. Yet in the twelfth year of the Constitution, at the fourth election for President, the first that had been at all disputed, the provisions so universally approved and boasted of were found to fail, were materially altered, and, even so amended, are now admitted to be highly imperfect. This is but a new proof to the many existing in various countries of the earth, that written codes are but instruments of inefficacy, when they are not founded on pre-existing facts in accordance with the opinions and the experience of mankind. The Constitution was, in fact, a compromise, to harmonise as much as possible the contending views of different parties ; not a pact emanating from a spirit of national unanimity. It does not therefore command the reverence of the national mind : and the various parties who build their several claims to public confidence on their interpretations of this great charter, find the best excuse for their own fluctuations in its undeniable ambiguities.

After the Constitution was adopted, a new division of parties gradually arose, built on the preceding one, but not altogether identical with it. Of those who had opposed the adoption of the Constitution, multitudes became its friends. Of those who favoured its adoption, many ranged themselves with the party which was for giving the most limited construction to its powers. Thus the two new parties differed mainly on the construction of the Constitution in reference to such measures as the funding system, the assumption of the state debts by the federal government, and the incorporation of a national bank. The name of Federalists was retained by the party who advocated a liberal construction of the fundamental law. Anti-Federalism, having originally denoted opposition to the new frame of government, fell gradually into disfavour, and no other name was immediately substituted. The term Democratic was occasionally used by individuals of the party of which Jefferson was the leader, but it was made odious by the Democratic Societies founded by Genet, the minister sent to the United States by the French Directory, whose insolent assumption of authority gave general disgust. Patrick Henry said, in July, 1795, "Though a democrat myself, I like not the late Democratic Societies."

After the name of Anti-Federalists was dropped, as inappropriate, that of Republicans was the first denomination assumed by Mr. Jefferson and his friends. In his correspondence he sometimes calls his friends "the Whigs;" but Republican was the party name officially adopted. On both sides there was a disposition to deny the right of the opposite party to the name they respectively assumed. Jefferson, in one of his letters, January 26, 1799, alludes to the party supporting the administration of President Adams as "the Federalists, self-called," evidently considering the name as belonging of right to all the friends of the Constitution; while Washington, in writing to his nephew, May 5, in the same year, on the subject of the changes of opinion in Virginia. says, "I am sure there will be no relaxation on the part of the Republicans, as they have very erroneously called themselves;" meaning to imply that the party had no exclusive right to that designation.

In fact, almost the whole country at this period being unanimously attached to the republican government, and to the union of the states, political parties required more definite and distinctive appellations than either of those then in use. They had not yet commenced to *call* names, but only to adopt them, in the new-formed nation; and so things remained for about twenty years or more.

From the breaking out of the French Revolution till the close of the war with England in 1815, party differences turned almost wholly upon questions connected with the foreign relations of the country. The old controversies as to the construction of the Constitution lost much of their interest. When the Republican party came into power, under the Presidency of Jefferson in 1801, they were naturally much less jealous of the powers of the general government than they were during the tenure of office by the Federalists; while the latter, on the contrary, became, in opposition, much less favourable to the same powers than they were while in place. At the return of peace new interests began to be developed. Some questions were settled by time and the public convenience, such as the necessity of a national bank, while the rapid growth of the western country called for the adoption of the system known by the name of internal improvements. The capital invested in manufactures during the war required protection. The war had caused the creation of a large national debt, a military establishment, a great increase in the navy, and permanent fortifications for the defence of the coast: out of all these grew the necessity of a more liberal system of public expenditure. And from the application or misapplication of the national resources arose new causes for party hostility, and new conflicts between the prerogatives of the executive and the popular power.

On the elevation of Mr. Munroe to the Presidency in 1817, Utopian views as to an amalgamation of parties began to prevail. And General Jackson, then becoming prominent on the stage of public affairs, in a letter to the new President, urged him to seize the auspicious moment to exterminate "the monster party."

We can scarcely suppress a smile at this advice, from such a man, in such a country. Party names just then fell into disuse; but the things they designated were silently pushing into growth. Party spirit seemed to slumber; but it was like the open-eyed sleep of the hare. Mr. Munroe was re-elected, almost unanimously; but at the period of the succession to his second Presidential term, the existing organisation of parties began; and from that time to this the struggle has been upheld with untiring vigour, but disgraceful virulence.

The opposing interests of different portions of the Union greatly enhance the difficulty of party consistency on general principles involving the well-being of all. The free states and the slave states, the producing and the manufacturing districts, the shipping and the agricultural interests, in so wide an extent of territory, can scarcely find any common point on which to concentrate their views. It is thus that in no country in the world is there so much inconsistency among public men or political parties, such changing of position, such contradiction of opinions, such abandonment of principles, as in the every-day example of the United States of America.

One sentiment alone exists, susceptible of a general application, sufficient to keep together in a bond of moral action, the influential body which was formerly called the Federal, but for many years known as the Whig party. That is the absurd, but I fear invincible, desire to follow the example of their European ancestors, in establishing a separate and privileged class; forgetting that what grew up spontaneously with the feudal institutions of the old world is incompatible with the genius, as it is adverse to the true interests of the American people.

This desire is, in fact, but a family weakness, so to speak, with many of the immediate descendants of the revolutionary leaders. It may be excusable in the sons of the men who, on the establishment of independence in 1783, wished to confer a crown on Washington, and who immediately afterwards formed the order of the Cincinnati, with him at its head; an order of knighthood, with insignia and distinctive marks of honour, and which it was proposed to convert into an order of nobility, by making those honours hereditary.

The tendencies of such men, however they might be concealed for the purpose of conciliating and hoodwinking the mass, must have long lingered in their early direction; and they were naturally shared in by many of their children. The first Federalists had been, before the revolutionary war, in tastes and habits Englishmen, and subjects of a monarchy, whose political institutions gave their colouring to the social state of the colonists as well as to the mother country. To fight for liberty was a glorious excitement to them. To have gained independence a noble enjoyment. The equality of the battle-field or the bivouac, is the natural condition of men in arms; but to carry it into the forms and customs of civil life was a necessity against which many proud and stubborn spirits revolted. However the men who made the revolution might have been satisfied, and many of them reluctantly submitted, that it should result in a Republic, there were numbers of them who were strongly opposed to its sinking into a Democracy. But the force of things obliged the men of the last century to yield. The resistance of the Federalists was overborne by the popular impulse. Yet their successors, the Whigs, in choosing a new title, less likely to shock the public feeling, could not divest themselves of the inherent passion which, though unavowed as a principle of the party, is even to this day boasted of by every individual who has the honesty to speak his mind.

This feeling is absurdly adopted by thousands of the *parvenus* who have long abounded in the Whig party, and in whom it is but an assumption, not a sentiment. The mingled pretension and meanness of such persons are highly offensive. These qualities are, in the first instance, concealed from passing observers. A foreigner, who travels rapidly through the country, cannot penetrate the motives of those who invite him to their houses, whose attentions seem so generous, and whose *empressement* takes the form of hospitality. The deficiencies in their manners and entertainments are not objected to, as long as they are believed to be in keeping with homely thoughts and humble desires. It is only when we discover that these individuals hold most inflated notions of their own importance, and assume a profound contempt for the people from whom they or their fathers have sprung, that we lose all confidence in the party of which they form the main strength.

Let it be disguised or disavowed as it may, this foolish and fatal longing for aristocratical distinction and exclusive power, is the one strong cement that has hitherto kept this great party together. The events of the last twenty-five years have considerably loosened the connection ; and it is now splitting off into fragments, under the influence of the Democratic spirit which spreads so rapidly.*

The early struggles of the principles adopted by Jefferson against those inherent in Washington and Hamilton, and congenial to the feelings of the wealthy and well-born among the first republicans, need be only adverted to here, to fix the reader's mind upon the shifting scenes of party conflict, from those days down to the period of General Jackson's first election to the Presidency in the year 1828. It is not my purpose to treat of the many questions which, during that interval, were considered the rallying points of the Federal party. I shall rather confine myself to those which have been adopted and avowed since that remarkable epoch of democratic ascendancy. Looking behind those questions, my endeavour has been to come at the secret spring of the various movements, so complicated and contradictory ; and I have no doubt that all may be resolved into that dominant

* Boston, one of the strongholds of Whiggism, offered in the winter of 1844—1845 a striking evidence of this spirit. In despite of all the repeated efforts of the dominant party to elect a Mayor from their leading men, heretofore a matter-of-course, they were defeated three several times, and as many of their candidates rejected, to make way for a watchmaker named Davis, who died in possession of his civic honours.

desire, just now alluded to, of creating—by the force of time and through the agency of banks, monopolies, extravagant expenditure, and sinister legislation—a distinct order—patrician, equestrian, no matter what it might be called—with separate influences and interests from those of the people at large.

Such has undoubtedly been the influence of the Federal and Whig leaders, and it has affected in a less absolute degree the opinions of their less wealthy but as ambitious followers; while the millions of artisans, farmers, and working-men who swell their ranks, have been actuated by the numerous local and selfish motives which lead men to adopt and cling to measures that they believe to be for their benefit. The example of the leading Whigs has of course great influence on the numerous class who admire their talents, respect their wealth, esteem their personal virtues, or depend on their patronage. Hence it is that their great force lies in the large towns, where they chiefly reside, where their money is spent, their eloquence listened to, and their business operations carried on.

An intense opposition to this deep design of the Whigs (which although never reduced to a system or publicly proclaimed, was early seen through and unflinchingly denounced) has been the life-spring of the popular party; and it is from necessity, rather perhaps than from choice, the creed of those educated persons whose ambition urged them into the political arena, and whose talent assured them the foremost position in the Democratic ranks. Many of those leaders have been, from time to time, men of independent means. But the great mass of property and the associations of "gentle blood" and family pride are to be found more conspicuously in the other party, particularly in the northern and eastern portions of the

Union. The foundation of the democratic party is the broad basis of the population at large. The people of the interior, farmers, planters, persons out of the atmosphere of commerce and manufactures, mostly belong to it. Men of property are no doubt to be largely reckoned in its ranks, and many of those, defying the prevalent influences of "fashionable society" and aristocratic pretensions, must be there from feelings of real conviction.

But whatever may be the varieties of dissent, or the manifold discrepancies between Whigs and Democrats, it will be found that all party differences have their source in the broad line of distinction between the moneyed and the working-classes—the would-be patricians, and the must-be plebeians. The operation of various constitutional measures causes at times anomalies which appear very puzzling, and the more so from the shameful tergiversations of public men, who constantly labour to mix up all political questions into a confusion that may hide their own inconsistencies. But the two principles, of encroachment on the one hand, and resistance on the other, will be sure to be found at the bottom of all disputes.

And strange as it may sound to English ears, it is no less true, that the Democratic is at the same time the Conservative party in the United States. It stands on the solid ground of republican rights, and it holds by the universal liberty and equality which they have guaranteed. But the Whigs, in the meantime, cannot be justly called Radicals. They do not attempt to root up the tree of the Constitution. They would only graft upon it the extraneous branches of a foreign growth. The Whigs are innovaters rather than reformers. They do not pretend that the political structure wants repair—but only improvement. They merely advocate ornament.

They would put a Corinthian capital on a Doric shaft. The Democrats prefer a simple column, of solid strength and congruous proportions, rejecting all that is composite, as out of keeping with the great design of the Temple of Freedom raised by their fathers, and in which they worship.

From these observations it may be inferred that I can find no analogy between the designations of parties in England and those in the United States. The one which professes what is with us called Toryism is there called Whig. The most extreme Democrats are there called Tories and Radicals, at one and the same time. In fact, in thus borrowing from the mother-country these and other political *sobriquets*, and applying them in slap-dash confusion, the Americans servilely adopt English phrases wholly out of keeping with their institutions and their manners. But this is only worth remarking as another proof of the spirit of imitation which is allied with their assumed superiority.

There are, however, two original nicknames very commonly applied by the opposing parties to their adversaries, viz., Locofocos and Coons. These, like political nicknames generally, are ignoble in their origin; and they have no moral signification whatever, being only indicative of the vulgarity and feebleness of party spite. At a democratic meeting in New York, some twenty years back, a few Whigs, by a dexterous trick, stopped the gas-pipes, and left the room for a while in total darkness. But several of the members of the meeting having been apprised of the intended manœuvre, had supplied themselves with candles and boxes containing a newly invented kind of match, called *locofoco*. With these they soon remedied the mischief; numerous lights were produced;

and the designation of Locofoco was attached generally to the party, a portion of which had so much benefited by the use of the matches so called.

The word Coon was, on the other hand, applied by the Democratic party to the Whigs, because some stuffed skins of that animal (the racoon) had been hoisted by them, as emblems of hunting prowess, during the Presidential contest in 1840, and because a ludicrous fable (the point of which consisted in a racoon calling out to a marksman who levelled his rifle at it, "I'm a gone 'coon!") was turned in derision on those who adopted so questionable an emblem, they themselves being looked on as so many "gone 'coons," when the aim of the Locofocos was unerringly fixed on them, and so likely to bring them down from their temporary elevation. Many other designations of party have since been adopted, such as Barnburners, Old Hunkers, Hard-shells, and Soft-shells, all as meaningless as they are vulgar.

The leading subjects of difference until very lately subsisting in the United States were almost altogether financial. A national bank, a federal exchequer, distribution of the public lands among the several states, a tariff of protection for manufactures, and the assumption by the whole country of the debts due by individual states, and the creation of a national debt for their liquidation, were the main points of debate and discussion between the Whig and the Democratic parties.

To subdivide and classify these several points of dispute into a code, upheld by one party and opposed by the other, is quite beyond my capability. The ramifications are so intricate, that I cannot undertake to disentangle them. The nearest attempt I can make at elucidation is by stating that paper money and the credit system on a most extensive scale seem to be the essence of Whig principles, all the various objects above enumerated being the machinery required for carrying them out ; while a a specie currency and ready-money dealings being the basis of the Democratic doctrines, they are in direct opposition to the various auxiliary measures advocated by the Whigs.

But the great difficulty opposed to a clear comprehension of the matter, arises from the frequent changes of opinion among the Whigs themselves. Smarting under the failure of most of their designs, they have all become impatient—some of them desperate ; and personal antipathies combining with party disappointments, they fell into a state of most deplorable disunion ; so much so, indeed, as to make it impossible to define the policy by which, as a party, they were guided, The Democrats, on the contrary, are in compact opposition to all the great measures which so divide their opponents. But many incidental questions of great moment exist, on which there is much diversity of opinion in both the parties. Among these are the policy or impolicy of the veto power, as granted by the constitution to the President ; and the privilege of re-election to his office for a second term of four years, immediately after the expiration of the first term.

The exercise of the veto power, by President Tyler, on three occasions within a very short period of his accession, brought the first of these questions strongly before the public ; and it acquired greater importance from being the subject of denunciation on the part of Henry Clay, himself a candidate for the Presidency. President Harrison, in his inaugural address, introduced this topic in a way to show that he was unfavourable to the frequent exercise of the privilege. But Harrison was not a great authority ;

and no particular attention was given to his remarks, nor even to his solemn disavowal of an intention to become a candidate for re-election ; had he lived to complete his first term of four years. Subsequent Presidents, down to the actual incumbent Buchanan have entertained varying opinions on this subject. But many other questions in connection with party differences arise, and require another chapter for their due development.

CHAPTER XIX.

PARTY DESIGNS—PRESIDENTIAL ELECTION.

The Whig Party—Its Objects—The United States Bank—Its Origin and History—War waged against it by President Jackson—Its Destruction—Rally made by the Whigs in 1839—Harrisburg Convention—Presidential Elections of 1840—General Harrison—Great Whig Meeting at Bunker's Hill—Democratic Meeting on Dorchester Heights—False Confidence of the Democratic or Locofoco Party—Election of General Harrison.

THE old Federal party in the United States having been broken up by the force of democratic principles, became merged, as before stated, in the combination of opinions which constituted the party known as the Whigs.

This Whig party, as I found it on arriving in America in 1839, was formed of most incongruous elements. Ci-devant Democrats like Henry Clay, old Federalists like Daniel Webster, Virginian theorists, nicknamed "Abstractionists," like John Tyler, former "Jackson Men," like William C. Rives, Conservatives like Talmadge, men of all possible inconsistencies like John Quincy Adams, had joined together, under various conflicting influences, to make one mass of opposition to the existing Democratic or "Locofoco" party, and force its chief, Martin Van Buren, from the Presidential chair, which he had filled for the three preceding years.

It would require considerable space and time to detail the proceedings of this extraordinary coalition. In giving a short sketch of those proceedings, I must remark that that coalition was entirely identical with the portion of society which is so anxious to establish an "aristocracy" and its concomitant associations. Aware, as before stated, of the obstacles to the completion of their design, even at a remote period, they had nevertheless laboured, for a long time and with great industry, to lay the foundation for the social structure they could not hope themselves to raise. Measure after measure was proposed, and some of them from time to time carried, in spite of the vigilance of the Democratic party, all tending to a state of things which, if upheld, would have inevitably led to the realisation of their projects. The establishment of joint-stock companies all over the country, for every conceivable purpose of commercial or manufacturing speculation, and of a system of banking institutions unparalleled in extent; and the endowment of these "corporations," with exorbitant privileges in the conduct of their affairs, formed a multitude of compact monopolies, all bound together by a common tie of moneyed influence, however particular rivalries might have here and there embarrassed their general action on the public interests. The universal regulator—the avowed oracle—of this swarm of exclusive institutions had been the second Bank of the United States, established at Philadelphia in the year 1816, and for several years under the dictatorship of the celebrated Nicholas Biddle, nominally assisted by a board of satellite directors.

It is not my intention to minutely discuss the merits or demerits of this great but long since defeated scheme. Suffice it to say, that the mighty moneyed class hoped through its agency to sap the foundations of the Democratic system, with which that class had held such a strenuous tug for supremacy ever since the days of

Jefferson; and under the insidious influence of the money power the cause of the people was beyond doubt in imminent jeopardy, when the election of Andrew Jackson to the Presidency of the Union, and the defeat of his fantastic opponent, John Quincy Adams, in the year 1829, changed the whole face of affairs, and was, I firmly believe, the salvation of the country from its then perilous position.

The elevation of this clear-sighted and strong-minded man, so sudden and so unexpected, was one of those events that look like interventions of Providence for a nation's safety. Principles adverse to the continuance of the Republic on its original plan were, beyond doubt, gaining a footing throughout the Union. The most lavish expenditure of money was carried on, nominally for works of internal improvement, but truly for purposes of party jobbing on a gigantic scale, the funds to carry on which were all borrowed from European capitalists on the security of the bonds of the various states, until the whole Union was nearly mortgaged to those foreign creditors. A course of reckless extravagance was pursued; and while, under the delusive pretext of prosperity, the national debt was extinguished, a series of state liabilities was instituted, which left the country virtually indebted to an extent that nearly amounted to its insolvency.

It would be impossible for me to enumerate the specific instances of wholesale profligacy, or to argue deeply the case of either party, in the furious financial war which was waged for twelve years from the date last mentioned, namely, from 1829 until 1841. The Bank of the United States and Nicholas Biddle, its manager, must be taken as the types of one of those belligerent parties. Andrew Jackson, President of the United States during the first eight of those years, and Martin Van Buren, his successor for the last four of them, must stand as the representative of the other.

And the British public, who so deeply suffered, may even now, were it only by way of warning, tolerate a brief notice of the origin and progress of that celebrated institution, whose existence and decease have had such influence on monetary affairs.

The creation of a national bank was a prominent topic of consideration, even before the establishment of the Constitution of the United States. And both then and for a long time after, the measure met with the opposition of some of the leading men of the country.

The convention that framed the Constitution expressly refused, by a vote of eight states against three, the power to make a bank or erect any other kind of corporation. *Vide* the "Madison Papers," vol. iii. pp. 1576-77.

On two occasions, and in two distinct forms, August 18th and September 14th, 1787, a motion was brought forward in Congress to give that body power to erect a corporation; and it was voted down by the framers of the Constitution. John Hancock and Samuel Adams adopted and insisted on this anti-corporation doctrine in the Massachusetts Convention of 1788. Jefferson's opinions against it are well known. So also are those of Calhoun, in direct opposition to the entire system of banking, and specially to the creation of a national bank. In 1812 Henry Clay "could nowhere find in the Constitution the vagrant power to create a bank." Nor could Webster in 1816, and as late as 1832; for he even then stated that "of all the contrivances for cheating the labouring classes none have been more effectual than that which deludes them with paper money, the most effectual of all inventions to fertilise the rich man's field with the sweat of the poor man's brow."—*Speeches*, vol. ii. p. 81.

Yet Clay and Webster were in 1841 jointly labouring with might and main to establish a national bank, and make paper money the currency of the country. In that year Webster forcibly advocated a national bank at a great public meeting in the city of New York, chiefly on the ground that "its odour of nationality" would secure the confidence of the people. But such are the rapid shiftings of political opinions in the United States, that I heard Webster declare, in Faneuil Hall, Boston, in October, 1842, that even then the proposal of re-creating a national bank had become "an obsolete idea."

The original plan of a national bank in the United States was started by Alexander Hamilton some time in the winter of 1778-9, to be founded on a foreign loan of two millions of dollars, and two hundred millions of paper money, to be valued at ten millions in specie. Many persons of intelligence and good sense were satisfied at that period of the advantages and facilities obtained by the governments and people of Europe from the establishment of such institutions. But they forgot that they had arisen there under circumstances far different from those in which the United States were then placed. Even the Bank of England had not been established for the purpose of restoring a fallen credit, but to give stability to one in danger of being impaired. Hamilton's object was to re-build, by such an institution, a confidence shaken almost to its foundation. His views were clearly expressed; but they were too bold and too much in advance of the financial knowledge of the time.

Robert Morris of Pennsylvania submitted to Congress another plan, in June, 1780, of a far more restricted nature than that of Hamilton, for he expressed himself satisfied with an institution founded on a moneyed capital alone ; and the Bank of Pennsylvania was established on that basis. Gouverneur* Morris proposed the Bank of North America in May, 1781 ; but it was reserved for Hamilton, soon after he was chosen Secretary of the Treasury during Washington's first Presidency, to submit to Congress his definitive report on the formation of a national bank, on the 13th of December, 1790. His opponents, headed by Madison, laboured hard to defeat his plan ; and the fact that the Constitution gave no direct authority to Congress to create a bank was eagerly seized on and adroitly used. But all was in vain. Washington, taking on himself to decide between the fluctuating opinions of his divided cabinet, adopted Hamilton's plan, and the charter of the bank received the President's signature.

The two questions connected with the establishment of a national bank, first its constitutionality, secondly its expediency, have caused much discussion, fierce debate, and party difference, from that time to the present. The topic has been one of absorbing interest, drawing almost every other into its vortex. The low state of national credit in the early days of American independence, seems to have justified the resort to this financial experiment, which certainly in the first instance fulfilled the purpose of its creation. Commerce revived. The intercourse between the states was facilitated by an equalisation of the exchanges, and became more intimate and secure. The price of the debt rose to its par value. The resources of the government were placed beyond the reach of peculation, and disbursed in the most distant parts of the Union

* A family name, not a title.

without loss. In short, all the great objects of a national bank were answered, from the one important fact that its operations were honestly managed.

The charter of the first national bank having expired, the government were forced to the necessity of proposing the project of a second, in the year 1814, in consequence of the financial difficulties arising from the war then declared against England. The leading features of this new plan were a capital of 50,000,000 of dollars, to consist, with the exception of a few millions of specie, entirely of the stock issued by the government for loans made to carry on the war. This project met with strong opposition in Congress, particularly from Mr. Calhoun, and after various attempts being made to pass a variety of bills, the whole scheme was frustrated.

On the conclusion of the war in 1815, this favourite measure was again introduced; and a national bank was formally recommended by the President, Mr. Madison (its early opponent), in his annual message to Congress. The great majority of that body concurred with the government, and even Calhoun, though adverse to the system in the abstract, yielded to the opinion that under existing circumstances a bank was indispensable, and having long argued in one sense, he now voted in the other. The separation of the government from the bank was then out of the question; nor was it possible to collect the taxes and dues in specie. The bill was passed, and the second national bank was chartered in 1816, for a period of twenty years. It was made by its charter the fiscal agent of the government for the collection, distribution, and safe-keeping of the public funds, unless otherwise ordered by the Secretary of the Treasury, and in that case it was provided that he should report to Congress his reasons for so doing. This condition of the bank's creation led to the memorable struggle between General Jackson and the legislature, as well as with that institution which had so powerful an influence on the financial, commercial, and political fate of the Union. The President in the year 1834, assuming on himself an entire and uncontrolled authority, ordered the removal of the government deposits from the Bank of the United States, and their transfer to certain state banks selected for that purpose, out of some hundreds then in existence ; having previously removed Mr. Duane, the Secretary of the Treasury, whose opinion was an obstacle to this decisive act of presidential despotism.

A powerful opposition was made to this bold measure ; but the obstinacy of General Jackson prevailed. Calhoun joined his efforts to those of Clay, Webster, and the whole federal party, to curb the President's assumption and exercise of absolute power. But he refused to sanction Webster's attempt to obtain a renewal of the bank charter for six years. Every successive effort to effect that proposition failed. Jackson was invincible. And the final veto which he put on the bill that subsequently passed both Houses of Congress for re-chartering the bank, completed his victory, and sealed the fate of that institution for ever.

Great confusion of facts and misrepresentation of arguments abound on this intricate subject, and sins were laid at the doors of each of the great actors respectively. Biddle, who was vanquished in the contest, has been charged with designs and identified with mischiefs in which he had no hand. The main ground established by this great financial schemer was that a national bank was necessary to restrain the excess of state banking ; that it was the real balance wheel of the paper currency of the states; that while the states held the power of chartering banks without limitation in number or capital, and consequently of augmenting or diminishing the currency at any time and to any extent, nothing could save the country from the mischievous operations of expansion and extension but a bank created by Congress, with sufficient capital to control all the operations of the State Banks.

The ground taken by General Jackson was, that a national bank was unconstitutional, unless it were necessary as a fiscal agent of the federal government; that it was not thus necessary, because the functions of such an agent could be performed better by the state banks; that the multiplication of the state banks was one of the best modes of rendering a national bank useless; and that the banking power was much more dangerous to liberty when connected with one national institution, than when diffused among several institutions under the control of the various states of the Union.

Jackson, the son of an Irish settler in the west, was strong-willed and impetuous, a man of little learning, but of intuitive quickness of apprehension; originally a poor attorney, subsequently a petty judge in his wild district; then an officer of militia, and quickly promoted to be a general in the regular army, and military governor of a large territory; and he was, in every one of those situations, a most remarkable person. Of calm bearing but undaunted courage—the latter amounting at times to ferocity—he had been noted for some daring acts of personal encounter, "street fights" and deliberate duels, in one of which he killed his opponent on the spot. The events of his career in his Florida campaigns against the Indians, and in his memorable defence of the city of New Orleans against the English forces in 1813, stamp his character with marks of superior power, which neither factious hostility to the man nor conscientious disapproval of his particular deeds can efface.

His elevation to the Presidency of the Union was looked on, both in America and Europe, with great alarm by all the lovers of peace and order. His previous violence of character and conduct amply justified their fears. But I need not dwell on the mild and peace-preserving contrast presented to them by his whole Presidential career. One great object of domestic policy absorbed his mind.

His ruling principle of conduct, on assuming the office of chief magistrate of the republic, was the destruction of the Bank of the United States. His motives for this object have been the subject of many different opinions. Mine is that he saw in that institution, and in the man who wielded its immense resources, the most dangerous instruments of national corruption which had come into play since the formation of the Republic; and that seeing all this, he felt it both a duty and a pleasure to complete their ruin. The sense of duty without the personal enjoyment had not probably been enough to ensure his perseverance. But he never flinched or turned aside. His success was perfect; and subsequent developments fully justified his hostility.

The labours of Hercules were but a type of this great work. The Nemæan Lion and the Augean stable did not present obstacles more formidable, or more foul, than Nicholas Biddle and his profligate establishment. He was, beyond doubt, a powerful man, of great ambition and experience in the world's ways. Backed by an illimitable command of money, credit, and reputation, and by a party containing talent, wealth, and influence, the war waged against him and his supporters was an undertaking of infinite boldness. But Jackson had the strength of a just cause and an earnest population at his back: his own firmness and their good sense carried him through; and he so thoroughly scotched the financial monster which held the nation in its folds, that Martin van Buren, when he succeeded to the Presidential chair, had little to do but look on and see it die. No one had the merit of actually killing it. It went out like an exhausted firework, with a lurid flash, and in bad odour. Under the title of "Bank of the United States," it was re-chartered by the legislature of Pennsylvania, in defiance of Jackson's veto; and under that false character it continued to be the means of deluding many an unfortunate European speculator, long after the Americans had ceased to have the slightest confidence in it, until its utter extinction in the year 1841.

But before this consummation, the Whig party had made that amazing rally to which I have already alluded, and in December 1839 they elected a number of delegates from all parts of the Union, to meet at Harrisburg in Pennsylvania, for the purpose of fixing on a candidate for President of the United States. The judicious management of that important convention was another striking illustration of the practical good sense of this people on any great necessity. The Whig expectants for nomination were Clay, Webster, Scott, and Harrison. Webster's name was soon withdrawn. He had not the remotest chance of success. Clay had a large body of adherents, and could have commanded the votes of several of the states. Scott also had some supporters; and Harrison his partisans. Had an election taken place between these three, Clay would no doubt have been the successful competitor. But he could not have commanded anything like a sufficiency to have entered the lists as the chosen Whig candidate against Van Buren with the hitherto enormous majority of the Democratic party; for the Scott and Harrison portions of the Whigs were inveterately hostile to Clay's success, and never would have rallied round him. Scott laboured in a minor degree under a similar difficulty. Such were the party divisions of that day; and the Harrisburg Convention soon came to the conclusion that, if they started either Clay or Scott, the triumph of Van Buren and the Democracy would have been complete. They accordingly nominated General William Henry Harrison, as, in their own phraseology, "the most available candidate;" and John Tyler, of Virginia, was fixed on for the office of Vice-President. The decision was acquiesced in with perfect apparent satisfaction by Clay, Scott, and their respective friends. And thus was an instance afforded, on a point of the most important and tender nature, of that amazing spirit of discipline and self-control, on which I have elsewhere enlarged as one of the most striking characteristics of the American people.

No sooner was the result of the Harrisburg Convention made known to the country, than the whole Whig party joined as one man in a jubilee of rejoicing. Harrison was immediately proclaimed to be a masterpiece of perfection. As warrior, statesman, orator, and scholar, he was lauded beyond all rational bounds; and so many various qualities were discovered in him, that those who had known him long and well were bewildered at the gross amount. There was no use in analysing his character, separating its component parts, or measuring them with each other. The enthusiastic estimate of general opinion was admitted and adopted, and idol-worship in this instance reached its loftiest height.

The Whig party, however, did not expend their

enthusiasm in mere idolatry. They joined to it a practical energy that made them irresistible. Enormous sums were subscribed by the wealthy. Men of small means were largely taxed for contributions. No bounds were placed to the popular expense. Every one who had ever spoken in public, and many who had never done so, hurried to the meetings which were convened all through the Union, for the promulgation of the views of the party —at least of such of them as the party chose to proclaim. Stump oratory had never been tried by such distinguished declaimers as were now to be heard in every street and at every cross-road. City orators and country orators of every grade, members of congress, senators and representatives, and governors of states, were made evident as open and clamorous demagogues. The Whig presses groaned under the weight of labour. Eloquence of all varieties, from "moral 'suasion" to fierce invective was poured forth in rushing streams. Portraits of Harrison in every form, fixed or portable, were profusely displayed. In these he generally figured in equestrian dignity, as the conqueror at "Tippecanoe" or "the Thames" (pronounced Thaymes), or some other of the petty skirmishes with the British or the Indians, which gave him the title of the hero of a hundred fights. But these pictures were as much things of fancy as the glories they blazoned forth. The manly, portly personage of the print or the transparency was no more like the living original, than "the Thames" was like Marengo or "Tippecanoe" like Austerlitz. But the purpose of these devices was answered. The Whigs believed Harrison to be very much of a hero, and not a little of a Hercules. Yet all this would have been insufficient to have secured his election, had not the democrats lent him most powerful means of success, by an error in tactics of which the Whigs took effective advantage.

By a too common practice in political warfare, the Democratic party affected to undervalue their over-praised opponent. Ridicule was unsparingly poured on him. He was insultingly called in the Van Buren papers, and by some of the Locofoco orators, a coward, an imbecile, an old woman; his victories rated at a low value (but probably above their real worth); and his talents as beneath criticism. All this might have failed to produce a great reaction in Harrison's favour. But his adversaries went farther—and there was their fatally false step. Some virulent editor spoke with contemptuous irony of Harrison as a poor farmer, living in a log cabin, and only able to afford to drink hard cider, the meanest American beverage. An attack like this at once enlisted in favour of its object the sympathies of thousands who, but for it, had probably remained neutral. The Whig leaders, assuming (but unconsciously, for very few of them had ever heard of it) the part played by the *Gueux* of Belgium in the sixteenth century, immediately adopted those sarcastic reproaches as the rallying cry of their party. And as the *Gueux* took the wallet of beggary for their emblem, so did the Whigs now adopt the log cabin and cider barrel for theirs. Effigies of Harrison were soon everywhere seen, in a totally new character and costume. The military chief was transformed into "the Farmer of North Bend," the name of his residence on the Ohio River. There he stood in his smock frock, holding his plough with one hand, while the other was stretched forth to greet a wooden-legged soldier, who claimed the hospitality of the log cabin, seen hard by, with a cider barrel close to the open door. Prints of this nature were profusely scattered through the country. Transparencies decorated the windows at night. And in the numerous processions by day, dozens of banners to the same effect were displayed. Then Whig songs were written and sung all over the Union, in honour of "old Tip," the familiar pet name for the hero of Tippecanoe; and the first verse of the most popular of them ran as follows:—

What has caused the great commotion,
Motion all the country through?
It is the people gathering all,
Responding to the country's call,
To put down the Locos' cry and hue—
And they'll do it all, with Tippecanoe.
Tippecanoe,
And Tyler, too.

Which words were shouted in every street, by all the musical and unmusical men and boys throughout the country.

From every testimony worthy of credit, I have reason to believe that the political excitement during this Presidential contest, was greater than any that had ever before or since been experienced in the United States. The efforts made by the Whig party were altogether unprecedented. Innumerable meetings were held in each of the states. Gatherings of many thousands were common. The masses were never so absolutely appealed to, particularly by that party which affects to hold them cheap. The conventions at Baltimore in May, and at Boston on the 17th of September, 1840, were the most numerously attended. The latter must have brought together 50,000 men, independent of the city population. Fully one half of that number rode or walked in party procession to Bunker's Hill on the latter occasion, where they were addressed by

Daniel Webster, as president of the meeting, and many others more or less eminent.

The immense assemblage, increased by lookers-on of all parties to double the number of those who regularly marched in procession, covered the surface of that memorable elevation. And had the object been one of patriotism instead of mere party, the moral effect would have been as sublime as the material appearance was imposing. There was a "chief marshal" with numerous assistant "marshals," like staff and field officers, all mounted, and wearing the insignia of command, swords, cocked hats, and scarfs of blue or pink, and dressed in suits of black. Many other grades, equivalent to those of regimental rank, had their regular places at the head of sections and platoons. There were several bands of music, and innumerable banners; while the whole array marched and manœuvred in sundry complicated evolutions, with great precision, only wanting uniforms, accoutrements, and weapons to be, in all intents and purposes, an army.

There was not the slightest appearance of military or police force; yet such was the decorum of the day, that not a single breach of the peace nor a single accident occurred, although large numbers of the opposite political party were abroad.

I had obtained admission, through the complaisance of the managing committee, into the garden of a gentleman whose house was on the most elevated inhabited part of Bunker's Hill, where the hustings were erected for the speakers to address the multitude thickly crowded on its surface. I was, therefore, close to the busiest portion of the scene, and I heard perfectly the various speeches. The eloquence did not strike me as of a high order. It was quite *ad captandum*, and rather common-place: and I could not help reflecting that of all the immense throng before me, excited and hurried away by the political feeling of the hour, there was not perhaps one whose mind reverted to the scene of glorious celebrity acted on that very hill sixty-five years before, or who looked up, as I inadvertently did, to its granite monument, with the fervour of historic reverence.

But the dispersion of this great meeting was the most picturesque of its many associations ; wrapped up in their enthusiasm (if I must give it that name) and listening intently to the speeches of the several orators, the immense crowd seemed insensible to the threatening aspect of the heavens, and the distant mutterings of the thunder which rolled far away to the westward. In that quarter, however, and to the north, the clouds were becoming livid and louring. The sunshine, which till three o'clock had lighted the magnificent panorama of city, sea, and country, now became fainter in the deep shadow of the sky. The brilliancy of the silken banners floating over the dense masses was by degrees obscured. The granite column rising above them grew more sombre, and a moaning wind swept across the crowd, and seemed to sway the thousands of heads to and fro.

Myself and two gentlemen unconnected with the active business of the meeting, perceiving these elemental warnings, agreed to retire from the scene, and making our way from the platform where we stood, and over the garden wall, we worked our passage across the broken surface of the hill in the direction of the timber yard, the least obstructed portion of its large space. Loud claps of thunder and vivid lightning had by this time aroused the gathering to the necessity of a retreat ; and the bands striking up, the several companies began to file off from the ground in excellent order. Thousands of lookers-on were also in motion homewards, and before we reached Charlestown (the city suburb close under Bunker's Hill) the approach to the two long wooden bridges connecting it with Boston was crammed with the retreating crowd. We were soon mixed with the rest; and a scene of great but most picturesque confusion took place. The wind increased to a hurricane. It gave me the idea of a tropical tornado. Columns of dust were whirled into the air, and the wild gusts sweeping it and us before them, enveloped us in partial gloom. The sea at either side of the bridges was lashed into foam, and the spray driven up among the throng. The rain came down in rattling torrents. The lightning streamed all round. But the heavy tramp of the thousands rushing across the wooden bridges deadened the thunder, and the mixture of deep sounds was most impressive. But among them was no utterance of voices. No one spoke. Not an exclamation of impatience broke forth. Every one seemed intent on his business, which was to reach his home as fast as he could. The Yankee character was strikingly exemplified in this whole scene. But my fancy was all the time busily at work in conjuring up the image of some flying military host: and as I marked the dripping marshals pushing along on horseback or on foot, the draggled banners, the musicians of the various bands, and the indiscriminate mass of badged and ribboned men, I thought of the Borodino, and many another scene of rout and ruin; while the flashing lightning and the loud thunder-peals realised the notion of a hostile artillery pouring its vengeance on the fugitives.

By good luck we found refuge in a wooden hovel which served as a kind of public office of *octroi*, close to the further end of the bridge. The obliging functionary recognising me, proceeded as soon as the storm subsided a little, to get a carriage for me at a neighbouring livery stable. But while my companions and myself awaited in our shed of shelter, and on our drive home, I remarked that of the many hundreds we saw, drenched to the skin, their best suits spoiled, and their day's sport broken up, not one gave the slightest symptom of dissatisfaction, or seemed to have lost his or her temper.

The inference to be drawn from the scene I have described, and the many similar ones acted at the same epoch throughout the country, was that a party which could combine so much union with such energy, must be almost sure to carry its point, against opponents who stood on the defensive in possession of office, and in a degree blinded by the confidence which possession always gives.

In several of the States the Whigs obtained majorities in the elections for governors, members of Congress, and of the State Legislature, during the months of August, September, and October, 1840, successes for which the democratic party was wholly unprepared. The best informed among that party were, to my knowledge, quite at fault in their calculations. But when the Locofocos saw the torrent flowing fast upon them, they certainly made vigorous efforts to stem it. They were by no means so boisterous or animated as their opponents ; but their meetings were frequent, serious, and ardent. One of those which I attended, was almost as picturesque as the Whig gathering on Bunker's Hill, although in most of its circumstances an absolute contrast to it.

The meeting I allude to was held in the old fort (now going fast to decay) on Dorchester Heights, close to the suburb called South Boston, and a couple of miles from the city. This fort is remarkable, as having been erected under the immediate orders of Washington, while the royal forces were in possession of the town, and the English squadron, consisting of several ships of war, lay in the harbour. The unexpected appearance on these heights, at daybreak one morning, of a battery hastily thrown up the previous night, and their occupation by a large body of the patriots under the command of their immortal chief, struck a complete panic into the royalists. The vessels immediately left the harbour, which was thus commanded by the enemy's guns ; and the evacuation of Boston was the speedy consequence of Washington's bold measures. The site made memorable by these events was a fitting place of meeting for a body calling themselves, *par excellence*, the patriots of the land. And there did about 5000 of the Locofocos repair in procession one dark night in October 1840, with bands playing, banners streaming, and abundance of torches gleaming—the whole regularly organised, commanded, and manœuvred, and producing an effect highly melodramatic and striking. Far less gaudy in dress and decoration than the Whig assemblage, which numbered the whole force of the wealthy "aristocrats" and their retainers, there was something sombre and almost desperate in the tone of this democratic night-gathering, which made it, as a mere *spectacle* perhaps, more impressive.

I accompanied this procession, but of course did not walk in it, with George Bancroft, the then collector of the Port of Boston, and the historian of his country. The march from Boston to the heights of Dorchester, through long streets, many of the houses illuminated in honour of the occasion, and across the wooden bridge connecting the city with the suburb—the torches throwing their glare upon the water—then winding up the steep hill, and finally crossing the dry ditch and entering the narrow pathway into the fort, was altogether a picture which has left a vivid impression on my mind.

The area within the crumbling walls was soon densely filled, as well as the earth-formed ramparts rising round, on which sundry of the banners were planted and waved gloomily, while a thick canopy of smoke from the many flambeaux hovered over the throng, brought out by the lurid gleams into strong and fierce relief.

The speakers—with one exception men of low station and small talent—stood on the portion of the rampart just above the gateway. Several persons addressed the meeting in the usual style of party oratory. It was altogether a most indifferent display. But Bancroft rarely failed in those exercises of *the stump* to throw in occasional scraps of talk above the commonplace of his colleagues. Still I could not help lamenting, as shouts of applause rose up after every pause in the several addresses spoken, that no subject of real patriotism awoke any of the nobler passions in the thousands of men around me. When I reflected on the objects at stake in this presidential contest for which they worked so hard and paid so dearly, I was, as usual, forcibly struck with the littleness of the contest that was waging; at the same time admitting to myself how lucky the people on both sides were, and how happy they ought to feel, in having nothing more serious to dignify with the name of politics.

Could I, as a stranger seeking information on all hands, reading everything that appeared, and mixing with men of both parties on familiar terms, have ventured to form an opinion as to the probable results, I should have said that the approaching election must have been favourable to the Whig party. But I had seen so many erroneous estimates made beforehand, on both sides, as to the majorities and minorities in certain localities, that I hazarded no foretelling on my own judgment. To show that I was justified in my hesitation, I subjoin a few extracts from letters received by me from intimate acquaintances employed in important offices under the Administration.

One of those persons wrote to me on September 12th, in reference to a conversation between us some months preceding :—

You remember my prediction to you last winter, respecting the re-election of Van Buren? The time is rapidly drawing near when the result will establish to your satisfaction that the Whigs do not understand the people of the United States.

On the 16th of October the same individual wrote to me, in spite of the various State elections favourable to the Whigs, in the intervals between the two letters :

Do not forget my confident prediction of the election of Van Buren. He will be re-elected, and our party will make merry over the long faces of your friends the Whigs.

A fortnight later I received a letter from another, an older and more intimate acquaintance, an active and intelligent partisan of the Administration, long employed in diplomacy, and, at that time, in the centre of the best political information. He wrote as follows :

New York, October 29th, 1840.

Hitherto we have lost only states in which none of our party, save the over sanguine, expected to prevail. We depend confidently on having the electoral votes of the three great democratic States,

Virginia, Pennsylvania, and New York. Even two of these will give us the presidency. The late disclosures of election frauds in New York city, in 1838, make this State as certain on our side as Virginia and Pennsylvania. My decided opinion is, that we shall re-elect Van Buren.

Another letter, confidentially written on the 30th October, by one influential office-holder in New York to another in Boston, was shown to me by the latter the following day. It said positively, "We (the Van Burenites) are sure of carrying this State. Have you any hope of Massachusetts?"

It is not to be supposed that all these instances were so many proofs of wilful deceit on the part of the writers. I am quite certain of the sincerity with which they deceived themselves. On the other hand, the Whig leaders were so confident of success, that Mr. Webster and others told me they reckoned on twenty States out of twenty-six composing the Union, as theirs beyond a doubt, and each of them by an overwhelming majority.

In the meantime the electioneering went on all over the country; with all the usual vices and devices, crimination and recrimination, false reports and fictitious votes, abuse, libel, slander, expense, debauchery—all the evils, in fact, of which such a contest is susceptible except fighting. During the whole of the Presidential election, from one end of the Union to the other, I heard of but one serious personal encounter, and that was a momentary collision between a procession of Whigs and a small party of Democrats in the streets of Baltimore, in which a man was killed by a chance blow of a staff—the only one, I believe, which was struck on the occasion.

It is certainly great good fortune for any country to be exempt from all the really serious subjects of domestic quarrel which cause those passion-stirring scenes that lead to riot and bloodshed. It is quite amusing to hear the people of the United States talk of their "political excitement." The newspaper abuse, the brawling at "caucuses" or "pow wow gatherings," as they call their public meetings, the hard names they bandy backwards and forwards, and the shouts they expend during their processions, form the sum total of the "excitement" they are so prone to boast of. They are very fond of being excited to this extent; but they scarcely ever go beyond it. It is a pastime to them indulged in thus far. Did they pass these bounds, it would become a business; and Americans enter into no business that does not promise a return of profit. They do not appear to me to be susceptible of that middle state of feeling that exists between the inclination for amusement and the calculation of gain. They rush to the theatres, the lectures, the caucuses, the meeting houses—all from the same motive, the want of what they call excitement—which is, in fact, but the sense of *ennui* requiring a change. But they scarcely ever get into personal conflicts, even when political processions of opposing parties meet in the public ways. In short, there is little or no impulse in anything they do. Whatever it be it is done advisedly. There is always a reason, good or bad, to justify or excuse it. No one forgets himself; no one is hurried away. Trifling local riots take place at times. But I do not expect to hear of any serious national outburst properly so called.

A remarkable feature in this memorable Presidential election before glanced at, consisted in the Tippecanoe songs, shouted by the Whigs from one end of the Union to the other. A popular vocalist, of the name of Russell, known since in England as "American Russell," but really an Englishman, with a good voice and a shrewd sense of his own interest, attached himself to the prominent party, and became a distinguished performer at various of the festive meetings, from Massachusetts to Mississippi,

"Tippecanoe, and Tyler, too,"

was the *refrain* in every one's mouth ; and

"Poor little Van
Is a used-up man,"

was another, which made the streets, roads, and rivers vocal. The Whig minstrel Mr. Russell, not contented with the honour of making this doggrel popular, claimed the authorship of it. He boasted that to him (almost alone) was owing the Whig success ; and even talked loudly of his expectation of a large grant of land in the far west as his reward. This episode in the history of the election is only worth recording as another proof of the clap-trap expedients to which its result may be, in a great measure, attributed. No other event of serious importance to the country was ever accomplished by means so undignified, in comparison with the object. The sober sense of the nation was completely overborne by a combination of trickery and tom-foolery, in which the most prominent men played the principal parts. The great Democratic majority which had for the twelve preceding years held the destiny of the country in its hands, was for a time stultified by the din and clamour of its opponents ; and it dwindled down to a powerful, but still insufficient body of voters, out-numbered in nineteen out of the twenty-six States comprising the Union ; and even in many where it was believed to be invincible.

The final result of the election was as follows:

The whole number of States was twenty-six, containing altogether 294 electoral votes, which were given in the following proportions,—

For Harrison . . .	19 states,	234	electoral votes.
For Van Buren . . .	7 „	60	„
Majority for Harrison	12 „	174	„

On the first blush, or on a partial glance, this record would seem to give an overwhelming majority for the Whig candidate. Taken by a comparison of State and State votes it undoubtedly does so. But if the aggregate amount of the "popular" votes throughout the Union be looked at, the appearance is far less flattering for the successful party; and it turns out that the contest was a very close one indeed. In an aggregate of nearly two and a half millions of voters the majority for Harrison was but 125,000. The account stood thus:

	Popular Votes.
For Harrison	1,274,428
For Van Buren	1,149,428
Majority for Harrison . .	125,000

So that, supposing this election to have been a fair test, and admitting that the distinctions of Whig and Democrat fairly designated the differences of political opinion throughout the country, it results that the population was, at the epoch of the election, divided into nearly two equal parties. But when it is considered that this majority of 125,000 votes throughout the Union was obtained by means of an excitement highly artificial, by an unparalleled junction of various factions, seriously opposed to each other on details; that it rested on no solid indestructible principles of government, and that those which it avows are beyond doubt opposed to democratic institutions, and subversive of republican interests, it cannot be believed that such a majority was a genuine manifestation of the public mind.

The truth is, that the people, impatient at the fluctuations in public affairs, and uncertain as to what measures, what men, or what party were best adapted for the management of the national concerns, were disposed to try something new. The most plausible theories were urged upon them by the Whig orators and writers. The unanimity of these men, who had been so long at variance with each other on sundry points, had something imposing in it. The influence was highly favourable to their object; and the millions who had in previous years given so many triumphs to Democratic candidates, now conscious that things were in great embarrassment, resolved on the experiment of a change, satisfied that after four years of Whig trial they could come back again to the old system.

Another material cause for the defeat of the Democratic party was the incompetency of its candidate to create any enthusiasm in his favour. Van Buren was a dry, cold, cautious man of business, respectable in conduct and talent; but possessed of no qualities to rouse the feelings or excite the admiration of the public. All his appeals were to the reason and the interests of men; none to their hearts and their passions. He had shrewdness enough to act on his countrymen's strong points. But he had no tact to work on their weak ones; and it was precisely those that were then in the ascendant.

Under these influences the Whig party gained their

victory in the Presidential Election of 1840. They came into power on the 4th of March in the following year, when William Henry Harrison was duly inaugurated into his high office, amidst the acclamations of his adherents, and the unmurmuring assent of those who laboured so hard for his defeat, but who now silently submitted to the great law of Republicanism—the will of the majority.

Among the many striking features of the contest thus terminated, was the ready submission of the discomfited candidate and his party; and it was the more so from their efforts to establish the charge of dishonest practices against the victors. Positive statements were made accusing the Whigs with every species of fraud in various parts of the Union. If a tithe of these stories were true, there is no doubt that General Harrison obtained his honours by most unhallowed means, and that his election was morally void.

My own opinion, however, is, that there was small ground for these wholesale denunciations. That occasional instances of corruption took place on either side is certain. That men voted, unduly qualified themselves at the cost of a false oath, and personated the dead and the dying at the polling places, there can be little doubt; but that any broad and general system of electioneering profligacy was practised on this occasion, or that any such system exists in the United States, I do not believe.* In the first place, I have never known it to be thoroughly proved. In the second, I do not think it possible from the particular nature of the election arrangements. In the

* This opinion is not affected by the recent outrages committed at the so-called elections in Kansas, by hordes of "border ruffians" from Missouri, who violated all acknowledged principles of law and usage.

third, to cut short the question, and omitting many other considerations, I am satisfied that the people of the United States would not submit to that worst kind of political tyranny, that would enable any party to make the multitude their tools for public dishonour and national destruction.

CHAPTER XX.

INAUGURATION OF PRESIDENT HARRISON.

Crowded state of Washington—Visits to Mr. Van Buren, and the retiring Ministers—Inauguration Ceremonies—President Harrison's Discourse—The Greeks and Romans—Consular Compliment—Political Aspirants—Inauguration Ball—The President's facility for Promising—Difficulty of Managing him—Diplomatic Reception—Henry Clay, Dictator in the Senate—Departure from Washington—Reflections on the Comparative State of Society there.

HAVING visited Washington during the rule of democracy and the reign of Van Buren, I was desirous of seeing the capital again, under the influence of a new party and a new President. I availed myself of a like wish on the part of some friends, near connections of one of the leaders of the dominant faction, and in company with them I set out from Boston in the latter end of February, 1841; and after a pleasant journey, with a few days' delay on the road, we reached our destination, in good time for the grand work of the Presidential inauguration.

If ever Washington appeared to any advantage, if ever its vast space had a chance of being considered in some degree filled up, if ever it had any pretension to the air or character of a metropolis, it was assuredly on this occasion. Its ordinary population was certainly trebled, and two-thirds of those composing the whole were idlers and money-spenders, even unto that large proportion of the visitors who came under the appellation of "office-seekers;"

the American epithet for the indefatigable tribe of men, in England yclept place-hunters.

On reaching Gadsby's Hotel, where I had lodged during my former visit, making my way through the crowd of smoking and dram-drinking loungers at *the bar*, and asking what accommodations I could have, I was informed by the obliging proprietor that he could favour me with bed No. 16 in parlour No. 4. But he at the same time put into my hand a billet, which relieved my anxiety on the subject of lodgings, for it was an invitation from a gentleman to take up my quarters at his house. I very gladly accepted the offer ; and I enjoyed for a fortnight the hospitality of this gentleman and his amiable and handsome wife ; and, with the exception of detestable weather, all things were entirely satisfactory during the whole period. But such odious varieties of heat and cold, snow, rain, frost, and thunder-storms, have rarely, I must believe, been crowded into so short a space of time, in any other given portion of the globe.

My first visit, the day after my arrival, was paid to the still acting chief magistrate, Mr. Van Buren. He received me with his constitutional good-temper and *sang froid;* showing no symptom of disappointment or low spirits at the approaching renunciation of his honours. There was nothing about him to make one feel regret at his fallen fortunes. He merely gave one the notion of a cool-headed gambler, who had played a bold *coup* on calculation, and lost his stake, without emotion enough to excite pity in the beholders. My next visit was really a painful one. It was to Mr. Forsyth's, where the contrast presented by his half-unfurnished and half-inhabited house to what it appeared when I had last seen it, was a serious illustration of the ups and downs of political life. The change was of material injury to Mr. Forsyth, whose private circumstances were not flourishing ; and a few brief months put an end to his mortal career, and deprived his party of one of its most gentleman-like supporters. I took care to make calls on Mr. Poinsett and others of the seceding members of the government ; and I was then ready to pay the proper quantum of homage to the rising sun of Whiggery.

The bad weather began on the 4th of March, a few days after my arrival. This memorable day of Harrison' glory was one of pinching cold ; but it was favourable enough for the formation of a long procession, formed of horsemen and footmen, firemen and artillery-men, banners and music, which according to custom escorted the new President from the White House to the Capitol. The *corps diplomatique* assembled at the house of M. de Bacourt, the French Minister. I went with Mr. Fox, whose carriage led the way, being followed by those of the other members of the diplomatic corps ; and we soon took our places in the crowded senate chamber, on chairs appropriated to our use in front of the President's seat. There Mr. Tyler, Vice-President of the Union, and *ex-officio* President of the Senate, was installed. And shortly afterwards the hero of the day, of " Tippecanoe," and " the Thames," came into the hall—a little, gray-headed, respectable-looking man of between sixty and seventy, plainly dressed. He moved briskly forward, ascended the steps leading to the President's chair, and after some hasty words of ceremony, retired. Mr. Tyler then made an address to the assembled senate, in which the only thing remarkable was his Virginian pronunciation of the word chair. When he, for the third time in the course of his address, professed his intention to act with independence as long as he might have the honour to occupy that "cheer," I could not help remarking to a person beside me, that Mr. Tyler had very properly given three cheers for the Vice-President.

Our whole assemblage quickly moved from the comfortable senate-room to the chilling air of the platform erected out beyond the vestibule of the Capitol, which looks to the extensive court-yard. Here was the place fixed on for the grand display. Large accommodations were effected for all the state dignitaries, judges of the supreme court, senators, members of the legislature, *corps diplomatique*, and "distinguished strangers." And there did General Harrison take the solemn oath to observe the constitution; and then and there did he deliver his lengthy oration—and indeed his last speech—of seven-eighths of two hours duration, in a loud voice and with bare head, to a shivering circle around and a symphathising multitude below him.

From a very old acquaintance of mine, one of the President's relatives and stanch adherents, and from another more confidential source connected with one of his "advisers," I knew a great deal in anticipation of his almost interminable speech. It had formed a subject of serious argumentation between the President and his cabinet; he being in the first instance resolved on having it entirely his own, and not to allow a change being made "in the dotting of an i or the crossing of a t." This harmless obstinacy was so far submitted to. But other changes of somewhat greater consequence were urged upon the President, and some of them were reluctantly conceded by his good nature rather than his good sense. Certain it is that this very first subject of consultation between him and his constitutional advisers (if an American board of secretaries, being merely so many *chefs de bureau*, are entitled to that dignity) taught the latter that they had a very arduous task before them, in their hope of managing the chief magistrate for their own purposes or that of the party.

On one point General Harrison was inflexible. He would not consent to leave out "the Greeks and Romans," those indispensable inflictions in a genuine American oration. Accordingly, almost the very first sentence contained an allusion to the act of one of the Roman consuls.

"What does that mean? What's that about Consuls?" asked a classical colleague of mine, an ex-member of Parliament, recently appointed to his post, and who sat close to me on this occasion.

"Oh, only a little compliment to the foreign Consuls present," answered I, with a chattering of the teeth.

"Ah!" said my colleague, "and must we answer it?" his Parliamentary propensities rising above the range of the thermometer.

"Certainly," I replied, "and you, as the newest appointed, will have the compliment paid you of being the spokesman."

My friend sank into thoughtfulness; and frequently, during the time consumed in the President's oration, I remarked his lips moving, and his brows compressed, as if he were engaged in the concoction of his own. To me, and the many others who had not that pleasant illusion to beguile the time, the suffering of the scene was intense. Poor Mr. Fox, unprovided with a cloak, shivered in his unbuttoned uniform coat, white waistcoat, and canary-coloured trousers, each garment of the loosest pattern and most threadbare texture, and the last mentioned having shrunk, from repeated washings, to considerably above his ankles.

The platform on which this scene was enacted afforded abundant materials for observation. The concentrated force of the Whig party was there, and perhaps not one individual of them was attending to the President's discourse, while all were occupied with their personal objects; no doubt a very general one was to keep the blood in circulation on that bitter day. And for that purpose, or with that excuse, the strict order of the arrangements was quickly disturbed, almost everyone, after a short time, quitting his seat and walking up and down, joining some companion, or with others forming groups for passing talk, or deep discussion. I thought I could perceive much of the true spirit of ambitious intrigue in what was going on; and I fancied that in the bent brow and unquiet glance of more than one of the chief actors on that stage, I read exciting anticipations of what was expected to come, in four years after that memorable day.

Under a salute of artillery, and the loud shouts of the crowd, the solemnity broke up, and the long procession returned to the President's official dwelling, the White House, which Harrison now entered as temporary tenant, little thinking that the ceremony which had just given him his title to possession also set the seal upon his frail tenure of life. The exposure and fatigue he had gone through on that occasion, laid the germs of the disease which carried him off exactly a month from that day.

But the labours of the day were by no means at an end. Crowds pressed to pay their respects and their court in the promiscuous enthusiasm of pleasure at the President's elevation, and in hope at the prospect of their own. Many of those partisans shared the hospitable dinner of their chief; and at a large and brilliant public ball in the evening, the indefatigable President again made his appearance early, and for hours went the rounds of a hundred little circles, all so many eddies of delight in which he sported unrestrained. At this ball there were full a thousand persons. As the price of the tickets was as high as ten dollars each, it might be supposed that the company would have been somewhat select. But it formed a most curious mixture, being composed of contingents from all parts of the Union. And strange varieties they were. Groups of fine ladies from Boston, New York, Baltimore, and Philadelphia, overloaded with ornament and in flaunting colours, were contrasted with specimens from the wild West, in dresses as gaudy in pattern, but more uncouth in cut. The hanging sleeves and flowing flounces in satin and gauze, with rich embroidery and lace garnitures, were opposed to tight muslin or cotton gowns made in defiance of all modern taste, while flowers, feathers, and the most fantastic combinations of head-gear, threw an air of inconceivable burlesque over the whole display. Female beauty, in every shape and hue which the country could furnish, was there, from the bright-skinned New Englander to the New Orleans brunette; while sprigs of dandyism from the Atlantic cities were in amusing contact with rough western men, or down-east delegates, in the glorious equality of semi-civilisation. The uniforms of diplomatists and military and naval officers gave their usual bright relief to the mass of black cloth coats and black satin vests. The building was large and straggling and of rude construction. The walls were covered with mere white-wash, which, with a profusion of spermaceti lights, threw an intense glare upon the crowded company, and I think

I never saw so true a picture on a large scale of elation and enjoyment as was presented by this motley assembly. Harrison was the main attraction, for it was in celebration of his election that the ball was given. But there were men there of far more note—Clay, Webster, Scott, in whom the present joy, and the glimmering chances of the future, must have been dimmed by the too vivid feeling that the actual honours of the scene were not for them.

Harrison looked, during all the different occasions of the day, animated, kind-hearted, and happy, and it was so pleasant to see a man of his years and experience give loose to his natural feelings, that it left one no inclination to criticise his deportment or tone. There was certainly no dignity, as it is generally understood, in President Harrison. He had not even the cautious coolness of manner which stood in its stead with his predecessor Van Buren ; nor the measured monotony of Tyler, doomed so soon to succeed him. He was, on the contrary, brisk and affable ; seemingly unconscious that his position required, or probably of opinion that it would not receive, any additional importance from a more reserved demeanour. It was, however, evident to all who remarked his familiar air, and more particularly to those who came in official contact with him, that though his frankness might conduce to popularity, it made him likely to be a very unmanageable chief magistrate. Whether he had penetration enough to see how he was considered by those nearest to him I know not ; but it was unfortunately clear to them that the thick layers of eulogy which had been laid on him had found in his real qualities no materials solid enough against which to *stick.* I very soon perceived that those who had puffed and praised him the most before they got their places from him, were conscious of the difficulty they had made for themselves, and that although they might continue to blow the bellows, they had a very impracticable instrument to play upon.

But all this was only the by-play of the drama acted before the public. The festivities and gaieties went on, and the poor old President worked hard to perform his part; he, however, being the only one of the company in whom there was really no acting. His natural kindness of disposition was seen at every moment. Whoever called to pay him a visit was sure to be asked to dinner; whoever asked for a place was sure to get a promise; whoever hinted at a want of money was sure to receive a draft; until it became the common talk that the President was over-drawing his account, over-promising his partisans, and over-feeding his friends.

During my stay at Washington, I had few opportunities of closely remarking him. He was, for the first week or two, so beset by a crowd of expectants, by whom he was shown no mercy, that he could not fix a day to give an official dinner, from which his rather questionable familiars could have been excluded. I do not know that he gave one such entertainment during his short reign. A few days after his inauguration he received the *corps diplomatique* at a regular morning *levée,* held for the occasion. We assembled in great force, and the President listened decorously to an address, read by Mr. Fox, as senior of the ministers present, and he replied with decent brevity, without a single allusion to *Grec ou Romain*. M. Bodisco, the Russian minister, chose to absent himself from this ceremony, on the excuse of indisposition; but he obtained a private and particular audience a couple of days afterwards, for the purpose of making his own little speech, and no doubt the worthy President took his revenge on the Plenipotentiary of the Autocrat, by an outburst of classical allusion which he had repressed before the representatives of the limited monarchies of the Old World and the Republics of the New.

After the diplomatic ceremony, a general reception took place, of members of Congress and others, mixed with ladies, which made a very off-hand kind of *mélange*. The President was, as was his wont, bustling and familiar. When I was presented, he, as usual, shook hands, and said a few civil things, and this being the only occasion on which I exchanged a word with him, I cannot pretend to form any opinion of him on grounds of personal knowledge.

The subsequent days of my stay in Washington were passed in a round of visiting, dinners, and attendance on the debates in Congress. The chief interest afforded by the latter was in the observance of Henry Clay, in the proud possession of that dictatorship over his party, which they conceded, and which was the by-word of bitter reproach on the part of his foes. He was indeed in his proper place, at the head of his adherents, and paying back the hatred of his enemies with defiance and scorn.

Whether this is an enviable position or not, or whether he who maintained it then was right or wrong in his opinions, I will not here discuss; I can, however, safely say, that such a position seemed to be Clay's fitting element, and that I have met no other man in the United States who appeared to me at all adapted for it.

Day by day, after the inauguration, the crowd of idlers began to dissolve, and the over-loaded railroad cars bore away the witnesses of Whig triumph, to carry their delusive notions of permanent ascendancy to the extremities of the Union. The hotels and boarding-houses grew empty, the "messes" were one by one broken up; and the time allowed by my friends and myself for our visit having been somewhat exceeded, we set off for the North once more, and pursued, with trifling impediments, and small delays, our way to Boston.

And as we went along, on railroad or in steam-boats, and although there was at least one person of our party for whom I felt a more than ordinary interest, I found leisure to reflect on this second visit to Washington, and to contrast it with the first, before recorded. It was scarcely possible to make such a direct comparison between the different circumstances as would allow of positive conclusions. But I saw enough to convince me that, though parties had shifted and places were changed, *the people* was identical and the same. As far as social organisation went, the orderly possession of power by the Democrats in 1840, was undoubtedly more respectable than the harum-scarum scramble of Whig ascendancy in 1841. The well-regulated hospitality of the White House during Van Buren's occupation, was superior to the indiscriminate feasting of Harrison. If "*le style c'est l'homme*" be true as to authorship, it is scarcely less so as to housekeeping. The tone was imperceptibly given and caught up from the respective establishments of the Presidents. And as with them, so was it in regard to Mr. Forsyth's dinner in comparison with Mr. Webster's (the rival Secretaries of State), and the same with the entertainments of other functionaries. And when I came to test the boasts of my Whig friends, as to the superior air and tone of their party over those of the ousted Locofocos, I was much disappointed; for, if any preference were due to either, I really thought it should be given the other way. The truth is, that if judged by an European standard, both parties would be pronounced lamentably deficient, either boisterous or formal, under-doing or over-doing the thing, and, with very rare exceptions, scarcely ever hitting that medium which is instinctively felt and acknowledged to be good breeding—a quality of blood which training may improve and modify, but cannot, as is sometimes believed, create. The general run of manners everywhere was inelegant; and a couple of years' experience was fast convincing me that no equivalent of frank cordiality and true warm-heartedness were to be found in the "high life" and the "fashionable society" of America. This conviction began insensibly to produce its effect on me. I liked most things and many persons at first sight, less from any positive attractions than from the hope of those compensations which were rarely forthcoming. As long as the excitement of change of scene and of society lasted, I enjoyed it; but, once over, the monotony and the superficialness of the whole produced a disheartening effect. And I began to feel thus early, that however pleasant the country may appear to hasty travellers or for a short sojourn, it would to any European without pursuits of an elevating nature, and a family to love and be loved by, be a bad resting-place indeed. During my whole residence in the United States I never met one foreigner who did not agree with that sentiment.

CHAPTER XXI.

THE NORTH-EASTERN BOUNDARY QUESTION.

Six Subjects of Serious Dispute between England and the United States—The Boundary Question the most dangerous—Its Origin and Progress—Left to Arbitration—Award of the King of the Netherlands — Accepted by the British Government—Rejected by the United States—Diplomatic Trickery —The Question in abeyance for Ten Years—Imminent danger of a Collision and of War—British Commission for Survey—Report of Commissioners— Exasperation in America — Appointment of Lord Ashburton as Special Minister — His Arrival in Washington — Commissioners from Maine and Massachusetts.

Of the six subjects of serious dispute between England and the United States during the last twenty years, from 1838 to 1858—the North-Eastern Boundary Question, the Oregon Question, the Fishery Question, the Central American Question, theRecruiting Question, the Search of American Ships Question—by far the most difficult and dangerous was the first mentioned, that of the boundary dividing the State of Maine from the British North American provinces of Canada and New Brunswick.

A brief historical sketch of that question, its negotiation and settlement, will, I think, have considerable interest for those who were contemporary with it; and it ought to be instructive to all time for whoever would rightly understand, or may have to cope with, the practices of American diplomacy.

The question itself was in existence for about sixty years, from the treaty of Paris in 1783, establishing the Independence of the United States and defining the boundaries of the Union, to the Ashburton treaty of Washington in 1842; but the dispute as to the boundary meant to be defined in 1783 can be said to have actually commenced only at the conferences of Ghent in 1814, from which time it lasted until 1842, a period of twenty-six years.

There are few examples of a question more complicated, a controversy more acrimonious, or a settlement more expedient. The enormous mass of Parliamentary debates, correspondence, reports, pamphlets, articles in Reviews and Newspapers, public speeches and private letters to which this matter gave rise is appalling. It became my duty to study this accumulation of documentary materials; and I can therefore speak at once fairly and feelingly, on the incessant labour of full three years, involving several visits to Washington and to Canada, in search of documents or for personal communications.

To unravel the tangled web of argument was an occupation that I entered on with zeal—considered to be a fatal quality in an official man; and I followed it up with industry—which is too often, like virtue in the abstract, its own reward. The State of Massachusetts, the jurisdiction of my consulate, was formerly the possessor of a portion of what, previous to the formation of the State of Maine in 1820, became the disputed territory; and the two States were, at the time of my appointment, entitled to a joint interest in the lands comprised in the claim which was contested by England.

I was not without some previous knowledge of this subject, for I had happened to be resident at the Hague during the winter of 1830—1831, at which period the King of the Netherlands, William I., in the midst of the revolutionary troubles which deprived him of more than half of his dominions, was busily employed in studying this North American dispute, which had been left to his arbitration by the governments of England and the United States, in pursuance of an article in the treaty of Ghent in 1814. King William had laboriously devoted himself to his task; and, to the surprise of all those interested in the question, he announced himself ready, on the 10th of January, 1831, the day originally fixed by him, to pronounce his award.

During the whole of that winter I had enjoyed an intimate intercourse with Sir Charles Bagot, the British Ambassador, as also with Mr. Preble (a judge of the State of Maine), the American Minister, and his Secretary of Legation, Mr. Davezac; as well as an acquaintanceship with Sir Howard Douglas, formerly Governor of the Province of New Brunswick, and sent specially to the Hague, to assist Sir Charles Bagot with his local knowledge on the question. From all these sources I was well supplied with information, on an affair which was of deep interest to them all, sufficient to divide the anxiety universally felt in the progress of the Dutch and Belgian question itself, the paramount political event of the day.

Without encumbering this portion of my work with an elaborate detail of the Boundary Question, it will be enough to state that it mainly rested on the interpretation to be given to that passage in the treaty of Paris of 1783, which declared the Northern frontier of the United States to be formed by a line, drawn from a certain point, "along the highlands which divide the rivers that empty themselves into the river St. Lawrence from those which fall into the Atlantic Ocean."

The question requiring solution was, which was the range of highlands so defined—there being two ranges dividing rivers, at a distance of about one hundred miles from each other, and to each of which it was on either hand argued the description might apply ; England claiming that on the South, the United States that to the North. I shall give in the Appendix my own reasonings on this point, with a greatly condensed statement of the question, as they appeared in a pamphlet printed for private circulation in New York, in the year 1843, with a map of the territory, and the various lines claimed and agreed to. It is sufficient to state here that the King of the Netherlands, puzzled, as well he might be, by the conflicting arguments of the negotiators, and despairing of arriving at the truth, made an award, which avoided a decision on the question actually submitted to him ; and instead of fixing on one or the other of the two ridges of highlands, to which alone his decision could be logically confined, he recommended a splitting of the difference between the parties, and that the boundary line should be for a long extent the middle of the St. John river, the course of which lies between, but not equidistant from the rival ridges.

If ever some reminiscences of mine, personal and political, relative to a long residence on the continent of Europe, see the light, a not unamusing mention will be found of the manner in which King William's award was received by the chief negotiators. Sir Charles Bagot accepted it with pleasure, as a reasonable, though to England an unfavourable, settlement of a troublesome dispute ; and the same view was taken by Lord Palmerston, then Secretary of State for Foreign Affairs, and speaking the sentiments of the British Government. Far different, however, were the feelings of Mr. Preble. He indignantly repudiated the King's award, against which he made an immediate protest, which he laid before His Majesty and transmitted to his own Government at Washington. No sooner had he been brought down to a moderate state of calm, by the caution of his wily Secretary of Legation, and I may truly add by my own efforts, than he prepared his despatches for the Federal Government at home, with all the details of his late proceedings. These being carefully made up, were sent off by the very longest and most tedious route, *viá* Brussels, Paris, and to some southern port of France, to New Orleans and thence to Washington, the seat of Government, where the President, General Jackson, and Congress were, or were not as the case might be, at the time of the arrival of this most important intelligence.

But, *en attendant* the slow movements of this official budget, another account, brief, and to the full as explicit, was expedited by the short, straight road of London, Liverpool, and New York, on board one of the fast-sailing packets of that line, for the Governor of the State of Maine, with a pressing recommendation to have a protest by the Legislature drawn up, voted, and approved, refusing their consent by anticipation to any award, by any foreign power or potentate, that might in any way infringe on the integrity of the national territory. So that, long before the official news of King William's award reached the Federal Government and Congress, the independent protest of Maine should be promulgated to the country, and a contingency be provided against before its existence could be publicly suspected. This *ruse*, so very diplomatic, in the worst sense of the term, was completely successful. The Protest of Maine was marked, learned, and inwardly digested throughout the Union, with admiring sympathy, some weeks before Preble's Protest reached the disgusted President, to be by him officially announced to Congress.

The embarrassment caused by this *mauvais tour*, played by my two friends from North and South (Preble and Davezac) in a style worthy of the most practised political jugglers, is well known in the history of the Boundary Question. General Jackson was much annoyed by it, as well as all the rational members of Congress. The matter caused serious deliberation in the Cabinet and Senate. To fly in the face of the Maine Protest, in its lofty assertion of States' rights, was a course too daring for the majority of the national legislature; while "Old Hickory" himself, fierce and obstinate as he was on various occasions, yielded on this one to that fatal subserviency to the public vote, so general among the politicians of America, who are dependent for their places on a popular election. General Jackson was then canvassing for nomination for a second term to the office of President. He could not risk the loss of the vote of the comparatively insignificant State of Maine. And therefore, although highly approving the compromise recommended by the Royal arbitrator, and thoroughly aware of its advantages to his country, he had not the boldness to brave the hostility of the "Down-Easters," but gave his sanction to their disingenuous course in this affair, and joined a majority of the Federal Senate in rejecting the award of the King of the Netherlands, on the ground that he had exceeded the powers given him by the articles of arbitration; and the settlement of the Boundary Question was thrown back for ten years or more.

Thus, a most desirable termination of what threatened to become a dangerous difficulty was thwarted, by the narrow-minded obstinacy of one or two men, giving the tone to State selfishness, by courtesy called State right, and acting on the personal purposes of the Presidential candidate and his friends. Jackson was re-chosen, for a second term of four years, the State of Maine and Judge Preble reposed on the laurels of their Protest, the question lay in abeyance, and the disputed territory, barren in almost everything but timber, became a fertile source of controversy and ill-will.

It contained about seven million acres of land, comprehended between the two lines of highlands. Up to the year 1792 this district was but a wilderness of lakes, morasses, and dense forests, known only to the scattered Indian tribes; but about that period the citizens of portions of the country since included in the present State of Maine began their encroachments upon it, and put forward pretensions to the highlands north of the St. John as the treaty boundary established in 1783. To the few persons, out of the United States, who considered the subject seriously, it appeared inconsistent with probability that the British negotiators on that occasion, or the King's government, would have consented to a frontier line running within twenty miles of the St. Lawrence, cutting off the established military and post routes leading from the Provinces of Nova Scotia and New Brunswick to Quebec, and giving to the Americans various military positions, almost overlooking the river, and actually menacing that fortress. Such a frontier was totally unnecessary for the United States, and antagonistic to the whole spirit of the treaty. Yet the universal people of the Union soon caught at the pretension put forth by the down-east borderers, adopted it as a doctrine of national belief, and on every possible occasion promulgated their determination to maintain it against all the world.

During the short war between the United States and

England, which began in 1812 and ended in 1814, this frontier dispute did not excite much attention, and by the treaty of Ghent in the latter year it was left, as before mentioned, to arbitration ; the American Commissioners, during the preliminary negotiations, never swerving from the full amount of the national pretensions, and not admitting any doubt as to their validity. In pursuance with a convention subsequently signed, the King of the Netherlands was named as the arbitrator, and he accepted the office and fulfilled its duties as before stated. For some years after the rejection of his award by the United States Government, that of England made several unsuccessful efforts to adjust the dispute, to carry out a new joint survey of the territory, and to cut the matter short by dividing it between the two countries. All these efforts having no result, Lord Palmerston directed the then minister at Washington, on the 30th October, 1835, to announce to the President that "the British Government withdraws its consent to accept the territorial compromise recommended by the King of the Netherlands." From that period a series of transgressions took place on the part of the rapidly-increasing populations of Maine and New Brunswick, arising from their avidity to push on towards those points which contained the finest and most available stock of timber.

The forests covering this vast district were of considerable value when the trees could be felled and floated down the rivers, to be subjected to the operation of sawing-mills, and finally transported by sea. On these rivers various small settlements were formed, of adventurous wood-cutters from the rival state and province. Among those hardy speculators violent quarrels and fierce feuds arose. The magistrates and forest functionaries, on both sides, interfered with all the virulence of partisans. Military posts were simultaneously established, and rashly advanced into the wild country which both parties considered their own; till at last what was for so long a time merely debatable ground assumed the character of an incipient battle-field. Redoubts, block-houses, and barracks, were erected on several points. Reinforcements of troops from either side poured in. The public mind in the United States became inflamed. The too ready cry of "British outrages" was loudly proclaimed in all quarters, and reckless politicians of every party joined, as they ever do on all plausible occasions, to lash the national spirit into fury. Their sporadic efforts soon spread far and wide. The people in the whole length and breadth of the Union were to a man convinced of the justice of their claim, and of the manifest wrong intended by Great Britain. The nation at large was ready and anxious for war; and had a skirmish taken place on the frontier involving the death of a dozen men, the whole available population would have hastened to the scene of conflict, and for a while at least settled the question, by overrunning the adjoining British province, and plunging the two nations into hostilities, the end of which no man then living could have foreseen.

During this transatlantic fermentation the English people were quite calm, and almost apathetic. With a vague notion of the locality of the disputed territory, a total ignorance of the merits or demerits of the dispute, a profound contempt for the blustering and abuse of American politicians and newspapers, and somewhat of an inclination to try their strength once more with their quarrelsome "cousins" (as it is the fashion to call them), the "Britishers" (as those distant relations call their kith and kin) were perfectly content to leave the affair in the hands of the Government, trusting to the ministers for its management, and probably ashamed to make any public demonstration on the subject, not well knowing what it was all about.

The Government, for their part, not very much better informed than the people at large, were satisfied to let the matter rest in the department of Foreign Affairs, to which it legitimately belonged, and of course it was then entirely in the hands of the head of that office.

It would be unbecoming in a subordinate employé to pronounce on the motives of his chief; and any criticism even on his public conduct should be made with much reserve. The complicated business of one great department, and its intricate connection with the others, can be but imperfectly known to any subaltern in one of them. The various reasons which must influence a minister are therefore generally a sealed volume to those who act under him. But it will be admitted that any man of ordinary intelligence stationed in a foreign country, and with opportunities of observing the national character, sifting the objects of party, and examining the career of individuals, may be better qualified than the high state officer to whom he reports, to judge of the details of a question, the chief effects of which are felt on the spot where he resides. It is therefore that I think I may, without undue presumption, give my opinion on some of the points in which Lord Palmerston appeared to be mistaken in reference to the affair I am now discussing.

To acquire a better understanding of the true nature of the dispute, which had led to some able and much flippant argument between English official writers and their American opponents, Lord Palmerston wisely resolved to send a couple of Commissioners to make a survey of the country and frame a report, on which the British Government might rely with confidence, and act with decision. One of the persons chosen was a Colonel of Engineers, entirely suited, no doubt, for the surveying and defining a given tract of land, and drawing a line from point to point. The other was also an Englishman, but who had been for many years employed in the service of the United States, in some geological inquiries, which in some degree prepared him for such scientific observations as he had now to make. But I may say, without impugning the motives of these Commissioners (and especially of the latter of them), that they were totally deficient in the main qualification for their mission—an unbiassed spirit of inquiry into the real question at issue, the true line of boundary intended by the framers of the treaty of Paris of 1783.

The gentlemen now employed by Lord Palmerston were but partisans, with opinions ready formed, satisfied of the justice of the British claim to the line contended for, scouting the American arguments *in toto,* and apparently not anxious to assuage the irritation that existed, or to discard the superciliousness that inflamed it. They proceeded with a numerous staff of assistants to the disputed territory; they returned to England after some months; and they produced a report, confirming the claim of Great Britain to the southern line, and founding their reasonings on grounds in some instances indisputably just, in some liable to contradiction, and in others quite untenable.

This Report was officially communicated to the Government of Washington, in June 1840. It was received throughout the United States with derision and defiance.

It was universally considered as so preposterous in some of its assumptions, and so apparently "made to order," that its adoption by the British Government was looked on as nearly tantamount to a declaration of war.

The only point to which I think it necessary to call attention in this place is, that these Commissioners strenuously maintained the identity of the line defined in the Royal Proclamation of George III. of the 7th October, 1763, as the southern boundary of the then British Province of Quebec (or Lower Canada) with that of the Treaty of 1783, which defined the boundary between Canada, Nova Scotia, and the UNITED STATES. The same identity between the line of 1763 and the line of 1783 was uniformly asserted on the part of the United States. And thence the whole foundation for the controversy—the sole cause of the mutual obstinacy and error, the difficulties, self-contradictions and inconsistencies of the innumerable disputants on either side of the question. The fact was, that both were partly right and both partly wrong. The Americans right, in maintaining that the northern line was that of the Proclamation of 1763; the British right, in claiming the southern line as that of the Treaty of 1783. So that had the British Commissioners in 1839 seen that they could, with perfect safety to their object, have admitted the views of the Americans as regarded the earlier of the two lines, instead of labouring to controvert them by a series of untenable statements as to the physical geography of the country in dispute, the claim which they (the Commissioners) most justly advocated to the later line, as that forming the true boundary of 1783, would have been evident to all unprejudiced and rational inquirers. Had that truth been arrived at sooner than it was, a vast amount of argument and sophistry would have been spared. Had a positive document of sufficient weight to have *proved* the truth been avowed when it *was* discovered, the treaty of Washington of 1842 would have had a far different basis than it has. But I am anticipating.

The Report of the British Commissioners was perhaps exactly what was expected by the British Government. It no doubt confirmed the previous opinions of the Minister for Foreign Affairs, and strengthened his determination to maintain the claim of England at all risks. The amount of those risks he assuredly could not have thoroughly understood. His mind, absorbed by great questions of European politics, the Continent still palpitating from recent agitation, and always requiring the utmost stretch of attention, Lord Palmerston may be well excused if he adopted somewhat too hastily a plausible but shallow Report, and looked rather lightly on the distant obscurity of transatlantic disputes, and measured them rather by the scale of Colonial insignificance than by that of national magnitude. His subordinates naturally took the tone from him. Mr. Fox, the Minister at Washington, where he was held in small consideration, kept up a constant and caustic correspondence with the American Secretary of State. Lord Sydenham, Governor General of Canada, maintained a style of haughty assumption.* The functionaries of New Brunswick were not more conciliatory. The British press was generally

* On my paying him a visit at Kingston, a very short time before his death, to communicate a proposition for a line of boundary, made to me by an influential Senator to Congress from the State of Maine, and for which Lord Sydenham was then considered the best channel of transmission to England, he peremptorily rejected the proposal, saying, with strong emphasis, "the Americans shall never touch the St. John;" a prophecy belied by the result, and somewhat inconsistent with the fact of a portion of that river having been long previously accepted as the boundary by the British Government.

irritating, true to the tone of contemptuous superiority inherent in the British mind, and too largely developed towards America, in all international disputes, since the early days of those which led to the Revolutionary war. All, in short, on our side of the question was supercilious pride; on that of the United States aggressive coarseness.

Every day increased the danger of such a state of things, and any hour might have produced a crisis beyond the power of diplomatic interference. Fortunately for both countries, in as far as this particular question was involved, a change of ministry took place in England. Sir Robert Peel came into power, and the settlement of the north-eastern boundary dispute became at last a fixed principle of the British Cabinet.

The unfitness of Mr. Fox to adjust a question he had so much contributed to make a vexed one was manifest. Equally so was the necessity of appointing a negotiator likely to consider the whole bearings of the case in a liberal spirit, and with personal influence among Americans sufficient to soothe their violence on the matter he had to manage. Lord Ashburton was the person so chosen; a nobleman well adapted to the occasion, from his connection by marriage and property with the United States. He was not a trained ambassador; but his general knowledge of business, straightforwardness, and good sense, were qualities far more valuable than those to be generally found in professional diplomatists, whose proceedings so often embroil instead of conciliating.

The intended mission of Lord Ashburton produced a great sensation in the United States. It was admitted to be a practical proof of the pacific intentions of the British Government, and it went far to counteract the mischief caused by the Report of the Commissioners. In the States of Maine and Massachusetts an evident disposition prevailed towards an amicable settlement, and in favour of a deviation from the extravagant territorial claims heretofore put forward, an equivalent in money being, however, always suggested as the price of the concession, and the free navigation of the St. John as an auxiliary stipulation. The state legislatures of Maine and Massachusetts adopted an improved tone in their various resolutions. Those of the latter, instead of ascribing the claim of England to "grasping cupidity," now admitted that "it emanates perhaps from convictions as honestly entertained as our own;" and instead of invoking armed force and the aid of the Federal Government, the appeal was made to "the justice of England," and the hope of a settlement was founded on "an alteration in her policy." While, in a report of the land agent of Maine to the government of that state, a proposition was actually made for a compromise of the dispute by a conventional line of boundary.

Under circumstances so encouraging, Lord Ashburton arrived at New York in the month of March, 1842, and immediately went on to Washington, where he delivered his credentials to President Tyler, and put himself into communication with Mr. Webster, the Secretary of State. They soon proceeded to the preliminary portions of their business; and the admitted understanding between them was, that frankness and fair-play were to be the basis of the negotiation; that subterfuge was to be discarded; that everything was to be done by conversation, not writing; and, in short, that all honest means were to be taken for a prompt solution of the dispute, and the conclusion of a reasonable treaty. Such were assuredly the intentions of Lord Ashburton, and every step he took in the transaction bore out those views. Had Webster been equally sincere, and had they to settle the question entirely between themselves, they would probably have made short work of it, and the treaty of Washington of 1842 might have formed a parallel to that of the Triple Alliance of 1699, concluded between Sir William Temple and De Witt after five days' personal intercourse—that marvellous instance of prompt and honest negotiation which still stands alone in its fame.

But the nature of the federal constitution of the United States gave Lord Ashburton no opportunity of being prompt, and Webster no chance of being honest. The States of Maine and Massachusetts having joint rights in the disputed territory, were invited by the President to send to Washington Commissioners to share in the negotiations; and the United States Senate being endowed with executive functions as regards all treaties with foreign powers, many complicated obstructions were now to be overcome. Seven Commissioners were appointed by the partner States of Maine and Massachusetts, to proceed to Washington and partake in the negotiations to be there carried on, and watch over the interests of their constituents. They were chosen from the Whig and Democratic parties, all having a common object on this occasion, and being expected to merge political hostility in the national interests now at stake.

Prominent among them was Judge Preble. Indeed, although all were on a nominal equality, he must be considered to have been *primus inter pares*; and his well-known obstinacy of character and fixed opinions on the matter now to a great degree under his control, offered a doubtful prospect of settlement to his less prejudiced or more pliable colleagues.

The other members of the Commission were Governor Kent, Governor Kavanagh, and Colonel Otis, from Maine, and Mr. Abbott Lawrence, Mr. Allen, and Mr. Mills, from Massachusetts. I was personally known to the majority of these gentlemen, and some of them were aware how earnestly I had devoted myself to the study of the Boundary Question, but not of the many communications I had made to Lord Ashburton on many points of which he was previously uninformed. But, although Judge Preble had called on me the day of his arrival, accompanied by his fellow-commissioners from Maine, and although I had talked freely with them, as well as with Mr. Abbott Lawrence relative to their mission, I was quite unprepared for their proposing to me, on the 7th of June, to accompany them to Washington the following day, to assist in the important negotiation they were about to enter on.

Taken by surprise by this gratifying proof of confidence on their part, I nevertheless met it cautiously. I explained my exact position, the entirely unofficial manner in which I must entertain their proposition, the possibility of Lord Ashburton not approving of any personal interference on my part, and the doubt as to the light in which it would be viewed by Lord Aberdeen, the Minister for Foreign Affairs; to say nothing of Mr. Fox, the regularly established minister at Washington, who had been so cavalierly superseded in an important portion of his functions. I thanked the Commissioners for their proposal, and the kind expressions with which it was coupled, and I required four-and-twenty hours to consider it.

During that time I turned the matter over in my mind. I was satisfied that I might do good service to Lord Ashburton at Washington in a semi-official way, and by, in some degree, acting as a check on Judge Preble's dogmatical obstinacy—an important point—for unanimity among the Maine Commissioners, on all the questions to be discussed, was required by their instructions. Any one of them, like a dissentient juryman, had power to paralyse the decision of his fellows; and, in the present case, the associates of my old friend Judge Preble were in mortal fear of his stern and uncompromising temper, and delighted at the chance of management which my influence with him held out.

On the other hand, I had some reason to reckon on the Foreign Office approving of my going to Lord Ashburton's assistance, for he had already reported favourably of the information I had given him, and I had received assurances of the satisfaction at home with my previous communications. Altogether, I decided on accompanying the Commissioners, and I set out with them the next day, having previously written to Lord Ashburton to expect me at Washington, and to Lord Aberdeen to explain the motives which induced me to take this unauthorised step, so unusual in the history of routine.

We left Boston on the 8th of June, and almost immediately on our arrival in New York the next day, a visit was paid to the Commissioners by Professor Renwick, a gentleman of great respectability, who came from Washington, on the part of Mr. Webster, with a confidential communication, which proved the first stumbling-block to our negotiation, and was very nearly cutting it short, so to speak, even before it began.

Judge Preble, hurrying to my room in the hotel (to which I had retired as soon as Professor Renwick had announced to my fellow-travellers the nature of his visit), opened on me with an explosion of anger—mild, however in comparison with his burst of fury on receiving the King of the Netherlands' award so many years before. He now spoke of Mr. Webster in terms of great reprobation, for the proposal he had the temerity to intrust to Professor Renwick; and its nature he at once divulged to me, in the shape of a map of the disputed territory, with a suggested line of boundary, which it seemed had been previously communicated to a secret committee of the legislature of the State of Maine. This line ran far to the south of the St. John River, and included fifteen townships of six square miles each, and was of course far more favourable to England even than the rejected award of the King of the Netherlands. I was, therefore, not surprised at the reception given to this proposal by Judge Preble; and it was with great difficulty I prevented him from at once quitting New York, retracing his steps to Maine, resigning his appointment, and publicly denouncing Webster as a traitor. Mr. Renwick disappeared. Mr. Preble's colleagues never afterwards ventured to touch on the subject of this untoward *feeler* put forth by Webster. I, for my part, found in it matter for much conjecture as to what might be going on between him and Lord Ashburton at Washington, little imagining the occult cause for this extraordinary deviation from the claim insisted on by all the public men of the United States, to a boundary line so enormously more favourable to them. Pondering over this strange affair, and paying minute attention to the incessant discussions among the Commissioners, I with them proceeded on the journey, and we reached Washington on Saturday, June 11th, when I immediately called on Lord Ashburton.

I was much pleased by his reception of me, his approval of the step I had taken, and his request that I would remain as long as I found it convenient. I thought, nevertheless, that though he was glad to avail himself of my assistance, he might not be quite at his ease, on the score of my being supposed to have anything actually official to do with the negotiation. So, at our next interview the following day, I took care to satisfy him that he had nothing to apprehend from my interference, and I was prepared to withdraw from Washington on the slightest appearance in any quarter of anything that might compromise my official position, or personally affect me. With this understanding, my co-operation actively commenced, and the division of labour was perfectly carried out, I continuing at Washington at Lord Ashburton's repeated urgent request, while he devoted himself to discussions with Webster. I gave myself up entirely to the seven Commissioners: I lived with them in the same hotel; I listened patiently to all their statements; I studied their documents, reports, such maps as they produced, and everything bearing on the controversy. I strove to reconcile their conflicting notions, and bring them all to bear upon a favourable construction of the English claims. On some points I successfully endeavoured to persuade them to changes of opinion; on others I admitted the justness of their views. On none whatever did I *dispute* with them; and altogether our intercourse was harmonious and satisfactory. The pertinacity of Preble and the pomposity of Lawrence required some management. The five others were exceedingly forbearing, unassuming, and gentlemanlike.

CHAPTER XXII.

THE NORTH-EASTERN BOUNDARY QUESTION—CONTINUED.

Negotiation and Conclusion of the Treaty of Washington—Attacked in both England and America.

LORD ASHBURTON gave frequent dinners to the persons most interested or mixed up with the affair he was managing so actively, including some gentlemen from New Brunswick. The President and Mr. Webster also entertained them hospitably. At these repasts everything went on with decorous cordiality. The Commissioners enjoyed the conviviality which is so great a softener of political asperities. The members of the Government mixed freely in those evening relaxations from the business of their respective bureaux. Mr. Fox was an occasional guest at Lord Ashburton's table during this period; and whatever might have been his jealousy of those concerned in the negotiation, in which he bore no part whatever, it in no way affected his amusing conversational qualities.

But under this unruffled surface of social enjoyment there was more than one current of disunion and discontent, on political and personal grounds, which are, however, not worth minutely recalling. Not only was the Secretary of State at variance on some points with the Commissioners, but they also had serious differences among themselves; and although I was, from time to time, able to discover this, from my constant intercourse with them, their discretion and my own sense of propriety prevented any undue confidence on their part, and any unfair exercise of curiosity on mine. In fact I was studious to maintain a great reserve in our communications, frequent and familiar as they were, in order to give no alarm to the suspicion, any more than to disturb the caution, which form two main ingredients of Yankee character, whether in New England or the district of Columbia.

Lord Ashburton's great object was to obtain a better line of boundary than that awarded by the King of the Netherlands. Mr. Webster was evidently disposed, from the first, to acquiesce in that desire. If his approval of Professor Renwick's proposal had not been sufficient proof of this, the somewhat "bullying" tone he assumed with the Commissioners (I use the word of one of them) left no doubt of it. This fact, in a great measure explained by after circumstances, created at the time a suspicion that means might have been used for influencing the Secretary of State, out of the legitimate pale of diplomatic persuasion. Although myself satisfied, from long study of the question, that the British claim to the boundary line along the highlands south of the St. John River was in accordance with the treaty of 1783; and although the written arguments in its favour placed by me in Lord Ashburton's hands were, as I believed, conclusive to him, I well knew that his Lordship had not, any more than myself, such documentary proof as would establish the validity of my reasonings. The many maps in his possession, as well as those belonging to the Commissioners, and more than one which I had discovered in Canada and in the state department in Boston, were most puzzling and contradictory. One map, to which I attached much importance, that mentioned in the published letters of Dr. Franklin as having been sent by him to Mr. Jefferson at Washington, and accurately tracing the boundary line, had, as I was assured there by Mr. Forsyth, the then Secretary of State, (some time previously to the Ashburton Negotiation) mysteriously disappeared from the Archives, and was nowhere to be found. Such a map, furnished soon after the signing of the treaty of 1783, to the then Secretary of State, by Dr. Franklin himself, the chief negotiator, would have carried a weight with it entirely official and reliable, and worth a dozen others, no matter of what pretensions. One of my journies from Boston to Washington, during the course of my researches, was expressly for the purpose of inspecting this missing map. I found nothing else there to compensate me for the disappointment of its loss ; and I had continued to grope my way very much in the dark, baffled by the negative as well as the positive obstacles towards an elucidation of the subject. When, at length, the true solution of the complicated difficulty became clear to me, I found ample confirmation of it, for my own satisfaction, as I advanced step by step in the inquiry. But I saw, nevertheless, that it would be impossible to convince against their will, by mere discussion, any of the American statesmen, legislators, or politicians, who were mixed up in the affair ; and I was not surprised at the reiterated assurances of the several Commissioners, of Mr. Webster, and sundry senators and representatives, of their steady conviction in the justice of the American claim in its totality.

Notwithstanding all this, more than one of the Commissioners expressed to me a willingness to accept of less territory, if more could not be had, than was contained in King William's award, on obtaining an ample equivalent in money. And one of them traced a line on a map which he, in plain terms, told me he was ready to accept, had Judge Preble been less obstinate. But nothing could remove his determination in the early stages of the negotiation to hold fast to his conviction in the identity of the lines of 1763 and 1783, that that was the one only true line, and that any variation from it was a mere diplomatic figment to be treated with entire contempt. Absolute as was the resolution avowed by the Commissioners, in many of our conferences, never to yield any territory south of the St. John, and convinced as I was that they dared not so far brave the indignation of the people of Maine and Massachusetts, I yet discovered a wavering in some of these gentlemen, a willingness to listen to my reasonings even on that point, and an anxiety that I should impress on Lord Ashburton an acknowledgment of this docility, which baffled my comprehension, although I was certain there must have been some strong motive for it, stronger than their avowed wish for an amicable settlement, so sudden a contrast to the previous unyielding pretensions.

Lord Ashburton, on his part, had early assured me in positive terms, that his instructions did not allow of his consenting to the St. John as a boundary, in that part of its course which would necessarily consign to the United States the moiety of the settlement made at Madawaska on both sides of the river, composed of stragglers from Lower Canada, about two thousand of whom were located on the right or southern bank. Satisfied that it was but loss of time to contend for this point, I showed him the necessity of his instructions being modified, and he wrote home accordingly. As to the other parts of the line, regarding which I saw a disposition to yield, I confess I attributed it in some degree to the arguments I had the opportunity of putting forward, and which could not, I thought, fail to bring conviction to any one less obdurate than Judge Preble.

With reference to that impracticable person, Lord Ashburton had much anxiety. He attached great importance to my influence with him, which, however, went no further than to keep him on tolerable terms with his colleagues, and several times to prevent his abruptly breaking up the negotiations, besides obtaining his consent to various minor concessions. But on his fixed opinion regarding the main point of the dispute I could produce no effect. Lord Ashburton, on my showing him a map, with the line which I had reason to know would be consented to by all the Commissioners, and a duplicate of which I had previously transmitted to Lord Aberdeen, had assured me with strong emphasis that "that line would never do," that "he could give them nothing like that," nor could he "abandon the Madawaska settlement." He then said he would "contrive to have some private and unofficial talk with Preble," and asked me, with a smile, significant of more than I could quite understand, "if I thought he would listen to reason ?" I replied that that was about the very last thing he would listen to ; and I assuredly did not suspect that it could "take any shape" at all likely to influence him on the point then chiefly in question.

It was not, in fact, to be expected that any of the United States authorities, whether federal or local, would consent to give up to England the portion of the only established community in the disputed territory which had been assigned to their jurisdiction by the award of the King of the Netherlands, who was himself at the time considered by Americans rather as the subservient instrument of England than the independent arbitrator between two rival nations. The terms of compromise he recommended, though giving about two-thirds of the territory to the United States, were considered by its people as a most unfair division. "The whole, and nothing but the whole," was the general cry; and the bewildered monarch, in awarding so much a larger portion to America than to England, was believed to have virtually admitted the justice of the exorbitant demand, and to have assigned what he did to England only as a bribe to influence the British Government in the arrangement of his own pending quarrel with Belgium.

On the other hand, it was out of the question to ask England to take less than had been so awarded. The political storm had blown over in Europe. The separation between Holland and Belgium was effected. The former country had retired within those original limits in which all its ancient fame and modern prosperity had been acquired, had reinstated the dynasty of its old predilections, and had been removed from the false position imposed upon it by the treaties of 1814 and 1815, under the imposing fiction of "an increase of territory." The new kingdom of Belgium had been relieved from the insulting stigma implied in that last-quoted phrase. It had chosen a King, whose eminent qualities were already patent to admiring Europe, and under whose influence the new-formed state was established, as an integral portion of its political civilisation. India and China, no doubt, were just then the scene of contests which caused some embarrassment to the otherwise unobstructed power of

Great Britain, and threatenings of a rupture with France on Eastern subjects, gave some inquietude. But altogether the nation was fully capable of any struggle that national honour might demand, and was therefore the better able to accede to a dignified adjustment of a dispute so disproportioned to her power and pride. The United States, recovering from a terrible crisis of financial difficulties, and busy in reorganising their disturbed commercial operations, were well disposed to prove to the world, and particularly to England, their readiness to give fair play to their tottering credit, by establishing the existing, but threatened peace, on a still firmer basis. Both nations were thus in a mood and a position to justify the mutual acceptance of a compromise of the only matter which then contained the germs of a rupture.

But while the negotiations at Washington were in progress, the country began to show impatience. Doubts of various kinds were openly expressed as to several propositions and counter-projects, the Conference, and the correspondence which day by day thickened the plot. Senators and members of the House of Representatives from Maine and Massachusetts, and leading politicians belonging to other sections, little by little mingled their interference with the legitimate proceedings. Many hints and suggestions reached my ears, mixed up with innuendos as to the secret doings between the members of the Government and the Senate. It was clear that some decisive measures must be taken to bring the affair, one way or another, to a close. Public opinion was all the while as obstinate as ever. It did not abate one jot of its pretensions. The Report of the British Commissioners was continually held up to the country by influential speakers and writers as a tissue of weak and false assertions unworthy of the least consideration ; while a second "Private and Confidential" production, coming direct from Downing Street, and the work of the same hand, would not, as Lord Ashburton avowed to me, be for a moment tolerated or even read, had he ventured to produce it in support of his own communications. This "confidential" report was thus completely suppressed. I found that it contained no small portion of the most material of my own communications to the Foreign Office, which were unceremoniously appropriated by the author, without the least acknowledgment ; but Lord Ashburton had already received a duplicate of them, and much more direct from the source, whatever it may have been worth.

Judge Preble became day by day more intractable. His colleagues were in serious apprehension of a total failure of the negotiations. Mr. Webster, whose political existence was dependent on their success, grew very uneasy, and found it necessary to show his zealous activity to the country at large, and Lord Ashburton, contrary to my urgent recommendation, allowed himself to be drawn into a correspondence on the old arguments as to the treaty of 1783, in contravention of the agreement early entered into that all was to be done by conversation alone. He had no chance in a written controversy with Webster and the Commissioners.

Lord Ashburton's letters were clear and ingenuous. He showed his knowledge of the subject, and stated his case with ability ; but he was borne down by the elaborate style of Webster, ambitious, and straining for effect, and the long and heavy common-place of the Commissioners. The odds were too great against the British negotiator. He appeared to be defeated on all points ; while his chief and overpowering adversary, Webster, solemnly reiterated his own belief, and that of all the branches of the American Government, in the justice of their claim, and that that belief arose from *an honest conviction that it was founded in truth,* and that it accorded with the physical geography of the country, and the intentions of the negotiators of the treaty of 1783. Webster said in one of his letters :—

"I must be permitted to say that few questions have ever arisen under this Government in regard to which a *stronger or more general conviction was felt that the country was in the right,* than this question of the north-eastern boundary. The question before us is whether these confident opinions, on both sides, of *the rightful nature and just strength* of our respective claims, will permit us, while a desire to preserve harmony and a disposition to yield liberally to mutual convenience strongly incites us, to come together, and to unite on a line by agreement."

Language so conciliatory and so plausible as this could be met only by confidence on the part of any candid or honourable man. It had considerable influence on Lord Ashburton, and it was by him represented to his Government in the light in which he himself viewed it. Impelled by this feeling, he threw no obstructions in the way of a settlement, which now went rapidly on, step by step; the hitherto recalcitrant element in the Council of the Commissioners subsiding with a suddenness that seemed almost magical. Lord Ashburton wisely availed himself of this change. The two extra subjects embraced in the negotiations relative to the slave trade and the extradition of criminals, were easily settled. Lord Ashburton yielded his claim to the southern line of highlands. He accepted the middle channel of the St. John River as the dividing line in the chief portion of its course. He granted its free navigation where it formed the dividing line. He gave up a moiety of the Madawaska settlement. In so far he confirmed the acceptance of the King of the Netherlands' award by the Government of Great Britain in 1831, when Lord Palmerston filled the office of Secretary of State. But in one most important point he secured far better terms than those at that time accepted.

By that memorable but impotent award, the St. John was made the boundary along the accepted portion of its course as far as the river St. Francis, and inasmuch as that related to the preservation of the British communication, it was satisfactory; but the boundary was directed to proceed up the river to its source in the highlands, and thence by the highlands to the sources of the Du Sud, surrendering to the United States, for a distance of sixty miles, the right to overlook the valley of the St. Lawrence from the military position there. This was the most objectionable part of the award; and by Lord Ashburton's treaty, as will be seen by a reference to the map in the Appendix, that portion of the line was successfully objected to; and another was with startling unanimity agreed to by the Commissioners, the Secretary of State, and the President, granting an unthreatened frontier to the whole of the province of Lower Canada, and not in any part of it approaching nearer than sixty miles to Quebec.

Thus it will be seen that by the Treaty of Washington, concluded and signed on the 9th of August, 1842, a boundary has been established, securing every essential object for which England had so long contended, and every advantage indispensable to the safety of her North

American Colonies, the highly objectionable portion of King William's award has been abrogated, and the American Government has withdrawn from the exorbitant claim, which was felt to be so dangerous, and all suggestions for a money equivalent to be paid by England were abandoned. It is true that the English negotiator, on his part, relinquished our revived pretensions to that large district of country lying between the southern bank of the St. John and the ridge of highlands, which were shown to our own satisfaction to be those of the treaty of 1783; but for the positive establishment of our right to which no authenticated title could then be produced by us. The territory was accordingly divided into two moieties as nearly as could be calculated, and to each country was assigned that portion contiguous to, and most necessary to its interests.

The whole area of the disputed territory was estimated to be 6,750,000 acres. By the award of King William there was assigned to England 4,119 square miles—2,636,160 acres.

The actual distribution of the territory by the treaty of Washington is in the proportion of—

To the United States . . .	3,413,000 acres.
To Great Britain	3,337,000 „
The difference in favour of the United States being . . .	76,000 „

Of which twice or thrice that amount in the part ceded to the United States consists of lakes and morasses.

By the compromise which was thus effected, it is clear that besides the acknowledgment of our title to all the military positions upon the frontier, England retains about

700,000 acres more than were assigned to her by the King of the Netherlands; and it is thus undoubted that the mission of Lord Ashburton was successful in its merely diplomatic and material objects. But a far more important and more elevated purpose was effected. A harassing and irritating subject of contention between the two countries was got rid of; a threatened war was averted; and an immense tract of country was secured to tranquillity, industry, and civilisation.

These were great results, of which every philanthropist might well be proud, and with which assuredly every British statesman ought to have been satisfied. For those who played the principal parts in the transaction, some degree of self-gratulation was perhaps pardonable, such as a surgeon might feel, on the final closing of a dangerous wound, which had tested his skill and menaced his patient's life. For myself individually, a mere subordinate, with no responsibility, and small pretensions, I had every reason to be gratified. I had received repeated expressions of approval from the Foreign Office for the communications I sent home during several years. I had seen my urgent representations of the necessity for a settlement justified. I had received the warm acknowledgments of Lord Ashburton and the Commissioners for the services I rendered. I had obtained the tepid thanks of the Secretary of State for Foreign Affairs, for my somewhat hardy and hazardous move from Boston to Washington without previous authority, and for the part I bore in these transactions.

Lord Ashburton, delighted with the consummation of his arduous task, paid successive visits to the Atlantic cities. I had the pleasure of receiving him at Boston, and, aided by some of the influential citizens there, of doing the honours of the place; and in a less formal and still more gratifying way, I had an opportunity of enabling him and Lord John Hay, the commander of the frigate which bore him out to America, to meet some of the gentlemen then residing at Nahant, and of initiating them into the beauties of that favourite resort of mine. Finally I accompanied them back to New York, and assisted at a grand banquet given there, in celebration of the treaty, and in honour of its negotiators.

In the meantime, however, a series of attacks were simultaneously made in the British Parliament and a portion of the London Press against Lord Ashburton and his work of "peace and goodwill towards men." It appeared strange and inconsistent, even to those accustomed to the excesses of party-feeling, that the foremost volunteer in those forensic assaults should be Lord Palmerston himself, who, in 1831, had given his prompt adhesion to the award of the King of the Netherlands, and had in 1835, authorised the British Minister at Washington to propose the arrangement before adverted to, for an equal division of the territory, and which was assuredly less advantageous to England than that now so happily secured and so unjustly assailed. An elaborate pamphlet in reply to those attacks was issued by the Foreign Office, under the auspices of Lord Aberdeen, the author of which was no other than the identical Commissioner of former days, whose Report, put forth under the ministry of Lord Palmerston, was the very basis of the strictures he was now ordered to refute. But individual instances of party spirit and literary pliancy were of small moment. The satisfaction of the public at large was the best reward sought for by the noble and honest negotiator, who bore unruffled the afflatus of political enmity, and received complacently the thanks of both Houses of Parliament.

And not only to this most estimable public servant was justice generously done by English opinion. The conduct of the American Government, and especially of its Secretary of State, Mr. Daniel Webster, was highly extolled. The skill with which he was believed to have managed the sometime restive Commissioners, and to have led them and the governments and legislatures from whom their functions were derived, to adopt his own views, and for the sake of the world's repose to sacrifice pretensions they believed (with him) to be of "such rightful nature and just strength," was felt and admitted to be above all praise.

Not so, however, was his conduct considered in the United States. The most violent opposition was made to the terms of the treaty; the most opprobrious language applied to the negotiator. While the factious in England pronounced Lord Ashburton to have been "sold," those in America declared that Webster had been bought. Every part of the treaty was denounced, wholesale, or bit by bit; and it became at last doubtful if the Senate would ratify it. That final consummation was, however, suddenly effected, almost, it might be said, *per saltum;* the Senate coming to its decision by an unexpected majority of thirty-nine to nine, after several days of *secret debates.* The sanction of the Queen and the British Government had been given without hesitation. Lord Ashburton returned to England. The Maine and Massachusetts Commissioners retired to their respective homes. The people at either side of the Atlantic were well satisfied with the termination of the long and virulent dispute; and the North-Eastern Boundary Question would soon have sunk into the archives of diplomatic history, as a monument of English moderation and American magnanimity, were it not that the system of political publicity in the United States makes it impossible to stifle truth altogether, however it may be for a time concealed. *Veritas visu et morâ.* Like murder, it will out. A practical application of the proverb to the present case was soon experienced; and it so happened that, as far as the British Government and public were concerned, I had the fortune to be the medium for dispelling the illusion that had for some months prevailed.

CHAPTER XXIII.

THE NORTH-EASTERN BOUNDARY QUESTION—CONTINUED.

Discovery of Franklin's Map, tracing the true Line of Boundary, and of others confirming its accuracy—Secret Debates in the American Senate—Debates in the British Parliament—Effrontery of American Speakers and Writers—Honourable Exceptions—Concluding Reflections.

AN American gentleman, whose acquaintance I had made in Europe, and had cultivated to considerable intimacy in Boston, whose reputation has gradually increased, as his fine talents and high principle have had the Senate Chamber of the United States for their display, voluntarily made me a communication on the subject of the recent treaty, which I felt it to be my duty at once to transmit to my Government, and the correctness of which was soon confirmed by the publication of the proceedings of the Senate at Washington, during their secret debates, leading to the ratification of the treaty, on the 17th and 19th of the preceding month of August.

It will have been obvious to all persons familiar with controversial discussions on boundary lines, that most important, as well as most contradictory, evidence in such disputes is founded on surveys and maps. I have already mentioned the conflicting testimony of those which were connected with the question I have undertaken in the preceding chapters to elucidate. I also called attention to the strange disappearance of that one transmitted by

Dr. Franklin to Mr. Jefferson, in October, 1790, with the true boundary line traced on it. It was, therefore, with great astonishment I learned from the confidential communication just alluded to, that during the whole of the negotiation at Washington, while the highest functionaries of the American Government were dealing with Lord Ashburton with seeming frankness and integrity, pledging their faith for a perfect conviction of the justice of their claim to the territory which was in dispute, Mr. Webster had in his possession, and had communicated to them all, President, Cabinet, Commissioners, and Senate, the highest evidence which the nature of the case admitted of, that the United States had never had a shadow of right to any part of the territory which they had so pertinaciously claimed for nearly fifty years. This evidence, as my conscientious informant told me, was nothing less than a copy of an original map, presented by Dr. Franklin to Count de Vergennes, the minister of Louis XVI., on December 6, 1782 (six days after the preliminaries of the Treaty of Paris, of 1783, were signed), tracing the boundary, as agreed upon by himself and the other Commissioners, with a strong red line south of the St. John, and exactly where a similar line appears in an *unauthenticated* map, discovered in London subsequent to Lord Ashburton's departure on his mission.

This was the revelation which so amazed me, and an account of which I at once forwarded to Lord Aberdeen.

My informant gave unmeasured expression to his indignation, which he assured me was fully shared by his friends Judge Story and Dr. Channing, with both of whom I was well acquainted. The latter of these truly distinguished and most virtuous men was unfortunately at the time confined by illness to what was too soon to become his death-bed. Had his fragile state of health but given him time, his powerful pen would have denounced to the whole world the deceptive transaction. Judge Story entirely sympathised in Dr. Channing's reprobation of it. I saw him immediately on the subject, and he expressed himself without reserve on Webster's conduct as "a most disgraceful proceeding;" and said he "greatly apprehended the ill effect it would have in future transactions between England and the United States, and that he was even prepared for the British Government insisting on a reconsideration, if not the annulling of the treaty." Other gentlemen of Boston who had heard of the affair, entirely coincided in those opinions. It was discussed at a dinner party by some of the leading persons there, and elicited different views, according to the different characters of the speakers, but no one of any great weight was found to justify what so many of respectability condemned.

The public attention being thus aroused, it was impossible to persevere in an official concealment of what had oozed out before its time. The injunction of secresy imposed by the Senate on its members was dissolved, and permission was given for the publication of the various speeches in the secret session of August 17, 19, 1842. The most important of those speeches was that of Mr. Rives, the chairman of the committee on Foreign Affairs. It was of considerable length, occupying five columns of the official paper in which it first appeared, and was an elaborate and a most successful effort to overcome the obstacles towards the ratification of the treaty. His principal argument with his colleagues was like that used by Mr. Webster, with the Commissioners (as I subsequently learned) that if they did not consent to receive what was conceded to them by Lord Ashburton's treaty, they would compel the dispute to be referred to a second arbitration, with very great danger of their losing the whole; "*Mr. Webster, the Secretary of State, having communicated to him to be laid before the Senate*, a copy of the map presented by Dr. Franklin to Count de Vergennes."

"It therefore appears to the Committee," said Mr. Rives, "in looking back to the public and solemn acts of the government, and of its successive administrations, that the time has passed, if it ever existed, when we could be justified in making the entire line of boundary claimed by us the subject of a *sine quâ non* of negotiation, or of the *ultima ratio* of an assertion by force. Did a second arbitration, then, afford the prospect of a more satisfactory result? If such an alternative is contemplated by any one, as preferable to the arrangement which has been made, it is fit to bear in mind *the risk and uncertainty*, as well as the inevitable delay and expense, incident to that mode of decision. Is there no danger, in the event of another arbitration, that a further search into the public archives of Europe might bring to light some embarrassing (even though apocryphal) document, to throw a new shade of plausible doubt on the clearness of our title, in the view of a sovereign arbiter? Such a document has been already communicated to the Committee; and I feel it to be my duty to lay it before the Senate, that they may fully appreciate its bearings, and determine for themselves the weight and importance which belong to it. It is due to the learned and distinguished gentleman (Mr. Jared Sparks of Boston) by whom the document referred to was discovered in the archives of France, that the account of it should be given in his own words, as contained in a communication *addressed by him to the Department of State*." *

Mr. Rives then proceeded to read from the communication as follows;—

"While pursuing my researches among the voluminous papers relating to the American Revolution in the Archives des Affaires Etrangères, in Paris, I found in one of the bound volumes an original

* It may be mentioned here that Mr. Jared Sparks told me he had the copy of Franklin's map in his possession for six months before he sent it to Mr.

letter from Dr. Franklin to Count de Vergennes, of which the following is an exact transcript:—

"'SIR, PASSY, *December* 6*th*, 1782.

"'I have the honour of returning herewith the map your Excellency sent me yesterday. I have marked with a *strong red line*, according to your desire, the limits of the United States, as settled in the preliminaries between the British and American plenipotentiaries.

"'With great respect, I am, &c.,

"'B. FRANKLIN.'

"This letter was written six days after the preliminaries were signed; and if we could procure the identical map mentioned by Franklin, it would seem to afford *conclusive evidence* as to the meaning affixed by the Commissioners to the language of the treaty on the subject of the boundaries. You may well suppose that I lost no time in making inquiries for the map, not doubting that it would confirm all my previous opinions respecting the validity of our claim. In the geographical department of the Archives are sixty thousand maps and charts; but so well arranged with catalogues and indexes, that any one of them may be easily found. After a little research in the American division, with the aid of the keeper, I came upon a map of North America, by D'Anville, dated 1746, in size about eighteen inches square, on which was drawn a *strong red line* throughout the entire boundary of the United States, answering precisely to Franklin's description. The line is bold and distinct in every part, made with red ink, and apparently drawn with a hair-pencil, or a pen with a blunt point. There is no other colouring on any part of the map.

"*Imagine my surprise on discovering that this line runs wholly south of the St. John's*, and between the head waters of that river and those of the Penobscot and Kennebec. In short, *it is exactly the line contended for by Great Britain, except that it concedes more than is claimed.* The north line, after departing from the source of the St. Croix, instead of proceeding to Mars Hill, stops far short of that point, and turns off to the west, so as to leave on the British

Webster. Mr. Edmund Dwight, of Boston (as he himself told me), was the person who took it to Washington for Mr. Sparks, and Mr. Peleg Sprague (afterwards Judge Sprague) was the medium for communicating it to the Committee of the Maine Legislature; these three gentlemen being the only unofficial depositories of the secret.

side all the streams which flow into the St. John's, between the source of the St. Croix and Mars Hill. It is evident that the line, from the St. Croix to the Canadian highlands, is intended to exclude all the waters running into the St. John's.

"There is no positive proof that this map is actually the one marked by Franklin; yet upon any other supposition it would be difficult to explain the circumstances of its agreeing so perfectly with his description, and of its being preserved in the place where it would naturally be deposited by Count de Vergennes. I also found *another map* in the Archives, on which the same boundary was traced in a dotted red line with a pen, apparently copied from the other.

"I enclose herewith a map of Maine, on which I have drawn a strong black line, corresponding with the red one above mentioned."

When Mr. Rives produced this communication (of Mr. Sparks to Mr. Webster), Mr. Benton informed the Senate that he could produce a map of higher validity than the one alluded to. He accordingly repaired to the library of Congress, and soon returned with a map, which there is no doubt was the one sent by Dr. Franklin to Mr. Jefferson, already alluded to as having been surreptitiously removed and hid away from the archives of the state department some years before. An account of this map, thus "paraded" by Mr. Benton in his ignorant zeal, is given in the continuation of Mr. Rives's speech.

"A map," said he, "has been vauntingly paraded here, *from Mr. Jefferson's collection*, in the zeal of opposition (without taking time to see what it was) to confront and invalidate the map found by Mr. Sparks in Paris. But the moment it is examined *it is found to sustain, by the most precise and remarkable correspondence in every feature, the map communicated by Mr. Sparks.* The senator who produced it could see nothing but the microscopic dotted line running off in a north-easterly direction; * but the moment other eyes were

* This microscopic dotted line was, of course, that designating the boundary of the proclamation of 1763, found on all the maps previous to 1783, and copied into the one now in question.

applied to it, there was found, in bold relief, a strong red line, *indicating the limits of the United States according to the treaty of peace, and coinciding, minutely and exactly, with the boundary traced on the map of Mr. Sparks.* That this red line, and not the hardly visible dotted line, was intended to represent the limits of the United States according to the treaty of peace, is conclusively shown, by the circumstance that the red line is drawn on the map, all around the exterior boundary of the United States, through the middle of the northern lakes, thence through the Long Lake and the Rainy Lake to the Lake of the Woods; and from the western extremity of the Lake of the Woods to the River Mississippi, and along that river to the point where the boundary of the United States, according to the treaty of peace, leaves it, and thence by its easterly course to the mouth of the St. Mary's on the Atlantic. Here, then, is a most remarkable and unforeseen confirmation of the map of Mr. Sparks, and by another map of *a most imposing character, and bearing every mark of high authenticity.* It was printed and published in Paris in 1784 (the year after the conclusion of the peace) by Lattré, *graveur du Roi* (engraver of maps, &c., to the King). It is formally entitled on its face a 'Map of the United States of America, *according to the treaty of peace of* 1783 (*Carte des États Unis de l'Amérique, suivant le traité de paix de* 1783.) It is dedicated and presented (*dediée et présentée*) to his Excellency Benjamin Franklin, Minister Plenipotentiary of the United States of America, near the Court of France,' *and while Dr. Franklin yet remained in Paris, for he did not return to the United States till the spring of the year* 1785."

"Is there not, then," continued Mr. Rives, "the most plausible ground to argue that this map, professing to be one constructed according to the treaty of peace of 1783, and being dedicated and presented to Dr. Franklin, *was made out with his knowledge and by his directions*; and that corresponding as it does *identically* with the map found by Mr. Sparks in the archives of Paris, they both partake of the same presumptions in favour of their authenticity?" and Mr. Rives might well have added, had he ever read or remembered the letter of Dr. Franklin to Mr. Jefferson, accompanied by the map—"or what map so likely to be sent from Franklin to Jefferson as that one so peculiarly, as may be said, *his own*, and which Mr. Benton has now dragged from its concealment and brought here, 'to make assurance doubly sure.'"

Notwithstanding these cogent arguments of Mr. Rives, his colleague, Mr. Benton, doggedly refused to admit his belief in the authenticity of the maps discovered by Mr. Sparks; but he observed, with hypothetical sincerity, that "if they were really authentic, the concealment of them was a fraud on the British, and that the Senate was insulted by being made a party to the fraud;" and further, that, "if evidence had been discovered which deprived Maine of the title to one-third of its territory, *honour required that it should be made known to the British.*" *

* Soon after the existence of these maps was made known to the public, another, which had formerly belonged to Baron Steuben, a Prussian officer in the service of the United States, but which had been for many years in the possession of a gentleman of New York, was transmitted to the State Department in Washington. It also showed a line in strict accordance with those before mentioned; making the fourth map about that period discovered, coinciding in the main point of the boundary line intended by the treaty of 1783, and all confirmed as to the authenticity of the line, by the semi-official map published in London in 1785, by Faden, the Geographer to the King, the correctness of which had never been objected to by the United States Government.

During the public discussions relative to these maps, a gentleman of Boston called the attention of the author to still another with a red line, in connection with the negotiations of 1782, and which he supposed to be identical with the one discovered by Mr. Sparks. In reference to this map, there is in the official correspondence of John Jay (one of the Commissioners with Dr. Franklin, Mr. Adams, and Mr. Laurens, for the United States) an account of a conference between him and Count d'Aranda, the Spanish Minister at Paris, in July, 1782, at which it was agreed that the Count should send him a map, with a red line traced on it, in accordance with the boundary proposed by Spain for the western portion of the United States.

"A few days afterwards," writes Mr. Jay, "he sent me the map with his proposed line marked on it in red ink. He ran it from a lake near the confines of Georgia, but east of the Flint River, to the confluence of the Kanawa with the Ohio, thence round the western shores of Lakes Erie and Huron, and thence round Lake Michigan to Lake Superior."—*Life of John Jay, by his Son*, vol. ii. p. 472.

Mr. Jay further states that (Dr. Franklin agreeing with him that this line was

Mr. Woodbury and Mr. Buchanan, in their speeches, pretended to consider the maps in question as merely showing the old boundaries claimed by France in her colonial disputes with Great Britain. But this absurd assumption was self-refuted, by the obvious fact that the red line on all these maps goes out to sea beyond the exterior bounds of the American continent, *in accordance with the treaty* of 1783, which gives twenty leagues out beyond the sea-coast, for the jurisdiction of the United States.

Mr. Calhoun, with a candour widely contrasting with Buchanan's shallow hypocrisy, admitted that the discoveries of the maps were corroborating circumstances calculated "to add no small weight to the claim of Great Britain;" and that "it would be idle to suppose that these disclosures would not *weigh heavily against the United States* in any future negotiation."

As the several speeches referred to successively appeared, I transmitted copies of them to the Secretary of State for Foreign Affairs, thus confirming the information I had privately received. The reception of this intelligence in London, caused, as I was unofficially informed, a great sensation. The ex-commissioner and pamphlet writer of the Foreign Office added a supplement to his latest *brochure*, stating that "since the preceding pages were sent to press and made ready for publication, an unex-

preposterous on the part of Spain) he gave the map to Count Vergennes, on the 10th of August, 1782.

It is almost needless to remark that this could not well be mistaken by any one giving a thought to the subject, for the map sent by Franklin to the Count de Vergennes, on December 6th, 1782, after the preliminaries were signed, on which were marked the boundaries of the whole of the United States, totally different to those here proposed to the westward, and marking the line to the eastward and southward for twenty leagues out to sea, in accordance with the treaty of 1783, that discovered by Mr. Sparks being exactly so marked.

pected piece of information has transpired, so vitally connected with the late negotiations at Washington, that the author, even after the pamphlet had been announced for sale, has felt himself compelled by *its unparalleled importance* to lay it before the world."

However exaggerated this may be, it shows how my communications were considered by the Government. It is scarcely necessary to dwell on the commotion they excited in Parliament, on the strong opinions enunciated by the press as to the bad faith of the American negotiators, or on the efforts made by our own Prime Minister, Sir Robert Peel, not merely to slur over but to justify the whole course of Mr. Webster in the transaction, with a zeal far greater than he appears to have displayed in defending his own able and honest envoy, Lord Ashburton. The effect of this conduct in England was of small importance. The public was little surprised at the exposure of American trickery, or the loose defence of it, from mere political expediency, on the part of the Prime Minister. But his reference to one or two of those unauthenticated maps before referred to, on which ignorance or carelessness had continued to trace the old line of the Proclamation of 1763, as identical with the *new line* of the treaty of 1783,* and the jocular manner in which he

* Any comparison between the conflicting maps referred to as evidence during the long dispute, was futile. The Americans maintained (and in my opinion justly) that the line of the Proclamation of 1763 ran along the Northern Highlands, and that never was contested till long after the treaty of 1783. No map anterior to that latter date had any other frontier line traced on it. It was after that period that those red lines were traced on the several maps. But if, as the Americans insisted, no southern, or, in fact, no second line was meant to be drawn by the treaty of 1783, why should any maps show such a line as that of Franklin's traced on them? It could not have been for the purpose of contesting the line of the Proclamation of 1763, relative to which there had been no dispute. It must then have been to designate *some other* boundary, no other was in question but that of the treaty of 1783; and, therefore, no maps with the old line of *domestic* boundary traced on them were of the least importance in the con-

treated the subject of the *suppressio veri,* as an admitted practice in diplomacy, produced such consequences as might have been looked for, by any one acquainted with the style of American writers and speakers. Resting on the authority of Sir Robert Peel, the tables were completely turned upon England by newspapers and stump orators in the United States. The English Government were accused of exactly what Webster and his associates had done ; and effrontery went so far as to assert that he was the party deceived and America the country defrauded. One orator stated that "Great Britain, that grasping and avaricious country, *had cheated* the United States in the late treaty, and obtained the portion of Maine which she wanted."* And a democratic paper remarked that "since the discovery of the part played by the English Government, in the late negotiation for the settlement of our North-Eastern boundary, in which they claimed and obtained a tract of our territory, with the evidence of our title to it in their possession and concealed from us, Mr. Webster's reputation as a skilful and successful negotiator does not stand very high."

To such an extent were those written and spoken commentaries pushed by unscrupulous pens and tongues, such a mass of vituperation was poured out against England, and such unblushing attempts made to impugn the information and even the intellect of Benjamin Franklin himself, in the admitted supposition that he had traced the red

troversy, while those showing Franklin's line were of the very highest. But to have understood this, it was necessary to feel satisfied that the line of the Proclamation was altogether different from the line of the Treaty ; and to that truth every body had hitherto seemed utterly blind. It was therefore to be expected that all those who had contended for the identity of the lines designated in those documents should persist in their self-confusing arguments, and ignore those which put the matter in the true light.

* The Hon. Isaac H. Wright, at a public meeting in Faneuil Hall, Boston.

line,* that I was impelled to publish (but anonymously), in a pamphlet form, a condensed statement, before referred to, of what I had furnished to Lord Ashburton, to show that even before the discovery of the maps it had been possible to explain in plain but not irritating terms, that England had an honest and equitable claim to the territory, which these maps so clearly proved to have been hers. †

I had by this time ascertained from the best authority that the effect produced by the discovered maps upon Webster, before the negotiations of Washington, was such as to lead to Professor Renwick's mission to New York, with the proposed line of boundary; and also to Mr. Webster's "bullying" language to the Maine Commissioners, when, urging their consent to Lord Ashburton's first proposal (which conceded to England both sides of the St. John), "he turned short, and asked in a fierce tone, what better terms do you want or expect?" Abbott Lawrence and Mr. (afterwards Judge) Allen were also particularly influenced by Franklin's map; and it was only Judge Preble's obstinacy, in treating with scorn every argument and threat that clashed with his own opinions, that prevented an immediate surrender of Lord Ashburton's entire demand. But the sudden abandonment of the extreme American pretensions and of the King of the Netherlands' line, and the adoption of Lord Ashburton's modified proposals, were all in consequence of the evidence of the maps, and the conviction of all concerned

* "That Dr. Franklin did either not understand the line that had been agreed upon, or that he, together with the other negotiators, made a most egregious error in the language of the treaty in which they undertook to describe it, is most apparent to any one who will compare the two. As exhibiting such a blunder on the part of Dr. Franklin, this map is a remarkable and curious document."—*Boston Daily Advertiser.*

† See Appendix.

that a discovery of their existence before the conclusion of a treaty, would have given irresistible strength to the English claims.

That the statement I published should have been well received by British readers generally, was natural. Nor was it strange that it should be only coldly welcomed by those official writers whose ineffectual productions had produced but angry retort in America. Several publications in that country noticed, but could not refute, the case I made out. The North American Review, the only periodical of the Union at all known in Europe, admitted, in reference to it (No. CXIX., for April 1843), that "the argument on the British side of the Boundary Question, is stated with more method, clearness, and force, than we have ever seen anywhere in print."

Still stronger testimony in favour of my statement was afforded, in communications addressed to me by American gentlemen to whom I had sent copies of it. I might cite several living individuals, well known and more or less respected in England, were I not apprehensive of endangering their popularity in their own country. One letter from one of those, whose character for probity and talent stands very high, I will gratify myself by inserting here, and were I to ask his consent for the publication of his name, I am sure he would give it, for he has abundantly proved himself to possess *le courage de ses opinions.* The statesman alluded to was long a firm believer in the claim of the United States to the whole of the disputed territory. He had when in Europe converted to this belief several Englishmen, among the rest Lord Brougham, who, on the strength of this gentleman's authority, recklessly asserted in the House of Lords that England was *undeniably, clearly, and manifestly in the wrong.* Besides such private adhesions, this gentleman had gained great public success, by an ingeniously written argument in favour of his then conscientious conviction, in which he stated that "nothing I have heard or read has altered my opinion, formed after a deliberate survey of the whole matter, that the claim of the United States is clear, conclusive, and just." It was, therefore, no small satisfaction to me to receive from such an authority the following letter in the month of January, 1843, and I hope my egotism may be now excused, in consideration of the length of time I have suffered to elapse, during which I have resisted strong motives for publishing whatever is personal to myself in this whole subject :—

"I have read your observations on the question of boundary settled by the late treaty, and have been astonished at the strong case you were able to make out for your government, without any knowledge of the maps which have recently come to light. I am obliged to confess (though in doing so I abandon convictions most conscientiously maintained for several years) that these maps and your very able argument satisfy my mind of the validity of the English claim. *The land does not belong to us,* and I am very sorry that any portion of it has been given to us. I might add that our government seems to me to have urged a groundless claim ; but the case did not probably present itself to them as it does to others. The commissioners from Maine had so long been accustomed to regard only one side, that they would not have believed Dr. Franklin himself if he had risen from the dead, and designated the boundary line as claimed by England. Indeed, in his map he did rise from the grave.

"I am much obliged to you for the privilege of perusing your observations. I have never read anything on the English side calculated to produce so strong an effect. I had thought that the argument on the identity of 'the sea' in the proclamation of 1763, and 'the Atlantic Ocean' in the treaty of 1783 was unanswerable, and that of course 'the Atlantic Ocean' embraced 'the Bay of Fundy.' But you shake my strong convictions on this important point. But

I will not trouble you by a discussion of this *crambe recoctâ*, of which you must be heartily tired."

With several of the Maine Commissioners referred to in the foregoing letter I had frequent communications, verbal and written, both previously and subsequently to its date. They laboured hard (but I need scarcely say in vain) to exculpate themselves from the reproach of duplicity in the secreting of Franklin's maps on the score of the solemn pledge extracted from them by Webster. That excuse, if admitted at all, would justify the knavish hiding of any document, the concealment of any crime. It is a privilege conceded to Roman Catholic clergymen in the confessional, and has been assumed by counsel in court. But nothing can justify it, in priest or layman, before the open and upright tribunal of public opinion. Judge Preble, consistent to the last, told me in one of his letters that "this map of Dr. Franklin weighed but as a feather in the argument." I replied that "I agreed with him," but that "*it was just that last feather that breaks the camel's back;*" and further, that "had I been aware of its existence, establishing as it did the truth of my previous convictions, I would have exerted myself to the utmost to have prevented the compromise I so strenuously laboured for, and to have opposed any concession short of obtaining as a boundary line that memorable red one traced by Franklin's hand, the only one consistent with the equity, the common sense, and the letter of the treaty of 1783."*

* One last desperate effort was made to throw discredit on the map, and the red line traced by Franklin's hand, which had created such damaging effect upon the character of American statesmen. An "opposition" map was brought forward, said to have belonged to Mr. Jay, one of the Commissioners with Franklin in Paris in 1782. It did no doubt belong to that gentleman, and was preserved in his family, and had certain lines traced on it, among others that of the Proclamation of 1763. But it was entirely worthless as an attempted

The Boundary Question has now become matter of history, and a few obvious reflections suggest themselves on closing this account of its progress and settlement. Diplomacy had done its work in arguing and explaining it. But scarcely had the two nations ratified the final deed when the voice of discontent was raised, and doubts as to the construction of some portions, and dissatisfaction at the tenor of others, were heard in both hemispheres. Thus another important public document attests the almost unavoidable imperfections of those very acts which require the clearest exercise of human wisdom.

The objects of all such inquiries as that embraced in those negotiations should be the establishment of TRUTH. Such object was alone worthy of two great nations, who for more than a quarter of a century had been occupied in a laborious attempt to discover the real meaning of the most important document they ever jointly executed—the treaty which acknowledged the independence of the one country, and was meant to secure the peace of both. If in such an inquiry truth should be paramount to all other considerations, candour is the best, if not the only means by which it can be reached. Let argument or evidence tell as it may, the truth can be in the long run but for the common benefit; and it is in the hope that some effect on the future may be produced by what cannot disturb the

refutation of Franklin's maps; and the hardihood of stating it to have been "before the Commissioners in Paris in 1782," was great indeed, in defiance of the positive statement of Mr. Adams, another of those Commissioners, that "the *only* map before them during the negotiations was one of Mitchel's, of 1755." Yet such was asserted by Mr. Webster at a public meeting in New York on the 15th of April, 1833, when he also ventured to call the really genuine and all important document, on which he had rested all his labours of persuasion with the Maine Legislature, the Commissioners at Washington, and the United States Senate—"a bit of doubtful evidence."

past, that I have resolved to put the facts of this case before the world.

Of all the individual Americans engaged in the negotiations, whether denying the importance of the discovered maps, or convinced of the absolute proof they afforded of the justice of the English claim, not one proposed to communicate them to the British Minister. Nor did any among the fifty senators who secretly debated the question of the ratification of the treaty do so. A deep mystery was observed, unnecessary had the belief really existed that the maps were of no value as evidence, but proving the conviction of those persons in the overwhelming force of their testimony.

But if, as was so clearly implied in the speech of Sir Robert Peel, the suppression of truth, and the false assertion of pretended rights, infamous in private law-suits, are allowable between nations ; if everything be fair in diplomacy, as it is said to be in war, then there is no chance for negotiators of integrity and honour ; the loftiest intellects must be the dupes of the meanest ; diplomacy becomes at best a game of brag, and at worst—as in the present instance—a successful effort of chicane ; and the least treacherous, if not the safest umpire is the sword.

A counteracting authority of the highest nature is, however, extant, an antidote to this pernicious doctrine.

In the month of March 1841, above a year before the negotiations at Washington on the North-eastern boundary began, another disputed case of boundary—that between the States of Massachusetts and Rhode Island—was argued before the Supreme Court of the United States, in the same capital ; and it was then and there solemnly decided, in spite of the powerful pleading of the same Webster in defence of this other spurious frontier line, that no lapse of time is a bar against opening such a question, even in the case of a long-standing *mistake*. How much stronger is this decision, as against a case of FRAUD. And may not the day come when a civilised and powerful population on the north bank of the St. John river, will invoke the authority of that decision, and claim its rights in the opposite territory, by virtue of the positive precedent and in defiance of the negative fraud, recorded in these pages ?

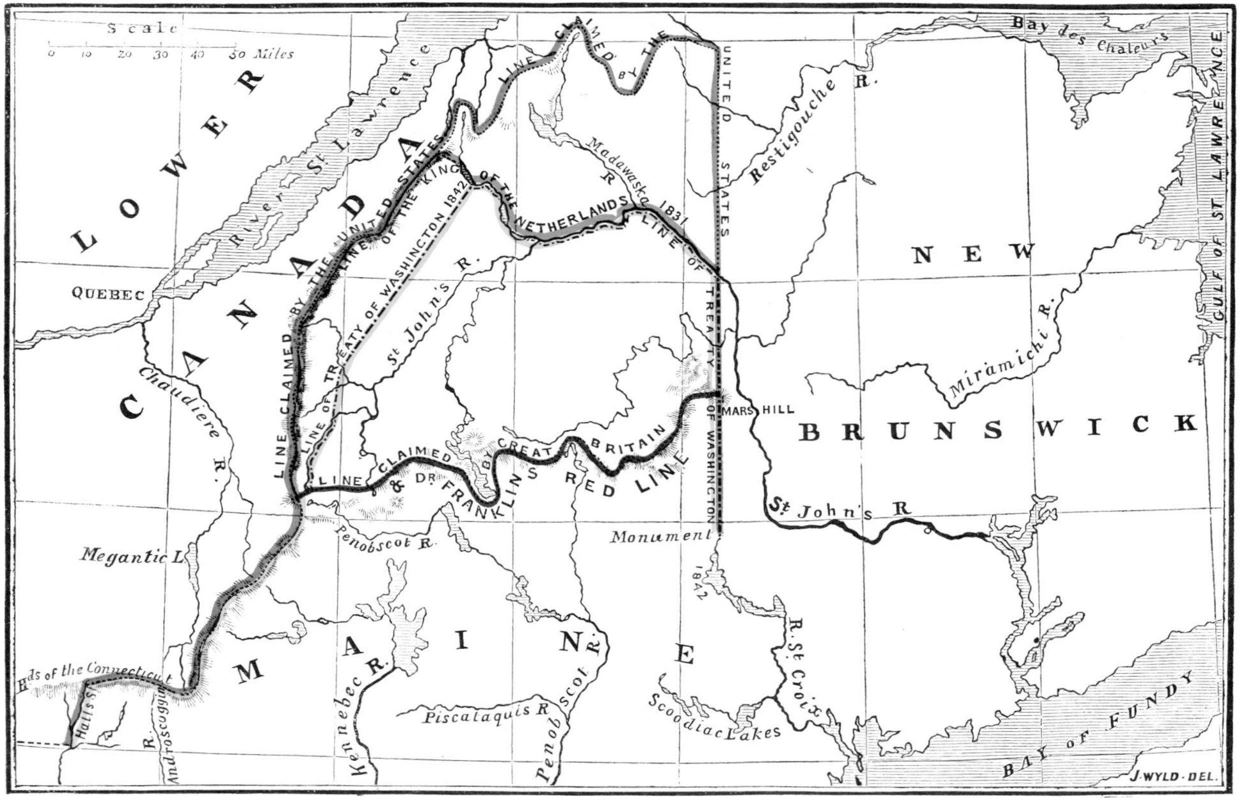

MAP OF BOUNDARY LINES.

Line claimed by Great Britain, coloured Red.
" " United States, " Blue.

Line claimed by King of Netherlands, coloured Green.
" of Treaty, 1842 . . . . . " Yellow.

APPENDIX.

TREATY OF WASHINGTON,

AUGUST 9, 1842.

A TREATY

To settle and define the Boundaries between the Possessions of Her Britannic Majesty in North America, and the Territories of the United States;—for the final suppression of the African Slave Trade;—and for the giving up of Criminals, fugitives from Justice, in certain cases.

WHEREAS certain portions of the line of boundary between the British dominions in North America and the United States of America, described in the second article of the treaty of peace of 1783, have not yet been ascertained and determined, notwithstanding the repeated attempts which have been heretofore made for that purpose; and whereas it is now thought to be for the interest of both parties that, avoiding further discussion of their respective rights, arising in this respect under the said treaty, they should agree on a conventional line in said portions of the said boundary, such as may be convenient to both parties, with such equivalents and compensations as are deemed just and reasonable:—And whereas, by the treaty concluded at Ghent on the 24th day of December, 1814, between His Britannic Majesty and the United States, an article was agreed to and inserted, of the following tenor, viz.: "Art. X. Whereas the traffic in slaves is irreconcileable with the principles of humanity and justice; and whereas both His Majesty and the United States are desirous of continuing their efforts to promote its entire abolition; it is hereby agreed, that both the contracting parties shall use their best endeavours to accomplish so desirable an object:"—And whereas, notwithstanding the laws which have at various times been passed by the two governments, and the efforts made to suppress it, that criminal traffic is still prosecuted and carried on; and whereas Her Majesty the Queen of the United Kingdom of Great Britain and Ireland, and the United States of America, are determined that, so far as may be in their power, it shall be effectually abolished:—And whereas it is found expedient for the better administration of justice, and the prevention of crime within the territories and jurisdiction of the two parties respectively, that persons committing the crimes hereinafter enumerated, and being fugitives from justice, should, under certain circumstances, be reciprocally delivered up:—Her Britannic Majesty, and the United States of America, having resolved to treat on these several subjects, have for that purpose appointed their respective plenipotentiaries to negotiate and conclude a treaty, that is to say: Her Majesty the Queen of the United Kingdom of Great Britain and Ireland has, on her part, appointed the Right Honourable Alexander, Lord Ashburton, a Peer of the said United Kingdom, a Member of her Majesty's most honourable Privy Council, and Her Majesty's Minister Plenipotentiary on a special mission to the United States; and the President of the United States has, on his part, furnished with full powers Daniel Webster, Secretary of State of the United States; who, after a reciprocal communication of their respective full powers, have agreed to and signed the following articles:—

Article I.—It is hereby agreed and declared, that the line of boundary shall be as follows:—Beginning at the monument at the source of the River St. Croix, as designated and agreed to by the Commissioners under the fifth article of the treaty of 1794, between the governments of Great Britain and the United States; thence north, following the exploring line run and marked by the surveyors of the two governments in the years 1817 and 1818, under the fifth article of the treaty of Ghent, to its intersection with the River St. John, and to the middle of the channel thereof; thence up the middle of the main channel of the said River St. John to the mouth of the River St. Francis; thence up the middle of the channel of the said River St. Francis, and of the lakes through which it flows, to the outlet of the Lake Pohenagamook; thence south-westerly, in a straight line, to a point on the north-west branch of the River St. John, which point shall be ten miles distant from the main branch of the St. John, in a straight line and in the nearest direction; but if the said point shall be found to be less than seven miles from the nearest point of the summit or crest of the highlands that divide those rivers which empty themselves into the River St. Lawrence from those which fall into the River St. John, then the said point shall be made to recede down the said north-west branch of the River St. John, to a point seven miles in a straight line from the said summit or crest; thence in a straight line, in a course about south, eight degrees west, to the point where the parallel of latitude of 46° 25′ north, intersects the south-west branch of the St. John's; thence southerly by the said branch, to the source thereof in the highlands at the Metjarmette Portage; thence down along the said highlands which divide the waters which empty themselves into the River St. Lawrence, from those which fall into the Atlantic Ocean to the head of Hall's Stream; thence down the middle of said stream till the line thus run intersects the old line of boundary surveyed and marked by Valentine and Collins previously to the year 1774 as the 45th degree of north latitude, and which has been known and understood to be the line of actual division between the states of New York and Vermont on one side, and the British province of Canada on the other; and from said point of intersection west along the said dividing line, as heretofore known and understood, to the Iroquois, or St. Lawrence River.

Article II.—It is moreover agreed, that from the place where the joint Commissioners terminated their labours under the sixth article of the treaty of Ghent, to wit, at a point in the Neebish Channel, near Muddy Lake, the line shall run into and along the ship channel between St. Joseph's and St. Tammany Islands, to the division of the channel at or near the head of St. Joseph's Island; thence turning eastwardly and northwardly around the lower end of St. George's or Sugar Island, and following the middle of the channel which divides St. George's from St. Joseph's Island: thence up the east Neebish Channel nearest to St. George's Island, through the middle of Lake George; thence west of Jonas' Island into St. Mary's River, to a point in the middle of that river about one mile above St. George's or Sugar Island, so as to appropriate and assign the said island to the United States; thence adopting the line traced on the maps by the Commissioners, through the River St. Mary and Lake Superior, to a point north of Ile Royale in said lake, one hundred yards to the north and east of Ile Chapeau, which last-mentioned island lies near the north-eastern point of Ile Royale, where the line marked by the Commissioners terminates; and from the last-mentioned point south-westerly through the middle of the sound between Ile Royale and the north-western mainland, to the mouth of Pigeon River, and up the said river to and through the north and south Fowl Lakes, to the lakes of the height of land between Lake Superior and the Lake of the Woods; thence along the water communication to Lake Saisaginaga and through that lake; thence to and through Cypress Lake, Lac du Bois Blanc, Lac la Croix, Little Vermillion Lake, and Lake Namecan, and through the several smaller lakes, straits, or streams connecting the lakes here mentioned, to that point in Lac la Pluie, or Rainy Lake, at the Chaudière Falls, from which the Commissioners traced the line to the most north-western point of the Lake of the Woods; thence along the said line to the said most north-western point, being in latitude 49° 23′ 55″ north, and in longitude 95° 14′ 38″ west, from the Observatory at Greenwich; thence, according to existing treaties, due south to its intersection with the 49th parallel of north latitude, and along that parallel to the Rocky Mountains. It being understood that all the water communications, and all the usual portages along the line from Lake Superior to the Lake of the Woods, and also Grand Portage from the shore of Lake Superior to the Pigeon River, as now actually used, shall be free and open to the use of the citizens and subjects of both countries.

Article III.—In order to promote the interests and encourage the industry of all the inhabitants of the countries watered by the River St. John and its tributaries, whether living within the province of New Brunswick, or the state of Maine, it is agreed, that where by the provisions of the present treaty the River St. John is declared to be the line of boundary, the navigation of the said river shall be free and open to both parties, and shall in no way be obstructed by either; that all the produce of the forest, in logs, lumber, timber, boards, staves, or shingles, or of agriculture, not being manufactured, grown on any of those parts of the state of Maine watered by the River St. John or by its tributaries, of which fact reasonable evidence shall, if required, be produced, shall have free access into and through the said river and its said tributaries, having their source within the state of Maine, to and from the seaport at the mouth of the said River St. John's, and to and round the falls of the said river, either by boats, rafts, or other conveyance; that when within the province of New Brunswick, the said produce shall be dealt with as if it were the produce of the said province;

that in like manner the inhabitants of the territory of the upper St. John, determined by this treaty to belong to Her Britannic Majesty, shall have free access to and through the river for their produce, in those parts where the said river runs wholly through the state of Maine: provided always that this agreement shall give no right to either party to interfere with any regulations not inconsistent with the terms of this treaty, which the governments, respectively, of New Brunswick or of Maine may make respecting the navigation of the said river, where both banks thereof shall belong to the same party.

Article IV.—All grants of land heretofore made by either party within the limits of the territory which by this treaty falls within the dominions of the other party, shall be held valid, ratified, and confirmed to the persons in possession under such grants, to the same extent as if such territory had by this treaty fallen within the dominions of the party by whom such grants were made; and all equitable possessory claims, arising from a possession and improvement of any lot or parcel of land by the person actually in possession, or by those under whom such person claims, for more than six years before the date of this treaty, shall in like manner be deemed valid, and be confirmed and quieted by a release to the person entitled thereto, of the title to such lot or parcel of land, so described as best to include the improvements made thereon; and in all other respects the two contracting parties agree to deal upon the most liberal principles of equity with the settlers actually dwelling upon the territory falling to them respectively, which has heretofore been in dispute between them.

Article V.—Whereas, in the course of the controversy respecting the disputed territory on the North-eastern Boundary, some moneys have been received by the authorities of Her Britannic Majesty's Province of New Brunswick, with the intention of preventing depredations on the forests of the said territory, which moneys were to be carried to a fund called the "Disputed Territory Fund," the proceeds whereof it was agreed should be hereafter paid over to the parties interested, in the proportions to be determined by a final settlement of Boundaries; it is hereby agreed that a correct account of all receipts and payments on the said fund shall be delivered to the government of the United States within six months after the ratification of this treaty; and the proportion of the amount due thereon to the States of Maine and Massachusetts, and any bonds or securities appertaining thereto, shall be paid and delivered over to the government of the United States; and the government of the United States agrees to receive for the use of, and pay over to the States of Maine and Massachusetts, their respective portions of said fund; and further, to pay and satisfy said states, respectively, for all claims for expenses incurred by them in protecting the said heretofore disputed territory, and making a survey thereof in 1838: the government of the United States agreeing with the states of Maine and Massuchusetts to pay them the further sum of three hundred thousand dollars, in equal moieties, on account of their assent to the line of boundary described in this treaty, and in consideration of the conditions and equivalents received therefor from the government of Her Britannic Majesty.

Article VI.—It is furthermore understood and agreed, that for the purpose of running and tracing those parts of the line between the source of the St. Croix and the St. Lawrence River, which will require to be run and ascertained, and for marking the residue of said line by proper monuments on the land, two Commissioners shall be appointed, one by Her Britannic Majesty, and one by the President of the United States, by and with the advice and consent of the Senate thereof; and the said Commissioners shall meet at Bangor, in the State of Maine, on the 1st day of May next, or as soon thereafter as may be, and shall proceed to mark the line above described from the source of the St. Croix to the River St. John, and shall trace on proper maps the dividing line along said river, and along the River St. Francis to the outlet of the Lake Pohenagamook; and from the outlet of the said lake they shall ascertain, fix, and mark, by proper and durable monuments on the land, the line described in the first article of this treaty; and the said Commissioners shall make to each of their respective governments a joint report or declaration, under their hands and seals, designating such line of boundary, and shall accompany such report or declaration with maps, certified by them to be true maps of the new boundary.

Article VII.—It is further agreed, that the channels in the River St. Lawrence on both sides of the Long Sault Islands and Barnhart Island, the channels in the River Detroit, on both sides of the Island Bois Blanc, and between that island and both the Canadian and American shores, and all the several channels and passages between the various islands lying near the junction of the River St. Clair with the lake of that name, shall be equally free and open to the ships, vessels, and boats of both parties.

Article VIII.—The parties mutually stipulate, that each shall prepare, equip, and maintain in service on the coast of Africa, a sufficient and adequate squadron, or naval force of vessels, of suitable numbers and descriptions, to carry in all not less than eighty guns, to enforce, separately and respectively, the laws, rights, and obligations of each of the two countries for the suppression of the Slave Trade; the said squadrons to be independent of each other, but the two governments stipulating nevertheless to give such orders to the officers commanding their respective forces, as shall enable them most effectually to act in concert and co-operation, upon mutual consultation, as exigences may arise, for the attainment of the true object of this Article; copies of all such orders to be communicated by each government to the other respectively.

Article IX.—Whereas, notwithstanding all efforts which may be made on the coast of Africa for suppressing the Slave Trade, the facilities for carrying on that traffic, and avoiding the vigilance of cruizers, by the fraudulent use of flags and other means, are so great, and the temptations for pursuing it, while a market can be found for slaves, so strong, as that the desired result may be long delayed, unless all markets be shut against the purchase of African negroes;—the parties to this treaty agree, that they will unite in all becoming representations and remonstrances with any and all powers within whose dominions such markets are allowed to exist; and that they will urge upon all such powers the propriety and duty of closing such markets effectually, at once and for ever.

Article X.—It is agreed that Her Britannic Majesty and the United States shall, upon mutual requisitions by them or their ministers, officers, or authorities, respectively made, deliver up to justice all persons who, being charged with the crime of murder, or assault with intent to commit murder, or piracy, or arson, or robbery, or forgery, or the utterance of forged papers, committed within the jurisdiction of either, shall seek an asylum, or shall be found within the territories of the other:—provided that this shall only be done upon such evidence of criminality as, according to the laws of the place where the fugitive or person so charged shall be found, would justify his apprehension and commitment for trial, if the crime or offence had there been committed; and the respective judges and other magistrates of the two governments shall have power, jurisdiction, and authority, upon complaint made under oath, to issue a warrant for the apprehension of the fugitive or person so charged, that he may be brought before such judges or other magistrates respectively, to the end that the evidence of criminality may be heard and considered; and if, on such hearing, the evidence be deemed sufficient to sustain the charge, it shall be the duty of the examining judge or magistrate to certify the same to the proper executive authority, that a warrant may issue for the surrender of such fugitive. The expense of such apprehension and delivery shall be borne and defrayed by the party who makes the requisition and receives the fugitive.

Article XI.—The eighth article of this treaty shall be in force for five years from the date of the exchange of the ratifications, and afterwards, until one or other party shall signify a wish to terminate it. The tenth article shall continue in force until one or the other of the parties shall signify its wish to terminate it, and no longer.

Article XII.—The present treaty shall be duly ratified, and the mutual exchange of ratifications shall take place in London within six months from the date hereof, or earlier if possible.

In faith whereof we, the respective Plenipotentiaries, have signed this treaty, and have hereunto affixed our seals.

Done in duplicate at Washington, the ninth day of August, Anno Domini One thousand eight hundred and forty-two.

Ashburton, (L.S.) Danl. Webster. (L.S.)

THE BOUNDARY QUESTION REVISED;

AND

DR. FRANKLIN'S RED LINE SHOWN TO BE THE RIGHT ONE.

BY A BRITISH SUBJECT.

The particular branch of the treaty of Washington, to which the following pages have reference, is the North-Eastern Boundary between the United States and the British North American possessions.

Almost everyone has heard of the discovery of certain maps relating to that subject, only made known to the public since the ratification of the treaty by the President and Senate of the United States and the Queen of Great Britain. The existence of these maps has been so made known by the publication in the Globe newspaper, at Washington, in December, 1842, of the speeches of Mr. Rives, chairman of the Committee of Foreign Affairs, on the 17th of August preceding, and of other senators, during the debate on the question of the ratification of the treaty.

The circumstances thus brought to light have led to numerous comments in the newspapers of England, the United States, and Canada. It is not the object of this publication to discuss the merits of the new question now at issue. No opinion is offered as to whether the maps alluded to were good evidence in favour of the British claim; or whether the government of the United States was justified in withholding all knowledge of those in their exclusive possession from Lord Ashburton during the negotiations; or whether Mr. Webster was justified in communicating those maps to the Senate and the Maine and Massachusetts Commissioners under a solemn injunction of secresy, and in arguing against the claim of England, and resisting Lord Ashburton's first proposal for a line of boundary far short of the line he considered England to be entitled to, while the department over which Mr. Webster presided possessed evidence in favour of the English claim, which Mr. Rives declared to the Senate he considered "of a most imposing character." The object of the author in this brief inquiry is to treat the subject as one of history. And he has been led to this publication from the recent promulgation of arguments, which not only impugn the intellect and the information of Benjamin Franklin, but which also imply, in contempt of all former reasoning on the part of Great Britain, and in despite of the several maps before alluded to, the belief that the claim of England had no honest or equitable foundation.

Now, the author of the following observations believes firmly that the claim of Great Britain to the line of boundary so long contended for was in accordance with the spirit, the letter, and the common sense of the treaty of 1783; and also with "all equity, good conscience, and honour;"* and that consequently the red line traced on the map discovered by Mr. Sparks, and confirmed by the several other maps which have simultaneously come to light, is the right one. He, therefore, offers these pages to the public to show what he believes to have been the rightful pretensions of England on the question, and

* The words of John Adams's letter to Lieutenant Governor Cushing, of Massachusetts, dated October 25, 1784, in reference to the river meant as the St. Croix, of the treaty of 1783.

the manner in which the arguments of the American Secretary of State and of the Maine Commissioners, during the negotiation with Lord Ashburton, could have been replied to.

Every word of the text of the following observations was written some months before Mr. Sparks's discovery was known to the author, and during the negotiations at Washington. A few notes subsequently added will speak for themselves. The manuscript was never shown to any citizen of the United States until after the confirmation of the treaty by both governments. For although the writer was convinced of the justice of the British claim he felt that it would have been useless to discuss the question on mere theoretic grounds of probability, no *evidence* then existing of force sufficient to satisfy the immense majority of the American people that they were mistaken in their unanimous belief in the validity of their own pretensions. Therefore it was, that he was one of those who was most anxious for the compromise of a dispute, which there seemed so little chance of otherwise terminating without a national quarrel and a war.

The author rejoiced in the conclusion of the treaty of Washington. He thought the terms of settlement good, under the circumstances of the case; and he hoped that the boundary was thenceforward for ever settled. The materials of this publication are selected from a great mass of notes on the subject, accumulated during three years tolerably constant attention to it. They would never have been printed but for the revival of the question by the recent discoveries. They are offered to the public not for the provocation of argument, but to show an old truth in somewhat of a new aspect, and by a series of easy probabilities, leading to the conviction that Franklin's red line *was* the right one. They do not pretend to embrace the many incidental questions which have arisen from the main ones. But it is believed that they will be found to condense and simplify the principal arguments; and reference will be frequently made to other sources, for the information of those who might like to consult them.

From a minute examination into the merits of the boundary question, I am convinced that it admits of two diametrically opposite opinions, on conscientious grounds. Reason and illustration have been brought to bear on either side with a bewildering plausibility. But I hold that no power of sophistry could so far pervert a series of positive truths, as to throw them into a chaos of doubt in the minds of candid and disinterested inquirers, if there was not an inherent obscurity in the questions at issue. This goes far to absolve the persons who have been officially concerned in this matter for the last quarter of a century, from much of the odium which deservedly attaches to quibbling statesmen or pettifogging negotiators.

A question like this should be examined broadly, and fairly discussed. It is too important to admit of any narrow issue. The boundary between two nations does not come within the limits of retail dealing. Yet many of the publications to which this question has given rise, abound in all the littleness of special pleading. This has necessarily involved many of the points in contradictions and inconsistency. Few writers on either side have admitted the reasonings of their opponents: and some, on both sides, have in fact more than once felt themselves forced to prove too much. The Americans have all laboured to establish that the north-eastern boundary line of the United States, as fixed by the treaty of 1783, is identical with that which was traced by the Royal Proclamation of 1763, and confirmed by the Quebec Act in 1774, establishing the boundaries between the then British provinces of Quebec and Nova Scotia; and that the line they now insist on is identical with it.

British writers have differed among each other on this point; some endeavouring to show that the line of the Proclamation of 1763 is not only different from that of the treaty of 1783, but that the line now claimed by the United States is different from both of them. Others pretend that the line of 1763, and that of 1783, are exactly the same, and that the line now claimed by England is identical with it.

Various contradictions have arisen from such conflicting opinions; but they do not affect the truths of the question.

I consider it necessary, in attempting to argue the various points of the treaty of 1783, to place one's self as much as possible in the position of the framers of that treaty, reasoning as they may be supposed to have reasoned, on such documents as were known to them, and with such views as to the physical features of the country as they must be believed to have entertained. Later researches and after discoveries ought not, I think, to affect the main question, viz: What were the intentions of the framers of the treaty? * And data

* See paragraph 2, p. 14, of the Statement on the part of the United States submitted to the King of the Netherlands, dated Washington, June 1st, 1829. And if higher authority be required, the following extract from Vattel can furnish

which were unknown to them, though they may corroborate, ought not to be suffered to shake our convictions, reasonably formed, as to what the framers of the treaty knew, and what they meant to express.*

We can only reach their intentions, to a certain extent by conjecture. But this must not be objected to as a mere flight of fancy. Imagination, founded on probabilities, is reasoning. It is, moreover, reasoning of the highest order. For by its ingenuity, in tracing analogies and penetrating motives, it becomes far superior to that process which is confined to the classification of facts, or the arrangement of things evident, and relative to which there can be no doubt.

I will now briefly state the main points of the controversy:

The Royal Proclamation, before alluded to, was issued on the 7th of October, 1763, the whole of Canada, and all the possessions claimed by France in that portion of North America having been ceded to Great Britain by the treaty of peace between the two countries of the month of February preceding.

The object of this proclamation was the establishment of the colony, province, or government of Quebec, including the country subsequently called Lower Canada; and the boundaries of that government were, by said proclamation, fixed as follows:—

"Bounded on the Labrador coast by the river St. John; † and from thence by a line drawn from the head of that river, through the Lake

it:—"Since the sole object of a lawful interpretation of a deed ought to be the discovery of the thoughts of the authors of that deed, whenever we meet with any obscurity in it, we are to consider what probably were the ideas of those who drew up the deed, and to interpret it accordingly."

* To prove the great difficulty of understanding the intentions of the framers of treaties, from the dry wording of the treaties themselves, we have only to refer to the difference now existing between the governments of the United States and Great Britain, as to Art. VIII. of the Treaty of Washington, executed a few months back—(9th August, 1842). Arguments are put forth by the President, to prove that England intended to abandon her views of the right of visitation, because no mention is made of it in the above-named article. But when the British negotiators assumed that the intention of England in the treaty of 1783 was to maintain the connection between their provinces, to secure the whole course of the river St. John in these provinces, &c., they were invariably met by the argument, that we must look to the letter of the treaty, in which those objects have no mention. See statement on the part of the United States, p. 27.

† Not the river of the same name which falls into the Bay of Fundy, but a stream which falls into the mouth of the river St. Lawrence.

St. John to the south end of the Lake Nipissing, from whence the said line, crossing the river St. Lawrence and Lake Champlain, in forty-five degrees of north latitude, passes along the highlands which divides the rivers that empty themselves into the said river St. Lawrence from those which fall into the sea, and also along the north coast of the Bay des Chaleurs and the coast of the Gulf of St. Lawrence, to Cape Rosiers; and from thence, crossing the mouth of the river St. Lawrence, by the west end of the Island of Anticosti, terminates at the aforesaid river St. John."

The boundaries of the province of Quebec were enlarged in another quarter by the Act of Parliament of 14 George III. chap. 83 (1774), commonly called the Quebec Act. But those adjacent to Nova Scotia and Massachusetts, were, by that Act, defined in words nearly similar to those used in the proclamation of 1763.

By Article I. of the Treaty of 1783, His Britannic Majesty acknowledged the thirteen United States therein mentioned, to be free, sovereign, and independent States; and relinquished all claims to the government, propriety, and territorial rights of the same, and every part thereof.

Massachusetts Bay was one of those States. A very important question, therefore, in the true understanding of the Boundary question, is, what were, at the time of the negotiations which ended in the treaty of 1783, the acknowledged and admitted territorial rights of the province of Massachusetts Bay?

Article II. of the Treaty of 1783 is as follows:—

"And that all disputes which might arise in future on the subject of the boundaries of the United States may be prevented, it is hereby agreed and declared that the following are and shall be their boundaries, viz: from the north-west angle of Nova Scotia, viz: that angle which is formed by a line drawn due north from the source of the St. Croix river, to the highlands; along the said highlands which divide those rivers that empty themselves into the river St. Lawrence from those which fall into the Atlantic ocean, to the north-westernmost head of Connecticut river; * * * * *

"East, by a line to be drawn along the middle of the river St. Croix from its mouth in the Bay of Fundy to its source; and from its source directly north to the aforesaid highlands, which divide the rivers that fall into the Atlantic ocean from those which fall into the river St. Lawrence: comprehending all islands within twenty leagues of any part of the shores of the United States, and lying between lines to be drawn due east from the points where the aforesaid boundaries between Nova Scotia on the one part, and East Florida on the other, shall respectively touch the Bay of Fundy and the Atlantic ocean; except such islands as now are, or heretofore have been, within the limits of the said province of Nova Scotia."

The above extracts from Article II. of the treaty of 1783 contain the germ of the long dispute between England and the United States. No less than five points therein mentioned led to directly opposite opinions between the two governments, viz :

1st. The North-West angle of Nova Scotia.

2nd. The true source of the St. Croix river.

3rd. The Highlands.

4th. The north-westernmost head of Connecticut river.

5th. The distinction between the Atlantic Ocean and the Bay of Fundy.

The United States have contended that the N.-W. angle of Nova Scotia of the treaty of 1783 is to be found at a spot 145 miles north of the source of the river St. Croix; that is to the north of the river St. John, which falls into the Bay of Fundy, and of the river Restigouche, which falls into the Bay of Chaleurs.

One American writer * on the subject, however, contends that the Restigouche ought not to be considered as included among those rivers which empty into the Atlantic Ocean, and that consequently the due north line from the source of the St. Croix, should instead of intersecting the Restigouche, stop at a point terminating on the Highlands south of it, and full fifty miles south of the point to which it has been run by the government of the State of Maine.

These opposing opinions would pretty clearly indicate that the north-west angle of Nova Scotia was not a positive and well authenticated geographical position even after the date of the treaty of 1783. It is admitted on all hands that previous to the date of that document the north-west angle of Nova Scotia might have been sought for on the banks of the river St. Lawrence, in accordance with the ancient boundaries of the colony of Massachusetts Bay, according to its charter dated 1691, and at the source of the river St. John according to the propositions made by the Congress of the

* This writer is Mr. Nathan Hale, one of those who assailed Franklin's "blunder," and the article in which he thus gives his opinion as to the true situation of the north-west angle of Nova Scotia is to be found in the American Almanac for 1840.

United States in view to a negotiation for a treaty of peace with Great Britain in 1779.

England has, however, all along maintained that the point designated in the treaty of 1783 as the north-west angle of Nova Scotia (but which is, correctly speaking, only the north-east angle of the United States), is to be found where the due north line from the river St. Croix strikes the ridge of Highlands which are to be found upwards of one hundred miles south of those claimed as the true boundary by the United States.

Amidst this diversity of assertion it was all along clear that the main object was to ascertain what was the line of Highlands meant by the framers of the treaty of 1783, and at what particular portion of them a line drawn due north from the river St. Croix would strike.

In order to accomplish this object it was agreed by the treaty of amity, commerce, and navigation of 1794, commonly called Jay's treaty, that Commissioners should be appointed by each nation to ascertain what was the river designated in the 2d article of the treaty of 1783. Two Commissioners were accordingly named; and on their disagreeing an umpire was chosen, who recommended a compromise, and in consequence the most northern source of the river was fixed on as the starting point whence to trace the due north line to the Highlands.

From this most erroneous, though well meant decision, all the subsequent embarrassments arose.

Had the due north line been traced from the westernmost of the Scoodiac lakes, in accordance with the original grant of Nova Scotia to Sir William Alexander of 1621, and which had ever been considered and followed as the real title deed for ascertaining the boundaries of the province, the line must have struck "the Highlands," as no doubt the framers of the treaty of 1783 meant it to do, at a point about twenty miles distant, which would have left no room for further contest. But by starting from the northern source of the St. Croix, the line, running considerably to the eastward, passed clear of the Highlands, and only came close to a detached elevation called "Mars Hill," which was but an isolated point geologically connected with the main chain of Highlands, but not forming a visible portion of it.

At this point the British Commissioners for running the due north line claimed that it should stop, and that the range of Highlands westward to the head of Connecticut river formed the second boundary line of the treaty.

The American commissioners insisted that no actual ridge of Highlands having been struck by the due north line it should still run on, intersecting the river St. John, and never stopping till it reached the Highlands beyond the source of the river Restigouche, and close to the river St. Lawrence, as before mentioned.

Finding it impossible to conciliate these two conflicting claims, the two governments agreed, by the fifth article of the treaty of Ghent, December 24, 1814, to provide for a final adjustment of the boundaries by the nomination of two Commissioners to ascertain and determine the disputed points; and that in the event of the Commissioners differing, a reference to a friendly sovereign was to take place.

The Commissioners appointed in conformity with the said article could not agree; and on the 29th of September, 1827, the two powers signed a convention making provision for a reference, and the King of the Netherlands was chosen, and he accepted the office of arbiter.

The statements and counter-statements on either side, laid before the royal arbiter, were drawn up with consummate skill and ingenuity. These documents with their appendices and the award of the arbiter, printed but not published, form a folio volume of about 600 pages. The diplomatic correspondence, reports of Commissioners, and various detached publications official or professional, pamphlets, articles in reviews and newspapers, would almost form a library. To attempt an abridgment of the whole, preserving anything like the spirit of the several arguments, would be altogether futile.

The King of the Netherlands delivered his award on the 10th of January, 1831, at the Hague in Holland, to Sir Charles Bagot the British ambassador, and Mr. Preble the American minister. The British minister accepted the award. The American minister protested against it (January 12, 1831), on the ground that the arbiter had exceeded his powers in recommending a compromise, his duty being confined to the fact of choosing one or the other of the adverse claims.*

Several years passed over in vain attempts at a settlement by

* The author of these observations happening to be at the Hague at that time, and enjoying the confidence of both the British ambassador and the American minister, was thus early initiated into the respective merits of the Boundary Question.

negotiation. New Commissioners of survey and exploration were appointed; new reports made; new views brought forward; but nothing definitive was done till the appointment of Lord Ashburton by the Queen of Great Britain, on a special mission to the United States, to settle this and other points of difference between the countries. His lordship arrived at Washington in April, 1842. Four Commissioners from the state of Maine and three from Massachusetts repaired to the scene of negotiation on the 11th of June following; and the negotiations were almost immediately afterwards begun between Lord Ashburton and Mr. Webster, United States Secretary of State, and through him with the seven Commissioners.

In the correspondence which ensued some of the old grounds of argument, in connection with the treaty of 1783, were entered on; and four particular subjects were discussed at some length, viz.:

1st. Is the Restigouche an Atlantic river?

2nd. What was meant by the American Congress in 1779, when they instructed their Commissioners to propose the river St. John, from its source to its mouth, as the eastern boundary between the United States and Nova Scotia?

3rd. Were the words "The Sea," as used in the Proclamation of 1763, and the words "The Atlantic Ocean," as used in the second article of the treaty of 1783, identical with each other?

4th. Was it intended by the treaty of 1783, that the river St. John should be included, in its entire course, within the British possessions?

The consideration of these four points embraces the entire merits of the question so long in dispute, viz., What were the intentions of the framers of the treaty of 1783? and I now proceed to notice them *seriatim*.

I pass over the manifest geographical errors in the treaty, particularly in its second article, which defined the boundaries. But I am satisfied that its framers believed (in common with their contemporaries and the generation preceding them) that the country between the river St. Lawrence and the ocean, which they were then about to portion out, was essentially a hilly, or highland, country, and that there was running through it, from the head of Connecticut river, for an extent of seventy or eighty miles up to the forty-sixth degree of north latitude, a line of Highlands, which at that point branched off into two distinct ranges, one running to the northward, parallel to the course of the river St. Lawrence, and the other considerably south of it, running to the north-east, and tending towards the bay of Chaleur.*

The first of these ranges, taken from the heads of the Connecticut river to its termination near the bay of Chaleurs, may be fairly considered, in general terms, to separate the rivers emptying into the St. Lawrence from those which fall into the sea, including the Restigouche, and all rivers south of it.

The second, or southern line of Highlands, from the heads of Connecticut river to the heads of the St. Croix, absolutely separates the rivers flowing into the St. Lawrence from those flowing into the Atlantic Ocean, viz., Connecticut river, the Androscoggins, Kennebec, and Penobscot.

The application to any ridge of highlands of the description "dividing, or separating rivers," did not require that such ridge should so divide rivers in *every* part of its course. It is sufficient if rivers flow from one side of the ridge all through its course, and from both sides of the ridge in parts of its course.

Nor is it necessary that a well understood ridge of Highlands should be a continuous chain of mountains from one end of its course to the other. Occasional breaks in the general line of elevation may and in fact do always exist without depriving the line of its character of a Highland ridge.

Both the ridges of the disputed territory viewed in this aspect, amply bear out the description of "highlands dividing rivers."

I believe that the first or northern branch of highlands formed the "Highlands" designated by the Proclamation of 1763; and that the second or southern branch formed the "Highlands" meant by the treaty of 1783.†

* See Governor Pownall's "Topographical Description of the Middle British American colonies," published in 1776, in which he expressly specifies two ridges. "All the rivers which have their sources amidst the *northern ridge* of this great range, fall into Canada or St. Lawrence river, as the St. Francis; Chaudière, and many others, all which have their sources amidst the *southern ridges*, fall into the Bay of Fundy, or into the main ocean."

This extract contains absolute evidence as to the two ridges of highlands, and as to the distinction between the Bay of Fundy *and* the Atlantic Ocean.

† To enter fully into the reasoning which has confirmed me in these opinions would lead me far beyond the limits I have prescribed to myself. It is sufficient to say, that the arguments of American writers as to the first point, and of English writers as to the second, along with my own close examination of the various questions at issue, have led me to these conclusions.

I think that the rivers alluded to in the Proclamation of 1763, and in the treaty of 1783, as emptying into the St. Lawrence, were the St. Francis and the Chaudière: but that the small streams to the northward of the latter were not considered as coming under the denomination of "Rivers."

I think the words "the Sea" were used in the Proclamation to show that the "Highlands" therein mentioned had reference generally to all the rivers of Nova Scotia and New England; but that the words "the Sea" were not meant to imply that the northern portion of those highlands, that is to say, from the forty-sixth degree of latitude upwards, divided from those rivers and their sources other "Rivers" emptying into the St. Lawrence, the small streams in that portion of the line of highlands being too insignificant to be designated as *rivers*, in the broad geographical sense of the term.

In briefly stating my own opinions, I do not attempt to explain or refute the various contradictions and conflicting opinions of others who have examined the subject, written on it with so much talent, and given evidence of such minute research.

My conviction is that the line designated by the Proclamation of 1763, is nearly identical with that claimed by the United States, and that the line meant by the treaty of 1783 is nearly identical with that claimed by Great Britain.

That a "New Boundary" was meant by the treaty of 1783, is, I think, clearly demonstrable, for the following reasons:—

1st. Because the minister, Mr. Townsend, positively asserted in the debates in the British Parliament (February 17th, 1783), that "a new line of boundary was intended by the treaty." And Lord North also stated that a new boundary was granted.

2d. Because the variations in the wording of the treaty of 1783, from the language of the Proclamation of 1763, are obviously designed to show that a new boundary was intended.

3d. Because, had not a new boundary line been intended, the description in the treaty would assuredly have followed, word for word, that of the Proclamation of 1763 and of the commissions to the various governors of Nova Scotia.

4th. Because the *domestic* line of boundary, so to call it, between the British Provinces designated by the Proclamation of 1763, would have been utterly and manifestly unfit for a boundary line between two independent nations, cutting off the communications between two of the provinces (Quebec and Nova Scotia) which remained faithful to the mother country, and giving territory between those two to a third province (Massachusetts Bay), which had successfully revolted and shaken off its allegiance.

5th. Because all the negotiations and projects for peace, from 1779 to 1782,* indisputably prove that the Congress of the United States never imagined the possibility of England conceding, as a boundary between her provinces and those which had successfully revolted, the entire line of the Proclamation of 1763: but that, on the contrary, ample documentary evidence notoriously exists, to show that the Congress itself was the proposer of other lines of boundary, and that it never attempted to propose an adherence to the provincial line designated in the Proclamation of 1763, the Quebec Act in 1774, and in the commissions to the Governors of Nova Scotia.

6th. That the second article of the treaty of 1783, which defines the boundaries, although it contains several geographical errors, is yet most specific in describing the highlands which were to form one portion of the "new boundary," and in laying down what the framers of the treaty meant, as the point which was then to form the north-east angle of the United States, erroneously called in that article, the north-west angle of Nova Scotia: and

7th. That the words of that second article of the treaty of 1783 can leave little, if any, doubt on the mind of a candid and careful inquirer that the southern ridge of highlands was the line meant as that with which the intersection of the due north line from the source of the St. Croix was to form the angle from which the boundary was to be traced westward to the head of Connecticut river.

I will now revert to the four branches of the subject particularly discussed in the written communications between Lord Ashburton and the Maine Commissioners, through the medium of Mr. Webster.

With regard to the first of these questions, taken on its own merits, and to refute the opinion of the Commissioners that the Restigouche is an Atlantic river, it may be enough to refer to the article in the American Almanac, for 1840, communicated by Mr. Nathan Hale, and already alluded to.

Secondly, as to the pretension that the United States' Congress, in the instructions to their Commissioners, in 1779, to propose the river St. John as the boundary, meant to indicate the river Madawaska, as

* See the instructions from Congress to the Commissioners, dated 14th August, 1729.—*Secret Journals,* vol. ii., p. 225, and 15th June, 1781. *Ibid.*, p. 445.

the northern branch of the St. John,* I must observe that this is not, as it appeared to Lord Ashburton, "a new discovery," of the Maine Commissioners.† The notion was put forward in an article in the North American Review, for April, 1841; but this pretension was originally started at page twenty-eight of the "Definitive Statement," on the part of the United States, laid before the King of the Netherlands.

Now, no map, I believe, calls the river Madawaska by any but its present name, as a tributary, not a branch, of the St. John. On Mitchell's map, the course of the St. John from the westward is clearly, though not accurately, traced and named. This assumed northern branch has no name at all affixed to it on Mitchell's map; but in the United States' Official Map (by Dashiel) of the State of Maine, and the adjacent British provinces, this river is called the Matawaska; and referring to the "Definitive Statement" of the American Commissioners (Messrs. Gallatin and Wm. P. Preble) we find at pp. 83, 84, that "the various upper branches of the river St. John have no other distinctive names but those of West, North-west, South-west branch, &c., while one of them is exclusively distinguished by the name of South or Maine Branch." Now as these designations have no possible reference to the Madawaska, Mr. Preble appears thus to have in some measure refuted by anticipation the present pretension that the Madawaska was considered a *branch* of the St. John. But a still stronger evidence exists on this subject. On the 19th of January, 1765, a petition was addressed to the Governor of the province of Quebec, on the part of the tribe of Maracitte Indians, representing that they were encroached upon by the Canadian inhabitants hunting beaver on their lands—"which tract begins at the Great Falls of St. John's, and runs as far as Femisquata, including the Wolf river (or *Rivière du Loup*) and the *river Madawaska*, which rivers *discharge themselves* into the river St. John." See the *Quebec Gazette*, Jan. 24, 1765.

But in another point of view this pretension of the Maine Commissioners is untenable. The proposition of Congress to make the St. John the boundary was for the purpose of giving a boundary between the British provinces and the United States, *more satisfactory* to England than the old *domestic* boundary of the Proclamation

* See the letter from the Maine Commissioners to Mr. Webster, June 29

18

† See Lord Ashburton's letter to Mr. Webster, July 11, 1842.

of 1763, and one more fitting to fulfil the great object of securing an unobstructed communication between Nova Scotia and Canada. Now a line from the source to the mouth of the St. John (supposing that source to have been at the Lake Medousa of Mitchell's map), would obviously have been a worse boundary for the British possessions than the line due north from the St. Croix to the highlands near the St. Lawrence. It would have given nothing towards the north of the least consequence to England, while towards the south it would have given all the territory between the St. John and the St. Croix to the United States. But the river St. John in its entire extent (admitting its source to be as laid down in Mitchell's map, far to the westward of the Madawaska and Lake Medousa) would certainly have been a better boundary for England than the domestic boundary of the proclamation of 1763, because it would have given a considerable extent of country between the highlands therein meant and the river St. John, in the entire of its upper course.

There can be therefore no doubt as to what Congress meant. They meant to propose the St. John of *Mitchell's map*, from its source pretty near the northern or upper range of highlands;* and that being rejected by England they next sought out the next best boundary for the satisfaction of England.

What, then, did they next fix on? and what principle regulated their new proposal? They undoubtedly fixed on the southern range of highlands, dividing the rivers which flow into the St. Lawrence from those which empty themselves into the Atlantic; and that they specially meant, in Article II., of the treaty of 1783, to designate that *southern* range is, I think, nearly demonstrable.

In pursuing this inquiry it must be observed that the two important phrases "the Atlantic Ocean" and "the North-west angle of Nova Scotia" (as points of description in the projected new boundary), were first used by the American Congress, in their instructions and proposals, and that this was their origin. Also that a great object in

* The following extract from the correspondence of John Jay, seems to leave no doubt on this point:—

"On the 24th of October, 1782, I dined at Passy with Dr. Franklin, where I found Mr. Rayneval [Count de Vergenne's principal secretary]. He asked us what boundaries we claimed? We told him the river St. John to the east, and ancient Canada, as described in the Proclamation, to the north. He contested our right to such an extent to the north." Jay's Life and Correspondence, vol. ii., p. 492. This proves that the American Commissioners did not claim the whole line of the Proclamation of 1763.

framing the Proclamation of 1763, and the treaty of 1783, had been to adopt natural boundaries—rivers and mountains. Therefore, the range of highlands near the St. Lawrence, never having been proposed by Congress, and the St. John river having been rejected by Great Britain, the course of the river St. Croix and *the nearest chain of highlands to it* dividing rivers were selected, as preferable to any imaginary line to be traced through the wilderness from the sources of that river to the westward.

Again, it must be borne in mind that at no time between 1697, the date of the treaty of Ryswick and 1783, had England admitted the claims of Massachusetts Bay to the territory eastward of the Kennebec, but had always insisted on the right of the crown to that extent, as a portion of the ancient property of Sagadahock. And this may be a fitting place to advert to the claims put forward by the colony of Massachusetts Bay for the extension of its territorial rights, not only to the eastward but to the north as far as the river St. Lawrence. The charter to the New Plymouth Company was dated 1606. The territorial rights under this charter having been forfeited, the new charter dated 1691 to the province of Massachusetts Bay restored them, and extended to the province of Nova Scotia or Acadia, to the province of Sagadahock, formerly granted by Charles II. in 1664 to his brother the Duke of York, and to the province of Maine, originally granted to Sir Ferdinande Gorges in 1639, and purchased from him by the colony of Massachusetts in 1677. But these being all merely war grants many of them subject to equal pretension of right on the part of France, the claim of Massachusetts to Nova Scotia was nullified by the treaty of Ryswick, 1697, by which that province was restored to France, and the grant of the Sagadahock territory was at the same time annulled. But even if it were not so, the charter of 1691 (under which Massachusetts claimed) gave no territorial rights to the colony farther northward than the heads of the river Sagadahock or Kennebec. To understand the arguments which confirm this opinion the various documents just mentioned should be consulted, as well as the opinions of the law officers of the crown on several occasions for above a century back, and of individuals more or less connected with the question.

The principles which actuated the framers of the treaty of 1783, in as far as the north-eastern boundary was concerned, were:—

1st. To satisfy the territorial rights of the thirteen United States, the independence of which was about to be acknowledged by Great Britain.

2nd. To secure a free and uninterrupted communication between the provinces of Canada and Nova Scotia, which had remained loyal.

3rd. To give to each country the free course of the great rivers emptying into the sea in their respective territories in conformity with the usage of all nations; as examples of which it may be enough to cite the various negotiations between France and England as to their American possessions, and between France and Spain, and the stipulation of the treaty which fixed on the Pyrenean chain as the boundary between them.*

Now, what were the admitted territorial rights of the province of Massachusetts Bay at the time of negotiating the treaty of 1783 ?

The claim of the United States to the boundary specified by the Proclamation of 1763 as the identical boundary traced by the treaty of 1783, rests on the assumption that that Proclamation and the commissions of the governors of Nova Scotia defined explicitly the north-eastern boundaries of Massachusetts Bay, in defining the southern boundary of the province of Quebec and the western boundary of Nova Scotia. And they further maintain that the treaty of 1783 fully confirmed their title to those boundaries.

But there are two documents frequently and triumphantly referred to by the United States and the State of Maine, to aid in proving that the northern range of highlands was that intended by the Proclamation of 1763, which while, in my opinion, fulfilling that object, defeat altogether the claim in favour of the assumed right of Massachusetts Bay, founded on that Proclamation.

The first of these documents, the royal commission to Governor Wilmot of Nova Scotia, dated 21st November, 1763, (the Proclamation being dated the 7th of the preceding month) specifically states that although the westward boundary of the province is formed "by the St. Croix and a line drawn due north from its source to the southern boundary of the colony of Quebec," yet that the said

* "Dans de pareil cas, la regle la plus usité et la plus convenable, est d'etendre les limites dans l'interieur des terres, jusqu'a la source des rivieres qui se dechargent a la cote, c'est-a-dire; que chaque nation a de son cote les eaux pendantes," &c.

Memorial of the Marquis de la Galissoniere and M. de Silhouette (Commissioners of the King of France) upon the limits of Acadie, dated 4th October, 1751.

province of Nova Scotia "doth of right extend as far as the river Pentagoet or Penobscot."

This clearly establishes that whatever might be the pretensions of Massachusetts Bay, they were not confirmed, or even *admitted* by the Proclamation of October 1763, or the commission of Montague Wilmot of November 1763, to extend further eastward than the river Penobscot, or further northward than the sources of that river; the Crown reserving to itself, while restricting the limits of the province of Nova Scotia, the right of territorial jurisdiction between the St. Croix and the Penobscot, maintaining its right to erect the territory between them into a separate government.*

The second of the documents so triumphantly brought forward by the United States, is the letter from Mr. Jaspar Mauduit, agent of Massachusetts Bay, to the Secretary of the province, dated London, 9th June, 1764, eight months subsequent to the date of the Proclamation.

It is by that letter incontestably proved, that even then negotiations were going on between the same agent and the Commissioners of the Board of Trade, for the final establishment of the territorial rights of the province of Massachusetts Bay. The province was, even at that date, urging its claims under its disputed charter to the "lands on the river St. Lawrence," as well as the "lands between the Penobscot and St. Croix." It is, therefore, evident that the Proclamation of 1763 was issued without any reference whatever to the final boundaries of the province of Massachusetts Bay; that the government of Great Britain only meant by that Proclamation, as far as it had reference to the tract of country now in question, to establish the southern boundary between the colony of Quebec and Nova Scotia, leaving the pretensions of the province of Massachusetts Bay to the unsettled territory towards the north and east of the Penobscot wholly in abeyance, and reserving to the Crown the right to erect said territory into a separate province if it thought fit so to do, as was (several years subsequently) strongly recommended and urged by Governor Hutchinson. How the negotiation of Mr. Mauduit, in 1764, terminated, there exists no proof; but it is quite

* It is to be remarked that the MS. letters of Governor Hutchinson, of Massachusets, of the years 1770, 1771, 1772, bear out this view in the amplest manner, and strongly recommend that course to the Home Government. These letters, remarkable in more points than one, are preserved among the public records in Boston.

clear that its result did not lead to an acquiescence with his demands.

The Quebec Act of 1774, with respect to the portion of boundary now in question, merely repeated the definition of the Proclamation of 1763. The principle of right on the part of the Crown to the Sagadahock territory, between the St. Croix and the Penobscot, laid down in Wilmot's commission, was never abandoned; and being once laid down it was not considered necessary or fitting to repeat it in the commissions to succeeding governors. The words formerly quoted as inserted in Wilmot's commission were omitted in Governor Parr's commission, dated 29th July, 1782, which proves that they were not so omitted by virtue or in consequence of the treaty of 1783. The territory in question was consequently a disputed matter between the Crown and the province of Massachusetts Bay, when the war of the Revolution broke out in 1775. It is unnecessary to say that so it remained during the war.*

* Extracts from an attested copy of a letter from Edmund Burke (then parliamentary agent to the state of New York) to the Committee of Correspondence for the General Government of New York, giving a full account of the debates in parliament on the passage of the Quebec Act, and the discussions on the various amendments:—

" BEACONFIELD, *August 2nd*, 1774.

" I must observe to you that the proceedings with regard to the town of Boston, and the province of Massachusetts Bay, had from the beginning been defended on their absolute necessity, not only for the purpose of bringing that refractory town and province into proper order, but for holding an example of terror to the other colonies."

He then states the predominant feeling among men in power, to check the growth of the colonies. He says, " it was not thought wise to make new grants of land but upon the weightiest considerations, if at all: prerogative was to be strengthened as much as possible."

He continues, " I next inquired upon what principle the Board of Trade would, in the future discussion which must inevitably and speedily arise, determine what belonged to you and what to Canada.

" I was told that the settled uniform doctrine of the Board of Trade was this: that in questions of boundary when the jurisdiction and soil in both the litigating provinces belonged to the Crown, there was no rule but the King's will, and that he might allot as he pleased in both the one and the other. They said also, that under these circumstances, even where the King had actually adjudged a territory to one province, he might afterwards change the boundary, or, if he thought fit, erect the parts into separate and new governments at his discretion. They alleged the example of Carolina; first one province, then divided into two separate governments, and which afterwards had a third, that of Georgia, taken from the southern division of it. * * * *

" Although doubting the soundness of some of these principles, at least in the

And when the American Congress thought they could advantageously negotiate for peace, what were their propositions with respect to "the rights of the Massachusetts Bay?" Does not every line of the various instructions to their Commissioners, from 1779 to 1782, prove that the rights of the Massachusetts Bay were altogether matter of conjecture and argument? Did they put forward the old claims to "the lands on the St. Lawrence?" Did they even ask for the Highlands of the Proclamation of 1763 (the southern boundary of Quebec), in their entire extent, as a boundary for the State of Massachusetts Bay? No. Their first demand was, as we have seen, for the river St. John, from its source to its mouth, and the Highlands to the northward, close adjoining; and this proposal, notwithstanding the great desire of peace on the part of England, was peremptorily rejected.

The British government, so far from swerving from their original pretensions to the Sagadahock territory, or yielding to the claims of Massachusetts Bay, under their then obsolete charter, all rights under which were really forfeited by the cession of Nova Scotia to France, by the treaty of Ryswick, in 1697, actually claimed (during the negotiations of 1782), *farther westward*, on the part of England than

extent in which they were laid down, I certainly had no cause to doubt that the matter would always be determined upon these maxims by the Board of which they were adopted. The more clearly their strict legality was proved, the more uneasy I became of their consequences. By this Bill, a new province under an old name was in fact erected: the limits settled by the Proclamation of 1763 were cancelled. On your side a mere constructive boundary was established; and the construction, when examined, amounted to nothing more than the King's pleasure.

"I did not press to have the line called the boundary between New York and Canada, because we would again fall into discussion about the bounds of the other colonies. It would be asked why the line along Nova Scotia, New Hampshire, and the northern Massachusetts' claim, was not called the boundary of those provinces as well as of New York! It would be said that the Act was to settle a constitution for Quebec, and not for adjusting the limits of the colonies; and in the midst of this wrangle the whole object would have infallibly escaped."

This letter has never yet been published. It was communicated to me by a gentleman of Boston, forming a portion of the vast store of materials collected by him from public and private sources, for the completion of a work, the three already published volumes of which have secured to him the foremost place among American historians. This letter, carefully considered in reference to the claims put forward by American writers, that the Proclamation of 1763, and the Quebec Act of 1774, in defining the southern boundaries of Quebec, defined the northern boundary of Massachusetts Bay, seems to me a conclusive refutation of those claims as matter of acknowledged right.

they had done in 1764; for they claimed first as far westward as the Pisquataqua river, then as far as the Kennebec, refusing all admission of the asserted rights of Massachusetts Bay to any territory east and north of that river. And as late as the 8th of October 1782, seeing the extreme difficulty of coming to an understanding, one of Dr. Franklin's proposals to Mr. Oswald was that "the true line east between the United States and Nova Scotia, should be settled by Commissioners after the war;" which proposal was at once rejected, by the British Government, to whom Mr. Oswald had referred it.

It was, then, with these pretensions that England went into the negotiations for peace in 1782; and it was in this admitted uncertainty as to territorial rights, on the part of the United States, that the long-disputed boundaries were, on the one hand, brought down, step by step, from the river St. Lawrence to the Highlands near its banks; then to the river St. John; and finally to the southern range of Highlands: and on the other hand, advanced from the Pisquataqua, to the Kennebec, thence to the Penobscot, and thence to the St. Croix. The treaty of 1783 was, in fact, a treaty of compromise.

The second principle in framing the treaty of 1783, was to secure the communication between the provinces of Canada and Nova Scotia. Nothing short of the last mentioned lines of boundaries could have thoroughly effected this; and thus it was that England insisted on these lines, and that the American Congress, from whom the various proposals for boundaries emanated, modified their several propositions to meet that object.

They first hoped that the river St. John would satisfy England on that point. Finding their mistake, is it not preposterous to suppose that they would *go back* and propose *for the first time* the Highlands near the St. Lawrence, and the line of provincial boundary as between Quebec and Nova Scotia? Assuredly it is. And there is not an iota of evidence to establish that such a proposition was *ever* contemplated during the negotiations.

Such a proposition, besides being altogether inadmissible as regards the second principle before mentioned, would have been destructive to the *third*, namely, the securing the free course of the rivers to the respective countries. The St. John was cut across by the north line of the commissions to the governors of Nova Scotia; a matter of small importance, as long as the whole of its course lay within the British Possessions; but a consequence not to be contemplated, when part of those possessions were to be declared independent of Great Britain.

Did England, when she yielded her claims to go westward to the Kennebec or the Penobscot, ever dream of demanding a boundary line running east to west, that would cut either of those rivers across, leaving their upper parts in her territory, and their lower course and mouths in that of the United States? No. True to the principles which have invariably presided over the framing of boundary lines, she accepted "the Highlands" which divided the sources of those rivers from the sources of other rivers; as the American Congress, acting on the same obvious principle, when they found that the St. John could not be obtained as a line, had proposed the said highlands as the natural boundary that would secure all the principles involved.

I may now observe that it was in the first proposition of Congress, namely, for the St. John's river from its source to its mouth, as the north-eastern boundary, that the words, "rivers which fall into the Atlantic Ocean," were first brought into use. These words were chosen advisedly and *of necessity*. The words, "which fall into the Sea," would have failed to convey a description of the restricted boundary agreed upon; besides which, they had been previously and properly used in the Proclamation of 1763. The object now being to show that a different line of Highlands from those of the Proclamation was intended, and two lines being recognised at that day, the description of them inserted into the 2nd article of the treaty was at once simple, and, as the framers of the treaty no doubt thought, not to be misunderstood.

To imagine that "the Sea," and the "Atlantic Ocean," as applied *to the two distinct ranges of Highlands*, were ever considered convertible terms, appears to me to be beyond belief. Let any candid inquirer look at any map, which may be believed to have lain before the Congress, who proposed the line of Highlands now in question. Are not the words "ATLANTIC OCEAN" in connection with the range of Highlands from whence the rivers Connecticut, Penobscot, and Kennebec flow, so prominent that no other could be well used in describing them clearly; while the same Congress knew full well, that the words, "the Sea," formerly used to specify the northern line of Highlands, could not, without confounding both ranges, be applied in a description of the southern range, with which they now had to deal.

If a different line of boundary from that of 1763 was not intended in 1783, why alter the words, "the Sea," into the words, "the Atlantic Ocean?" Had a larger range of boundary been intended, and had "the Atlantic" borne a more extended sense than "the Sea," the propriety of the change would have been admitted at once. But the case was the very reverse; and the manifest object being to give a restricted boundary, and "the Atlantic" being evidently a less extensive term, the change that was made seems so obviously required by the circumstances of the case, that all further argument to prove its propriety and necessity appears to me superfluous. But, *for the sake* of argument, it may be still asked, why, if no change of boundary was meant, was Mitchell's map, published in 1755, eight years anterior to the Proclamation, and of course not showing the boundary specified in that document, *alone* used by the Commissioners who framed the treaty of 1783, in their official consultations together, as it was proved to be by the testimony of John Adams?

I think abundant reasons have been given to show that the boundary line of the Proclamation, and of the Quebec Act, could not have been intended by the treaty; but supposing even that the lines were identical and that the words, "the Sea," and "the Atlantic," are synonymous, for what possible object could the latter have been substituted for the former? It cannot be pretended that this occurred accidentally, in a cautiously prepared, well considered, solemnly executed, document. It must have been done by design; and if so, there must have been an object. To prove that the change was designedly made in the treaty, we have only to look to the commissions of the governors of Quebec, subsequent to its date. In all of these the same change of words is made; "the Atlantic Ocean" being substituted for "the Sea," in the description of the southern boundary of Quebec, proving that instead of the highlands which formerly formed the boundary, other highlands—and no one can be mistaken as to *what* other highlands—were substituted. But in the commissions to the various governors of New Brunswick, after the western portion of Nova Scotia was formed into a separate province under that name, no variation is made from the wording of the previous commissions to the governors of Nova Scotia; the words being invariably "from the St. Croix due north to *the southern boundary of the province of Quebec.*"

If, then, I would ask again, no change was made by the treaty of 1783 from the Proclamation of 1763, why did not the description of the eastern boundary of the United States in the treaty merely mention "a line due north, from the St. Croix to the southern boundary of the province of Quebec?" Because the southern boundary of Quebec was itself changed, from the northern range of highlands to the southern range, and because it became necessary to specially describe that southern range by words that proved the difference between the two.

But it will be observed, that the words of the commissions of the governors of New Brunswick, after the treaty, remained the same as in those of the previous commissions to the governors of Nova Scotia, because it was indifferent to *them* where the southern boundary of Quebec lay. To *it* their proper jurisdiction extended, be it where it might. For the governors of Quebec, however, the change was absolutely essential, because it brought down their jurisdiction from the northern to the southern range of highlands. It was, consequently, necessary to specify, as is clearly done in their commissions subsequent to the treaty, the highlands, which had become the southern boundary of the province.*

The framers of the treaty were, no doubt, satisfied that the range of southern highlands was very clearly described by their being called "highlands separating rivers that empty into the Atlantic Ocean," in contradistinction to the other well known range previously described as "highlands separating the rivers that empty into the sea." Had the framers of the treaty foreseen any possible plea of ambiguity in the change they made, they would, no doubt, have designated the highlands as "the southern range," or have stated the parallel of latitude in which they had their course. It is to be regretted that they did not so describe them; but they cannot be blamed for the omission of what they must have thought, under all the circumstances of the case, and in perfect understanding with each other, a mere waste of words.

The United States' authorities and the Maine Commissioners contend that the northern range of highlands answers the description

* Great stress has been laid by American writers on the disputes about jurisdiction existing ever since the date of the treaty of 1783, between the provinces of Quebec [or Lower Canada] and New Brunswick. These disputes prove nothing but a difference of opinion as to the extent of jurisdiction; and that very difference shows, that the Governors of Lower Canada considered that their rights under the treaty of 1783 extended far to the southward of the southern boundary of Quebec according to the Proclamation of 1763.

of the treaty of 1783, that is to say, that it divides the rivers of the St. Lawrence from the Atlantic rivers. Argued as a question of logic, and admitting the major to include the minor, perhaps that assertion may be true, for the Atlantic Ocean is, no doubt, a portion of the sea. But the framers of the treaty were not chopping logic. They were describing territorial boundaries in geographical terms, taken from the words printed on the map that lay before them; and, assuredly, in that point of view the northern highlands do not answer the description applied by the treaty to the southern range; nor could they do so in a geographical sense unless the southern range had happened to be entirely abraded, or swallowed up by an earthquake.

The expression, "the highlands which divide the rivers that empty into the St. Lawrence, from those which flow into the Atlantic Ocean," of course means *all* the rivers. The phrase "*the* rivers" can mean nothing less. Now, even admitting (again for argument sake), that the Restigouche, the Miramichi, and the St. John, are Atlantic rivers; and, allowing that the northern range of highlands separates *them* from some of the St. Lawrence rivers, it cannot be pretended that it so separates the north and east branches of the Penobscot, which, unquestionably, flows into the Atlantic from the southern range of highlands. It therefore appears that the northern range can have no pretension to be considered the range of highlands described in the treaty, when viewed in comparison with the southern range, which does completely separate all the *rivers* flowing into the St. Lawrence, from *all* the rivers flowing into the Atlantic. It must, I think, be admitted that it does fulfil the brief, but ample description given of it in the treaty of 1783; and had the due north line from the St. Croix been run, as must have been intended by the framers of the treaty, in accordance with the ancient boundary of Nova Scotia, mentioned in the grant (the model from which all the subsequent designations of boundaries has been borrowed,)* to Sir William Alexander, in 1621, from "the westernmost source" of that river, no question could have arisen as to what highlands it would strike. The manifest error made by the Commissioners, under the treaty of amity, 1794, of adopting the northern branch of the St. Croix, instead of the westernmost source, is not further insisted on here, though it may be fairly stated as the main cause of the long

* See Statement on the part of the United States, p. 16.

pending dispute, and as having given the principal pretext for the claim set up by the United States.

I will not go further into the discussion as to the relative meanings of the words "the sea," and "the Atlantic Ocean." There is only one point dwelt on by the Maine Commissioners, as proving them to be synonymous terms, and which point was long ago made, in page 26 of the American Statement, laid before the King of the Netherlands, namely, the passage in the Proclamation of 1763, quoted in the note of the Maine Commissioners of July 16, 1842.*

This point does not, I think, penetrate very deep into the argument. Terms, to be synonymous, must be susceptible of being applied indifferently. Now, if the positions of the two divisions of the passage quoted by the Commissioners be reversed, will the words *sea* and *Atlantic* bear transposition, and still preserve the sense of the whole? Certainly not. Every one knows that the Atlantic Ocean is part of the sea; and that all rivers flowing into the Atlantic flow at the same time into the sea (as before admitted), and, therefore, a sentence specifying "the Atlantic Ocean" might, very appropriately, be referred to in a subsequent sentence, in which it is called "the sea *as aforesaid*." But the question now at issue, namely, the geographical application of the words "the sea," and "the Atlantic Ocean," in describing separate objects, is in no way whatever affected by this passage of the proclamation. The admirable reasoning of "the British statements," laid before the King of the Netherlands, on the distinction between the Atlantic Ocean and the Bay of Fundy, obviate the necessity of all further remark on that branch of the subject; though even that reasoning might be strengthened by a reference to the usual descriptions in the geographies and gazetteers of rivers flowing into the Bay of Biscay in contradistinction to others flowing into the sea, or the Atlantic Ocean.

But as one individual, an agent on the English side of the dispute, has been quoted in the American "Statement" before alluded to, as having used the expression "rivers which fall into the sea *or*

* "No governor of our other colonies or plantations in America do presume to grant warrants of survey, or pass patents for any lands beyond the heads or sources of any of the rivers which fall into the Atlantic Ocean, from the west or north-west," &c. And the proclamation then proceeds to declare that the king does reserve under his sovereignty and dominion, for the use of the Indians, "all the lands and territories lying to the westward of the sources of the rivers which fall into the sea from the west and north-west, as aforesaid," &c.

Atlantic Ocean," I will just refer to the American map of the State of Maine, by Osgood Carlton (founded on the first survey of the country subsequent to the treaty of 1783), which in its title professes to show the course of the rivers flowing into "the Atlantic Ocean *and* the Bay of Fundy." *

These individual errors, discrepancies, or admissions, or whatever else they may be called, are most numerous on the part of the agents at both sides of the question, and cannot affect the real principles at stake, which are to be thoroughly understood only by long and minute investigation of the subject.

I will add a word or two with respect to *maps*, as they have been brought into the late discussion. If Faden's map of 1785, which traces the boundary line in accordance with the British claim, was influenced by his appointment to be Geographer to the King (as insinuated by the Maine Commissioners †), it, at any rate, proves that, even within *two years* after the ratification of the treaty of 1783 England put forth the claim to the disputed territory, which it has been over and over asserted on the part of the United States, she never dreamt of putting forward until during the negotiations for the treaty of Ghent in 1814.

Passing by, however, the numerous maps brought forward in evidence on either side, I must remark that one map has been often alluded to, the production of which would have given me more satisfaction *than all the others put together*. That is Dr. Franklin's *own* map, a section of which, containing the line of boundary marked out with his own hand, was sent by him to Mr. Jefferson, then Secretary of State, with a letter dated Philadelphia, April 8th, 1790. This letter, the last public one which, I believe, he wrote, may be found in the last page, vol. vi. and last, of Duane's edition of Franklin's works, Philadelphia, 1827.

To see this original section of so remarkable a document in this controversy, was one of my chief objects in going to Washington in April, 1840, soon after I began to study this subject. The late Mr. Forsyth, then Secretary of State, assured me that the map was not to be found in the Department ‡. I thought it strange that so

* I found this original map in the Massachusetts Land Office, Boston, where it now still is, I have no doubt.

† See their letter to Mr. Webster, June 29, 1842.

‡ I have since learned from good authority that it was to be seen there as late as the year 1828. Its disappearance dates from that year, and I may here mention that in the American "Statement" so often before referred to, it is

important a document should have been lost; but I was shown by Mr. Forsyth and some gentlemen in his office, a large map by Mitchell, which they all said they believed to be the identical map that was before the Commissioners at Paris or Passy, during the negotiations in 1782 and 1783. On this map a pencil line was traced, through the line of highlands and watercourses, in accordance to what I believed to have been the boundary of the Proclamation of 1763. The next and last time I saw this map, it was in the possession of the Maine Commissioners at Washington, during the negotiations in June 1842. Judge Preble, one of the Commissioners, considered it as of the first importance to the question, and affirmed his belief that it was the identical map mentioned by Dr. Franklin in his letter to Mr. Jefferson, and that the pencil line was *the* line traced by Franklin's own hand, as the boundary of the treaty of 1783.

Now, independent of Mr. Forsyth's statement that Franklin's *section* of map sent to Mr. Jefferson was lost, I must observe that this map in Judge Preble's possession was *an entire* copy of Mitchell's map, the several sections all bearing the same discolouring marks of age, and all pasted on canvas. I would moreover observe, that Dr. Franklin states in one of his letters (see the appendix to the Statement of the American Commissioners submitted to the King of the Netherlands), "I am perfectly clear in the remembrance that the map we used in tracing the boundary was brought in the treaty by *the Commissioners from England*."

It is therefore clear that the large map lately in Judge Preble's possession was not the *section* of Dr. Franklin's map sent by him to Mr. Jefferson; it is very doubtful that the map which belonged to the British Commissioners found its way to the State Department at Washington; and there is not an iota of proof that the pencilled line on the large map in question was meant to trace the boundary of the treaty of 1783, or that it was traced by any one employed in negotiating that treaty.*

stated that "some maps may have escaped notice; but not a single one has been omitted that has come within the knowledge of the American Government," p. 30. And this passage conveys a very strong, though a negative, admission of the obligation under which the Government felt itself, to produce *all maps*, which might be considered as evidence on the question at issue.

* There seems to be great probability that the map discovered in one of the public offices in London, after Lord Ashburton's departure for America, was the map in question, as used by the Commissioners in Paris in 1783.

I cannot conclude these observations, without a remark or two in relation to the north-west angle of Nova Scotia.

That the framers of the treaty of 1783 *could* not have considered that angle as an " understood," " determined," " well known " point, is admitted by the Maine Commissioners, when they state that previous to the treaty of 1783 there had been *three* several admitted or proposed north-west angles of Nova Scotia ; viz. the first, where the due north line struck the river St. Lawrence; the second, where it struck the highlands of the Proclamation of 1763 ; the third at the source of the St. John river.

It consequently became necessary in framing the treaty to give a *description* of the point (as it was established *anew* by that treaty) from which the boundary was to commence ; and therefore the introduction of the words "from the north-west angle of Nova Scotia, viz., that angle which is formed by a line drawn due north from sources of the River St. Croix to the highlands which divide those rivers that empty themselves into the St. Lawrence from those which flow into *the Atlantic Ocean*." I will not now stop to prove that it was in reality a north-east angle of the United States, not a north-west angle of Nova Scotia; nor is it necessary again to advert to the north-west angle of Nova Scotia attempted to be established by Mr. Nathan Hale, with much more appearance of reason certainly than attaches to the north-west angle of the other American writers on the subject.

Among the arguments brought forward by various American writers against the line of highlands claimed by Great Britain, one very much relied on is the series of reproaches addressed to the English ministers in the year 1783, by certain members of both houses of Parliament, for having conceded a line of boundary identical with that now claimed by the United States. Two particular debates (those of Feb. 17th, 1783) are cited, and relied on as " conclusive of the question," to use the words of a recent American writer. The meagre reports of these debates which are extant, contain statements of a very vague and general nature in reference to the line of boundary specified in the treaty of 1783. The impression on my mind relative to those debates has always been, that the reproaches in question were chiefly founded on the cession to the United States of the district of country between the Kennebec and the St. Croix; and that *they had no reference whatever* to the country north of the line of highlands claimed as the boundary by

Great Britain. There is *nothing* in the report of the debates to warrant the latter construction; but almost every one of them attentively considered bears out the former one. Yet it has been repeatedly taken for granted by American writers, that those reproaches were founded on *the admitted fact* that the provisional articles of the treaty of 1783 conceded to the United States the very line of highlands she now claims north of the St. John river.

So many efforts have been made in the discussion of the boundary question to ascertain the general state of opinion in relation to it which existed at the period of the treaty of 1783, that whatever can throw any light on that particular branch of the inquiry may be considered worthy of observation. I am, therefore, induced to call attention to a pamphlet which I lately met with in a private library in the city of Boston, and which is, I think, altogether explanatory of the views of the opposition speakers in the debate alluded to, and strongly confirmatory of the interpretation which I have always given to them.

The title page of this pamphlet, published in London, shows no author's name; but it is signed "Portius," and bears the date on the 40th (which is the last) page, of Feb. 5, 1783. I will give an extract from the portion which relates to the North Eastern Boundary; and I think it furnishes convincing proof not only that the reproaches addressed to the ministers and the commissioners of that day, by the press as well as in parliament, had no reference whatever to the line of boundary at present claimed by the United States; but that the highlands of the treaty were understood at that period, even by those who disapproved of the treaty, to be the identical ridge claimed as the true line of the treaty by Great Britain. From the fact that the boundary line is pointed out in this pamphlet, as running "from the head of the river St. Croix, along the ridge of the highlands *at the back of Massachusetts Bay*, to the source of the Connecticut river," it is not to be believed that those who cavilled at the treaty had any notion that the boundary line crossed the St. John, or extended to the highlands to the north of that river.

It will be also perceived that the most serious reproaches made against Lord Shelburne, having reference to the north-east boundary, in this pamphlet, are for having given up to America "the vast tract of country extending from the St. Croix to the Kennebec, and the whole of the countries surrounding Lake George and Lake Champlain." But not a word of allusion is made to the district between the head of the St. Croix and the St. John, or to the large tract north of it, either in the pamphlet or in parliament; and it seems impossible to suppose that to the series of reproaches so minutely specified, would not have been added another for the cession of what is now "the disputed territory," had such a cession been believed to have been included within the boundaries agreed upon by the Commissioners who framed the treaty of 1783.

"However personally and peculiarly unpleasing to your lordship it may be, and however devoid of entertainment it may prove even to the public, yet so fatal are the concessions made by the limits agreed on between us and America, that I owe it to my country and myself, on this most important point, to go into a detail, with geographical precision, and to convince every impartial person, that no possible situation or circumstances could justify a minister in thus abandoning the interests of the empire. Here, at least, I renounce all declamation, and stand on facts. By the line of partition passing up the river St. Croix, *the vast tract of country extending from that river to the Kennebec*, is given up to America. It is true, indeed, that this country was included in the original charter of the province of Massachusetts Bay; but the general court could not grant any part of it without the consent and permission of the crown of England; and no grants were ever attempted beyond the river Penobscot. By the passage of the line FROM THE HEAD OF THE RIVER ST. CROIX, *along the ridge of the highlands at the back of Massachusetts Bay to the source of the Connecticut river*, and passing thence through the 45th degree of northern latitude into the river St. Lawrence, the whole of the countries surrounding Lake George and Lake Champlain, with both those lakes, and the two forts of Crown Point and Ticonderago, are ceded to America," &c.—*Letter to the Earl of Shelbourne on the Peace*, London, 1783, 2d edition, pages 16, 17, 18.

HAND-BOOK OF THE COTTON TRADE.*

From the "Times" of Oct. 7, 1858.

At present, as everyone knows, Great Britain and Continental Europe obtain most of their raw cotton from the United States.

* "A Hand-book of the Cotton Trade," &c. By Thomas Ellison. Longmans, &c., 1858.

Within a century this import has grown to its present enormous dimensions. Archæological inquiry has ascertained that there were seven bags of cotton shipped from Charleston as early as 1747—8, and that again eight were imported into Liverpool in 1764. Twenty years later, when 71 bags were shipped from the United States to Great Britain, they were seized on their arrival into Liverpool by the Custom-house authorities, on the ground that all America *could not produce so much.* At this day, on the average of the last three years, the United States export 1,136,042,959lb. of the same product, though whether this comprises exports to other places besides Great Britain, the table referred to does not sufficiently indicate. At all events, Great Britain has always received a large proportion of the American crops of cotton, even allowing for a large deduction for the home consumption of the United States. The proportional distribution of the last five years is stated at the close of a table (which, by the way, we should observe requires some fractional correction in addition to that given in the *errata*) as averaging,—

Great Britain	51·28
France	13·24
North of Europe	6·84
Other foreign ports	5·91
Consumption of the United States	23·58

What proportion Great Britain obtains of the cotton grown in other parts of the world we are unable to ascertain, for it is not to be expected that *data* should exist which would enable ourselves or the author to make this computation. At all events, our imports from the whole of the world besides, positively large as they are, and comparatively large as they may be, fall very far short of those from the United States of America.

But here the practical question is obtruded by some further tables, which show that the exports of raw cotton from the United States to Great Britain have not of late years been to the same *proportional* extent as formerly. In fact, there has been a gradual decrease in the proportion received during the years 1851 to 1857. In 1851 Great Britain received 58·72 per cent. of the total yield; in 1857 the exports to this country had dwindled to 46·74 per cent.; the average for the four years ending 1853 being 53·68, and for those ending 1857 being 51·28 per cent. This is, indeed, no conclusive proof of an actual deficiency of supply at this moment, or that the whole imports into Great Britain are falling short of its demand;

but if we turn to another table we shall find statistical proofs of this tendency, to be suspected from the phenomenon which alarmed the millowners of Manchester—viz., proofs of a general deficiency of raw material in the recent increase in the price of that portion of it which comes from America. Thus, from 1806 to 1848, we find that its price decreased, speaking summarily, from about 20*d.* to 4¼*d.* per pound. But from 1848 prices have gradually advanced, middling Orleans being worth 7*d.* per pound in June, 1858, after having reached as high as 9⅝*d.* per pound in September 1857. The deficiency thus indicated has been less felt, no doubt, in consequence of the mercantile crisis and the suspensions of 1857. But it *is* felt, nevertheless, and is differently regarded from the opposite points of view of the producer and consumer. An advance of 1*d.* per pound on the price of American cotton is welcomed by the slaveowner of the Southern States as supplying him with the sinews of war for the struggle now waging with the Northern Abolitionists. This mere advance of 1*d.* on our present annual consumption is equivalent to an annual subscription of 16,000,000 dollars towards the maintenance and extension of American slavery. On our side it restricts the natural increase of consumption, and is a curtailment of the profits of the manufacturer and the wages of the operative, or it involves an equivalent increase of price to the home and foreign consumer.

Its prospective limitation of our cotton trade is that serious question which has been taken up by the Cotton Supply Association, to whom this volume will prove such a valuable auxiliary. If, on behalf of this movement, we review the capacities of the cotton zone, we come to these chief conclusions among many others worked out for us by the author. The localities of the Union most favourable to the growth of the cotton plant are at present under cultivation, nor can we from these lands expect any larger amount of produce than has been raised during the last eight years. If, however, the most favourable localities are already cultivated to the utmost, a table compiled in 1852 by the American Government estimates the southern regions of the United States as capable of producing an incomparably larger quantity than they raise already. But, in the first place, it is suicidal to rely upon any one source for a constant and increasing supply of a produce dependent on the uncertainty of seasons, which a late spring, too much or too little rain, early frost, insects, rot, &c., may materially curtail, and which possibly war might prevent our receiving direct from the places of export; and in the second place, a variety of considerations point to the conclusion that no immediate relief can be supplied from this quarter while immediate relief is required. On the other hand, the produce of the British and foreign West Indies has greatly decreased since the beginning of the century, nor is there a prospect in either of its speedy recovery. The cotton export of the Brazils had made some progress down to 1850, but from that date to the present there has been a perceptible decline. The want of roads has yet to be supplied by railways, and the non-importation of slaves to be compensated by the immigration of free settlers; in short, prospects now opened have yet to be realised. The export trade of Egypt is of modern origin and slow growth. The produce of Algeria within the last two years has perceptibly fallen off. Experiments are now proceeding in Morocco and Tunis and on the west coast of Africa, with more definite promise, under Mr. Clegg. Dr. Livingstone has been ascertaining in a more general sense the capabilities of the African continent as a cotton-growing country under conditions untried as yet. The European side of the Mediterranean, Asiatic Turkey, Australia, and the Pacific, are restricted from their possible production by impediments not easily removed. In fine, the conclusion is this, that we must look primarily to India, from which we obtain cotton already next in proportion to the United States; for "although Africa may in a few years be expected to contribute largely to our stock of raw cotton, and the West Indies considerably increase their present scanty rate of supply, India *alone* is capable of affording *immediate* relief to the manufacturers of Great Britain."

India, indeed, has doubled its exports in the last twenty years, but its progress has been tardy as compared with the United States, which have apparently quadrupled theirs. But India suffers, first, from the hindrances of careless cultivation; secondly, from the absence of a proper system of irrigation; thirdly, from the want of an efficient system of roads; fourthly, from the want of a fixed tenure of land; fifthly, from the apathy of English manufacturers. Some of these hindrances are and some are not remediable by the judicious intervention of the Government, and practically the most valuable portion of Mr. Ellison's Handbook is his summary of the facilities in this behalf, a summary which occupies forty of his 200 pages, and which he pertinently applies in a dedication to Lord Stanley as the statesman whom they most concern, and who is known to be most deeply impressed by their importance. The East India Company in this respect fell short of their opportunities, and truly, as Mr. Ellison holds, the country looks to Lord Stanley to make up for their shortcomings and to multiply the ties of cotton between Great Britain and her great dependancy.

END OF VOL. I.